The Basque Country
Pages 122–147

**Navarra
and La Rioja**
Pages 148–173

Bordeaux

Bayonne

Toulouse

Narbonne

FRANCE

Perpignan

HE BASQUE
COUNTRY

Pamplona (Iruña)

)

roño

NAVARRA
AND
LA RIOJA

CENTRAL AND EASTERN
PYRENEES

Huesca

Girona

Zaragoza

Barcelona

SPAIN

Tarragona

**Central and Eastern
Pyrenees**
Pages 174–197

Valencia

*Mediterranean
Sea*

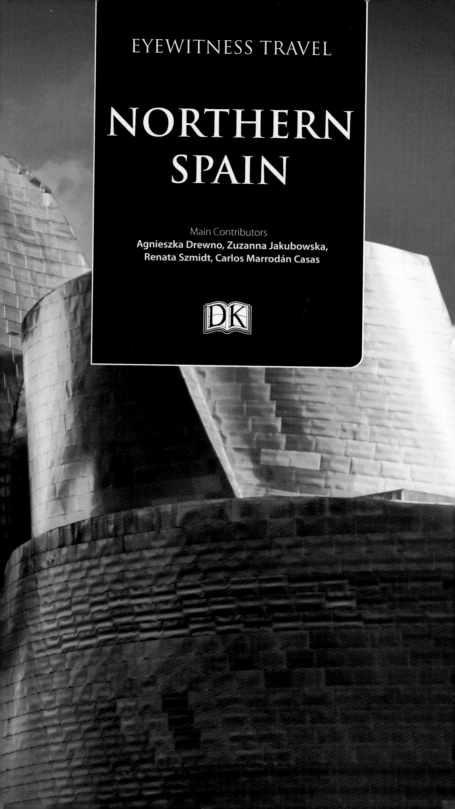

EYEWITNESS TRAVEL

NORTHERN
SPAIN

Main Contributors
**Agnieszka Drewno, Zuzanna Jakubowska,
Renata Szmidt, Carlos Marrodán Casas**

LONDON, NEW YORK,
MELBOURNE, MUNICH AND DELHI
www.dk.com

Produced by Hachette Livre Polska sp. z o.o., Warsaw, Poland

Senior Graphic Designer
Paweł Pasternak

Contributors
Agnieszka Drewno, Zuzanna Jakubowska,
Renata Szmidt, Carlos Marrodán Casas

Cartography
Magdalena Polak

Photographers
Dorota and Mariusz Jarymowicz

Illustrators
Michał Burkiewicz, Paweł Marczak

Editor
Maria Betlejewska

Typesetting and Layout
Elżbieta Dudzińska

Printed and bound in China.

First American Edition 2007

Published in the United States by
DK Publishing, 375 Hudson Street,
New York, New York 10014

15 16 17 18 10 9 8 7 6 5 4 3 2 1

Reprinted with revisions 2009, 2011, 2013, 2015

Copyright ©2007, 2015 Dorling Kindersley Limited, London
A Penguin Random House Company

ISSN: 1542-1554

ISBN: 978-1-4654-2722-9

MIX
Paper from
responsible sources
FSC™ C018179
www.fsc.org

Front cover main image: Church of Nuestra Señora de la Asuncion, Labastida, Basque Country

◀ The striking architecture of the Guggenheim Museum in Bilbao

Contents

Coat of arms, Sos del Rey
Católico town hall

Introducing
Northern Spain

Lighthouse in the fishing village of
Cudillero, on the Asturian coast

A picturesque *ría* in the vicinity of San Vicente de la Barquera

Sculpted figures in the portal of
San Bartolomé in Logroño

A figure in the Iglesia de Santa María
del Palacio in Logroño

Cathedral of Santiago de Compostela
(see pp66–7)

HOW TO USE THIS GUIDE

This guide will help you get the most from your stay in Northern Spain. It provides both expert recommendations and detailed practical information. The guide maps the region and sets it in its historical and cultural context. The important sights are described, with maps, photographs and illustrations. Suggestions for food, drink, accommodation, shopping and activities are given, as well as tips on everything from the Spanish telephone system to travelling to and getting around the region.

Northern Spain Region by Region

In this guide, Northern Spain has been divided into five regions, each of which has its own chapter. A map of these regions can be found inside the front cover of the book. The most interesting places to visit in each region have been numbered and plotted on a Regional Map.

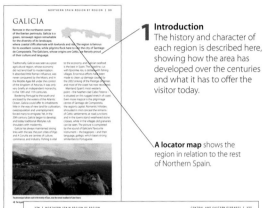

1 Introduction
The history and character of each region is described here, showing how the area has developed over the centuries and what it has to offer the visitor today.

A locator map shows the region in relation to the rest of Northern Spain.

Each area of Northern Spain can be quickly identified by its colour coding.

2 Regional map
This gives an illustrated overview of the whole region. All the sights are numbered, and there are also useful tips on getting around by car and public transport.

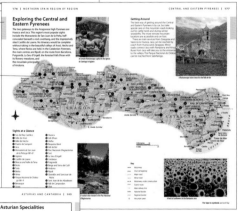

Features give information on topics related to each region.

3 Detailed information on each sight
All the important towns and other places to visit are described individually. They are listed in order, following the numbering on the Regional Map. Within each town or city, there is detailed information on important buildings and other major sights.

4 Major towns

All the important towns and other places to visit are described individually. They are listed in order, following the numbering on the map. Within each town or city, there is detailed information on important buildings and other major sights.

A Visitors' Checklist gives contact information for tourist offices, transport information, details of market days and dates of local festivals.

The town map shows all major through-roads as well as minor streets of interest to visitors. All the sights are plotted, along with the bus and train stations, parking, tourist offices and churches.

A suggested route for a walk covers the most interesting streets in the area.

5 Street-by-Street Map

Towns or districts of special interest to visitors are shown in detailed 3-D, with photographs of the most important sights, giving a bird's-eye view of the area.

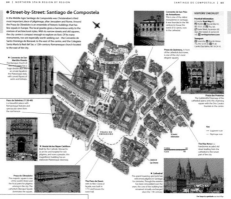

For all the top sights, a Visitors' Checklist provides the practical information you will need to plan your visit.

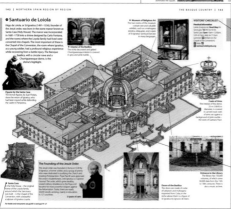

6 Top sights

These are given two or more pages. Important buildings are dissected to reveal their interiors.

Stars indicate the works of art or features that no visitor should miss.

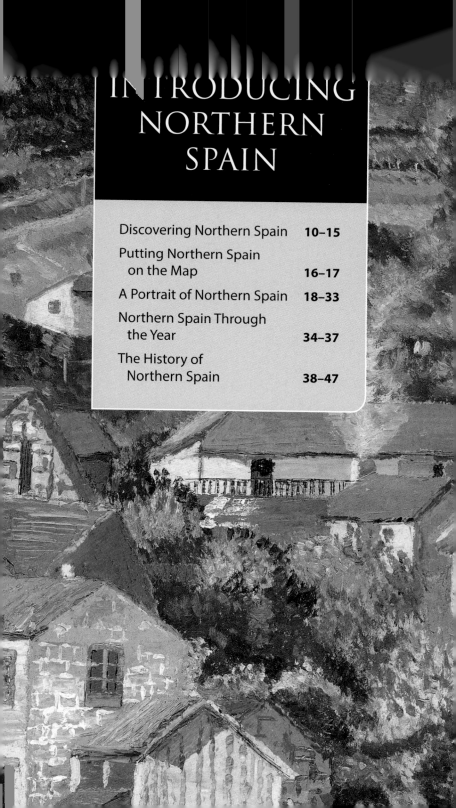

INTRODUCING NORTHERN SPAIN

DISCOVERING NORTHERN SPAIN

The following tours have been designed to take in as many of Northern Spain's highlights as possible, while keeping long-distance travel to a minimum. First come three two-day tours of Northern Spain's most alluring cities: Bilbao, home of the world-famous Guggenheim Museum; San Sebastián, set around a beautiful bay and celebrated for its superb cuisine; and Santiago de Compostela, a breathtaking medieval city of cool grey stone. Next come three seven-day tours, covering the pilgrim routes and wine regions of Navarra and La Rioja; the glorious Asturian and Cantabrian coastline; and the historic towns and villages of the Aragonese and Catalan Pyrenees. Pick, combine and follow your favourite tours, or simply dip in and out and be inspired.

Costa Verde

- Admire some of the most spectacular coastal scenery in Spain at **Ribadeo**'s Praia das Catedrais beach.
- Visit the delightful fishing village of **Cudillero**, with its pretty houses spread steeply around the harbour.
- Enjoy the serenity of **Oviedo**'s outstanding Visigothic churches, and feast on great tapas in the city's historic quarter.
- Watch cider being poured from great heights, in traditional style, at a *sidrería* (cider house) in **Villaviciosa**.
- Soak up the sun on **Santander**'s El Sardinero beach, a marvellous stretch of white sand backed by belle époque buildings.
- Tuck into superb seafood at one of the restaurants overlooking the picturesque harbour of **Castro Urdiales**.

Key

— Vinyards and Pilgrim Paths

— Costa Verde

— Castles and Mountains

Cueva de Tito Bustillo
Remarkable prehistoric paintings line the walls of these caves in Ribadesella, which date back to 22,000 BC.

Santander
Strolling along the harbour of Cantabria's capital is a pleasant way to spend some time in this lively city.

◀ *The Environs of Bilbao* 1918, by Benjamin Palencia

Vineyards and Pilgrim Paths

- Explore **Pamplona**'s enchanting Old Town, and tuck into some of the best tapas in Spain.

- Take a tour of a bodega in **Logroño** or **Haro**, where much of the world-famous Rioja wine is produced.

- Be dazzled by the lavish monastery in **Santo Domingo de la Calzada**, where a live cock and a hen are still kept in honour of a miracle attributed to Santo Domingo.

- Admire the royal palace in **Olite**, a handsome medieval town still partly ringed by ancient walls.

- Enjoy a picnic by the river in the beautiful **Valle de Salazar**.

- Hike through the **Bosque de Irati**, where you might catch a glimpse of some red deer.

- Visit **Roncesvalles**, an ancient mountain town, where Charlemagne was defeated in the 8th century.

Haro
The grapes grown in Haro, the capital of the Rioja Alta region, produce full-bodied wines.

Castles and Mountains

- Visit **Jaca**'s art-filled cathedral, and follow the medieval walls in the city's historic quarter.

- Admire the fabulous mountain views from the **Castillo de Loarre**.

- Spend a day hiking amid the Pyrenean peaks of the **Parque Nacional de Ordesa**.

- Marvel at the murals in the medieval churches of the **Vall de Boí**.

- Explore the villages of the **Vall d'Aran**, and tuck into the excellent local cuisine.

- Enjoy thrilling whitewater rafting along the Noguera Pallaresa River in the Catalan mountain town of **Sort**.

Castillo de Loarre
A Romanesque church lies inside the walls of this 11th-century castle built on a rocky promontory in the Aragonese Pyrenees.

2 Days in Bilbao

The Guggenheim Museum may hog the limelight, but Bilbao has many cultural highlights, plus an Old Town packed with tapas bars.

- **Arriving** Bilbao Airport is located 5 km (3 miles) north of the city centre. Buses run to the city.

- **Transport** Bilbao is easy to explore on foot. However, there is also an excellent public transport network. Get the CreditTrans card if you plan to use the metro, buses and trams.

- **Booking Ahead** Book tickets for the Guggenheim Museum Bilbao ahead of your visit to avoid queues. Bilbao's biggest fiesta, Aste Nagusia (Semana Grande) takes place in the last fortnight of August; book accommodation and special restaurants well in advance.

Day 1
Morning Spend the morning at Bilbao's biggest attraction, the **Guggenheim Museum Bilbao** (pp128–9). Take a stroll around the building first, admiring the Frank Gehry-designed titanium swirls from the nearby Puente de la Salve, before heading in to enjoy the spectacular interior and the changing exhibitions. There are several nearby restaurants where you can enjoy an alfresco lunch by the river.

Afternoon Explore the Siete Calles (Seven Streets), the original medieval streets that make up the **Casco Viejo** (pp126–7), Bilbao's atmospheric historic quarter. Don't miss the fascinating **Museo Vasco** (pp130–31), set in a handsome Baroque building, and the **Catedral de Santiago** (p130), a splendid Gothic building topped by a slender tower. For dinner, enjoy tapas in some of the many traditional tapas bars that are crammed into this lively district.

A sculpture at the entrance to the Museo de Bellas Artes in Bilbao

Day 2
Morning Head to one of Spain's finest museums of fine arts, the **Museo de Bellas Artes** (p131), which hosts fascinating temporary exhibitions to complement its excellent permanent collection. Have a break in the museum's café, which overlooks the pretty Parque Doña Casilda, then take a stroll around the park to admire the duck pond and the shady walkways. Have lunch in the **Ensanche Bilbaíno** district (p131).

Afternoon Head out of town on the metro (get off at Areta), and visit the Puente Colgante in **Portugalete** (p131). Continue on the metro to the Niguri stop to reach the charming seaside town of **Getxo** (p131), where you can enjoy a pleasant wander around the narrow streets and the port. Tuck into a delicious seafood dinner overlooking the harbour.

2 Days in San Sebastián

Glamorous San Sebastián, full of restaurants and tapas bars, is a haven for gourmets; it also boasts elegant architecture and a stunning beach.

- **Arriving** San Sebastián has a small airport, located 22 km (14 miles) from the city centre and connected by local buses. However, most people fly to Bilbao, then take the express bus (about 1 hour) or the train (about 2 hours) from Bilbao city centre to San Sebastián.

- **Transport** San Sebastián is ideally explored on foot, but it is also well served by a bus network.

- **Booking Ahead** Book accommodation ahead during local festivals.

Day 1
Morning Explore the beautiful **Old Town** (p138), the maze of narrow streets behind the port. Drop in at the **Museo San Telmo** (p139), with its fine collection of artworks and displays on traditional life. At the centre of the Old Town is the **Plaza de la Constitución** (p137), where the balconies are still numbered, recalling the days when bull-fights were held right on the square. For lunch, you can take your pick of any one of the area's fantastic traditional restaurants.

A view of the Ribera Bridge spanning the Ría de Bilbao river, in Bilbao

Afternoon Escape the crowds by strolling up **Monte Urgull** *(p138)*, a hill criss-crossed by delightful walking paths, and enjoy the wonderful views from the summit, where there's a bar and some castle ruins to explore. Head downhill and into the **New Town** *(p139)*, laid out in the 19th century and dominated by the handsome Neo-Gothic **cathedral** *(p139)*. This area has a good selection of smart restaurants and tapas bars where you can have dinner.

Day 2

Morning Take a long stroll around the marvellous **Bahía de la Concha** *(p138)*, stopping to sunbathe or have a dip in the sea, if the weather allows. If you're feeling adventurous, you could take a boat out to the nearby island of Santa Clara. At the southern tip of the bay is Eduardo Chillida's huge sculpture *The Comb of the Winds*.

Afternoon Head up **Monte Igueldo** *(p139)*, either on foot or by the charming, century-old funicular, to enjoy the views and perhaps have some fun in the delightfully old-fashioned funfair. There are a couple of restaurants at the top of the hill where you can dine accompanied by fabulous views. Alternatively, head back to the city centre for dinner.

A 16th-century painting in the vaults of the Museo San Telmo, San Sebastián

The cathedral of Santiago de Compostela seen from Praza Quintana

2 Days in Santiago de Compostela

A breathtakingly beautiful city, Santiago de Compostela is packed with palaces and churches.

- **Airport** Santiago de Compostela Airport is 10 km (6 miles) from the city centre. Buses run to the city.

- **Transport** The historic heart of Santiago is easy to explore on foot.

- **Tip** Note that the pilgrim's mass at the cathedral takes place daily at noon.

Day 1

Morning Head straight to the city's main attraction, **Santiago Cathedral** *(pp66–7)*, a vast, magnificent church built between the 11th and 18th centuries. Explore the interior, admiring its exquisite chapels and doorways, then visit the **Cathedral Museum** *(p68)*, full of religious artifacts. Have lunch on one of the city's many beautiful squares.

Afternoon Visit the **Pazo de Xelmírez** *(p68)*, the medieval Archbishop's Palace, and take in the amazing views over the city's ancient domes and spires from its rooftop. A short walk away is the **Museo das Peregrinacións** *(p69)*, where you can discover more about the famous pilgrimage route that has attracted thousands of pilgrims annually for more than a millennium. Have dinner at a seafood restaurant.

Day 2

Morning Immerse yourself in the atmosphere of this ravishing city by strolling through its ancient streets and squares, including the **Praza das Praterias** *(p65)*, named after the goldsmiths' workshops that once lined it, the **Praza do Obradoiro** *(p64)* and the **Praza Quintana** *(p68)*. Don't miss the lavish Baroque **Convento de San Martiño Piñario** *(p69)*, which boasts a richly carved façade.

Afternoon Visit more of the city's cultural attractions. Find out about local life and traditions in the **Museo do Pobo Galego** *(p69)*, housed in a 17th-century church. Then, for a change of pace, head around the corner, where you'll find the bold, modern building that houses the **Centro Gallego de Arte Contemporáneo** *(p69)*, a striking collection of contemporary art.

Extend your trip...

Hire a car for a three-day coastal round-trip from the city (325 km/202 miles). Head to **Cabo Fisterra** *(p60)* via the medieval town of **Noia** *(p70)*; spend the night in Fisterra. Continue north along the scenic **Costa da Morte** *(p60)* to the fishing town of **Camariñas** *(p60)* and the elegant seaside city of **A Coruña** *(pp58–9)*. Soak up the nightlife here and stay overnight before returning to Santiago de Compostela.

The walkways and turrets of the Palacio Real in Olite

Vineyards and Pilgrim Paths

- **Duration** Seven days.
- **Airports** The nearest international airports are Biarritz (France), 115 km (72 miles) from Pamplona, and Bilbao, 155 km (96 miles) away.
- **Transport** A car is essential.

Day 1
Explore the Navarran capital of **Pamplona** *(pp156–9)*. Walk along the ancient narrow streets of its Old Town, home to several pretty medieval churches and a splendid cathedral. Take a break in the gardens surrounding the Ciudadela, a 16th-century fortress, and don't miss out on the city's fantastic tapas bars.

Day 2
Drive south to the enchanting pilgrimage town of **Estella** *(p161)*. Stop for lunch, then press on to **Logroño** *(p164)*, famous for its many bodegas that produce the area's world-renowned Rioja wines. Take a **wine-tasting tour** *(pp168–9)* at one of the bodegas.

Day 3
Spend the morning at another bustling wine town – **Haro** *(p167)* has an excellent wine museum and a clutch of eminent bodegas. After lunch, take a leisurely drive to **Santo Domingo de la Calzada** *(p167)*, a small village named after a medieval martyr whose relics are buried in the lavishly decorated 12th-century church.

Day 4
Head east to **Calahorra** *(p165)*, one of the oldest cities in the region. Press on to prettier **Olite** *(pp162–3)*, where the kings of Navarra kept a royal residence, the magnificent Palacio Real de Olite, then on to **Sangüesa** *(p160)*, another well-preserved medieval town.

Day 5
Follow the **Valle de Salazar** *(pp154–5)*, a beautiful, verdant valley shaded with beech forests and scattered with charming villages and handsome country houses. Stop for lunch at a rural restaurant, or bring a picnic and enjoy it by the river. Travel to **Ochagavía** *(p154)*, the loveliest of all the villages in these parts, which preserves six stone bridges.

Day 6
Spend the morning exploring the magical **Bosque de Irati** *(p154)*, Spain's largest primeval forest, which is home to an abundance of bird and animal life and full of wonderful walking paths. Take the twisting mountain road to **Roncesvalles** *(p154)*, an ancient pilgrim town on a mountain pass near the French border, where you can visit the Colegiata Real, the burial place of Sancho VII.

Day 7
Enjoy the many beautiful walks around Roncesvalles, admiring the spectacular mountain scenery, before returning down another scenic mountain road back to **Pamplona**.

Costa Verde

- **Duration** Seven days.
- **Airports** The nearest international airport is Asturias Airport in Oviedo, 93 km (58 miles) from Ribadeo.
- **Transport** A car is essential.

Day 1
Ribadeo *(p56)* enjoys some of the most spectacular coastal scenery in the area, particularly the rock formations at the Praia das Catedrais beach. Drive east to **Luarca** *(p89)*, a whitewashed fishing port, where you can enjoy a delicious seafood lunch. Continue east to another picturesque fishing town, **Cudillero** *(p89)*, piled steeply around a charming harbour.

Day 2
Spend the day in **Oviedo** *(pp92–7)*, famous for its **Romanesque churches** *(pp96–7)*, which sit in the hills overlooking the town. Stroll around the winding streets of the Old Town, admiring the handsome mansions and churches, then visit the beautiful Gothic cathedral and the excellent Museo de Bellas Artes.

Day 3
Back on the coast, modern **Gijón** *(pp90–91)* boasts plenty of attractions, including its old fisherman's quarter, known as Cimadevilla, and the fascinating Museo del Pueblo de Asturias, which gives an insight into traditional life in the region.

The dramatic landscape at the beach of Praia das Catedrais, Ribadeo

Colourful buildings and market stalls around Plaza Daoiz y Velarde, Oviedo

Day 4
Follow the Ría de Villaviciosa river to reach the pretty town of **Villaviciosa** (p99), the cider capital of Spain. Stop for lunch at a local *sidrería* (cider house), then head inland to **Cangas de Onís** (p106), a small historic town, and nearby **Covadonga** (p106), where the Moorish advance was halted in 722.

Day 5
Drive back to the coast and stop at the seaside town of **Ribadesella** (p102), with great tapas bars, a beautiful beach and the Cueva de Tito Bustillo, a series of caves that contain remarkable prehistoric paintings. Drop in at nearby medieval **Llanes** (p102), before heading east to **Comillas** (p108) to see unusual Modernista buildings.

Day 6
Travel to the harbour town of **Santander** (pp114–15), elegantly arranged around a beautiful bay. The Cantabrian capital offers museums, a fine cathedral and the Playa el Sardinero, a stunning white-sand beach.

Day 7
Continue along the coastline to **Laredo** (p115), a popular resort with a glorious 5-km- (3-mile-) long beach. There are more wonderful beaches to discover on the way to **Castro Urdiales** (p115), where fabulous seafood restaurants surround the picturesque harbour.

Castles and Mountains

- **Duration** Seven days.
- **Airports** The nearest international airports are Pau (France), 112 km (70 miles) from Jaca, and Zaragoza, 150 km (93 miles) away.
- **Transport** A car is essential.

Day 1
Explore the attractive town of **Jaca** (p179), set against the peaks of the Pyrenees. Visit the pentagonal citadel and Spain's first Romanesque cathedral, and admire the Puente de San Miguel, a medieval bridge on the pilgrimage route. Spend the afternoon at the **Monasterio de San Juan de la Peña** (pp180–81), an imposing monastery that is said to have once guarded the Holy Grail.

Day 2
Spend the morning visiting the enormous **Castillo de Loarre** (p182), hugging a rocky outcrop and enjoying stunning views over the Ebro plain. Then drive east to **Huesca** (p191), a charming mountain town and former Aragonese capital, which is still home to a royal palace and the Iglesia de San Pedro el Viejo, burial place of several Aragonese kings.

Day 3
Take the 2-hour drive to **Aínsa** (p183), wriggling over the mountains via little villages such as Adahuesca and Arcusa. Meander through the cobbled streets of Aínsa, climbing up to its lofty castle, and enjoy a drink on the handsome Plaza Mayor, lined with stone houses.

Day 4
Drive up to the **Parque Nacional de Ordesa** (pp186–7) to enjoy a day's hiking in one of the most spectacular national parks in Spain. There are routes for walkers of all fitness levels, and you can bring a picnic to enjoy on a mountain top.

Day 5
Head across the Catalan border to the **Vall de Boí** (p193), which boasts UNESCO World Heritage status for its superb collection of Romanesque churches, filled with extraordinary murals. Most of the tiny villages boast their own beautiful church, but the finest are in Taüll.

Day 6
Continue north to **Vielha** (pp192–3), a handsome town filled with the grey stone and slate buildings typical of the **Vall d'Aran** (p192). Admire Vielha's fine churches and museums, then enjoy some local food, before continuing through the valley to reach the villages of Arties and Salardú.

Day 7
Drive south, along another beautiful road that follows the Noguera Pallaresa river, to **Sort** (p194), a small town famous for its rafting and watersports. From Sort, the mountain road winds east to **La Seu d'Urgell** (p194), home to Catalonia's only Romanesque cathedral and a clutch of elegant mansions.

The Monasterio de San Juan de la Peña, concealed under a rock overhang

Putting Northern Spain on the Map

The area described in this guide comprises the autonomous regions of Northern Spain – Galicia, Asturias, Cantabria, the Basque Country, Navarra and La Rioja – as well as the Central and Eastern Pyrenees, which lie in Aragón and Catalonia respectively. Northern Spain's varied coastline borders the Atlantic Ocean. The country's most northerly point, the headland of Estaca de Bares, is in Galicia.

Key

━━━ Motorway

━━━ Major road

━━━ International border

━━━ Regional border

--- Ferry route

Brive-la-Gaillarde
Saint-Flour
Valence
Bordeaux
A10
A89
Gujan-Mestras
Langon
Figeac
Montélimar
A7
Saugnacq-et-Muret
A65
N21
Agen
Rodez
N88
Avignon
FRANCE
Albi
A62
N106
A75
Mont-de-Marsan
Auch
A68
Nîmes
Arles
Biarritz
Dax
Toulouse
Montpellier
A9
San
A64
Sebastián
AP8
Pau
Tarbes
A64
A61
Béziers
Bilbao
PAÍS
VASCO
Vitoria-
Pamplona
Perpignan
Gasteiz
NAVARRA
ANDORRA
roño
A12
Jaca
La Seu
de Urgell
AP15
Figueres
LA RIOJA
Huesca
CATALUÑA
Girona
Tudela
A23
Vic
Genoa, Livorno,
Soria
ARAGÓN
N240
Manresa
AP7
Civitavecchia
A68
Zaragoza
A54
Calatayud
AP2
Lleida
A2
Barcelona
A2
N232
N211
AP2
Sitges
A23
Alcañiz
AP7
Tarragona
A2
Mediterranean
N211
Tortosa
Sea
N232
Teruel
Benicarló
Cuenca
N330
AP7
A40
Benicasim
Ciutadella
Menorca
A3
Castellón de la Plana
Alcudia
Mahón
Sagunto
Palma
ANCHA
Requena
Valencia
Mallorca
36
A3
PAÍS
A43
VALENCIANO
ISLAS
N322
Albacete
N330
A7
BALEARES
Gandia
Ibiza
A31
Xábia
Ibiza
Hellín
A31
Elda
Benidorm
322
A30
Alicante
AP7
MURCIA
A7
Murcia
Huéscar
AP7
Lorca
Cartagena
A92
A7
AP7
Águilas
Mojácar
Almería

For keys to symbols see back flap

Melilla, Nador
Ghazaouet

Europe and Northern Africa

NORWAY
SWEDEN
ESTONIA
LATVIA
NORTH
DENMARK
LITHUANIA
SEA
REP. OF
UNITED
IRELAND
KINGDOM
NETHERLANDS
POLAND
BELARUS
GERMANY
BELGIUM
CZECH
UKRAINE
REP.
ATLANTIC
SLOVAKIA
OCEAN
FRANCE
AUSTRIA HUNGARY
SWITZ.
ROMANIA
BOSNIA
SERBIA
HERZ.
ITALY
BULGARIA
MONTEN.
MAC.
PORTUGAL
Madrid
GREECE
SPAIN
TUNISIA
Canary
MOROCCO
Islands
ALGERIA
LIBYA

A PORTRAIT OF NORTHERN SPAIN

Spain's diversity is evident in its northernmost part, the source of many of the country's oldest and most fascinating traditions. The peoples of the north speak three languages – Galician, Basque and Catalan – as well as Spanish. And instead of sun-browned southern plains there are thickly wooded hills, facing a misty Atlantic Ocean.

Northern Spain is, above all, extremely lush and green, with pockets of abundance like the winelands of Galicia and La Rioja. Thanks to the steepness of its mountains and their proximity to the Atlantic, it gets plenty of rain, so much of the region is carpeted with woodland or rich pasture. Yet it is sufficiently far south for the weather to be often warm and mild.

The north was the only part of Spain not conquered by the Moors in the Middle Ages, and some of its peoples even resisted the Romans. The Basques are the longest-established people in Europe, having already been in their green mountain home for centuries when the Romans encountered them around 200 BC. The Celtic Galicians are only relative newcomers by comparison.

The other communities of the north took shape after the influx of the Moors into Spain in AD 711, when retreating Christians took refuge in the northern mountains. The tiny principalities and dukedoms formed in the valleys of Asturias and the Pyrenees were the cradles of the later states – Castile, Aragón, Catalonia – that eventually spread south to defeat the great Moorish kingdoms of Spain.

For centuries the regions west of Navarra were linked by the *Camino de Santiago*, the road to one of Europe's greatest pilgrimage sites, the shrine of St James at Santiago de Compostela. The abundant traffic along the *camino* during the Middle Ages encouraged the growth of striking cities with magnificent Gothic architecture.

View of the village of Roncesvalles surrounded by woodland, in Navarra

◀ The Rosa dos Ventos seen from the Torre de Hercules Roman lighthouse, in A Coruña, Galicia

The landscape near Fuente Dé in the Picos de Europa

Land and People

Once the tide of history moved south, large areas of northern Spain were left to themselves. As a result, today many parts of Galicia, Asturias and the Pyrenees feel distinctly remote, dotted with mountain farms and isolated villages whose buildings seem to have remained virtually unchanged since the 1600s. This remoteness has aided the survival of a rich vein of traditions. Both Galicians and Basques have their own extensive folklore and myths, and are known for witchcraft and magic.

These traditions are inseparable from the landscape. Abrupt mountainsides and narrow sea cliffs have imposed a special way of life. In Galicia the misty green countryside is a natural haunt for the many spirits of Celtic folklore, while to the Basques every inch of their beech-woods and valleys has some historical or mythological connection. The Cantabrian mountains, too, have ancient stories.

A woman in traditional
Galician costume

Besides the mountains, the life of the rugged north coast has been bound up with the sea. The Basques have historically been Spain's foremost seafarers, and furnished many of the skilled navigators who took Spanish explorers to the Americas. The Galicians have long relied on superb mussels and other inshore seafood as staples of their diet, and now outdo the Basques as deep-sea fishermen.

The port of Malpica on the Galician coast

The peoples of the north also share some characteristics of all Spaniards – especially their Iberian gregariousness. They are just as devoted to socializing, whether on an evening *paseo* (stroll) or eating out in a convivial group. These are some of the friendliest parts of the country, less jaded by tourism than Mediterranean regions.

The Guggenheim Museum, Bilbao's prestigious landmark

Northern *fiestas* – great showcases of local traditions and foods – are among Spain's most exuberant, from Pamplona's San Fermín to the flower parades of Cantabrian harbours.

Modern Times

In Spain's modern history the regions of the north have followed varying paths. Some joined the Industrial Revolution early in the 19th century, with shipbuilding, iron and steel in the Basque Country, coal mining and shipbuilding in Asturias. This made them centres of progressive dynamism in the struggle to make Spain a modern state, while areas like Navarra and rural Galicia were known for an unchanging conservatism. The rise of Basque nationalism also undermined faith in the status quo. Asturias was the base for a socialist revolt in 1934, and when the Spanish Civil War erupted two years later both it and the Basques resisted General Franco's right-wing army. The victorious Franco regime regarded them with intense suspicion; their rebelliousness was met with harsh repression.

The northern regions have continued to fare differently in the new

The bull run *(encierro)* during Pamplona's San Fermín festival

Spain created since 1975, integrated into the European Union and with a system of regional self-government *(Autonomías)*. For Spanish-speaking regions like Asturias and La Rioja the "Autonomies" have become useful arms of local government. In Galicia, nationalism has always been quite mild, but has lately become more demanding. The Basque government has greater powers than any other region in Europe, but a substantial proportion of Basques want total independence – although few sympathize with the militant nationalist group ETA. The declaration of a ceasefire by ETA in March 2006 briefly raised hopes of a permanent solution, but ETA called off the ceasefire less than a year later. In October 2011, ETA announced a definitive ceasefire, without conditions.

The north's economic transformation has been striking. The coal, steel and shipbuilding industries declined rapidly in the 1980s, causing severe hardship. Fishing, too, has come under pressure from EU quotas. However, tourism and Spain's industrial diversification have since opened up new possibilities. Most dramatic of all has been the revitalization of the now stylish Bilbao.

Architecture of Northern Spain

Northern Spain is remarkable for its exceptional architectural heritage. Preserved here are the foundations of Celtic homesteads and the ruins of Roman buildings, testifying to the region's ancient history. It is also here, especially along the pilgrimage route to Santiago de Compostela and in the Catalan Pyrenees, that beautiful Romanesque churches and lofty Gothic cathedrals are to be found. One of the area's most distinctive and visible features is the traditional architecture, unique to each region of Northern Spain, which reflects the terrain and traditional forms of livelihood – fishing, farming and agriculture.

Renaissance detail of the Hostal de San Marcos in León *(see p119)*

Pre-Romanesque & Romanesque (8th–13th Centuries)

Most notable among the pre-Romanesque buildings are the Asturian shrines. Romanesque churches built in the 10th–12th centuries in Catalonia, as well as along the pilgrimage route to Santiago de Compostela, feature massive walls, tall rounded arches, and few windows.

Santa Maria del Naranco *(see pp96–7)* is a pre-Romanesque church with slender proportions. Barrel vaults and columns around arcaded galleries are typical of the style.

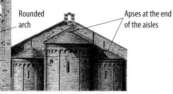

Rounded arch

Apses at the end of the aisles

Romanesque San Climent in Taüll *(see p194)*

Four-arched window

Stone corbels

The Palacio de los Reyes de Navarra in Estella *(see p161)*, built at the end of the 12th century, is one of very few examples of secular Romanesque architecture.

Gothic (12th–16th Centuries)

An ogival window

In most of Northern Spain, especially along the road to Santiago, where the French influence was strongest, the Gothic followed the French version of the Gothic style. It was based on verticality and the introduction of twin-towered façades and ribbed vaulting. Catalan Gothic had a heavier style of its own.

The nave of León Cathedral *(see pp120–21)*, whose construction began in 1254, is covered in ribbed vaulting and lit by colourful stained-glass windows covering a staggering 1,800 sq m (19,375 sq ft).

The Gothic retable in Ourense cathedral *(see p75)* was carved by Cornelis de Holanda at the beginning of the 16th century. A scene of the Deposition appears in one of its richly decorated sections.

Renaissance (16th Century) & Baroque (17th–18th Centuries)

The Renaissance, with its predilection for Classical proportions and harmony, was raised to the extremely decorative style known as Plateresque, said to replicate the effects of silverware *(plata)* in stone, with heraldic motifs, arches with complicated curves, and stone openwork ornamentation. The Baroque style brought with it grand ornamentation, dramatic religiosity and splendour.

Detail of the cathedral at Santiago de Compostela

Universidad de Sancti Spiritus in the Basque town of Oñati has a Plateresque façade adorned with figures of saints *(see p141)*.

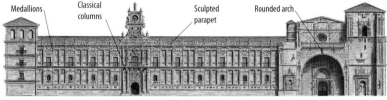

Medallions — Classical columns — Sculpted parapet — Rounded arch

The Hostal de San Marcos in León *(see p119)*, in the Plateresque style, with a long palatial façade

The Modern Era

The sheer variety of forms and harmonious integration with the environment typify modern architecture in Northern Spain, where increasing numbers of foreign architects are working, from Canadian-born Frank Gehry to Portuguese Alvaro Siza. Innovative forms are evident in practical architecture, such as in Bilbao's metro (by Norman Foster) and airport.

Modernist 1950s church in Arantzazu *(see p141)*

Rare materials, such as titanium, were used in the construction of the futuristic Guggenheim Museum in Bilbao *(see pp128–9)* by Frank Gehry.

Regional Architecture

Because so much of the North is mountainous, many regions are dotted with big farmhouses where livestock were kept on the ground floor, and the family lived above. On the Galician coast fishermen's equipment was kept downstairs, and the family lived above. Galicia also has many *hórreos* (granaries), while *teitos* (shepherds' huts) are a symbol of Asturias.

Hórreos, or granaries common in Galicia, are built on stone pillars to prevent rodents from eating the grain.

Teitos are traditional stone huts with thatched roofs, used by shepherds in Asturias.

Stone houses in Cantabria usually have wooden balconies, a broad entrance and projecting eaves to protect the walls from rain.

The Road to Santiago

According to legend the body of Christ's apostle James was brought to Galicia. In 813 the relics were supposedly discovered at Santiago de Compostela, where a cathedral was built in his honour *(see pp66–7)*. In the Middle Ages half a million pilgrims a year flocked here from all over Europe, crossing the Pyrenees at Roncesvalles *(see p154)* or via the Somport Pass in Aragón *(see p178)*. They often donned the traditional garb of cape, long staff and curling felt hat adorned with scallop shells, the symbol of the saint. The various routes, marked by the cathedrals, churches and hospitals built along them, are still used by travellers today.

19th-century painting of the Pórtico da Gloria in Santiago's cathedral

Astorga *(see p117)*, once a Roman city, was an important halt on the pilgrim route in the Middle Ages. The museum within its cathedral has a collection of gold and silver plate including a 13th-century gold filigree cross.

A certificate is given to pilgrims covering 100 km (62 miles) of the route on foot, or 200 km (125 miles) on horseback.

O Cebreiro *(see p78)* has a 9th-century church and some of the ancient *pallozas* the pilgrims often used for shelter.

León was one of the main pilgrim stops. Its cathedral *(see pp120–21)* contains one of Spain's finest collections of stained glass.

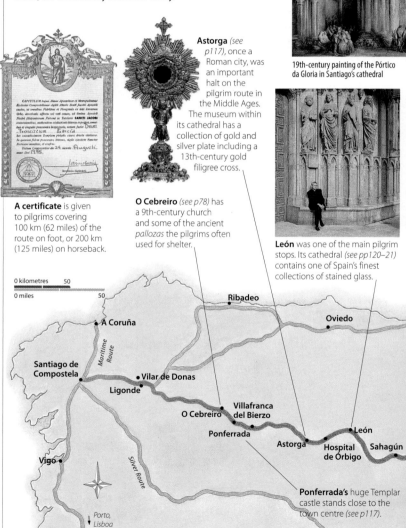

0 kilometres 50
0 miles 50

Ribadeo

A Coruña

Oviedo

Maritime Route

Santiago de Compostela

Vilar de Donas

Ligonde

Villafranca del Bierzo

O Cebreiro

Ponferrada

Astorga

Hospital de Órbigo

León

Sahagún

Vigo

Silver Route

Ponferrada's huge Templar castle stands close to the town centre *(see p117)*.

Porto, Lisboa

Romanesque Church Architecture

The Romanesque style of architecture (see p22) was brought to Spain from France during the 10th and 11th centuries. As the pilgrimage to Santiago became more popular, many glorious religious buildings were constructed along its main routes. Massive walls, few windows, round heavy arches and barrel vaulting are typical features of Romanesque architecture.

Octagonal lantern

Carved capital

Twin round towers

Barrel vault

Thick walls

Round arch

Façade

Cross-section

San Martín de Frómista

(see p170), built in the 11th century, is the only complete example of the "pilgrimage" style of Romanesque. The nave and aisles are almost the same height and there are three parallel apses.

Parallel apses   Aisle   Nave

Floorplan

Pamplona's (see p157) Gothic cathedral was one of the pilgrims' first stops after crossing the Pyrenees at Roncesvalles.

Santo Domingo de la Calzada's (see p167) pilgrim hostel is now a parador.

Puente la Reina (see p161) takes its name from the 11th-century humpbacked bridge (puente), built for pilgrims and still used by pedestrians.

Northern Route

Santander

Donostia (San Sebastián)

Biarritz, Bordeaux

Orthez

Bilbo (Bilbao)

Orreaga (Roncesvalles)

Frómista preserves one of the finest Romanesque churches on the French Route.

Tarbes, Arles

Iruña (Pamplona)

Lizarra (Estella)

Aragonese Route

Santo Domingo de la Calzada

French Route

Puente la Reina

Sangüesa

Jaca

San Juan de la Peña

San Juan de Ortega

Nájera   Logroño

Frómista

Burgos

Burgos has a magnificent Gothic cathedral (see pp172–3).

Routes to Santiago

Several traditional pilgrimage roads converge on Santiago de Compostela. The main road from the Pyrenees is known as the French Route, with the Aragonese Route as a variation.

Basque Culture

The Basques may be Europe's oldest civilization. Long isolated in their mountain valleys, they preserved their unique language, myths and art for millennia, absorbing outside influences while retaining their identity. Many families still live in isolated, chalet-style stone *caseríos*, or farmhouses, built by their forebears. Their music and high-bounding dances are unlike those of any other culture, and their cuisine is varied and imaginative. The ancient Basque laws were suppressed under General Franco, but since the arrival of democracy in 1975 the Basques have won great autonomy over their own affairs.

La Ikurriña – the Basque flag – symbolizes Christianity (white cross) and a battle won by St Andrew (green cross).

Basque cuisine is among the best in the world, and the region is known for its men's gastronomical societies that arrange cookery sessions and banquets. Traditional dishes are dominated by fish and seafood and exquisite *pintxos*, the distinctive Basque style of *tapas*.

A tome of Basque laws

Basque fishermen with oars and nets

The Museo Vasco in Bilbao presents examples of Basque art and folk crafts, as well as scenes from the everyday life of the Basques.

Traditional Law-Making

A ceiling in the historic parliament of Vizcaya (Casa de Juntas) in Gernika is covered by this 1985 stained-glass window. It depicts the great oak tree that was a symbol of Basque rights and liberties, around which representatives once gathered to engage in debate and to pass laws.

Picasso's *Guernica* was inspired by the tragic Nazi bombing (at Franco's request) of this Basque town in 1937, during the Spanish Civil War. The original painting is in the Museo Reina Sofía in Madrid; the one in Gernika is a copy.

Traditional Basque instruments include the *txalaparta*, a percussion instrument made up of two hollowed logs, that was used historically as a means of communication across mountain valleys. The four-hole flute known as the *txistu* is played with one hand.

Basque Language

The Basque language, *Euskera*, is believed by some linguists to be the only surviving pre-Indo-European language in Europe. Unrelated to any other tongue, it is exceptionally difficult to learn, requiring years of practice to become fluent. It has 11 grammatical cases and a highly complicated conjugation. Articles, adjectives, prepositions and other parts of speech are added to the ends of words, while surnames often refer to features in the landscape of the countryside.

Dances at fiestas are masterful displays of agility and rhythm, such as the various *espatadantza* or sword dances or the *aurresku* – a courtship dance performed by men. At fiestas you may also hear the *irrintzi*, a high-pitched shriek traditionally used to communicate across long distances.

In the Basque Country, road signs, street names, and information boards are in Euskera and Spanish. Euskera is also spoken in northern Navarra, which is counted as part of the wider Basque Country.

Gernikako Arbola – the sacred oak tree of the Basque people.

A coat of arms with an image of the oak tree

Parades, such as this one in Hondarribia, are a key element of every fiesta. Musicians dressed in colourful costumes march through the town playing flutes and drums.

The stained glass is framed by images of the most famous buildings in the Basque Country.

Basque farmers in traditional berets

Pelota is the world's fastest game. The ball, which can reach speeds of 300 km/h (186 mph), is hurled against a wall by hand, or with a bat or a special curved wicker basket.

Wines of Northern Spain

Spain's most prestigious wine region, Rioja, is best known for its red wines, matured to a distinctive vanilla mellowness. Some of the most prestigious bodegas were founded by émigrés from Bordeaux, and Rioja reds are similar to claret. Rioja also produces good white and rosé wines. Navarra reds, whites and especially rosés have improved dramatically, helped by a government research programme. The Basque region produces a tiny amount of the prickly, tart *txacoli (chacoli)*. Larger quantities of a similar wine are made further west in Galicia, whose best wines are full-bodied whites.

Repairing barrels in Haro, Rioja

Ribeiro, the popular everyday wine of Galicia, is usually fizzy. It is often served in white porcelain cups (tazas).

0 kilometres   50
0 miles   25

Key
- Rías Baixas
- Ribeiro
- Valdeorras
- Txacoli de Guetaria
- Rioja
- Navarra

Lagar de Cervera is from Rías Baixas, where Spain's most fashionable whites are made from the Albariño grape.

Wine Regions

The wine regions of Northern Spain are widely dispersed. Cradled between the Pyrenees and the Atlantic are the important regions of Rioja and Navarra. Rioja is divided into the sub-regions of Rioja Alavesa, Rioja Alta and Rioja Baja, separated by the Río Ebro. The river also cuts through the wine region of Navarra. To the north are some of the vineyards of the Basque Country: the minuscule Txacoli de Guetaria region. In the far west lie the four wine regions of wet, rugged Galicia: Rías Baixas, Ribeiro, Valdeorras, and Ribeira Sacra.

Wine village of El Villar de Álava in Rioja Alta

Gathering the grape harvest in the traditional way in Navarra

Remelluri, one of the new single-estate "château" Riojas, from the vineyards of Rioja Alavesa, is soft and not too oaky.

Chivite, from a family bodega in Navarra, is made from Tempranillo grapes and aged in the barrel, resulting in a style similar to Rioja.

Viña Ardanza is blended, as are most red Riojas. The best, like this *reserva*, are aged for two or more years in American oak casks.

Key Facts About the Wines of Northern Spain

Location and Climate
Rioja and Navarra are influenced by both Mediterranean and Atlantic weather systems. The hillier, northwestern parts receive some Atlantic rain while the hot Ebro plain has a Mediterranean climate. The Basque region and Galicia are both cool, Atlantic regions with high rainfall. Soils everywhere are stony and poor, except in the Ebro plain.

Grape Varieties
The great red grape of Rioja and Navarra is Tempranillo. In Rioja it is blended with smaller quantities of Garnacha, Graciano and Mazuelo, while in Navarra Cabernet Sauvignon is permitted and blends excitingly with Tempranillo. Garnacha, also important in Navarra, is used for the excellent

rosados (rosés). Whites of Navarra and Rioja are made mainly from the Viura grape. Galicia has many local varieties, of which the most important are Albariño, Loureira and Treixadura, which is now taking over from the inferior Palomino.

Good Producers
Rías Baixas: Fillaboa, Lagar de Fornelos, Martín Codax, Morgadío, Santiago Ruiz. ***Ribeiro:*** Cooperativa Vitivinícola del Ribeiro. ***Rioja:*** Bodegas Riojanas (Canchales, Monte Real), CVNE (Imperial, Viña Real Oro), Faustino, Marqués de Cáceres, Marqués de Murrieta, Martínez Bujanda, Paternina, Remelluri, Viña Ardanza. ***Navarra:*** Bodega de Sarría, Guelbenzu, Julián Chivite (Gran Feudo), Magaña, Ochoa, Príncipe de Viana.

Map labels
Llanes · Santander · Laredo · Bilbao · San Sebastián · CANTABRIA · PAÍS VASCO · Miranda de Ebro · Vitoria · Estella · Pamplona · NAVARRA · Haro · Logroño · Nájera · Calahorra · LA RIOJA · Tudela

Landscapes and Nature of Northern Spain

A mountain wall extends right across Northern Spain, through the length of the Pyrenees, the Basque Country and along the north coast in the Cordillera Cantábrica, before spreading out and turning south into the hills of Galicia. The mountains contain the most spectacular scenery, and separate Northern Spain from central Spain, creating the green, Atlantic climate that gives the northern regions their distinctive feel. Many parts of the northern mountains remain remote, thinly populated and thickly wooded, and so provide a home for a fascinating range of wildlife.

Medieval stone bridge across a fast-flowing river, Picos de Europa

Mountains

The mountains reach their highest points in two great massifs, the High Pyrenees and the Picos de Europa, much of them above 2,000 m (6,560 ft), and with alpine landscapes of massive rockfaces, gorges and near-infinite views. They are dotted with alpine flowers and animals found only in high mountains such as snow voles and chamois. High above fly eagles, falcons and vultures. On the lower slopes, meadows explode into colour with flowers and butterflies each spring.

The Picos de Europa, straddling Asturias and Cantabria, form Europe's largest national park. With an excellent network of paths and refuges, it's a fabulous area for walking and climbing, with beautifully contrasting scenery of peaks, meadows and valleys.

Eagle owls are recognizable by their large "ears", or tufts above each eye. Living in the woods around mountain valleys, they hunt for small birds and animals at dusk and at night.

Chamois live amid the highest peaks, on mountain grasses and flowers found in rock gardens between the bare crags and scree. Astonishingly agile, they can leap remarkably quickly into the rocks whenever eagles or other predators appear.

Blue, purple and yellow gentians are characteristic flowers of the high mountain pastures and rocky plateaux of the Pyrenees and the Cantabrian mountains.

Griffon vultures are a frequent sight in the Picos de Europa and the Pyrenees. In their search for prey they circle on huge wings high above the slopes, riding the rising air currents.

Rippling river in the Parque Nacional de Ordesa, the Pyrenees

Forest

Thanks to their remoteness, steep terrain and rainfall, huge areas of the northern mountains are still clad in forest. Mainly of beech, chestnut, ash and Pyrenean oak, they are among Europe's oldest broadleaf forests. They are also the refuge of Spain's rarest birds and wildlife – wildcats, wolves and bears.

Beech martens are shy and nocturnal, and so hard to see, but are still quite common in the lower forests. Asleep during the day, they emerge at night to feed on fruit, nuts and sometimes small mammals and birds.

The woods of Galicia, dense and often shrouded in rain and Atlantic mists, are closely associated with local folklore, as the homes of witches and Celtic spirits and fairies.

Gold and russet colours spread across the broadleaf forests each autumn. The colours are richest in the beech woods of the Basque Country, Navarra and Asturias.

Rock thrushes are plentiful from spring to autumn. Feeding on insects, they can be seen in the trees around meadows and other clearings in the woods.

The brown bears of Asturias – the last substantial bear population in western Europe – still number about 200, mostly in the Parque Natural de Somiedo.

The Coast

The mountains approach the sea in cliffs and giant headlands of granite and slate, separated by an enormously varied mix of deep, wooded inlets, rocky coves, rolling sand dunes and marshy wetlands. There are huge seabird colonies, especially on the tiny offshore islands. Sheltered estuaries provide feeding-grounds for many wading birds, and are visited by porpoises and dolphins.

View of the Rías Baixas from Mirador de La Curota, near Noia in Galicia

Sand dunes at Corrubedo in Galicia

Around Praia das Catedrais beach, near Foz in the Rías Altas of northern Galicia, the schist and slate cliffs have been eroded by the sea into spectacular rock "cathedrals".

The Atlantic Coast from Galicia to the Basque Country

Ruggedness and a green exuberance are characteristics of Spain's spectacular north coast. Majestic headlands, bizarre rock formations and massive granite cliffs loom up out of the ocean, but in between them there are soft-sand beaches in well sheltered bays, backed by tranquil woods and meadows. There are fabulous views at every turn, and the Atlantic air is invigorating. The coastal scenery is at its finest in Galicia, with its exquisite winding inlets, or *rías*, and wild capes, while the best beaches are in Cantabria and the Basque Country. The sea is also the source of many of Northern Spain's finest foods.

Cudillero is one of the most picturesque villages of the Asturian coast, with a dramatic lighthouse and a tiny harbour crammed into a steep cove below the cliffs.

Cabo de Peñas, just northwest of Gijón, is dotted with small villages, windswept cliffs and sand dunes rising up behind fine beaches that are pounded by crashing surf.

A Toxa island is the most exclusive resort in Galicia's Rías Baixas. The tiny, pine-covered island has luxurious hotels and villas, a casino, secluded beaches and a famous church covered entirely in scallop shells.

Cabo Fisterra, "the end of the world" is the westernmost point of continental Spain. Travellers to Santiago traditionally finished their pilgrimage here, to gaze at the vast horizons and fabulous sunsets.

Llanes is a charming fishing port that is now a popular small resort, with delightful beaches reached by footpaths along the cliffs.

San Vicente de la Barquera is a picturesque seafaring town in the foothills of the Picos de Europa. It has been a busy port since Roman times, and boasts many historic buildings as well as excellent beaches nearby.

Hondarribia has distinctive historic houses typical of the Basque fishing villages, with intricately carved and brightly painted woodwork, and balconies loaded with flowers.

Llanes
San Vicente de la Barquera
Santander
Cabo de Ajo
A8 Laredo
Costa Vasca
Hondarribia
de Europa
Torrelavega
A67
Bilbao
A8
San Sebastián
AP1
Cordillera Cantábrica
A68
Reinosa
THE BASQUE COUNTRY
Vitoria-Gasteiz
A1

The Atlantic Coast

The rocky crags and islands, sand dunes and sheltered estuaries and wetlands of this coast provide varied habitats for an enormous range of birds, both residents and migratory visitors.

0 kilometres 50
0 miles 25

Kittiwakes are members of the gull family. Each summer they breed in clefts in sea-cliffs, and spend all winter far out at sea, cruising the oceans for fish. There are large colonies on the islands off Galicia.

Snipes are most common in the marshes near Santoña, in Cantabria. In spring male snipes perform a strange diving display to attract females, making a drumming sound with their feathers.

Oystercatchers are easily recognizable by their black and white plumage and bright red beak – strong enough for them to crack open shellfish. They are common around cockle and mussel beds.

Ospreys are the only birds of prey that live solely on fish. They migrate between Northern Europe and West Africa, stopping over in Asturias and Cantabria each spring and autumn.

San Sebastián's La Concha beach is one of the most beautiful on the north coast. Forming an elegant curve, it faces the green promontories at the mouth of the bay, and is lined by a gracious promenade.

NORTHERN SPAIN THROUGH THE YEAR

Most Spaniards love a fun-filled fiesta. In Northern Spain every town or village has its patron saint whose day is celebrated with parades, *corridas*, singing and firework displays. Major religious festivals, such as *Semana Santa* (Holy Week), are occasions for spectacular celebrations. Some fiestas, such as the Sanfermines in Pamplona or St James' Day in Santiago de Compostela,

attract crowds of tourists. Many farming or fishing towns also celebrate the harvest or their catch with fairs, colourful rituals and displays of local produce. There are plenty of music, theatre, dance and film festivals, many internationally renowned, like the San Sebastián Film Festival. Check the dates with local tourist offices, as some vary from year to year.

Wild horses brought in from the countryside during the Rapa das Bestas

Spring

The inhabitants of Northern Spain enjoy outdoor life in spring. People turn out on streets and meet in bars and cafés. Fields burst forth with wild flowers after the winter cold. Eastertime abounds in colourful processions.

March

Festa da Arribada (*1st weekend Mar*), Baiona (Galicia). The re-enactment of the arrival of the *Pinta* – the 1493 caravel that brought news of the discovery of America – accompanied by a medieval fair.
Fiesta Santa Áurea (*11 Mar*), Villavelayo (La Rioja). The feast of the town's patron saint, with dancing to bagpipes and castanets.

Semana Santa (*Mar–Apr*). Holy Week is celebrated in grand style. Colourful processions are led by religious brotherhoods in brilliantly coloured robes and hoods. The biggest processions are those in Northern Castile and Navarra.

April

Aberri Eguna (*Easter Sunday*), the Basque Country. Basque National Day.
Güevos Pintos (*Easter*), Langreo (Asturias). Easter festival of painted eggs.
La Folía (*1st or 2nd Sun after Easter*), San Vicente de la

La Folía in San Vicente de la Barquera

Barquera (Cantabria). A statue of the Virgin is carried across the harbour in a procession of illuminated and decorated boats, to bless the sea.

May

White-water Rafting Day on the Esca River (*1–2 May*), Burgui (Navarra). Prominent figures from the world of science, sport or culture are presented with the Golden Rafter Award.
La Victoria (*1st Fri May*), Jaca (Pyrenees). Parades, banquets and medieval jousts celebrating a legendary 8th-century battle against the Moors.
Fiesta del Santo (*10–15 May*), Santo Domingo de la Calzada (La Rioja). The feast of the town's patron saint, who was believed to protect pilgrims travelling to Santiago, is celebrated with three days of colourful dances and processions. In the most famous, young girls carry baskets of fresh bread on their heads. Hearty feasts are centred on "the Saint's Lunch" of lamb and chickpeas.
Día das Letras Gallegas (*17 May*), Galicia. Celebration of the Galician language, in literature and culture.
Bicycle Marathon (*late May*), Cangas de Onís (Asturias).

Average Daily Hours of Sunshine

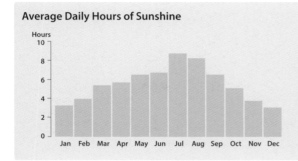

Sunshine Chart
July and August are the sunniest months in Northern Spain, and also the peak tourist season. December and January are the cloudiest, especially in Galicia and in the mountain areas.

Summer

Late summer is harvest time, with many fiestas celebrating crop gathering. August is a holiday month, and Spaniards flock to the coastal towns and beaches, or the mountains.

June
Corpus Christi *(Thu in May or Jun)*. Religious processions.
Festival of Flower Carpets *(weekend after Corpus Christi)*, Ponteareas & Gondomar (Galicia). Streets are laid with colourful carpets of flowers.
Wine Battle *(29 Jun)*, Haro (La Rioja). Manic fiesta in which thousands of people squirt wine at each other.

July
Rapa das Bestas *(various weekends, late Jun–late Aug)*, Pontevedra & Lugo (Galicia). Wild horses are rounded up to have their manes and tails cut.
Celtic Festival *(early Jul)*, Ortigueira (Galicia). Inter-national festival with music and piper parade.
Semana Negra *(1st or 2nd week Jul)*, Gijon (Asturias). This festival is entirely dedicated to noir fiction.
Coso Blanco *(1st weekend Jul)*, Castro Urdiales (Cantabria). Nighttime parade of carriages.
Los Sanfermines *(6–14 Jul)*, Pamplona (Navarra). Bull running, with festivities.
Festival de la Sidra *(2nd week Jul)*, Nava (Asturias). Cider festival with tastings.
International Jazz Festivals Getxo *(1st week)*; Vitoria *(mid-Jul)*; San Sebastián *(3rd week)*.

Pamplona's *corrida* during Los Sanfermines

Danza de los Zancos *(21–24 Jul & last weekend Sep)*, Anguiano (La Rioja). Costumed dancers on stilts walk the steep streets trying to knock each other off.
Feast of St James *(25 Jul)*, Santiago de Compostela (Galicia). Fireworks on the eve of the saint's feast day.

Cider being poured during the Festival de la Sidra in Nava

Fiesta Patronales *(end Jul)*, Tudela (Navarra). Bull running, dancing and singing takes place in honour of Santa Ana.

August
Festa María Pita *(Aug)*, A Coruña (Galicia). Month-long programme of concerts, *corridas*, medieval fairs and sea battles in honour of this war heroine.
Descent of the Río Sella *(1st Sat Aug)*, Asturias. Spectacular kayak and canoe race from Arriondas to Ribadasella.
Semana Grande *(2nd week Aug)*, Gijón (Asturias). Lavish festival with concerts, dances, parades and food displays.
Feast of the Assumption *(15 Aug)*. Festivities include a sardine feast at Sada (A Coruña) and El Rosario, a fishermen's festival in Luarca (Asturias).
Aste Nagusia *(3rd week)*, San Sebastián; *(last week)*, Bilbao. Week-long programmes of parades, music, dancing and Basque sports.
Romería de Naseiro *(late Aug)*, Viveiro (Galicia). Huge celebration of Galician cuisine.
Festival Internacional de Santander *(Aug)*, Santander (Cantabria). Cultural festival for lovers of theatre, opera, classical dance and ballet.
Batalla de Flores *(last Fri Aug)*, Laredo (Cantabria). Parade of extravagant floats, made of flowers, ending in a flower-throwing "battle".

Average Rainfall

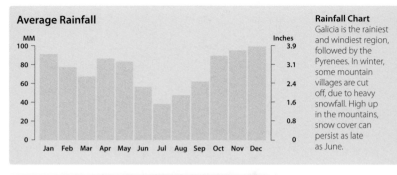

Rainfall Chart
Galicia is the rainiest and windiest region, followed by the Pyrenees. In winter, some mountain villages are cut off, due to heavy snowfall. High up in the mountains, snow cover can persist as late as June.

Visitors on a hike in the Picos de Europa

Autumn

Autumn marks the beginning of vine harvest festivities, and the first juice extracted from the grapes is blessed. The start of the mushroom picking season becomes evident in restaurants, and the hunting season also opens, continuing until February. In larger towns the music and theatre seasons begin, and San Sebastián hosts the famous film festival.

September

Vuelta Ciclista a España (late Aug–mid-Sep) Round Spain cycle race.

Regatas de La Concha (1st and 2nd Sun Sep), San Sebastián (Basque Country). Traditional Basque rowing races across La Concha bay.

Nuestra Señora de Covadonga (8 Sep), Picos de Europa (Asturias). People pay homage to the patron of Asturias.

Fiesta San Mateo (20–26 Sep), Logroño (Rioja). Rioja wine harvest is celebrated on St Matthew's day with food, drink, concerts and *corridas*.

The treading of grapes during the Fiesta San Mateo in Logroño

Día de Campoo (last Sun Sep), Reinosa (Cantabria). Celebration of Cantabrian folk music, costumes and traditions, with a parade of bullock carts.

San Sebastián Film Festival (last 2 weeks Sep), San Sebastián (Basque Country). One of the world's top film festivals, inaugurated in 1953.

San Antolín (1–8 Sep), Lekeitio (Basque Country). Wild goose festival, including a contest in which people try to hang onto the greased neck of a dead or rubber goose above the harbour.

October

San Froilán (1st & 2nd week), Lugo (Galicia). Food tasting, parades, dancing and singing.

Seafood Festival (1st or 2nd week), O Grove (Galicia). Seafood tasting and dancing in traditional costumes.

Virgen del Pilar (12 Oct). National day of the patron saint of Spain.

A woman in traditional costume

November

All Saints' Day (1 Nov). Traditional cakes are made the day before, and then people take flowers to cemeteries to remember deceased relatives.

Os Magostos (11 Nov) Galicia. Many towns and villages celebrate the sweet chestnut harvest.

Fiesta del Humo (last Sun Nov), Arnedillo (La Rioja). Bonfires and feasts in honour of St Andrew.

Gijón Film Festival (late Nov–early Dec), Gijón (Asturias). This film festival started in 1963.

Average Temperature

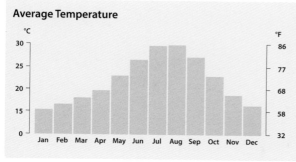

Temperature Chart
The warmest months are July, August and September, although the heat is less ferocious on the northern coast than inland. In mountain areas it can be cold even in summer, and the weather can change very rapidly.

Winter

Mountainous Northern Spain has fairly harsh winters. The mountain passes close to traffic, the skiing season starts, and Christmas brings family gatherings and religious reflections, before carnival starts.

December

Santo Tomás (21 Dec), Bilbao, San Sebastián and other Basque towns. Pre-Christmas fairs in celebration of St Thomas, with food and traditional products for Christmas.
El Gordo (22 Dec). Televised draw of the top prize in the Spanish lottery, "the Fat One".
Noche Buena (24 Dec). Christmas Eve is spent within the family circle in Spain.
Santos Inocentes (28 Dec). Spanish April Fool's Day.
Noche Vieja (31 Dec). New Year's Eve is an exuberant farewell to the passing year.

Women banging pots during a fiesta in honour of Santo Tomás

January

Fiesta del Aguinaldo (Guirria) (1 Jan), San Juan de Beleño (Asturias). This small town is visited by Guirria – a mysterious masked figure who, accompanied by 40 young horse riders, asks people for presents.
La Vijanera en Silió (1st Sun), Cantabria. The *Zarramacos* dressed in furs and with blackened faces parade through the streets noisily with big bells to frighten away the evil spirits of the past year.
Epiphany – Tres Reyes (6 Jan). Arrival of the "Three Kings" (wise men) celebrated everywhere with parades, presents and children's events.
La Tamborrada (19–20 Jan), San Sebastián (Basque Country). The feast of St Sebastian is celebrated with ear-splitting parades of pipe-and-drum bands and fireworks, commemorating the fire that swept the town during the Napoleonic Wars.

February

Carnival Procession (late Feb or Mar), Lantz (Navarra). Parade of large figures made of hay, burned ceremoniously afterwards. Famous and popular carnival celebrations take place in many towns throughout Spain.

Os Peliqueiros Carnival in Laza

Os Peliqueiros Carnival (last Sun of Carnival, Feb–Mar), Laza (Galicia). Os Peliqueiros wearing comical masks stroll along the town streets, beating passers-by with birch sticks.

Public Holidays

New Year's Day (1 Jan)
Epiphany (6 Jan)
Good Friday, Easter Sunday (Mar/Apr)
Labour Day (1 May)
Assumption (15 Aug)
Virgen del Pilar (12 Oct)
All Saints' Day (1 Nov)
Constitution Day (6 Dec)
Immaculate Conception (8 Dec)
Christmas Day (25 Dec)

THE HISTORY OF NORTHERN SPAIN

Inhabited from remote times, the regions of Northern Spain have played a significant role in the peninsula's history. It was from here that the Reconquest began, and from here that many of Spain's great navigators originated. The north was involved in the Carlist Wars, and was a Republican stronghold during the Spanish Civil War.

Prehistory

Remains of some of our earliest pre-human ancestors were discovered in caves at Atapuerca, in Burgos province, in 1976. They are estimated to be 800,000 years old. About 20,000 years ago, humans of Cro-Magnon type (very similar to modern humans) appeared on the Iberian Peninsula. Skilled artists, they decorated the walls of caves with engravings and polychrome paintings of animals. The finest of these caves is Altamira, in Cantabria, which was discovered in the 19th century.

At the end of the Ice Age, several thousand years ago, people began to abandon their nomadic lifestyle for a more settled existence. Instead of hunting animals they learnt to breed them, and to cultivate crops. They began to make increasingly sophisticated tools and to smelt metals.

Celts, Phoenicians and Greeks

In about 1200 BC Celts began to migrate south, settling in the peninsula. Over the following centuries they mixed with Iberian tribes, laying the foundations of the Celtiberian culture. In Northern Spain, particularly in Galicia, the Celts built distinctive hilltop settlements – *castros* – with round stone houses. The best-known Celtiberian tribe are the Arevacos, who famously defended Numantia against the Romans in 133 BC.

The peninsula's northeastern coast was colonized by Greeks, who established the colony of Emporion, near present-day Barcelona, in about 600 BC. The Phoenicians, who settled in the south, founded Cádiz, the oldest town in this part of Europe. They coined the name "Spain", meaning "Island of Rabbits", and they also introduced the grapevine, the olive tree and the donkey. Both the Greeks and the Phoenicians were interested in Spain's deposits of ore. Galicia, for example, yielded gold and tin, which was needed to make bronze. In time, the Phoenicians were displaced by the Carthaginians.

The origins of the mysterious Basques, who already inhabited the north, are not clear, but it's possible they are descended from the earliest inhabitants of Iberia (Cro-Magnon). The earliest written reference to them appears in Roman writings.

c.800,000 BC Pre-human presence in Atapuerca caves, Burgos	**c.5000 BC** Beginning of the Neolithic Revolution	**c.1200 BC** Celts start to settle in the Iberian Peninsula		*The golden helmet of a Celtiberian warrior*
800,000 BC	**200,000 BC**	**1000 BC**	**600 BC**	**228 BC**
Painting of a bison at Altamira cave.		**c.18–12,000 BC** Cave paintings at Altamira. Cantabria	**c.600 BC** Greek colony of Emporion founded on the coast of Girona	**264–241 BC** First Punic War between Carthage and Rome

◄ *Arrival of the Body of Saint James in Galicia* by School of Miguel Ximenez

Fragment of a Roman mosaic of the 4th century BC, now in the Museu Arqueològic in Girona

Roman and Visigoth Spain

The Romans entered Spain as part of their war with the Carthaginians (the Punic Wars), trying to control the whole of the Iberian peninsula. The tribes in the north, who occupied land rich in minerals, resisted the longest, but their lands were finally taken over.

The Romans also built an extensive network of roads, bridges and aqueducts. The towns of Astorga, in León, and Lugo, Galicia, still have their Roman walls, and Pamplona, founded in 74 BC by the Roman military commander Pompey, later became the capital of the kingdom of Navarra. Although Latin was widely spoken, the indigenous population continued to use local languages as late as the 2nd century (the Basques never stopped). Christianity began to spread, replacing the worship of local deities.

When the Roman Empire began to crumble, Germanic tribes invaded from the north. The Vandals and the Suevi occupied León and Galicia, but the Visigoths gained control, almost succeeding in creating the first unified state in Spain. However, the Visigoths failed to subjugate the Basques, who continued to expand their territory. In the final stages of the Visigothic state, Septimania (its northern part) attempted to break away. Civil wars fought under Wamba's reign hastened the kingdom's disintegration.

Moorish Spain

In 711 the declining Visigothic kingdom was invaded and quickly conquered by the Moors. Most of the Iberian peninsula became part of a vast Islamic empire. Christians who did not accept Muslim rule retreated into the northern mountains, which remained unconquered due to their terrain, fierce resistance and an inhospitable climate. In 756 Abd al Rahman I proclaimed an independent emirate on the peninsula, and made Córdoba its capital. For 300 years the Caliphate of Córdoba was Europe's most opulent society. Periods of peace

Portrait of Wamba, the Visigothic king who ruled from 672 to 680

219–201 BC Second Punic War. Expansion of Roman territory on the Iberian peninsula	**61 BC** Julius Caesar begins final conquest of Galicia and northern Lusitania		
	19 BC Agrippa conquers Cantabria and Asturias, completing the Roman conquest	*Visigothic relief on a Christian theme, 7th century*	

200 BC	**1 BC**	**AD 200**	**400**
155 BC Lusitanian War		**AD 74** Emperor Vespasian extends Roman law to the Spanish provinces	**476** Fall of the Western Roman Empire
219 BC Hannibal captures Sagunt	*Stone disk, 1st century BC*		**589** Reccared and the Visigothic nobility embrace Christianity; Toledo becomes capital of Visigothic Spain

and trade were interspersed with continual wars with the northern Christian kingdoms, and with the Frankish empire of Charlemagne from across the Pyrenees. In the late 10th century the vizier of Córdoba, Al Mansur, led 100 raids into the Christian territories,

A miniature from the *Cantigas de Santa María* by Alfonso X, the Wise

plundering towns across the north, including Santiago de Compostela (the site where St James' relics were discovered), and halting further Christian advances for another century. Around 1013 the Caliphate disintegrated into bickering emirates.

The Reconquest

The collapse of the Caliphate favoured the expansion southwards of the Christian states that had taken shape in the north. Among them was the kingdom of Asturias, whose origins date from the perhaps-legendary Battle of Covadonga in 722, when a small band led by the Visigoth Pelayo are said to have halted the Muslim advance. After the battle, seen as the starting point of the long 'reconquest' of Spain from the Moors, Pelayo became king of Asturias. This kingdom won its greatest victories against the Moors during the reign of Alfonso II (791-842).

In the 9th century, after a short period of Moorish rule in the Basque territories at the foot of the Pyrenees, the kingdom of Navarra came into being. Previously the Basques had demonstrated their independence on all sides by defeating the rearguard of

A 9th-century stone cross

Charlemagne's army at the famous Battle of Roncesvalles (778). Another part of Christian Spain developed around 800, when Charlemagne's armies crossed into the eastern Pyrenees, making the area the 'Spanish March' of the Frankish empire – the origin of the future Catalonia. Around this time vast numbers of pilgrims from all over Europe were journeying on the Road to Santiago, which resulted in Northern Spain becoming culturally and economically connected to the rest of Europe.

Battles for the expansion of territory gradually took on the status of crusades against the Muslims. In 1085 Alfonso VI, king of Castile and León, captured Toledo from the Moors, and expelled the Muslim rulers. His kingdom became the dominant power in central Spain. In the 12th century Muslim Spain was again unified under the rule of two militant dynasties from north Africa – the Almoravids and their successors the Almohads – who halted the Reconquest. But in 1212, the combined forces of several northern kingdoms crushed the Almohad army at Las Navas de Tolosa, paving the way for the final victory of Christian power in the Iberian peninsula.

711 Moors defeat Visigoths at Battle of Guadalete

c.810 St James' tomb supposedly discovered at Santiago de Compostela

1230 Ferdinand the Saint (El Santo) reunites Castile and León

905 Sancho I founds the kingdom of Navarra

1085 Alfonso VI takes Toledo

800 **1000** **1200** **1400**

778 Battle of Roncesvalles

1212 Combined Christian forces defeat the Moors at the Battle of Las Navas de Tolosa

722 Battle of Covadonga. The kingdom of Asturias founded

Illuminated manuscript, 9th century

The Northern Kingdoms and the Reconquest

The regions of the north were the only parts of Iberia not conquered by the Moors, and their identities were all formed in the difficult, centuries-long struggle to retake lands further south from Muslim rule. Political disunity among the Christian strongholds, their remote mountain locations, and a severe climate all made the effort to retake the lands that much harder. The main Christian states that took shape were Asturias, León, Castile, Navarra, Aragón and Catalonia.

Ferdinand the Great
By uniting León and Castile in 1037, Ferdinand created the first Christian coalition of significant military strength.

Navarra's troops were commanded by Sancho VII, the Strong.

Several Spanish kingdoms answered the Pope's call for a united campaign against the Moors. This war between Christians and Muslims assumed the character of a crusade.

The Almohad army was finally crushed by the Christian cavalry.

Pelayo the Warrior
The Reconquest began after the Battle of Covadonga (722), where Pelayo, a Visigothic nobleman, defeated a Moorish army. He became king of Asturias.

Santa María del Naranco
This imposing pre-Romanesque building near Oviedo was erected in the 9th century as the palace of Ramiros I, and was later converted into a church.

The Battle of Clavijo (844)
In this battle that probably only existed in legend, St James, known as the Moor-slayer, led Christian knights on to victory against the Muslims.

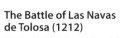

The Battle of Las Navas de Tolosa (1212)
Fired with Christian zeal and the backing of Pope Innocent III, the combined forces of the kingdoms of Castile, Aragón and Navarra defeated the Almohads at Las Navas de Tolosa. This victory, depicted in the above stained-glass window in the Colegiata Real in Roncesvalles, led to the collapse of Moorish power in Spain.

Cantigas de Santa María
This manuscript detail by Alfonso the Wise, king of Castile (1252–84), shows Christians confronting Moors. Alfonso encouraged cooperation between Christian, Arabic and Jewish scholars.

The combined armies
of Castile, Aragón and Navarra numbered 70,000 knights.

Cross of Angels (808)
This jewelled cross is an exquisite example of early Asturian art. Alfonso II, who bequeathed it to Oviedo Cathedral, had it inscribed:"Whosoever dares remove this cross from the place which my will destined for it shall be thunderstruck by God."

The Church of San Miguel in Estella
In the Christian kingdoms, religious architecture flourished along the pilgrimage route, an example being the late Romanesque church in Estella.

The Cathedral in Huesca
The *mudéjar* style developed in regions that were influenced by the Moors. One example of this style is the richly decorated gallery above the portal of the cathedral in Huesca.

The body of a
Moorish soldier

Shield with the coat of arms
of Sancho VII of Navarra

The Tomb of King Alfonso VII
Alfonso VII of Castile led many military campaigns in southern Spain. In 1147 he captured Calatrava, opening the way to Andalusia. He also occupied Córdoba and Almería.

The *Santa Maria*, Christopher Columbus's caravel

Discovery and Exploration

Through their marriage in 1469, the Catholic Monarchs – Fernando II of Aragón and Isabel I of Castile – united almost all the territories of the peninsula. The process was completed when Navarra was incorporated in 1512. When Christopher Columbus discovered America in 1492, this marked the beginning of Spain's overseas expansion. Many of the ships and navigators came from the Basque Country and Cantabria. Among notable seamen were Juan Sebastián Elcano – the first to circumnavigate the globe after Magellan died during his journey – and Juan Sebastián de la Cosa, who sailed with Columbus and mapped the new lands.

Juan Sebastián Elcano

In 1517 Carlos I, of the Habsburg dynasty, inherited the thrones of Spain, Austria and Burgundy, giving him huge territories across Europe. Under him, Spain acquired vast lands in the Americas, becoming the first world-wide empire. His successor, Felipe II, made Madrid the capital.

The Golden Age

The discovery voyages led to growth in trade, which encouraged the development of north coast towns. Growth was somewhat limited by the king's insistence that all large-scale trade with the American colonies go through Seville. The Spanish Empire also engaged in constant wars – in the colonies, against the French, Turks and Protestants. The Dutch wars started in the 1560s, and in 1588 part of the Spanish Armada set out from Vigo to attack England. In 1589, Francis Drake led attacks on Vigo and A Coruña, in response to the Armada.

The north provided a lot of Spain's soldiers. Related to this militarism was the founding of the Jesuits by the Basque Saint Ignatius, himself a soldier once. The constant wars exhausted the country, however, and by 1650 the process of inexorable imperial decline began, following defeats against the Dutch and French.

El Escorial, the palace designed by Juan de Herrera

1502 Expulsion of unconverted Moors from Spain	**1512** Annexation of Navarra completes the unification of Spain	**1618** Spain joins the Thirty Years' War against France
1491 Birth of St Ignatius of Loyola, founder of the Jesuits	**1521** Basque seaman Juan Sebastián Elcano completes circumnavigation of the globe	

1400	**1450**	**1500**	**1550**	**1600**	**1**6

1492 Columbus discovers America	**1540** Founding of Basque university in Oñati	**1659** Peace of the Pyrenees signed with France
1500 Juan de la Cosa creates the first map of the New World	*Isabel I, Queen of Castile (1474–1504)*	

A 15th-century knight

Fernando VII agreeing to accept the Constitution

Bourbon Spain

In 1701 Carlos I died without an heir. In the subsequent War of the Spanish Succession, Castile and most of the north supported Felipe V (of the French Bourbon dynasty). Catalonia, Aragón and Valencia supported the Archduke Charles of Austria, who promised to restore their traditional rights. Felipe V was victorious, and in 1715 made Spain into a unified state, abolishing the local rights of Catalonia, Aragón and other regions. In return for their loyalty, however, the Basque Country and Navarra were allowed to keep their local rights.

The 18th-century Bourbon kings and ministers sought to reform Spain's adminstration and halt the country's decline. Most important was Carlos III (1759–88), who in his efforts to encourage economic expansion ended Seville's monopoly on trade with Spanish America. This had an immediate effect in the north, which saw vigorous expansion in ship-building, trade and agriculture.

The French Revolution was the start of a traumatic period. Initially Spain joined European monarchies in attacking Republican France, with heavy losses.

Later, unpopular PM Godoy allied Spain with Napoleon. In 1808 Napoleon kidnapped the Spanish royal family and declared his brother, Joseph, king of Spain, triggering the Peninsular War, with Spain aided by Britain. During the war, a *Cortes* or parliament met in Cádiz and approved Spain's first constitution in 1812.

At the end of these wars in 1814 Spain's institutions were severely weakened. The restless 19th century also saw the awakening of nationalist sentiments in the Basque Country. Galicia and Catalonia sought to rescue their languages and traditions from the dominance of the official Spanish-speaking culture.

Carlist Wars

When Fernando VII died in 1833, a dispute arose over his successor – his brother Don Carlos or daughter Isabel – and civil conflict, the Carlist Wars, began. The Carlists had support in the northern provinces, particularly in the Basque Country, Navarra and north Catalonia, which opposed state centralization. The Carlists were defeated; the First Republic was proclaimed in 1873.

A battle between loyalists and Carlists during the Carlist Wars

1767 Jesuits expelled from Spain and its empire by Carlos III

1846–9 Second Carlist War

1898 Following the Spanish-American War, Spain loses the last of its major colonies

1702–14 War of the Spanish Succession

1833–9 First Carlist War

1700

1750

1800

1850

1900

Felipe V (1700–24), the first of the Bourbon kings

1808–1814 War of Independence with Napoleon

1812 Promulgation of liberal constitution in Cádiz leads to uprising

1875 Bourbon dynasty restored

1872–6 Third Carlist War

General Primo de Rivera, who ruled Spain from 1923 to 1930

Unrest and the Second Republic

In the first 30 years of the 20th century, during the reign of Alfonso XIII, the country was plagued by strikes and political crises. Successive governments were incompetent, and disorder grew. During World War I Spain remained neutral, which boosted the economy but also encouraged demands for reform, with violent confrontations between the government and radical forces. In 1923 General Miguel Primo de Rivera suspended the constitution and declared himself Dictator, with the support of the king. He ruled with an iron hand, curtailing civil liberties and banning regional languages.

In 1930 Primo's dictatorship collapsed, and the following year local elections showed huge support for Republican candidates. The king was forced to leave the country, and in 1931 Spain's Second Republic was proclaimed, amid high hopes that it would deal with the country's problems. Reforms proved ineffective, however, and the country was rocked by outbreaks of anticlericalism, and unemployment rose.

Civil War and Franco

In 1936, when the general election was won by the left, the army rose in revolt, starting the Spanish Civil War. In much of southern Spain, Madrid, Catalonia, and part of the Basque Country, Cantabria and Asturias Republican forces defeated the initial revolt. The rest of the country was controlled by the Nationalists (the army and the right), led by General Francisco Franco. The war dragged on for three years, the Nationalists supported by Germany and Italy, and the Republicans, much less so, by the Soviet Union. The International Brigades fighting on the Republican side included volunteers from many other countries.

In the north, the Basque Country, Cantabria and Asturias were cut off from the rest of the Republican-controlled zone, and

The Basque town of Gernika (Guernica), after the bombing of 1937

Second Republic election poster

1923–30 Dictatorship of General Primo de Rivera

1937 Battle for Madrid rages; on 27 April Nazi planes bomb Gernika

1939 National Army enters Madrid on 28 March; Franco declares the war ended on 1 April

1900	1920	1940	1960

1909 Semana Trágica (Tragic Week) in Barcelona

1934 Revolution in Asturias, suppressed by General Franco

1936 Start of the Spanish Civil War

Post-World War II ration card

were gradually overrun by Franco's forces during 1937. One of the most notorious episodes of the war was the Nazi bombing of the Basque town of Gernika.

The Nationalists ultimately triumphed. With the end of the war in 1939, Franco's dictatorship began. Devastated and impoverished, the country stood in international isolation until the 1950s. Republicans suffered repression and many were forced into exile. In the centralized state, regional diversity was repressed. The use of the Catalan and Basque languages was prohibited, there was moral censorship, and political parties were banned. The 1960s saw the emergence of the violent campaign of the Basque separatist group, ETA.

Modern Spain

Franco died in 1975, having named Juan Carlos I (grandson of Alfonso XIII) as his successor. The country's transition to democracy was relatively peaceful. Political parties were legalized, and in 1978 a new constitution declared Spain a parliamentary monarchy. The constitution granted autonomous status to Spain's regions, which enabled the Basque Country, Galicia, Asturias and Cantabria to set up local administrations from 1979 onwards. However, in the Basque Country this still did not satisfy ETA, and terrorism became one of Spain's constant problems.

Mass demonstration against ETA, the Basque separatist group

In 1982 Spain elected its first Socialist government, led by Felipe González. In 1985 it joined NATO, and in 1986 became a member of the European Union. The Olympic Games were staged in Barcelona in 1992.

The 1996 general election was won by the centre-right People's Party (PP), led by José María Aznar. Spain enjoyed further economic success, but his decision to send troops to Iraq was unpopular.

In March 2004 Islamic extremists blew up four suburban trains in Madrid. Aznar's

King Felipe VI and Queen Letizia at an official function

government initially blamed ETA, but as the truth emerged this only increased the popularity of the Socialists (PSOE), led by José Rodríguez Zapatero, who were voted into power. In November 2011, the centre-right PP came into power again led by Mariano Rajoy, who has promised to tackle Spain's economic problems. In 2014, King Juan Carlos I abdicated in favour of his son Felipe VI.

1979 Catalonia, Basque Country and Galicia granted autonomy

1997 Museo Guggenheim opens in Bilbao

2002 Spain adopts the euro

2004 On 11 March Islamic extremists carry out a terrorist attack in Madrid; on 14 March PSOE wins the general election

2006 In March ETA declares a permanent ceasefire

2007 ETA breaks ceasefire

1980

2000

2020

1975 Death of Franco (20 Nov)

1986 Spain joins the EEC (now the European Union)

2003 As an ally of the USA, Spain sends troops to Iraq

2008 Zapatero's PSOE party re-elected

2014 King Juan Carlos I abdicates; his son ascends to the throne to become Felipe VI

2011 ETA declares another permanent ceasefire; Mariano Rajoy of the PP wins the general election

General Franco

NORTHERN SPAIN REGION BY REGION

Northern Spain at a Glance

Increasing numbers of visitors are drawn to Northern Spain, where the climate is milder than in the southern Iberian Peninsula, and the autonomous regions offer all the ingredients of a wonderful holiday. The Atlantic coast boasts attractive sandy beaches, while the mountain ranges are criss-crossed by numerous footpaths. Magnificent examples of Romanesque architecture mark the famous pilgrimage route to Santiago de Compostela, while in the region's cities fine modern buildings can be seen. Fiestas and festivals take place throughout the year in Northern Spain, many of them hailed as important international events.

Santillana del Mar *(see pp110–11)* is one of the region's most picturesque towns, with beautifully preserved medieval houses. Inside the Convento de Regina Coeli is a museum with a rich collection of painted figures of saints. Near the town are the famous Cuevas de Altamira.

The Picos de Europa mountain range *(see pp104–7)* dominates the landscape of Asturias and Cantabria. The towns, situated in beautiful valleys, boast a plethora of pre-Romanesque buildings, while hiking trails lead through the spectacular scenery of the national park.

Map labels:
Viveiro
Ferrol
A Coruña
Vilalba
Ribadeo
Avilés
Gijón
Llanes
Santander
Santillana del Mar
Bilba
Santiago de Compostela
Lugo
ASTURIAS AND CANTABRIA *(See pp84–121)*
Reinosa
Padrón
GALICIA *(See pp52–83)*
Miranda Eb
Quiroga
Vigo
Ourense

The Rías Baixas form one of Northern Spain's prettiest coastlines. Around the towns and villages here are many quaint *hórreos* – wooden granaries raised on stone stilts *(see p23)*.

Santiago de Compostela *(see pp64–9)* attracts thousands of visitors each year. In the Middle Ages, the cathedral in Santiago was one of the most important places of pilgrimage in Christendom.

◄ One of the impressive rock formations at Praia das Catedrais, in Ribadeo, Galicia

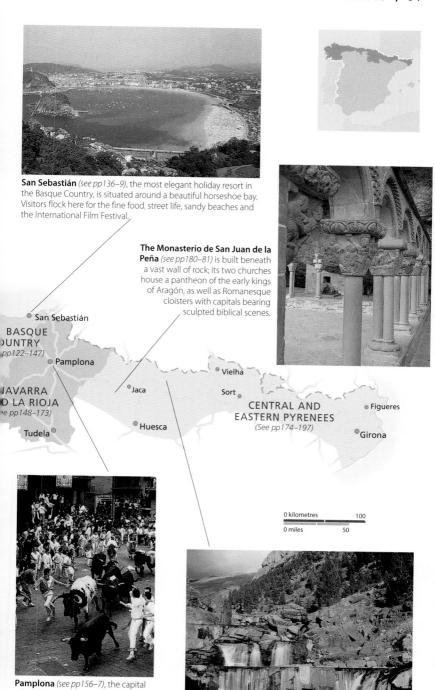

San Sebastián (see pp136–9), the most elegant holiday resort in the Basque Country, is situated around a beautiful horseshoe bay. Visitors flock here for the fine food, street life, sandy beaches and the International Film Festival.

The Monasterio de San Juan de la Peña (pp180–81) is built beneath a vast wall of rock; its two churches house a pantheon of the early kings of Aragón, as well as Romanesque cloisters with capitals bearing sculpted biblical scenes.

San Sebastián

BASQUE COUNTRY (pp122–147)

Pamplona

NAVARRA AND LA RIOJA (see pp148–173)

Tudela

Jaca

Huesca

Vielha

Sort

CENTRAL AND EASTERN PYRENEES (See pp174–197)

Figueres

Girona

0 kilometres 100
0 miles 50

Pamplona (see pp156–7), the capital of Navarra, is best known for its annual fiesta, *Los Sanfermines*, immortalized by Ernest Hemingway. The highlight of each day of riotous celebration is the *Encierro*, in which bulls stampede through the streets.

The Parque Nacional de Ordesa (see pp186–9) in the Aragonese Pyrenees is a haven for walkers and hikers. The rocky massifs are enchanting, and in the mountain valleys many species of flora and fauna can be seen.

GALICIA

Remote in the northwest corner of the Iberian peninsula, Galicia is a green, rainswept region remarkable for the diversity of its landscape, where coastal cliffs alternate with lowlands and *rías*. The region is famous for its excellent cuisine, while pilgrims flock here to visit the city of Santiago de Compostela. The Galicians, whose origins are Celtic, are fiercely proud of their culture and language.

Traditionally, Galicia was seen as a poor agricultural region, whose economy did not lend itself to modernization. It absorbed little Roman influence, was never conquered by the Moors, and in the Middle Ages fell under the control of the kingdom of Asturias. It was only very briefly an independent monarchy, in the 10th and 11th centuries.

Bordering Portugal to the south and enclosed by the waters of the Atlantic Ocean, Galicia could offer its inhabitants little in the way of new land for cultivation; overpopulation and unemployment forced many to emigrate. Yet, in the 20th century, Galicia began to develop, and today traditional lifestyles rub shoulders with modernity.

Galicia has always maintained strong links with the sea; the port cities of Vigo and A Coruña are centres of culture, commerce, and industry. Fishing is vital to the economy, and Galician seafood is the best in Spain. The coastline, cut with fjord-like *rías*, is dotted with fishing villages. Enormous efforts have been made to clean up damage caused by the 2002 sinking of the Prestige oil tanker, and most of the coast has now recovered.

Mainland Spain's most westerly point – the heather-clad Cabo Fisterra – is situated on this rugged stretch of coast. Even more magical is the pilgrimage centre of Santiago de Compostela, the region's capital. Romantic hillsides shrouded in mist conceal the remains of Celtic settlements; at road junctions and in the towns stand weathered stone crosses, while in the villages old granaries can be seen. The picture is completed by the sound of Galicians' favourite instrument – the bagpipes – and their language, *gallego*, which bears strong similarities to Portuguese.

The picturesque Galician coast in the vicinity of Ézaro, near the remote headland of Cabo Fisterra

◄ The façade of the Convento de San Martiño Pinario, in Santiago de Compostela

Exploring Galicia

Santiago de Compostela is Galicia's major tourist attraction. This beautiful city is the centrepiece of a region with many fine old towns, especially Betanzos, Mondoñedo, Lugo and Pontevedra. The resorts along the coastline of the wild Rías Altas, with their backdrop of forest-covered hills, offer good bathing. The Rías Baixas, the southern part of Galicia's west coast, have sheltered coves and sandy beaches, and excellent seafood. Travelling through the interior, where life seems to have changed little in centuries, is an ideal way to spend a peaceful, rural holiday.

Coat of arms, Colexio de San Xerome in Santiago

Getting Around

Galicia is served by airports at A Coruña, Vigo and Santiago de Compostela. A network of modern highways connects Vigo, A Coruña and other major towns, and also links Galicia to the rest of Spain and to Portugal, though traffic along the coast can be heavy. Rail lines link Galicia's major cities and towns on the north coast, as do coach services.

Key

━━━ Motorway
= = Motorway under construction
━━ Major road
⋯⋯ Minor road
━━ Scenic route
━━ Main railway line
━━ Railway line
━━ National border
━━ Regional border

0 kilometres   25
0 miles   25

A stone cross on the Costa da Morte, northwest of Santiago de Compostela

Sights at a Glance

Tours

For keys to symbols *see back flap*

Amazing rock formations at the beach Praia das Catedrais, near Ribadeo

❶ Ribadeo

Lugo. **Road Map** C1. 🏔 10,000.
🛈 Rúa Dionisio Gamallo Fierros 7;
982 12 86 89. 🚌 Wed. 🎪 San Roque
(16 Aug), Santa Maria del Campo
(8 Sep). 🌐 **ribadeo.org**

Galicia's north coast, between
Ribadeo and Ferrol, is an area
of natural beauty known as the
Rías Altas, formed from *ría* inlets
and beautiful bays. The characterful fishing town of Ribadeo, with
its attractive harbour, occupies
a picturesque setting on the
banks of the Ría de Ribadeo.
Among the many observation
points here are the hill of Santa
Cruz, with its monument of a
piper, and **La Atalaya**, formerly
a bastion. The beach at **Praia
das Catedrais** is known for its
rock formations that recall
Gothic buildings and arches.
The waters of the *ría* can be
explored by pleasure boat from
the nearby haven of Porcillán.

The town itself is home to the
**Colegiata de Santa María del
Campo** (18th century), with
two Baroque altarpieces.
Inside are earlier elements –
Romanesque arches and two
Gothic portals with plant
ornamentation. Another
attraction is the Modernist
residence of the brothers
Moreno, which recalls the
work of Antoni Gaudí.

Environs
North of Ribadeo lies the
18th-century **fort of San
Damián**, which once
defended the mouth of the
ría. It is now a municipal
exhibition space. About

10 km (6 miles) west of Ribadeo
is the fishing town of Foz, which
also has fine beaches. Nearby is
the Romanesque Iglesia de San
Martín de Mondoñedo.

❷ Mondoñedo

Lugo. **Road Map** C1. 🏔 4,100.
🛈 Plaza de la Catedral 34; 982 50 71
77. 🚌 Thu & Sun. 🎪 As Quendas
(1 May), Rapa das Bestas (Jun), Fiestas
Patronales (2nd Sun in Sep), As San
Lucas (18 Oct). 🌐 **mondonedo.net**

Situated in a valley, this was
the provincial capital for nearly
four centuries, and as a result
has an unusual number of fine
buildings for such a small town.
Its oldest monument is the
13th-century Romanesque
Catedral de la Asunción, which
was remodelled during the
Gothic and Baroque periods.
It features 14th-century murals

The portal of San Martín de Mondoñedo

and a figure of the Virgin
brought here from St Paul's
Cathedral in London. Its **Museo
Diocesano** has works by
Zurbarán and El Greco, and the
18th-century **Palacio Episcopal**
contains a Neo-Gothic chapel.
Nearby is the **Fonte Vella**, a
16th-century fountain decorated with the coat of arms of
Charles V; beyond it extends
the old Jewish quarter.

🏛 **Museo Diocesano**
Plaza de la Catedral. **Tel** 982 52 10 06.
Open 10am–2pm & 4:30–6pm Tue–
Sun. 🎟 📷

❸ Viveiro

Lugo. **Road Map** C1. 🏔 16,000.
🛈 Avda Ramón Canosa s/n; 982 56
08 79. 🚌 Thu; 1st day and 3rd Sun of
the month. 🎪 Semana Santa (week
preceding Easter Sun), Rapa das
Bestas (1st Sun in Jul), San Roque and
Nuestra Señora (week of 15 Aug).
🌐 **viveiro.es**

Situated on the beautiful *ría* of
the same name, Viveiro is the
prettiest and most popular
town in the Rías Altas, with
good hotels and restaurants.
Fragments of its medieval walls
survive – their most beautiful
feature is the Plateresque Gate
of Charles V, by Maestro Pedro
Poderoso. It is decorated with
coats of arms, medallions and
an image of St Roch, the town's
patron saint. Facing the gate is
the 15th-century bridge, Ponte
de la Misericordia.

Of note is the Romanesque
**Iglesia de Santa María del
Campo**, with a Baroque belfry
and a 19th-century clock tower.
The Romanesque-Gothic
Iglesia de San Francisco has
a beautiful apse. On the Praza
Maior, where a cheese and
vegetable market is held each
Thursday, stands the town
hall, with a sundial and 17th-
and 19th-century houses.
Nearby rises the Renaissance
Casa de los Leones, with
lions on the coat of arms.

The district of Covas
borders a long white beach.
The hill of San Roque
overlooks the town and
offers fine views.

Houses in Ferrol with typical glass-enclosed balconies

Environs

The Ría de Viveiro constitutes the mouth of the Landro river and is part of the Rías Altas region. The area is characterized by high waves, beaches with fine white sand, and an abundance of fish. During a storm in the 19th century, two ships – the *Magdalena* and the *Paloma* – sank here.

❹ Ortigueira

A Coruña. **Road Map** B1. 🚉 6,500.
ℹ A Lagarea s/n; 981 42 20 89.
🛒 Thu. 🎭 Santa Marta (27 Jul–1 Aug), International Celtic Festival (2nd weekend Jul). 🆆 **concellode ortigueira.com**

The main attractions here are the fantastic beaches and the diverse landscape of fertile valleys, hills and steep cliffs. The town's architecture dates mainly from the 19th and 20th centuries, but in the **Museo Ortegalia** an exhibition traces the region's prehistory, including the oldest Galician megaliths (4400 BC). North of town lie the ruins of **Punta dos Prados** – a settlement dating from the 4th to the 1st centuries BC.

Museo Ortegalia
Avenida Francisco Santiago 6.
Tel 981 40 24 13. **Open** 11am–2pm & 5–8pm Tue–Fri, 11am–2pm Sat–Sun.
Closed public hols. ♿

❺ Cedeira

A Coruña. **Road Map** B1. 🚉 7,500.
ℹ Av. de Castelao; 981 48 21 87.
🛒 Sat & 2nd Sun of month. 🎭 Rapa das Bestas (Curro de la Capelada) (last Sun Jun), Fiestas Patronales and Nuestra Señora del Mar (around 15 Aug).

One of the prettiest villages in the Rias Altas, Cedeira spans the river Condomiñas, and has excellent beaches, exquisite seafood, a tiny fishing harbour and good conditions for watersports. The surrounding area is ideal for fishing and hunting.

In the medieval old town, fragments of the town walls are preserved. The parish **Iglesia de Nuestra Señora del Mar de Cedeira** dates from the 15th century.

Some 12 km (8 miles) away, perched above the Atlantic atop sheer surf-battered cliffs in wild, windswept countryside is the 12th-century **Monasterio de San Andrés de Teixido**, a Galician shrine that once belonged to the Knights of Malta. The earliest preserved fragments in the monastery are the late-Gothic north portal, and the murals depicting the martyrdom of St Andrew. It is customary for pilgrims to throw breadcrumbs into the nearby spring, which flows from underneath the church's altar. Legend has it that if a crumb floats, your wish will be fulfilled.

A figure of St Andrew in San Andrés de Teixido

❻ Ferrol

A Coruña. **Road Map** B1. 🚉 72,000.
ℹ Rúa Magdalena 56; 981 31 11 79.
🛒 Mon, Wed & 3rd Sun of month. 🎭 San Julián (7 Jan), A Noche de las Pepitas (18 Mar), Fiestas Patronales (31 Aug). 🆆 **turferrol.com**

Ferrol has strong links with the sea – some of the ships in the Spanish Armada set sail from its port. Yet it wasn't until the 18th century that the town became an important naval base, acquiring an arsenal, shipyards, and the castle of San Felipe, which defended the mouth of the local *ría*. The Magdalena district was laid out in symmetrical Neo-Classical style in the 18th century. It features many houses with glass balconies, plus the 18th-century **Iglesia de San Xulián** with Mannerist elements, designed by Julián Sánchez Bort.

Environs

Lying 10 km (6 miles) south of Ferrol is **Pontedeume**, an attractive medieval town that boasts a tower with a huge coat of arms, built in the 14th century in honour of Count Andrade. There is also an equally old bridge, in the middle of which once stood a hostel for pilgrims and a hermitage. Andrade's castle is nearby, while hidden in the forest is the 12th-century monastery of Caaveiro.

Fishing boats in a bay near the picturesque village of Cedeira

❼ A Coruña

The oldest town in Galicia, A Coruña is mentioned in Irish myths about a Celtic hero by the name of Breogán, who came to the Iberian coast and built a tower here. The famous lighthouse – Torre de Hércules – dates from the Roman period. A Coruña is also the birthplace of María Pita, who became a Galician heroine by leading local resistance to a raid by Sir Francis Drake in 1589. The town has been an important commercial port for centuries.

Plaza María Pita, lined with arcaded houses

Exploring A Coruña

A Coruña boasts the longest sea promenade in Europe, with magnificent red-pillared lighthouses and old trams running along its length. The most important historic monuments, as well as the town centre, are laid out on an isthmus leading to a headland.

🏛 Museo de Belas Artes

Tel 881 88 17 00. **Open** 10am–8pm Tue–Fri, 10am–2pm & 4:30–8pm Sat, 10am–2pm Sun. 🎫 (free Sat pm & Sun). 📷 ♿ 🛍 📸

This modern building houses Spanish and European paintings from the 16th to the 20th centuries, as well as 19th- and 20th-century Galician art. There are also prints by Goya and ceramics by the celebrated local factory of Sargadelos.

📷 Avenida de la Marina

The harbourfront promenade known as the Avenida de la Marina is one of A Coruña's great landmarks. Houses with gleaming glass-enclosed balconies, or galerías, run along its length; these are best viewed from the Real Club Náutico. At one end rises a memorial obelisk topped by a clock with four dials (1845).

📷 Plaza María Pita

This sumptuous, harmoniously designed square bears the name of Galicia's national heroine, who defended the town against the English, led by the navigator and buccaneer Francis Drake. A popular spot for pavement cafés, it is surrounded by houses with arcades that offer protection against the sun and rain. Here, too, is the monumental Neo-Renaissance

town hall (Palacio Municipal), with three huge domes. Spain's finest clock museum is housed within it. Beside the town hall rises the 17th-century Baroque Iglesia de San Jorge.

🏛 Iglesia de Santiago

Calle del Parrote 1. **Open** 8am–1pm & 5:30–7pm Mon–Fri, 10am–1pm & 4:30–7pm Sat–Sun.

Stone from the Torre de Hércules was used to build this Romanesque-Gothic hall church (12th–15th century) where, in the Middle Ages, the town council met. It is the oldest church in A Coruña, featuring three apses.

The Romanesque-Gothic tower of the Iglesia de Santiago

🏛 Colegiata de Santa María del Campo

The saint to whom this 13th-century church is dedicated is particularly venerated by sailors, who pray for her protection before setting off on a voyage. The main portal's decoration recalls the Pórtico da Gloria on the cathedral in Santiago de Compostela (see pp66–7). On the square in front of the church is a 15th-century cruceiro (stone cross), one of the oldest in Galicia.

🌳 Jardines San Carlos

The Romantic-style San Carlos gardens, laid out on the site of a fortress whose walls have survived to this day, form one of the most charming corners of A Coruña. Buried at their centre is the Scottish General John Moore, killed by the French at the Battle of Elviña (1809). Among the many trees are some especially fine elms.

Glass Houses in A Coruña

Houses with large glass balconies, glistening in the sun, are common all over Galicia, but the most famous ones are found here in A Coruña. It was this particular architectural feature that led visiting sailors to dub A Coruña the "City of Glass". These extensive glass

Houses with impressive glass balconies in the port area of A Coruña

galerías, which have been used in thousands of advertising photographs, were designed to face the harbour, and so are located at the back of the buildings. The façades face the Calle de Riego de Agua and Calle Real, streets that once formed the main axis of the town.

🏛 Museo Arqueológico

Paseo Parrote. **Tel** 981 18 98 50. **Open** Sep–Jun: 10am–7:30pm Tue–Sat, 10am–2:30pm Sun; Jul–Aug: 10am–9pm Tue–Sat, 10am–3pm Sun. 🐾

This museum, housed in the Castillo de San Antón, an 18th-century fortress, traces the history of Galicia. On show are exhibits from the Palaeolithic period up to the time of the Roman conquest, more exhibits present the culture of the *castros* (fortified villages) and medieval sculptures and coats of arms used to illustrate the most important events in A Coruña's history.

🏛 Domus

C/Santa Teresa 1. **Tel** 981 18 98 40. **Open** Jan–Apr: 10am–6pm Mon–Fri, 10am–7pm Sat & Sun; Jul–Aug: 10am–8pm daily; May–Jun, Sep–Dec: 10am–7pm daily. 🐾 ♿ ⊘

Also known as the *Casa del Hombre* (Museum of Mankind), this interactive museum is devoted entirely to the human being. The futuristic building in which it is housed was designed by the Japanese architect Arata Isozaki.

The modern building of the Museo Domus

🏛 Torre de Hércules

Avenida de Navarra. **Tel** 981 22 37 30. **Open** Oct–May: 10am–6pm daily; Jun–Sep: 10am–9pm daily. 🐾 (free Mon). 🐾

The Tower of Hercules is the world's oldest working lighthouse. Since the 2nd century it has warned sailors that they are approaching land. The lighthouse was built during the reign of the Emperor Trajan, but according to legend it was built by Hercules. Its current appearance is the result of renovation in the 18th century. The 59.5 m (180 ft) shaft rests on a square base; you can climb the 234 steps to the top.

Torre de Hércules lighthouse

VISITORS' CHECKLIST

Practical Information
A Coruña. **Road Map** B1.
🗺 246,000. 🅸 Plaza de María Pita 6. **Tel** 981 92 30 93.
📷 Fiestas de María Pita (Aug).
🆆 turismocoruna.com

Transport
✈ 902 40 47 04. 🚉 C/Joaquin Planells. 🚌 C/Caballeros 21; 981 18 43 35. 🚌 Avda. de la Marina 3; 981 21 96 21.

🏛 Aquarium Finisterrae

Paseo Alcade Francisco Vázquez 34. **Tel** 981 18 98 42. **Open** daily (from 10am Mon–Fri; from 11am Sat, Sun & hols); closing times vary. 🐾 🛈 ♿

At the edge of the ocean, this modern aquarium has fantastic viewing platforms for watching the waves. Inside, it is fun and educational. The circling sharks are a highlight.

🏖 Playas (Beaches)

On the other side of the isthmus from the harbour, but within walking distance, is the town's most important beach, Riazor-Orzán. Near the Tower of Hercules are the smaller beaches of Das Lapas and San Amaro.

A Coruña Town Centre

1. Museo de Bellas Artes
2. Avenida de la Marina
3. Plaza María Pita
4. Iglesia de Santiago
5. Colegiata de Santa María del Campo
6. Jardines San Carlos
7. Museo Arqueológico
8. Domus
9. Torre de Hércules
10. Aquarium Finisterrae
11. Playa das Lapas

0 metres 100
0 yards 100

For keys to symbols *see back flap*

Townscape overlooking the fishing port in Malpica

❽ Betanzos

A Coruña. **Road Map** B1. 🏘 13,500.
🚉 🚌 👢 Praza de Galicia; 981 77
66 66. 📅 Tue, Thu, Sat. 🎭 Medieval
Fair (2nd weekend Jul), San Roque
(14–25 Aug). 🕸 **betanzos.es**

At the centre of this fascinating town is the **Praza García Hermanos**, an elegant 18th-century square. The steep streets, which arose on the site of the former *castro*, are lined with old houses and Gothic churches. The tympanum of the 15th-century **Iglesia de Santiago** is decorated with an equestrian figure of St James. Hidden inside the aisleless 14th-century **Iglesia de San Francisco** are beautiful tombs, including that of Count Fernán Pérez de Andrade, supported on figures of a wild boar and a bear. The **Iglesia de Santa María de Azogue**, with a beautiful façade and rose window, has a 15th-century Flemish reredos.

Iglesia de Santiago portal, Betanzos

❾ Malpica

A Coruña. **Road Map** A1. 🏘 6,000.
👢 Avenida Emilio Gonzáles 1; 981 71
14 62 (Jul–Sep only). 🎭 San Adrián
(16 Jun), Nuestra Señora del Mar (last
Sun Aug). 🕸 **concellomalpica.com**

This small fishing town has good beaches and enchanting views of the nearby Sisargas islands – an important nature reserve especially rich in birds. Of interest is the Romanesque **Iglesia de Santiago de Mens**;

legend has it that the church was linked with Mens castle by an underground tunnel. Near Malpica is the partially destroyed **Cerqueda dolmen**.

❿ Camariñas

A Coruña. **Road Map** A1. 🏘 6,000.
🚌 👢 Praza da Insuela; 981 73 70 04.
📅 Wed, Sat. 🎭 Lace Festival (Easter),
Carmen (16 & 17 Jul).
🕸 **camarinas.net**

This pretty fishing town is known for the bobbin lace that is manufactured and sold here. In the local 18th-century **Iglesia de San Jorge** is a valuable reredos sculpted by José Ferreiro bearing images of saints.

Environs
Among the wild landscape of the **Cabo Vilán** headland, 5 km (3 miles) away, stands a lighthouse with the longest beam of all Galician lighthouses. Here, too, are wind turbines for electricity.

Costa da Morte

Between Cabo San Adrián, near Malpica, and Fisterra headlands extends the "Coast of Death", whose grim name is due to the many ships that have been smashed against the rocky shoreline over the centuries. The landscape here is characterized by a wild beauty; the steep cliffs, sea birds, stone *cruceiros* and gigantic *hórreos* will long remain in the memory. At great risk, fishermen scour the coast for barnacles for use in local cuisine.

Stone *cruceiros* on the Costa da Morte

⓫ Cabo Fisterra

A Coruña. **Road Map** A2. 🏘 5,000.
🚉 🚌 👢 Rúa Real 2; 981 74 07 81.
📅 Tue, Fri. 🎭 Virgen del Carmen
(8–10 Sep), Fiesta del Cristo (Easter
week). 🕸 **concellofisterra.com**

Known in English as Finisterre, and translated as "World's End", this cape with fabulous views was long considered to be Continental Europe's most westerly point, though in fact that distinction belongs to Portugal. The lighthouse, on the perilous Costa da Morte, is a symbol of Galicia.

A village of the same name lies 3 km (2 miles) from the cape. Nearby is the Romanesque **Iglesia de Santa María de las Arenas**, with a figure of the Santo Cristo da Barba Dourada (Christ of the Golden Beard). Before it stands a 15th-century *cruceiro* (stone cross). This is the last part of the Road to Santiago – here pilgrims traditionally burn the clothes they wore on the pilgrimage.

A lighthouse on the treacherous Costa da Morte at Cabo Fisterra

Regional Galician Architecture

Traditional buildings that reflect Galicia's own vernacular style give the region its unique charm. In A Coruña the glass *galerías (see p58)* are a common sight, but there are also distinctive, narrow, two-storey fishermen's cottages, which can be seen in Pontevedra. Visitors can experience the mansions known as *pazos*, some of which date back to the Middle Ages, as many have been converted into hotels or exclusive *paradores* (state-operated hotels). Beyond the larger towns, there are many reminders of times gone by: grain is still stored in stone granaries *(hórreos)* used as far back as Roman times; ancient stone crosses stand by the roadsides; and many villages feature *pallozas* – oval stone buildings with thatched roofs that survive as the oldest type of Galician architecture.

This **hórreo** (granary) in Carnota, dating from 1760 and extending 35 m (126 ft), is one of the largest in Galicia. *Hórreos* were built on stone legs to protect the grain from damp and pests. The cross is a decorative motif.

Pallozas are among the oldest structures built in Europe. Dating from Celtic times, these houses have thick walls and thatched roofs. The inhabitants used to divide the space into living quarters, animal stables and a food store.

Pazos are traditional stone mansions that form an attractive feature of this picturesque region. Nowadays many of them have been converted into hotels.

The distinctive **cruceiros** (stone crosses) can be found throughout Galicia, at places of worship, next to cemetery gates, by the Stations of the Cross (as in A Guarda), and on roadsides where accidents have occurred.

Many pilgrimage churches were built in Galicia, as various strands of the Road to Santiago pass through the region. The churches give the region a special charm.

These narrow two-storey houses with glass-enclosed balconies are common in fishing villages. Their functional plan creates living space on the upper floor, with storage for fishing equipment on the ground floor.

⑫ Street-by-Street: Santiago de Compostela

In the Middle Ages Santiago de Compostela was Christendom's third most important place of pilgrimage, after Jerusalem and Rome. Around the Praza do Obradoiro is an ensemble of historic buildings that has few equals in Europe. The local granite gives a harmonious unity to the mixture of architectural styles. With its narrow streets and old squares, the city centre is compact enough to explore on foot. Of its many monuments, two are especially worth seeking out – the Convento de Santo Domingo de Bonaval, to the east of the centre, and the Colegiata Santa María la Real del Sar, a 12th-century Romanesque church located to the east of the city.

★ Convento de San Martiño Pinario
The Baroque church of this monastery has a huge double altar and an ornate façade in the Plateresque style, with carved figures of saints and bishops.

Pazo de Xelmírez (1120–49)
is a beautiful palace with Romanesque features and spectacular views from the roof terrace.

★ Hostal de los Reyes Católicos
Built by the Catholic Monarchs as an inn and hospital for sick pilgrims, and now a parador, this magnificent building has an elaborate Plateresque doorway.

Praza do Obradoiro
This majestic square is one of the world's finest and the focal point for pilgrims arriving in the city. The cathedral's Baroque façade dominates the square.

The Pazo de Raxoi,
with its Neo-Classical façade, was built in 1772 and houses the town hall.

Convento de San Paio de Antealtares
This is one of the oldest monasteries in Santiago. It was founded in the 9th century to house the tomb of St James, now in the cathedral.

VISITORS' CHECKLIST

Practical Information
A Coruña. **Road Map** B2.
🏛 95,000. 🚹 Rúa do Vilar 63,
981 55 51 29. 🌐 Thu, Sat.
🎭 Easter Week, Ascension (40 days after Easter), St James (24 Jul). 🆆 **santiagoturismo.com**

Transport
✈ Lavacolla. 🚌 Rúa do Hórreo 75a, 902 32 03 20. 🚍 Pl. de Camilo Díaz Baliño, 981 54 24 16.

RÚA DE ACEVECHERIA

SACRA

Praza da Quintana, in front of the cathedral clock tower, is one of the city's most elegant squares.

Praza das Praterias
The Goldsmiths' Doorway of the cathedral opens onto this charming square with the Dos Cavalos fountain in the centre.

RÚA DE XELMÍREZ

RÚA NOVA

RÚA DO VILAR

RÚA DA RAIÑA

RÚA DO FRANCO

To tourist information

Key

— Suggested route
— Pilgrimage route

The Rúa Nova is a handsome arcaded old street leading from the cathedral to the newer part of the city.

| 0 metres | | 100 |
| 0 yards | | 100 |

Colexio de San Xerome

★ Cathedral
This grand towering spectacle has welcomed pilgrims to Santiago for centuries. Though the exterior has been remodelled over the years, the core of the building has remained virtually unchanged since the 11th century.

For keys to symbols *see back flap*

Santiago Cathedral

With its twin Baroque towers soaring over the Praza do Obradoiro, this monument to St James is a majestic sight, as befits one of the great shrines of Christendom *(see pp24–5)*. The core of the present building dates from the 11th–13th centuries and stands on the site of the 9th-century basilica built by Alfonso II. Behind the Baroque façade and through the original Pórtico da Gloria is the same interior that met pilgrims in medieval times.

"Passport" – proof of a pilgrim's journey

★ **West Front**
This richly sculpted Baroque façade was added in the 18th century in front of Mateo's Pórtico da Gloria.

KEY

① **The Santo Dos Croques** is a statue of Maestro Mateo, the cathedral's architect – touching it with the forehead was said to bring luck and impart wisdom.

② **Pazo de Xelmírez**

③ **Statue of St James**

④ **The twin towers** are the cathedral's highest structures at 74 m (243 ft).

⑤ **The botafumeiro**, a giant censer, is swung high above the altar by eight men during important services.

⑥ **The Mondragon Chapel** (1521) contains fine wrought-iron grilles and vaulting.

⑦ **Clock Tower**

⑧ **Cloister**

⑨ **Chapterhouse**

Museum entrance

★ **Pórtico da Gloria**
The cathedral's most impressive element is the sculpted Doorway of Glory, with its statues of apostles and prophets. It dates from the 12th century.

Crypt
The relics of St James and
two disciples are said to lie
in a tomb in the crypt,
under the altar, in the original
9th-century foundations.

VISITORS' CHECKLIST

Practical Information
Praza do Obradoiro.
Tel 981 58 35 48.
Open 7am–8:30pm daily.
Museum: **Tel** 981 56 93 27.
Open Apr–Oct: 9am–8pm daily;
Nov–Mar: 10am–8pm daily.

★ Porta das Praterias
Bas-relief sculptures of biblical
scenes cover the 12th-century
Goldsmiths' Doorway.

High Altar
Visitors can pass behind the altar
to embrace the silver mantle
of the 13th-century statue of
St James, and to access the crypt.

Tapestry Museum
Noteworthy within
this collection of
antique tapestries
is an exhibition of
Oriental medieval
weavings dating back
to the 13th century.

The two-level Praza Quintana behind the cathedral

Exploring Santiago de Compostela

The centre of Santiago is a pedestrianized zone. The most important monuments are found in the vicinity of the Praza do Obradoiro.

Praza do Obradoiro

This huge square is the focal point for arriving pilgrims. On the square's eastern side rises the cathedral's famous Baroque façade; to the west is the Pazo de Raxoi; to the north the Hostal de los Reyes Católicos (today an exclusive parador); and to the south the Colexio de San Jerónimo.

Convento de San Francisco

Rúa Campiño de San Francisco 3. **Tel** 981 58 16 34.

The founding of the monastery of San Francisco de Valdediós is traditionally ascribed to St Francis of Assisi, who came to Santiago in 1214. All that remains of the original structure are Gothic arches in the cloister and the tomb of the master mason Cotolay. The current buildings date from the 18th century. In the atrium is a *cruceiro* (stone cross) dedicated to St Francis. The monastery now houses a hotel.

Praza Quintana

Situated behind the cathedral, at the foot of a Baroque clock tower called the Berenguela, is this elegant square divided into two sections by steps. One side of the square is occupied by the monastery of San Paio de Antealtares, with its imposing façade sporting a row of windows with wrought-iron grilles. The Baroque Casa de la Parra, decorated with plant ornaments, is also here.

Cathedral Museum

Praza do Obradoiro. **Tel** 902 55 78 12. **Open** Apr–Oct: 9am–8pm daily; Nov–Mar: 10am–8pm daily.

The museum's rich collections cover religion as well as the cathedral itself. Preserved in the library are incunabula, manuscripts and two examples of a giant censer known as the *botafumeiro*. You can also see the cathedral cloisters, medieval reliquaries and old ornaments, which were taken down during construction of the new façade.

Pazo de Xelmírez

Praza do Obradoiro (part of Cathedral Museum, above). **Open** 10am–7:15pm Mon–Fri; 10am–2pm & 4–7:15pm Sat & Sun.

Dating from the 12th–13th centuries, this building is the most important work of secular Romanesque architecture in Galicia. Built as the Archbishop's Palace, it continues to fill this role. The severe appearance of the

Buildings of the Pazo de Xelmírez, housing the Archbishop's Palace

building contrasts with its lavish interior. On the ground floor is the Weapons Chamber. From the patio, stairs lead up to the cross-vaulted refectory with its magnificent reliefs depicting life in the Middle Ages.

Pazo de Raxoi

Praza do Obradoiro. **Closed** to the public.

Initially, this 18th-century palace was a residence for students of the seminary and choirboys; since 1970 it has served as the town hall. The palace was built on the former city walls, and the master-mason was Charles Lemaur. A curiosity here is the extraordinary variation in the height of the land on which the building stands. The long arcaded façade is supported on Ionic columns. A figure of St James designed by J. Ferreira is visible on the roof. The interior of the building is noted for its Rococo staircase.

The late-Romanesque portal of the Colexio de San Xerome

Colexio de San Xerome

Throughout its history, the Colexio de San Xerome has served many purposes: hospital, grammar school, art school, and later a hostel for poor students. Today, it accommodates the chancellor of the University of Santiago de Compostela. Preserved from the earlier, 15th-century building is a late Romanesque portal, richly decorated with figures of the Virgin and Child surrounded by saints. The structure you see today, dating from the 17th century, has an inner courtyard with a fountain.

⛪ Colegio de Fonseca

Rúa do Franco s/n.

The Colegio arose in the 16th century as one of the university buildings. The Renaissance design is the work of the architects Juan de Alava and Alonso Covarrubias, and was completed by Rodrigo Gil de Hontañón. The façade is decorated with the coat of arms of the Fonseca family, figures of saints (the Virgin, St James the Lesser, St Peter, St Paul), and the Church Fathers of Spanish origin (St Isidore, St Leander). For a time, the Galician Parliament was housed here. Today the university library is located here, and numerous exhibitions are held in the elegant cloisters.

🏛 Museo das Perigrinacións

Rúa de San Miguel 4. **Tel** 981 58 15 58. **Open** 10am–8pm Tue–Fri, 10:30am–1:30pm & 5–8pm Sat, 10:30am–1:30pm Sun. 🖼 (free Sat pm & Sun).

The Pilgrimage Museum, devoted to the cult of St James and the cultural impact of pilgrimages over the ages, is located inside the Casa Gótica (Gothic House). The eight rooms contain exhibits that describe the beginnings of the apostle's cult and the history of pilgrimages. They also display the iconography of St James (including several sculptures and *Santiago Peregrino* – the famous painting by Juan de Juanes) and even musical instruments reproduced from the cathedral's Pórtico da Gloria. The museum library has a rich collection of books, journals and photographs connected with St James.

⛪ Convento de San Martiño Pinario

Praza da Inmaculada 5. **Tel** 981 58 92 00. **Open** Oct–mid-Jun: 11am–1:30pm & 4–6:30pm daily; mid-Jun–Sep: 11am–7pm daily. 🖼

The imposing Benedictine monastery complex of San Martiño Pinario occupies more space than the cathedral itself. Its construction began during the Renaissance period, but it was given its current Baroque appearance by Gabriel Casas and Fernando Casas y Novoa. The superb church dome and grand interior were designed in the 17th century by Bartolomé Fernández Lechuga. The façade, which is supported on massive columns, is decorated with figures of saints, the evangelists, and the Church Fathers. There are two sets of cloisters within the monastery complex – one centred on a Baroque fountain. The monastery building itself is modest and rather severe.

The Baroque reredos at the Convento de San Martiño Pinario

🏛 Museo do Pobo Galego

San Domingos de Bonaval. **Tel** 981 58 36 20. **Open** 10:30am–2pm & 4–7:30pm Tue–Sat, 11am–2pm Sun. 🖼 🖼 (free Sun).

Housed inside the 17th-century Convento de Santo Domingo de Bonaval, this museum has an interesting collection of pieces illustrating the social history of Galicia. The thematic layout covers subjects ranging from the sea to the countryside, traditional occupations, costumes, music, architecture, painting and sculpture throughout Galicia. Inside the church is a pantheon of famous Galicians – among others, the local poet Rosalía de Castro is buried here.

🏛 Centro Gallego de Arte Contemporáneo

Rúa Valle Inclán. **Tel** 981 54 66 19. **Open** 11am–8pm Tue–Sun. 🖼 🖼 by appointment only.

Designed by Álvaro Siza, this interesting building houses a modern art centre, whose aim is to present trends in both Galician and international art since the 1960s. A variety of courses, concerts, workshops, conferences and film shows are offered. The centre also has a library, an audiovisual library and a film archive.

⛪ Colexiata Santa María a Real do Sar

Tel 981 56 28 91. **Open** 10am–1pm & 4–7pm Mon–Sat (8pm in summer), 10am–1pm Sun. 🖼

Huge buttressed arches support the walls of this simple 17th-century collegiate church; they were added in the 17th–18th centuries when the walls and interior columns began to lean dangerously. Near the main entrance stands a 12th-century baptismal font. Through the sacristy you emerge onto the cloisters, one wing of which is the only surviving Romanesque building of this kind in Galicia. Other elements of the building date from the 17th and 18th century. The sacristy and cloisters house liturgical and archaeological museums.

The Legend of St James

According to legend, the apostle St James was responsible for bringing Christianity to Spain. Though martyred in Palestine around AD 45, centuries later it was said that before his death the saint had visited Spain to bring the Gospel to her people, and that after his death his body had been brought to Galicia on a ship led by angels. In 814 a hermit claimed to have been guided to rediscover the saint's tomb by a shower of stars – (*compostela* means "field of stars") – and the bishop declared the miracle genuine. The tomb rapidly became a centre of pilgrimage.

St James (Santiago), the patron saint of Spain

The palm-lined promenade in Noia

⑬ Noia

A Coruña. **Road Map** A2. ⛰ 14,500.
🛈 Alameda s/n; 981 84 21 00. 🚌 Thu,
1st & 3rd Sun of month. 🎭 San Marcos
(25 Apr), San Bartolomé (24 Aug).

According to legend, this town
was founded by the great-
grandson of Noah; hence,
Noia's coat of arms features a
dove with an olive sprig in its
beak. The town's golden age
was in the 15th century, when it
was one of Galicia's main ports.
The medieval town plan and
houses bearing coats of arms
survive from that period.

Worth seeing is the late-
Romanesque **Iglesia de San
Martino**; its portal is richly
decorated with saints and biblical figures. The Romanesque
Santa María a Nova, dating
from the 14th century, stands
in the middle of the Quintana
dos Muertos, an exceptionally
interesting cemetery. In its
northern part rises Cristo de
Humilladoiro, a conical stone
chapel that contains a
16th-century *cruceiro* (cross).
The four columns supporting it
have fine decoration depicting
the phases of the moon and
injured animals fleeing from
hunters and hounds. In the
southern part of the cemetery,
which is overlooked by a second
cruceiro from the 13th century,
are some 200 gravestones; the
most interesting are those that
show the symbol of the guild to
which the deceased belonged.

Near Noia is the Celtic **Castro
de Baroña**, one of the best-
preserved stone fortifications
in Galicia.

⑭ Padrón

A Coruña. **Road Map** A2. ⛰ 8,800.
🚌 🚉 🛈 Avenida de Compostela;
646 59 33 19. 🚌 Sun. 🎭 St Isidore
(15 May); St James (25 Jul).

According to legend, the
name of this town derives from
the stone *(padrón)* to which
the ship carrying the body of
St James was moored when it
arrived in Galicia *(see p69)*. Many
Baroque buildings remain, such
as the town hall and Palace
of Alonso Peña Montenegro.
You can visit the **Casa-Museo
Rosalía de Castro** to learn

Room in Padrón's Casa-Museo Rosalía de Castro

Rías Baixas (Rías Bajas)

The southern part of Galicia's
beautiful west coast consists of four
large *rías*, or inlets, between pine-
covered hills. The beaches are good,
the scenery is lovely, the bathing safe
and the climate much milder than on
the wilder coast to the north. Though
areas such as Vilagarcía de Arousa
and Panxón have become popular
holiday resorts, much of the Rías
Baixas coastline is unspoiled, such as
the quiet stretch from Muros to Noia.
This part of the coastline provides some of Spain's most fertile
fishing grounds, and also produces excellent wines.

An unspoiled stretch of Galicia's
Rías Baixas shoreline

---

more about this 19th-century
poet. The **Fundación Camilo
José Cela** is devoted to Padrón's
other major writer.

Environs
The 17th- to 18th-century
estate of **Pazo de Oca** is a
fine example of Galician
architecture. It comprises a
palace, a Baroque church, and
workers' houses. The gardens
feature a pond divided by a
stone footbridge.

🏛 **Casa-Museo Rosalía de Castro**
La Matanza (Retén). **Tel** 981 81 12
04. **Open** Oct–Jun: 10am–1:30pm
& 4–7pm Tue–Sat, 10am–1:30pm
Sun & hols; Jul–Sep: 10am–2pm &
4–8pm Tue–Sat, 10am–1:30pm Sun
& hols. 🚫

🏛 **Fundación Camilo José Cela**
C/Santa María 22. **Tel** 981 81 24 25.
Open Sep–Jun: 10am–2pm Mon–Fri;
Jul & Aug: 10am–2pm & 5–8pm
Mon–Fri. 🚫 📷

⑮ Cambados

Pontevedra. **Road Map** A2. ⛰ 14,000.
🛈 Praza do Concello; 986 52 07 86.
🎭 San Bieito (11 Jul), Santa Margarita
(23 Jul), Fiesta del Vino Albariño
(1st weekend Aug).
🌐 cambados.es

In Cambados' his-
toric centre is the
Pazo de Bazán, a
manor house built
in the 17th century
by the ancestors
of renowned
19th-century writer
Emilia Pardo Bazán.
Today it is a parador.

A century older is the **Pazo de Fefináns**, decorated with Baroque coats of arms, in which one of the town's oldest bodegas has been established; the estate also comprises the late 16th-century **Iglesia de San Benito**. For a strange experience, visit the ruins of the roofless **Iglesia de Santa Mariña de Dozo**, which stands near the hill of A Pastora. Close by is the **Museo Etnográfico e do Vino**, where you can see exhibits connected with the region's history and culture and learn about wine production in the Rías Baixas.

In the Santo Tomé district, you can visit the ruins of the tower of San Sadurnino, dating from the 10th century.

🏛 **Museo Etnográfico e do Viño**
Avenida da Pastora 104. **Tel** 986 52 61 19. **Open** 10am–2pm & 4:30–7:30pm Tue–Sat (till 8pm in summer), 10am–2pm Sun. 🎨 📷 ♿

⑯ A Toxa

Pontevedra. **Road Map** A2. 🚌
ℹ Ayuntamiento, O Grove, Praza do Corgo; 986 73 14 15.
🚢 Fri. 🦪 Shellfish fiesta (weekend before 12 Oct). 🌐 **turismogrove.es**

A tiny pine-covered island joined to the mainland by a bridge, A Toxa is one of the most stylish resorts in Galicia. The *belle époque* palace-hotel and luxury villas add to the island's elegant atmosphere. A Toxa's best-known landmark is the small church covered with scallop shells. Aross the bridge is **O Grove**, a thriving family resort and fishing port on a peninsula, with holiday hotels and flats alongside glorious beaches.

⑰ Sanxenxo

Pontevedra. **Road Map** A2. 🚶 17,500.
ℹ Puerto Deportivo Juan Carlos I; 986 72 02 85. 🎉 Tourist Day (25 Aug); Santa Rosalía (4 Sep); Nosa Señora do Carmen (5 Sep). 🌐 **sanxenxo.es**

With its good restaurants, lively nightlife, big promenade and attractive beaches, Sanxenxo is one of the most popular

The picturesque coast near Sanxenxo

resorts in the Rías Baixas. **Silgar beach** has the most modern sports harbour in Galicia. Its Old Town features the 17th-century **Iglesia de San Xinés** as well as the 16th–18th-century **Pazo de los Patino**, with a tower, the coats of arms of its former inhabitants, and stone steps leading out onto a terrace.

The Sanxenxo area also enjoys a good reputation for its *albariño* white wine.

Environs

One of the best-known local beaches is **Praia da Lanzada** – a superb long beach that's a favourite with windsurfers. On Midsummer's Eve, near the Romanesque hermitage of Santa María, a colourful pilgrimage of women used to enter the sea to perform the ancient ritual of *bano das nove ondas*. Nine waves had to envelop the body of each woman, who during this time made a wish – single women wished for marriage, married women for children.

⑱ Illas Cíes

Pontevedra. **Road Map** A3.
ℹ Plaza Santa María s/n, Pontevedra; 886 21 17 00. 🚢

The three islands of Cíes are uninhabited, if you don't count the lighthouse keeper and guards. You can get here from Vigo by one of the boats moored at the improvised port on the Illa Norte (or Monteagudo), or from Baiona in summer. The Illa Norte is joined to the Illa do Faro by a sandbar and an artificial embankment along which runs the road. There is a campsite on Faro, which must be booked ahead on 986 43 83 58. The third island is called Sur or San Martín.

The entire archipelago is a national park and a paradise for waterfowl. It boasts breathtaking landscapes, beaches (also for nudists), the ruins of a Celtic *castro*, and an ancient Suevi monastery that was plundered by the Vikings and later by English pirates. The islands have a first-aid post, café and police station.

Rosalía de Castro and Camilo José Cela

These two writers from Padrón left a profound mark on Galicia. Rosalía de Castro (1837–85), a Galician national icon, was the foremost figure of the 19th-century renaissance in the Galician language, with such works as *Cantares Gallegos*. Her poetry was written in Gallego, and coloured by her difficult life. Born an illegitimate child, she herself lost seven children, and died prematurely of cancer after a lifetime of illness. Camilo José Cela (1916–2002), winner of the Nobel Prize in 1989, wrote in Spanish and was renowned for his superb mastery of language and knowledge of the human character.

The 19th-century Galician poet, Rosalía de Castro

⑲ Pontevedra

Pontevedra. **Road Map** B2. 📍 82,500.
🚇 🚌 *i* Marqués de Riestra 30; 986
85 08 14. 🗓 1st, 8th, 15th & 23rd of
month. 🎭 Fiestas de la Peregrina (2nd
week in Aug), Feira Franca (1st Fri & Sat
in Sep). W visit-pontevedra.com

According to legend,
Pontevedra was founded by
Teucro, one of the heroes of
the Trojan War, but in reality
it was the Romans who
constructed a bridge across the
Lérez river, around which the
town began to emerge. The
bridge – the restored A Ponte
do Burgo – remains to this day
one of the town's landmarks.

A tour of Pontevedra,
which is also the
provincial capital, is
best begun on the
Alameda boulevard –
the green lungs of
the city. Along here
stand numerous
19th-century buildings
that today house
important offices.
At the end of the
boulevard are the
**Ruinas do Santo
Domingo**, ruins of a Gothic
church that form part of the
Museo de Pontevedra, where
you can see Roman steles and
medieval coats of arms and

Façade detail from the Basilica
de Santa María la Mayor

tombs. The main
buildings of the
museum – regarded
as one of the best in
Galicia – are on the
Praza da Leña. The
collections include
Celtic gold bracelets
and necklaces, and
locally found Bronze
Age treasures.
Apart from
15th-century
paintings, the
artworks on display include
canvases by Zurbarán and
Goya. There are also several
works by the Galician painter
and writer Alfonso Castelao.
Near to the tiny Praza das
Cinco, sporting an 18th-
century *cruceiro*, is the huge,
partially treed **Praza da
Ferraría**, with a beautiful
fountain. Worthy of mention
here are the Renaissance
Casa das Caras, decorated
with sculpted faces, the
14th-century **Iglesia de San
Francisco**, and a branch of
the Ministry of the Economy,
which incorporates the Santo
Domingo gate from the
medieval town walls.
The greatest monument
of the Galician Renaissance

The huge Praza da Peregrina in Pontevedra

Pontevedra Town Centre

① Ruinas do Santo
   Domingo
② Museo de Pontevedra
③ Praza da Leña
④ Iglesia de San
   Francisco
⑤ Basilica de Santa
   María la Mayor

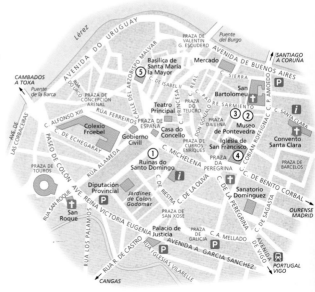

0 metres   200
0 yards   200

style is the 16th-century **Basilica de Santa María la Mayor**, with a Plateresque west façade, funded by the sailors' guild; its richly sculpted portico looks like a reredos. Next to it is the Jewish Quarter and cemetery.

The church dedicated to Pontevedra's patron saint – the Virgen de la Peregrina – is built to a circular plan and features a bow-fronted façade.

🏛 **Museo de Pontevedra**
Pasantería 2–12. **Tel** 986 80 41 00.
Open 10am–9pm Tue–Sat, 11am–2pm Sun.
Ruinas do Santo Domingo:
Open call ahead for opening hours.
W **museo.depo.es**

The ruins of the Gothic Iglesia de Santo Domingo in Pontevedra

⓴ Vigo

Pontevedra. **Road Map** A3.
🏔 297,000. ✈ 🚌 🚆 **i** Calle Cánovas del Castillo 22; 986 43 05 77.
🗓 Wed & Sun. 🎉 Festas da Virxe do Carme (16 Jul), Cristo de los Afligidos (3rd Sun Jul); Folk Festival (1st week Aug). W **turiturismodevigo.org**

Vigo is Galicia's largest city, with a vibrant fishing port and a busy industrial centre. The **Barrio de Berbes** is an old quarter of cobbled alleyways and superb *tapas* bars. On the **Praza de España**, the striking modern face of Vigo can be admired in the form of Juan José Oliveira's horses statue.

In the surrounding area there are up to 1700 *hórreos* and 30 *cruceiros*, as well as numerous dolmens and the remnants of Celtic settlements *(see p61)*.

Fishing in Spain

The Spanish eat more seafood than any other European nation except the Portuguese. Each year, some 61,000 fishermen and 16,000 boats land over a million tonnes of hake, tuna, lobster and other species popular in Spanish cuisine. Nearly half of the fish and shellfish caught in Spain is supplied by the modern Galician fishing fleet, one of the largest in the EU, but because fish stocks in the seas around Europe have become depleted through overfishing, deep-sea trawlers have been forced to look for new fishing grounds as far away as Canada or Iceland.

Fishing boats in the port at A Coruña

⓴① Baiona

Pontevedra. **Road Map** A3. 🏔 12,000.
🚌 **i** Paseo da Ribeira; 986 68 70 67.
🗓 Mon. 🎉 Festa da Arribada (1st weekend in Mar), Santa Liberata (20 Jul), Virgen Anunciada (1st Sun in Aug). W **baiona.org**

The *Pinta*, one of the caravels from Columbus's fleet, arrived at this small port in 1493, bringing the first news of the discovery of the New World. This event is commemorated in the Festa da Arribada.

Today Baiona, which is sited on a broad bay, is a popular summer resort, its harbour filled with pleasure and fishing boats. There are lovely beaches here, especially the long Praia America.

A royal fortress once stood on the Monterreal promontory, north of the town. Sections of its defensive walls remain, but the interior has been converted into a smart parador. There are superb views from here.

⓴② A Guarda

Pontevedra. **Road Map** A3. 🏔 10,500.
🚌 **i** Praza do Reloxo 1; 986 61 45 46. 🗓 Sat. 🎉 San Amaro (18 Jan), Festa do Monte (1–11 Aug).

At the end of the Miño river is this small fishing port. On the slopes of Monte de Santa Tecla (a steep climb) are the remains of one of the most complete Celtic *castros* (settlements) in Galicia, dating from the 1st century BC. Also here is the **Museo da Citania de Santa Tegra**, a Christian sanctuary.

🏛 **Museo da Citania de Santa Tegra**
A Guarda. **Tel** 986 61 00 00. **Open** 9am–9pm Tue–Sun (9:30am–7pm in winter). 🚗

Environs

Some 13 km (8 miles) north, by the beach at Oia, stands the 12th-century Cistercian **Monasterio de Santa María**.

The Cistercian Monasterio de Santa María de Oia, near A Guarda

㉓ Tui

Pontevedra. **Road Map** A3. 🚋 17,500.
🚌 🚍 *i* C/Colon s/n; 986 60 17 89.
🚢 Thu. 🎭 San Telmo (week after
Easter), rafting along the Miño river
(Aug). **W** concellotui.org

As the inhabitants of Tui like
to say, their small city is history
carved in stone. It lies on the
Miño river, on the border with
Portugal. The **old quarter**, with
its narrow streets and secret
passageways, has arcaded
houses with coats of arms,
churches and former manor
houses. Rising above this is
the fortress-like 12th-century
Catedral de Santa María.
 The town's defensive walls
and battlements lend it the
appearance of a fortress, and
indeed it performed this role
due to its border location.
The **Torre Soutomaior** affords
 a magnificent view over Tui,
the river, and the Portuguese
town of Valença do Minho.
The banks of the Miño are

A fountain in Tui along the border between
Spain and Portugal

linked by the iron **Puente
Internacional** (1884), a bridge
by Gustave Eiffel, and by a
modern motorway bridge.

Environs
Not far from Tui is the hill of
Aloia – a park with a wide
variety of flora and fauna.

Many archaeological finds
have been made here, including
Roman walls. The hill has good
observation points of the
Miño river valley.

㉔ Ribadavia

Ourense. **Road Map** B3. 🚋 5,500.
🚌 🚍 *i* Praza Maior 7; 988 47 12 75.
🚢 10th and 25th of each month.
🎭 Feria del Vino del Ribeiro (4th week
in Apr or 1st week in May), Virgen del
Portal (8 Sep). **W** ribadavia.net

Set in a fertile valley, Ribadavia
has for centuries produced
Ribeiro wines. It was also once
home to a Sephardic community, and a walk through the
Jewish quarter today is like
stepping back in time. The
modest houses, with perfectly
preserved façades, conceal
former *bodegas* within their
walls. The Jewish Information
Centre, housed above the
tourist information office, has
information and exhibitions.

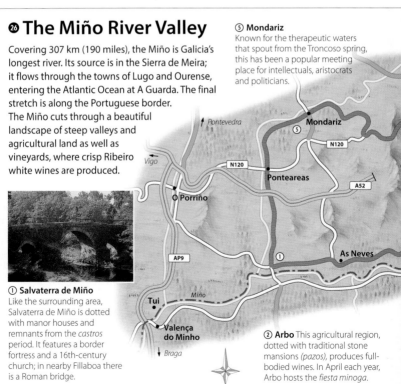

㉖ The Miño River Valley

Covering 307 km (190 miles), the Miño is Galicia's
longest river. Its source is in the Sierra de Meira;
it flows through the towns of Lugo and Ourense,
entering the Atlantic Ocean at A Guarda. The final
stretch is along the Portuguese border.
The Miño cuts through a beautiful
landscape of steep valleys and
agricultural land as well as
vineyards, where crisp Ribeiro
white wines are produced.

⑤ **Mondariz**
Known for the therapeutic waters
that spout from the Troncoso spring,
this has been a popular meeting
place for intellectuals, aristocrats
and politicians.

Pontevedra
Vigo
Mondariz
⑤
N120
N120
Ponteareas
A52
O **Porriño**
① **As Neves**
AP9
Tui
Miño
**Valença
do Minho**
↓ *Braga*

① **Salvaterra de Miño**
Like the surrounding area,
Salvaterra de Miño is dotted
with manor houses and
remnants from the *castros*
period. It features a border
fortress and a 16th-century
church; in nearby Fillaboa there
is a Roman bridge.

② **Arbo** This agricultural region,
dotted with traditional stone
mansions *(pazos)*, produces full-
bodied wines. In April each year,
Arbo hosts the *fiesta minoga*.

The Puente San Clodio in the area near Ribadavia

Located on **Praza Maior** are houses with characteristic arcades, a town hall with a wrought-iron belfry and 16th-century tower bearing a sundial, and the Baroque Pazo de los Condes de Ribadavia. Also preserved is the 15th-century **Sarmiento castle**. Important elements of the castle complex are the 9th-century rock-hewn tombs whose outlines reflect those of human figures, and fragments of the old town walls. The Gothic Casa de Inquisición – an 11th-century House of Inquisition – bears on its façade as many as five coats of arms of families connected with the Holy Office.

By the road leading out of town stands the **Monasterio de Santo Domingo**. The 14th-century monastery church, the best example of local Gothic style, contains medieval tombs.

㉕ Ourense

Ourense. **Road Map** B3. ⛰ 108,000. 🚊 🚌 ℹ C/Isabel la Católica 2; 988 36 60 64. 🗓 7th, 17th & 26th of each month. 🎉 Os Maios (1–3 May), Corpus Cristi (Jun), Os Magostos (San Martín, 11 Nov). 🌐 turismourense.com

Ourense was built around the thermal springs of As Burgas. In Roman times, visitors were also drawn by the abundance of gold in the Miño river. The Romans built a 307-m (1,007-ft) bridge here, now restored.

Built on the site of a Suevi temple, the Baroque **Iglesia de Santa María Madre** incorporates 1st-century columns.

The **Praza Maior** is lined with 18th- and 19th-century buildings, including the town hall and the former bishop's palace.

The 12th- to 13th-century **Catedral de San Martín** has several entrances. The main one (the Pórtico del Paraíso) has partially preserved polychrome decoration. By the high altar is a huge 16th-century Gothic-Renaissance reredos by Cornelis de Holanda.

The 14th-century **Convento San Francisco** houses the **Museo Arqueolóxico Provincial**, currently closed for renovation. Meanwhile, a representative sampling of the collection is on view at the Sala San Francisco.

🏛 **Museo Arqueolóxico Provincial** Sala San Francisco, Rua Xílgaros s/n (temporary location). **Tel** 988 22 38 84. **Open** 9am–10pm Tue–Sat, 9am–3pm Sun.

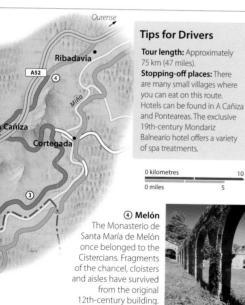

Tips for Drivers

Tour length: Approximately 75 km (47 miles).
Stopping-off places: There are many small villages where you can eat on this route. Hotels can be found in A Cañiza and Ponteareas. The exclusive 19th-century Mondariz Balneario hotel offers a variety of spa treatments.

0 kilometres		10
0 miles		5

④ **Melón**
The Monasterio de Santa María de Melón once belonged to the Cistercians. Fragments of the chancel, cloisters and aisles have survived from the original 12th-century building.

③ **Crecente**
Numerous Roman remains are found here, as well as medieval ones, such as the castle of Fornelos. Excellent observation points can be found in the surrounding area.

Key

≡ Motorway
▬ Tour route
▬ Scenic route
= Minor road

Detail of the high altar at the Catedral de San Martín in Ourense

Horses on the road to Celanova

㉗ Celanova

Ourense. **Road Map** B3. 🏛 5,800.
ℹ Praza Maior 1; 988 43 22 01.
🎭 As Marzas (1–3 Mar), San Roque (16 Aug). 🌐 **concellodecelanova.com**

This village of Celanova is known for its unusually large and grand **Praza Maior**. The Benedictine **Monasterio de San Salvador** was founded in the 10th century, though the current church dates from the 18th century. In the garden is the well-preserved 10th-century Mozarabic Capilla de San Miguel.

Environs
In Bande, 26 km (16 miles) south of the village, is the 7th-century **Iglesia de Santa Comba**, one of the few surviving Visigothic shrines in Europe. Built on the plan of a Greek cross, with thick walls, the barrel-vaulted church contains the tomb of St Torcuato.

㉘ Allariz

Ourense. **Road Map** B3. 🏛 6,000. 🚌
🚌 ℹ Paseo da Alameda; 988 44 20 08. 🎭 1st & 15th of each month. 🎭 San Benito (11 Jul); A Empanada (3rd weekend Aug). 🌐 **allariz.com**

The most attractive feature of Allariz is its location by the Arnoia river, crossed by a medieval stone bridge, next to which you can swim and hire rowing boats. The town is built on a medieval plan, with narrow streets and old houses

decorated with coats of arms. In the **Real Monasterio de Santa Clara**, visitors can admire a Gothic ivory figure of the Virgin and a crystal cross dating from the same period. Also worth visiting is the **shrine of San Benito**, with a lofty 17th- to 19th-century tower, and the **Parque Etnográfico do Río Arnoia**, in which there are museums of leather crafts and textiles as well as a mill.

The portal and façade of the Iglesia de Santiago in Allariz

㉛ The Sil River Valley

This picturesque Sil river valley, replete with chestnut and oak trees, is part of the wine-producing region of Ribeira Sacra. Fresh white wines from the *godella* grape, and a few reds using the *mencía* grape, are produced here. The region owes its name to the local monasteries – for centuries, the monks were involved in the cultivation of vines. The Sil valley and its branches are often extraordinarily steep, with vineyards seeming to climb up near-sheer valley sides.

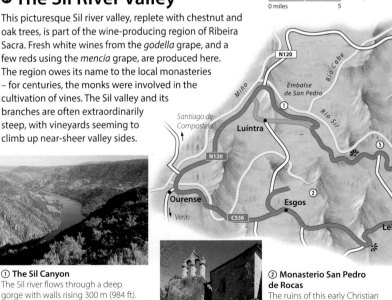

0 kilometres   10
0 miles   5

N120
Río Cabe
Miño
Embalse de San Pedro
Río Sil
Santiago de Compostela
Luíntra
N120
Ourense
Verín
C536
Esgos
Le
①
⑤
②

① The Sil Canyon
The Sil river flows through a deep gorge with walls rising 300 m (984 ft). According to legend, Juno disfigured the "face" of Galicia with a gorge so that Jupiter would not find it appealing.

② Monasterio San Pedro de Rocas
The ruins of this early Christian monastery include altars in the form of a table and eight anthropomorphic tombs.

**📷 Parque Etnográfico
do Río Arnoia**
Tel 988 44 08 59. **Open** early Jul–
mid-Sep: noon–2pm Tue–Wed & Sun,
noon–2pm & 7–9pm Thu–Sat; mid-
Sep–early Jul: noon–2pm & 5–7pm
Sat–Sun. 📷 📷 ⊘

㉙ Verín

Ourense. **Road Map** C3. 📷 14,500.
📷 ℹ Rua Imans da Salle; 988 41 16
14. 🗓 3rd, 11th and 23rd of the
month. 📷 Lázaro (after Easter), Santa
María la Mayor (15 Aug).

Verín is noted for its thermal
springs, which have therapeutic
powers. There are also many
17th-century arcaded houses
with glass-encased balconies
(galerías), but the area's biggest
attraction is **Castillo de
Monterrei**, some 3 km (2 miles)
to the west. It was built to defend
the border during the wars with
Portugal; within its three rings
of walls is a 15th-century square
keep, an arcaded courtyard, and
a 13th-century church with an
intricately carved portal.

The Monasterio de Santo Estevo de Ribas de Sil, set high above a gorge

🏰 Castillo de Monterrei
Closed until further notice. 📷

㉚ Monasterio de Ribas de Sil

Ourense. **Road Map** B2. 📷 San
Esteban de Sil (15 km/ 9 miles away).
📷 from Ourense (then 15-minute
drive); 988 01 01 10. **Open** daily.

Near its confluence with the
Miño, the Sil river carves an
exceptionally deep gorge
in which dams form two
reservoirs. A hairpin road
winds to the top, where
the Romanesque-Gothic
**Monasterio de Santo Estevo
de Ribas de Sil** is situated
high above the gorge.
Some elements of the
monastery exhibit different
architectural styles, such as
the Renaissance cloisters
and Baroque façade. The
building has been restored
and modernized (with a glass
wall in the cloisters), and is now
home to an exclusive parador.

⑤ Parada do Sil
The Monasterio de Santa Cristina
de Ribas de Sil and the Balcones
de Madrid observation point, with
splendid views, are found here.

④ Castro Caldelas
The town has a 17th-century
castle, from which three towers
and a wall still survive.

**③ Monasterio de
Montederramo**
The monastery buildings are
in Plateresque and Baroque
styles, while the church has a
Castilian Baroque façade.

Tips for Drivers

Tour length: Approximately
70 km (43 miles).
Organized excursions:
Tourist agencies offer guided
tours (including a meal) and
boat trips along the river;
these are arranged by Viajes
Pardo (www.riosil.com) and
by Hemisferios Viajes (www.
hemisferios.es).

Key

▬ Tour route

▬ Scenic route

═ Minor road

Quiroga

Río Sil

Ponferrada

N120

A Teixeira

④

C536

C536

A Pobra de Trives

❷ Monforte de Lemos

Lugo. **Road Map** C2. 🏔 19,500. 🚇
🚌 ℹ Rúa Comercio 8; 982 40 47 15.
🛒 6th, 16th, 24th & 30th of each
month. 🎏 Nuestra Señora de
Montserrat (mid-Aug), San Mateo (21
Sep). 🆆 **concellodemonforte.es**

On a hill overlooking the town
are the remnants of a fortress –
fragments of the massive walls,
the palace of the Lemos family
and the **Mosteiro de San
Vicente do Pino** are preserved
here. The monastery's Renaissance façade conceals a Gothic
interior. Of note is the 30-m
(98-ft) tower, from the 13th
century. Spanning the Cabe
river is a bridge supported on
semicircular arches. Originally
Roman, the current structure
dates from the 16th century.
　The **Convento de Santa Clara**,
dating from the 17th century,
accommodates a museum of
religious art with some fine
Italian reliquaries.
　In the suburbs of Monforte
stands the **Colexio de Nosa
Señora da Antiga**, a Piarist
(originally Jesuit) college in the
Herrera style, dating from the
early 16th century. The small
picture gallery within displays
two paintings by El Greco and
five works by the Mannerist
painter Andrea del Sarto.

The Colexio de Nosa Señora da Antiga
in Monforte de Lemos

Environs
The Cistercian **Mosteiro de Santa
María de Oseira**, one of many
monasteries in the area, was
founded in the 12th century. Its
name derives from the word *oso*
(bear), as bears once roamed the
remote area where it was built.
The complex includes a Gothic
church, remodelled during the

Imposing Monasterio de Santa María de Oseira, near Monforte de Lemos

Baroque period, with two huge
towers; its construction was
based on the cathedral in
Santiago de Compostela (*see
pp66–7*). The chapterhouse rooms
have columns with twisted shafts
and capitals resembling palm
leaves. The monastery also
features a well-preserved staircase in the Herrera style and three
cloisters – the Knights', Medallions'
and Pinnacles' cloisters, which
date from the 16th century.
Medicinal liqueurs are produced
by the monks who live here.

❸ Sárria

Lugo. **Road Map** C2. 🏔 13,500. 🚇
🚌 ℹ Rúa Vigo de Sárria 15; 982 53
00 99. 🛒 6th, 20th, 27th of each
month. 🎏 San Juan (23–27 Jun), Noite
Meiga (last Sat in Aug). 🆆 **sarria.es**

Sárria is a common starting
point for pilgrimages to Santiago
de Compostela, which lies 111
km (69 miles) away (100 km is
the minimum distance required
to receive the certificate of
completion of the pilgrimage).
　The town was established by
Alfonso IX, who died en route
to Santiago. Due to its location,
Sárria had many hostels for
pilgrims. The 13th-century hostel
near the **church** and **monastery
of La Magdalena** has been
transformed into a youth hostel,
as have many others. The
monastery has a Renaissance
façade and a late Gothic cloister.
Another building that spans
Romanesque and Gothic styles is
the 13th-century **Iglesia de San
Salvador**, beside the **fortress** of
the same period, of which only
the tower remains. The town
also has four medieval bridges.
In the surrounding area there are
many Romanesque churches.

❸ O Cebreiro

Lugo. **Road Map** C2. 🏔 16. **Tel** 982
36 70 25. 🎏 Virgen de O Cebreiro
(8–9 Sep).

High up in wild, windswept
mountain countryside, famous
for its volatile weather and
with wonderful mountain
views, is tiny O Cebreiro. Here
are several *pallozas* – Celtic
thatched stone huts.
　Many pilgrims begin the last
stage of the Road to Santiago
from here; the local church is one
of the oldest monuments on the
route. According to legend, the
9th-century pre-Romanesque
Iglesia de Santa María La Real
was the scene of a miracle
involving the transformation of
bread and wine into the flesh
and blood of Christ. Inside the
church is a 12th-century chalice,
known as the Holy Grail, in which
the transformation is said to
have taken place. One of the
pallozas contains the **Museo
Etnográfico**, which presents
the daily life of the settlement's
former inhabitants.

🏛 Museo Etnográfico
O Cebreiro. **Open** 11am–6pm (7pm in
summer) Tue–Sat.

A typical stone *palloza* with a thatched roof
in O Cebreiro

㉟ Reserva Nacional de Os Ancares

Os Ancares is a mountainous nature park lying on the border between Galicia and León. Thanks to its varied landscape, in which high, snow-covered mountains alternate with deep valleys and rivers and waterfalls, the region boasts an abundance of plants and wildlife, including such rare species as the capercaillie, deer and wild boar. The highest peaks reach an altitude of almost 2,000 m (6,562 ft).

Tips for Drivers

Tour Length: Approximately 55 km (34 miles).
Stopping off places: Albergue Campa da Braña, Degrada (**Tel** 982 18 11 35); Os Ancares Camping, Mosteiro (**Tel** 982 36 45 56); Hotel Piornedo, Cervantes (**Tel** 982 16 15 87)

⑤ Navia
Aside from the picturesque single-span bridge, several *castros* and the castle of the Altamira family are to be found here.

④ Piornedo
Reachable only on foot, Piornedo contains the pre-Roman oval or rectangular thatched huts known as *pallozas*.

③ Degrada
The Degrada trail encompasses the tallest peaks of Os Ancares – Pena Rubia, Tres Obispos, and Mustallar, good for experienced climbers.

Envernallas
Rao
Navia de Suarna
Son
Navia
↗ *Lugo*
A6
LU 722
San Román
Quindous
NVI
As Nogais
NVI
Sierra de Ancares
Pedrafita do Cebreiro
O Portelo
Ponferrada
A6

0 kilometres 5
0 miles 3

② Castro de Cervantes
The district of Cervantes is home to important historic monuments, such as the castle of Doiras and the *castro* of San Román.

① Becerreá
Nestled between steep hills and valleys, Becerreá is the starting point of most trails into the park. Here are also several bridges and the 17th-century Monasterio de Santa María. Look out for wildlife, including red foxes.

Key
▬ Motorway
▬ Tour route
▬ Scenic route
═ Minor road
–•– Park boundary

㊱ Street-by-Street: Lugo

Lugo is the oldest of Galicia's provincial capitals. A settlement already existed here 2,000 years ago, and its name is probably Celtic in origin (*Lugh* means "God of the Light"). The Romans built a wall here, which today encircles the Old Town. Apart from the fortifications in Ávila, it is the best-preserved old town wall in Spain; over the centuries, it enabled the city to be defended against the Suevi, the Moors and Norman pirates. Nowadays, visitors can walk along the top of the wall, from where there are good views of the city.

Porta Nova
This was the main northern gate, through which people would enter and leave the town. The current gate dates from 1900; it replaced the original gate, which had become unstable.

★ Museo Provincial
Housed in the former monastery of San Francisco, this museum has exhibitions of Celtic and Roman finds and a collection of sundials.

Porta Miña
One of 10 gates in the town walls, the Porta Miña is closest to its original form; also known as Carmen, it gives access to the Miño river.

CARRIL SAN FROILAN

CARRIL DE AMOR MEILAN

RUA BOLAÑO RIBADENEIRA

KOUIROS BALLESTEROS

RAMON Y CAJAL

RUA NOVA

RUA DO MIÑO

PRAZA PIOX II

Bishop's Palace

★ Cathedral
The imposing Romanesque-Gothic cathedral, dating from the 12th century, was modelled on the cathedral in Santiago de Compostela. It has a Neo-Classical façade and Baroque cloisters.

Key

— Suggested route

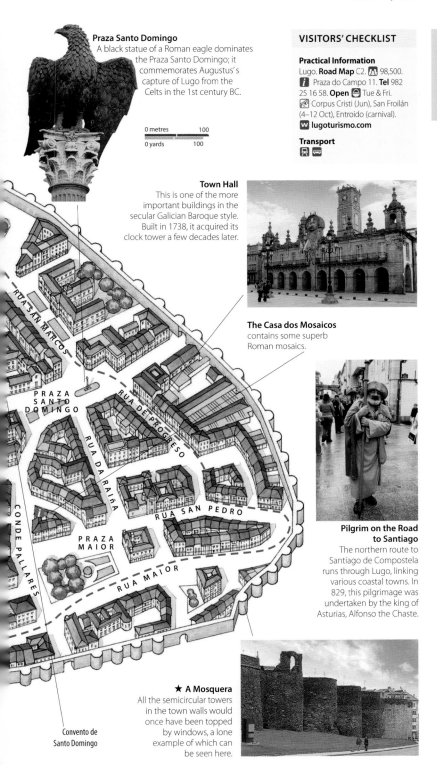

Praza Santo Domingo
A black statue of a Roman eagle dominates the Praza Santo Domingo; it commemorates Augustus's capture of Lugo from the Celts in the 1st century BC.

0 metres 100
0 yards 100

VISITORS' CHECKLIST

Practical Information
Lugo. **Road Map** C2. 98,500.
Praza do Campo 11. **Tel** 982 25 16 58. **Open** Tue & Fri. Corpus Cristi (Jun), San Froilán (4–12 Oct), Entroido (carnival).
lugoturismo.com

Transport

Town Hall
This is one of the more important buildings in the secular Galician Baroque style. Built in 1738, it acquired its clock tower a few decades later.

The Casa dos Mosaicos contains some superb Roman mosaics.

Pilgrim on the Road to Santiago
The northern route to Santiago de Compostela runs through Lugo, linking various coastal towns. In 829, this pilgrimage was undertaken by the king of Asturias, Alfonso the Chaste.

RUA SAN MARCOS
PRAZA SANTO DOMINGO
RUA DE PROGRESO
RUA DA RAIÑA
CONDE PALLARES
RUA SAN PEDRO
PRAZA MAIOR
RUA MAIOR

Convento de Santo Domingo

★ A Mosquera
All the semicircular towers in the town walls would once have been topped by windows, a lone example of which can be seen here.

For keys to symbols *see back flap*

Exploring Lugo

Lugo's main attraction is its town walls, but also well worth visiting is the maze of Old Town streets, including Rua da Raiña, opened in the 19th century by Isabel II, and the two squares – Praza Santo Domingo and Praza Maior (also known as Praza España), whose colonnades are home to cafés and restaurants. Be sure not to miss the charming Praza do Campo – the old Roman forum. On the Feast of St Froilán, the fountain here spouts wine, not water.

Town Walls

The 1st- to 2nd-century Roman fortifications are 2 km (1.2 miles) long, 4–7 m (13–22 ft) thick, and up to 12 m (39 ft) high. They are among the best-preserved town walls in Spain, with ten gates (five old and five new) as well as 71 towers. On A Mosquera tower, two broad windows have survived. Visitors can walk along the walls, which form an unbroken circle around the Old Town.

Cathedral

Museo Diocesano: **Open** 11am–noon Mon–Sat. compulsory.
The Romanesque-Gothic cathedral dates from the 12th century and was modelled on the cathedral in Santiago de Compostela *(see pp66–7)*. Over the centuries, it acquired elements of other styles, including a Neo-Classical façade and a Baroque cloister. The cathedral has a Renaissance chancel and altars, and a **Museo Diocesano** set in the cloisters.

Bishop's Palace

Rising opposite the cathedral on the beautiful Praza Santa María is the Baroque Bishop's Palace. The palace resembles an aristocratic *pazo* (stone mansion), while the Galician granite used in its construction lends it a certain dignified austerity.

The 12th-century Romanesque-Gothic cathedral in Lugo

Town Hall & Praza Maior

The Town Hall in Lugo is one of the more important secular buildings in the Galician Baroque style. It was built in 1738 by renowned master-mason of the day Lucas Ferro Caaveiro. The clock tower was added in 1873.

The Town Hall is situated on Praza Maior, which, together with Praza Santo Domingo, forms the hub of Lugo's Old Town. In Roman times, there was probably an amphitheatre on Praza Maior; a market was later established here.

The square is popular with local people, who come to relax in the nearby cafés, or stroll along the tree-lined boulevard that is guarded by two lions that once decorated Praza Maior's now-vanished fountain.

Casa dos Mosaicos

Rúa Doutor Castro 20–22. **Tel** 982 25 48 15. **Open** Sep–Jun: 11am–2pm & 5–7pm Tue–Sun (until 8pm Jul & Aug). Audiovisual guide: 11am, noon, 1pm, 5pm, 6pm. (free 1st Sat of month).

The remnants of a 1st- to 2nd-century AD Roman villa, which probably belonged to a wealthy nobleman, have been converted into an excellent contemporary museum. An audiovisual guide describes the history behind the superb mosaics, still dazzling after almost two millennia.

Iglesia de Santo Domingo

Open 6pm daily for mass only.
The monastery church of Santo Domingo dates from the 13th century. It was built in a combination of Romanesque and Gothic styles (this can be seen in the three apses with tall windows). The façade is hidden behind the monastery wall, which has 18th-century arcades. The chapel and altars are all Baroque; one of them contains a painting by the 18th-century Galician artist Antonio García Bouzas. Of note are the tomb slabs that are set in the walls and are framed by decorated arches, in particular the one of Fernando Díaz Rivadeneyra, which features a figure of the knight.

Museo Provincial

Praza da Soidade. **Tel** 982 24 21 12. **Open** 9am–9pm Mon–Fri, 10:30am–2pm & 4:30–8pm Sat, 11am–2pm Sun. **museolugo.org**

The museum is housed in the former monastery of San Francisco, of which the cloister, kitchen and refectory have survived. The museum's main aim is to present Galician art. The exhibits include Celtic and Roman finds such as jewellery, coins, ceramics from Sargadelos, sundials and paintings.

Walkers on the Roman walls that encircle Lugo

For hotels and restaurants see p204 and pp216–17

A wall painting of birds in Santa Eulalia de la Bóveda

⑨ Santa Eulalia de la Bóveda

Santalla de Bóveda s/n, Lugo. **Road Map** B2. **Tel** 982 23 13 61. **Open** 8am–3pm & 4–6pm Mon–Fri, 11:30am–7:30pm Sat & Sun (until 6pm in winter year-round).

Situated 14 km (9 miles) from Lugo, this small temple was originally pagan, was later put into use by early Christians, and then forgotten until its rediscovery in 1962.

One of the great mysteries of Lugo province, the building probably dates from the 3rd or 4th century AD, and its purpose has been the subject of various interpretations. Some suggest it was a bathhouse, others say it was a temple to the Phrygian goddess Cybele (the Roman equivalent of the Greek goddess Rea, the mother of all the gods). It is possible that sacrificial bulls and rams were slaughtered here, their blood being collected in a special shallow basin. Centuries later, the temple was used as a church for christenings.

Originally, the church had two storeys, but only the lower one has survived – an almost perfectly preserved square crypt, whose vaulting was damaged during the demolition of the chapel that had been added to the upper floor. Three sides of the crypt are covered with earth; the fourth has two small windows providing the only source of light, apart from the entrance.

Inside the church you can see the atrium leading to the semicircular entrance, the basin, a few columns, various bas-reliefs, and, above all, the barrel vaults covered with murals of birds. The symbolism of birds seemingly points to the cult of Cybele, but it also facilitated the Christianization of the temple, since St Eulalia is the patron saint of birds.

⑧ Vilar de Donas

Lugo. **Road Map** B2. 🚹 130. ℹ️ Carretera de Santiago 28; 982 38 00 01. Church: **Open** Easter–Oct: 11am–2pm & 3– 6pm Tue–Sun; Nov–Easter: ask priest for key (**Tel** 669 54 40 09). 🚌 📷 San Antonio (13 Jun), San Salvador (6 Aug).

In this hamlet on the road to Santiago stands the small, aisleless Romanesque **Iglesia de San Salvador**, dating from the early 13th century and built on the plan of a cross. Initially, it belonged to a convent,

The portal of the church of Vilar de Donas

inhabited first by nuns (hence the name – *Donas*) and later by the Knights of the Order of St James. The Knights' Chapter would meet here each year.

Tombs of the knights are preserved inside the church, as are 14th-century Gothic murals depicting biblical scenes and the figures of King Juan II and his wife with melancholy expressions. The external ornamentation comprises plant motifs, birds, figures that are half human and half bird, griffins and angels. The doors of the church bear the original Romanesque fittings – precise and elegant.

Notable, too, is the tower (a later addition) that is visible from afar, and the remnants of the portico, which stands in front of the main western entrance. The church was built of granite, which in places has now become covered with weeds.

Environs
West of Vilar de Donas, the village of **Palas de Rei** has an abundance of Romanesque churches and chapels; there are also several dolmens and *castros* here.

Galician Fiestas

Os Peliqueiros (Feb/Mar), Laza. Dressed in grinning masks and outlandish costumes, with cowbells, Os Peliqueiros take to the streets on the last Sunday of the carnival.
A Rapa das Bestas (May–Jul), various places. Semi-wild horses are rounded up by local farmers for their manes and tails to be cut.
Flower pavements (May/Jun), Ponteareas and Gondomar. The streets along the Corpus Christi procession are carpeted with designs in petals.
St James's Day (25 Jul), Santiago de Compostela. Firework display in Praza do Obradoiro the night before.

A band of folk musicians performing at a fiesta in Lugo

ASTURIAS AND CANTABRIA

The spectacular Picos de Europa massif sits astride the border between Asturias and Cantabria. In this rural region cottage crafts are kept alive in villages in remote mountain valleys and forested foothills. There are many ancient towns and churches, and pretty fishing ports on the coasts. Cave paintings, such as those at Altamira, were made by people living here over 18,000 years ago.

An ancient principality, Asturias is also known as the Costa Verde (Green Coast). The secluded mountain valleys and wooded hills have attracted settlers to the region since time immemorial. Asturias is proud that it resisted invasion by the Moors. The Reconquest of Spain is traditionally held to have begun in 718, when a Moorish force was defeated by Christians at Covadonga in the Picos de Europa.

The Christian kingdom of Asturias was founded in the 8th century, and in the brilliant, brief artistic period that followed many churches were built around the capital, Oviedo. Some of them still stand. In 1037 Asturias was absorbed into Castile.

Asturias was a strong player in the 19th-century industrial revolution in Spain, with coal mining from Gijón to Oviedo, and steelmaking and shipbuilding in Gijón. Though much of this industry has closed, its legacy is reflected in the Austurian character, which is rough-edged but friendly. Today Asturian towns have a lively cultural life.

Cantabria centres on Santander, its capital, a port and a lively resort. It is a mountainous province with a legacy of isolated Romanesque churches and well-preserved towns and villages such as Santillana del Mar, Carmona and Bárcena Mayor.

Mountains cover more than half of both provinces, so mountain sports are a major attraction. Expanses of deciduous forests remain, some sheltering Spain's dwindling population of wild bears. Equally beguiling is the beautiful coast, with pretty fishing ports and resorts, such as Castro Urdiales, Ribadesella and Comillas, and sandy coves for bathing.

A picturesque *ría* in the vicinity of San Vicente de la Barquera

◀ The Holy Cave of Covadonga, in the Picos de Europa, Asturias

Exploring Asturias and Cantabria

The biggest attraction in this area is the group of mountains that straddles the two provinces – the Picos de Europa. These jagged peaks offer excellent rock climbing and rough hiking. The coast offers sandy coves, spectacular cliffs and remote villages. Santander and Oviedo are lively university cities with a rich cultural life. There are innumerable unspoiled villages to explore, especially the ancient town of Santillana del Mar. Some of the earliest examples of art exist in Cantabria, most notably at Altamira, where the cave drawings and engravings are among the oldest to be found in Europe. It is also worth going slightly further afield to visit some interesting places that lie just outside the region, in Castilla-León, such as El Bierzo, with its medieval monasteries, the Roman town of Astorga, and León.

A flower-covered balcony in Bárcena Mayor, Valle de Cabuerniga

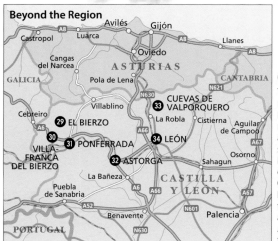

Getting Around

The main roads through the region are the A8 and the N634. Most other major roads run north to south. Minor roads are generally good but can be slow and winding. The private FEVE railway, which follows the coast from Bilbao to Ferrol, in Galicia, is extremely scenic. Brittany Ferries links Santander twice weekly with Portsmouth and weekly with Plymouth. Asturias has a small international airport near Avilés.

Sights at a Glance

The Virgin and Child, Convento de la Regina in Santillana del Mar

Key

— Motorway

— Major road

--- Minor road

— Scenic route

--- Main railway line

— Regional border

△ Summit

⌣ Pass

A view along the crowded beach of Playa del Camello, Santander

For keys to symbols *see back flap*

❶ Castropol

Asturias. **Road Map** C1. 3,700.
C/Vior, 670 55 80 14 (Easter and summer); Plaza del Ayuntamiento s/n, 985 63 50 01 (rest of the year).
Corpus Cristi (May–Jun).
castropol.es

This pretty fishing port, with its narrow streets and white-washed buildings, occupies the eastern bank of the Eo river, which marks the border between Asturias and Galicia. The town lies opposite Ribadeo in Galicia *(see p56)*. Its name derives from nine well-preserved *castros*, or ancient Celtic settlements with dwellings arranged in a circle.

For centuries, the town was an impor-tant commercial centre, where trade in grain, timber, iron, salt, wine and textiles flourished. The significance of the port was recognized by King Juan I of Castile, who in 1386 accorded it numerous privileges.

Castropol also played an important role as a town situated on the pilgrimage route to Santiago de Compostela. The parish **Iglesia de Santiago** dates from the 17th century, having been built on the site of an earlier church. Until the 19th century, it served as a shelter for weary pilgrims.

Also noteworthy is the **Capilla Santa María**, built in 1461, with a Gothic alabaster figure of the Virgin and Child inside. It was apparently the only building in the town to have escaped the devastating fire of 1587.

Of interest, too, are the palaces that once belonged to the port's richer inhabitants, such as the Palacio Vellador, the Palacio de los Marqueses de Santa Cruz, and the Palacio Villarosita, which bear family coats of arms on their façades.

The town's green space is the **Parque de Vicente Loriente**, opened in 1911; it is named after a Cuban émigré who undertook several initiatives to aid the town's development.

Detail of the monument to Fernando Villamil in Castropol

❷ Taramundi

Asturias. **Road Map** C1. 700.
Solleiro 14; 985 64 68 77. San José (19 Mar), Día del Turista (last Sun in Jul). **taramundi.net**

Situated in the remote Los Oscos region, on the border with Galicia, is the small village of Taramundi. In the surrounding forests visitors can admire not only the beautiful natural environment but also acquaint themselves with the tradi-tions of local craftsmanship at various forges. The tourist information office can provide information on five hiking routes through the area. Of particular interest is **Grandas de Salime** – 30 km (19 miles) to the southeast – where handicrafts are displayed in the local **Museo Etnográfico**. However, Taramundi is celebrated above all for its tradition of wrought-iron craftsmanship. Iron ore was first mined in the area by the Romans, and today there are approximately 13 forges in and around the village, where craftsmen can be seen making traditional knives with decorated wooden handles. Here, the skill of artistic smithery is still passed down from father to son.

Taramundi is also justly renowned for the high-quality liqueurs produced here.

Museo Etnográfico

Avenida del Ferreiro 16, Grandas de Salime. **Tel** 985 97 96 40. **Open** 11am–2pm & 4–7pm (until 7:30pm Jul–Aug) daily. (free Tue)

❸ Castro de Coaña

Asturias. **Road Map** C1. 5 km (3 miles) SW of Navia. **Tel** 985 97 84 01. **Open** Apr–Sep: 10:30am–3:30 Wed–Sun; Oct–Mar: 10:30am–5:30pm Wed–Sun. (free Wed). (Jul & Aug).

This is one of the most important centres of Celtic-Iberian culture. *Castros* were the most common type of settle-ment at the end of the Bronze Age, consisting of chaotically arranged circular dwellings surrounded by moats and palisades. The Castro de Coaña, with its 80 dwellings spread over a hillside in the Navia valley, dates from the Iron Age; the first archaeological digs took place here in 1877. The on-site museum displays many of the finds that have been unearthed.

Environs
Nearby, in a picturesque location at the foot of the mountains, is **Navia**, a typical Asturian fishing village. On 15 August is its festival of the cult of the Virgin, who, according to legend, saved a group of fishermen from drowning. The *fiesta* is a good time to sample the local delicacy – *Venera de Navia*, a beautifully decorated almond cake.

There are beautiful beaches just to the east at **Frexulfe** near Puerto de Vega.

The remains of a Celtic settlement in Castro de Coaña

The old harbourmaster's office near the seafront in Luarca

❹ Luarca

Asturias. **Road Map** D1. 🚶 4,000. 🚌
🚌 **i** Plaza Alfonso X El Sabio s/n; 985 64 00 83. 🚃 Noche Celta (last Sat in Jul), Rosario (15 Aug), San Timoteo (22 Aug). **w** turismoluarca.com

Luarca is nicknamed Villa Blanca de la Costa Verde (White Town on the Green Coast) on account of its houses with white façades. This picturesque fishing port, specializing in tuna, arose at the mouth of the meandering Río Negro, across which many bridges have been built. On a cliff overlooking the narrow beach are a chapel and an impressive lighthouse.

Luarca is considered to be one of the most attractive places on the northern coast. Its traditional character is reflected in the charmingly old-fashioned *chigres*, or *tavernas*, where one can sample the excellent local cider. The port is brimming with bars and restaurants offering inexpensive fresh fish, which is sold every day in the afternoon once the fishermen have returned with their catch.

The most beautiful building in Luarca is undoubtedly the **town hall**, which was commissioned in 1906 by an influential family who had returned after making a fortune in Spain's colonies. Some of the rooms have been converted into exclusive tourist accommodation. Luarca's most important *fiesta* is San Timoteo, which begins in the evening of 21 August with a fireworks display on the seafront.

❺ Cudillero

Asturias. **Road Map** D1. 🚶 5,500.
i Puerto del Oeste; 985 59 13 77.
🚃 Fri. 🚃 San Pedro (29 Jun).
w cudillero.org

With its streets winding down an impossibly steep cliffside to end at a picture-perfect harbour, this fishing village attracts large numbers of visitors, thanks also to its outdoor cafés and excellent seafood restaurants. The houses, with their red roofs, seem to merge imperceptibly with the hillsides that cascade down towards the sea.

Its name derives from the word *codillo* (elbow), referring to the shape of the village. The place looks most seductive in the evenings, when attractively lit – a pleasant walk can be made to the port and observation point, from where there is a panoramic view of the surrounding area. The view certainly inspired director José Luis Garci, who shot here some of the scenes for *Volver a Empezar* (1982) – the first Spanish film to win an Oscar.

The port boasts fine architecture. The oldest buildings are a 13th-century Romanesque chapel – the **Capilla de Humilladero** – and the Gothic **Iglesia de San Pedro**, dating from the 16th century. On 29 June, when a *fiesta* in honour of St Peter is held, locals meet on the plaza to describe to each other, in a humorous and ironic way, the events of the previous year in local dialect.

A verdant square in Pravia, near Cudillero

Environs
Some 10 km (6 miles) south of Cudillero is **Pravia**, with its charming 12th-century Capilla de la Virgen de Valle that has a terracotta statue of the Virgin.

The façade of the 16th-century Iglesia de Santa María in Salas

❻ Salas and Valle del Narcea

Asturias. **Road Map** D1. 🚶 5,600. 🚌
i Plaza de la Campa (Salas); 985 83 09 88. 🚃 Fiesta del Bollo (3rd week in Aug).

Salas is the birthplace of the Marquis de Valdés-Salas, the founder of the university in Oviedo and one of the main instigators of the Inquisition. The main highlight is the beautiful Old Town, built around the imposing **castle**, which once served as the residence of the archbishop.

The **Iglesia de San Martín** was consecrated in 896 and later rebuilt in the 10th century. Also noteworthy is the collegiate **Iglesia de Santa María**, which dates from 1549 and is situated on the main square.

South of Salas extends a beautiful, wild valley known as the **Valle del Narcea**. Green and secluded, it is an excellent place for walking, hiking and fishing. The villages here are known for fine ham and traditional crafts.

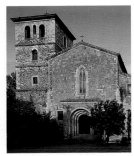

The 12th-century Iglesia de San Nicolás de Bari in Avilés

❼ Avilés

Asturias. **Road Map** D1. 🏛 83,000.
🛈 Calle Ruíz Gómez 21; 985 54 43 25.
🚉 Mon. 🎭 San Agustín (28 Aug).

Ringed by large factories, Avilés is an industrial town once known for steel production; it is also an important transport hub, with services to many destinations. Visitors should head straight for the Plaza de España in the delightful Old Town, which is surrounded by 14th- and 15th-century buildings. Here, too, are the majority of shops, bars and hotels, as well as the vast **Parque de Ferrera**, covering an area of 80,000 sq m (20 acres), which is maintained in the style of an English garden. Well worth visiting is the 12th-century Romanesque **Iglesia de San Nicolás de Bari**, occupying the site of an earlier pre-Romanesque shrine, which was built as part of a Franciscan monastery. The church contains a beautiful 14th-century chapel as well as the fine Spanish-Flemish tomb of the first Governor of the American state of Florida.

The town boasts four well-preserved palaces: the 14th-century **Palacio de Valdecarzana**, the oldest secular building in Avilés; the **Palacio del Marqués de Camposagrado**, completed in 1663 but Renaissance in appearance; the **Palacio del Marqués de Ferrera**, from the start of the 18th century, frequented by visiting royalty; and the early 20th-century **Palacio de Balsera**, which houses a music conservatory.

❽ Gijón

Asturias. **Road Map** D1. 🏛 278,000.
🚉 🚌 🛈 Calle Rodriguez San Pedro;
985 34 17 71. 🚉 Sun. 🎭 San Pedro (29 Jun), La Virgen de Begoña (15 Aug).
🔳 gijon.info

Gijón is Asturias' largest city, with a metal- and chemical-producing industry, but still an enjoyable place to visit. There are interesting museums, nice beaches and a lively nightlife. A good place to start a tour is the **Parque del Cerro de Santa Catalina**, which features the 1990 sculpture *Elogio del Horizonte* – the symbol of the city – by the Basque artist Eduardo Chillida.

Near the park is Gijón's most interesting building – the Baroque **Palacio de Revillagigedo**. Built between 1704 and 1721 at the initiative of Carlos Miguel Ramírez de Jove, the first Marquis of Esteban del Mar, it accommodates a Centre for Modern Art, opened in 1991. Opposite the palace stands a statue of Pelayo, the Visigothic ruler who began the Reconquest *(see p41)*. Nearby is the **Torre del Reloj**, a modern tower erected on the site of a 16th-century building; there are beautiful views of the city and its attractive surroundings from the top of the tower.

This part of Gijón, stretching out along a headland, is called **Cimadevilla**. Fishermen began to settle here in Roman times. Today, the district has preserved its maritime character, offering visitors one of the most

breathtaking views of the Cantabrian Sea. Narrow streets cluster around the Plaza Mayor, with its 19th-century town hall, near to which stands the **Museo Casa Natal de Jovellanos**. This 16th-century house is the birthplace of Gaspar Melchor de Jovellanos, an eminent 18th-century author, reformer and diplomat. The house, which dates from the end of the 16th century, abuts the walls of the medieval citadel. To the right of the Plaza Mayor are the **Baños Romanos**, or Roman baths, built in the 1st century BC.

The seafront leads to the long sandy beach, **Playa San Lorenzo**, which is popular with surfers.

The **Museo del Pueblo de Asturias**, opened in 1968, has a wealth of documentation as well as an archive and library. You can learn about the history of Asturias, see the interior of

The balcony of a house on Calle del Marqués de San Esteban, Gijón

The port in Gijón, with the Palacio de Revillagigedo in the background

a traditional Asturian cottage, or visit one of the numerous exhibitions on local history that are held here. Occupying an area of 35,000 sq m (376,700 sq ft) are two granaries, a period house from 1759 (Casa de los Valdés) and a typical homestead from the central part of the Asturian region, among other exhibits. In 1993, the pavilion that had showcased Asturias at '92 Expo in Seville was transferred to the museum premises. Today, it houses a permanent exhibition entitled "Asturians in

the Kitchen. Everyday Life in Asturias, 1800–1965". Part of the museum, in a house dating from 1757, is the **Museo de la Gaita** (Bagpipe Museum), which contains a collection of instruments from Europe and North Africa.

The **Acuario**, Gijón's modern aquarium, provides great family

The Museo de la Gaita in Gijón

entertainment, with huge tanks teeming with all kinds of sea life. As well as sharks, rays and exotic fish from distant oceans, there is also a small section called *toca toca* ("touch touch"), where children will enjoy being allowed to handle starfish and sea anemones.

Cabo de Peñas, the small peninsula between Avilés and Gijón, has good beaches, impressive dunes, and little resorts at **Luanco** and **Candás**.

🏛 **Museo Casa Natal de Jovellanos**
Plaza Jovellanos. **Tel** 985 18 51 52.
Open 9:30am–2pm & 5–7:30pm Tue–Fri; 10am–2pm & 5–7:30pm Sat–Sun.

🏛 **Museo del Pueblo de Asturias**
Paseo del Doctor Fleming 877, La Güelga. **Tel** 985 18 29 60
Open Apr–Sep: 10am–7pm Tue–Fri, 10:30am–7pm Sat & Sun; Oct–Mar: 9:30am–6:30pm Tue–Fri, 10am–6:30pm Sat & Sun. 🎟 (free Sun). ♿ 🌐 museos.gijon.es

🏛 **Acuario**
Playa de Poniente s/n.
Tel 985 18 52 20. **Open** Jul–Aug: 10am–10pm daily; Sep–Jun: 10am–7pm Mon–Fri, 10am–8pm Sat, Sun & hols. 🎟 ♿ 📷 🚫 🐟 🌐 acuario.gijon.es

---

Gijón City Centre

① Parque del Cerro de Santa Catalina
② Palacio de Revillagigedo & Torre del Reloj
③ Cimadevilla
④ Museo Casa Natal de Jovellanos
⑤ Baños Romanos
⑥ Playa San Lorenzo
⑦ Museo del Pueblo de Asturias
⑧ Museo de la Gaita

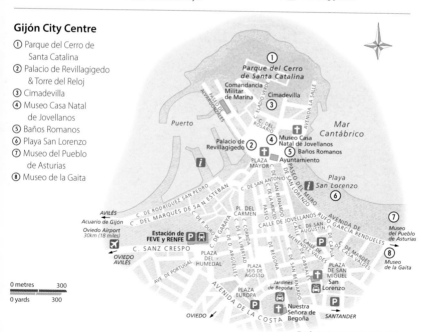

0 metres 300
0 yards 300

For keys to symbols *see back flap*

◉ Street-by-Street: Oviedo

Oviedo, considered to be one of the most beautiful cities in northern Spain, is also the country's oldest Christian city. Founded in the 8th century at the initiative of the Asturian ruler Fruela, son of Alfonso I, it soon became the cultural and commercial capital of the region. To this day, Oviedo boasts one of the best universities in Spain. The delightful Old Town, with its narrow winding streets, invites visitors to contemplate the rich artistic legacy of the capital of Asturias.

Palacio de Valdecarzana
The façade of this 18th- to 19th-century palace is adorned with a huge coat of arms of the Heredia family, the former owners of the residence.

Palacio de Camposagrado
This magnificent 18th-century building is today the seat of the regional court.

PLAZA DE PORLIER

JOVELLA

SAN JUAN

RAMÓN Y CAJAL

C. DE SAN FRANCISCO

To tourist information

ALTAMIRAN

PLAZA DE RIEGO

The Plaza de Porlier is home to *El Viajero*, a sculpture by Eduardo Úrculo.

Palacio de la Rúa
This small palace, dating from the 15th century, is the oldest secular building in Oviedo.

Ayuntamiento
Built in the 16th and 17th centuries, this imposing town hall was destroyed during the Civil War; it was meticulously rebuilt in 1939–40.

★ **Catedral de San Salvador**
Built from the late 14th to the early 16th centuries, the cathedral's flamboyant Gothic interior houses many works of Asturian art, including two gold crosses – the Cross of Angels and the Cross of Victory.

PLAZA ALFONSO "EL CASTO"

SANTA ANA

Monasterio San Pelayo
Inside this 12th-century monastery is an imposing sculpture of Pelayo – the ruler of the Visigoths and a national hero.

★ **Iglesia de San Tirso**
This 9th-century church has been rebuilt several times. Apart from the triforium in the eastern wall, it has lost its original pre-Romanesque appearance.

PLAZA MAYOR

The medieval Plaza de Alfonso II is the historic centre of Oviedo; the city's most important buildings are concentrated in its vicinity.

★ **Museo de Bellas Artes**
Opened in 1980, this museum houses rich collections of Spanish art from the 15th to the 20th centuries, as well as Asturian, Italian and Flemish works.

| 0 metres | | 50 |
| 0 yards | | 50 |

Key

— Suggested route

For keys to symbols see back flap

Exploring Oviedo

Many of Oviedo's historic monuments were destroyed during the Civil War, but the city centre still has several medieval churches and squares, as well as 19th-century tenements. Most of the buildings are located around the Plaza de Alfonso II, making it easy to explore the city on foot.

South of the Plaza Mayor is one of the oldest parts of Oviedo, with charming narrow streets that converge on the **Plaza del Fontán**, home to a lively food market and surrounded by striking old buildings above colonnade porticos, which have been restored and now house a range of restaurants and cafés.

🏛 Catedral de San Salvador

Tel 985 21 96 42. **Open** daily. Nov–Feb: 10am–2pm & 4–6pm; Mar–May & Oct: 10am–2pm & 4–7pm (6pm Sat); Jun: 10am–2pm & 4–8pm (6pm Sat); Jul & Aug: 10am–8pm (6pm Sat); Sep: 10am–7pm (6pm Sat). 🏛 Cámara Santa, museum & cloister.
W catedraldeoviedo.com

Dating from the 16th century, Oviedo's cathedral is the best example in Asturias of the flamboyant Gothic style. In the 9th century, Alfonso II ordered the construction of the Cámara Santa. Part of this chapel, meant to house reliquaries recovered from Toledo after the Moorish invasion, does indeed date from Alfonso's reign; the Romanesque part is the result of remodelling carried out in 1109. Alfonso II's

The medieval Plaza de Alfonso II "El Casto"

🏛 Iglesia de San Tirso

Also on the Plaza Alfonso II, "El Casto", to the left of the cathedral, stands the Iglesia de San Tirso, commissioned by King Alfonso II at the end of the 8th century. This aisled structure, on a basilican plan, was restored several times. It has consequently lost its original appearance, except for the triforium in the eastern wall, whose columns are adorned with plant motifs. Of note, too, is the Gothic chapel of St Anne, which was destroyed during a fire and later rebuilt by Juan Caeredo in the second half of the 16th century.

🏛 Plaza Alfonso II, "El Casto" & Palacio de la Rúa

Closed to the public. The nucleus of the medieval city is this stately square, also known as Plaza de la Catedral, though officially named in honour of the founder of the capital of Asturias, King Alfonso II. After defeating the Moors, Alfonso transferred the Asturian court to Oviedo in 792 and turned the town into an important pilgrimage centre. On the square stands the fortress-like Palacio de la Rúa, built by Alonso González, the treasurer to the Catholic Monarchs, Fernando and Isabel. This elegant and beautiful small 15th-century palace is thought to be the oldest secular building in Oviedo.

🏛 Palacio de Camposagrado

Plaza Porlier. **Closed** to the public. Commissioned by José Bernaldo de Quirós in the first half of the 18th century, the massive four-storey Palacio de Camposagrado was designed by two renowned architects: Francisco de la Riba Ladrón de Guevara and, after 1746, his pupil Pedro Antonio Menéndez de Ambás. The Baroque palace sports a Rococo façade embellished with masks, shields, cornices and fanciful recesses.

🏛 Palacio Toreno

Plaza del Portlier 5. **Open** for occasional exhibitions.
The palace was designed in 1663 for the Malleza Doriga family by the architect Gregorio de la Roza. Featuring an asymmetrical Baroque façade, the building accommodates the headquarters of RIDEA (Real Instituto de los Estudios Asturianos), the Royal Institute for Asturian Studies, which was established in 1946 to encourage research on Asturian culture. Within the building, which often hosts temporary exhibitions, is a patio with Tuscan columns.

🏛 The University

Oviedo's international university was founded in 1608 by the Inquisitor and Archbishop of Seville, Valdés-Salas; it was officially opened on 21 September 1608. The present rectorate building was designed by Bracamonte and Juan de Rivero. Especially impressive is the library, designed by Rodrigo Gil de Hontañón. In the 19th century, Oviedo University was one of ten universities in Spain; today, it is the only public institution of higher education in Asturias.

tomb is found inside the cathedral, as is a gilded altar of 1525 – one of the largest in Spain – by Giralte of Brussels.

The flamboyant Gothic Catedral de San Salvador

For hotels and restaurants see pp204–5 and pp217–19

The spacious interior of the Museo de Bellas Artes

🏛 Museo de Bellas Artes

Calle Santa Ana 1. **Tel** 985 21 30 61.
Open Jul–Aug: 10:30am–2pm &
4–8pm Tue–Sat, 10:30am–2:30pm Sun
& hols; Sep–Jun: 10:30am–2pm &
4:30– 8:30pm Tue–Fri, 11:30am–2pm
& 5–8pm Sat, 11:30am–2:30pm Sun &
hols. 🚻 🖥 museobbaa.com

In the city's old quarter, just
next to the cathedral, Oviedo's
Museum of Fine Art occupies
three buildings: the Palacio de
Velarde (1767); the Baroque
Casa Oviedo-Portal (1660)
by the Cantabrian architect
Melchior de Velasco; and a
building from the 1940s.
The museum, opened in 1980,
boasts the most exciting
collections in the region.
The permanent exhibition
comprises Spanish painting
dating from the 15th to the
20th centuries, Asturian art,
Italian and Flemish works from
the 14th to the 18th centuries,
as well as Spanish and Asturian
sculpture from the 15th to the
20th centuries. In total, the
museum's inventory numbers
8,000 items, including works
by Goya, Murillo, Zurbarán,
Picasso, Dalí and Miró.

🏛 Plaza Mayor and Iglesia San Isidoro

On this square, usually
known as Plaza Constitución
(Constitution Square), stands
the town hall, which dates from
the 16th–17th century. Almost
completely destroyed during
the Civil War, the town hall was
rebuilt in 1939–40. Looming

over the square is the tower of
the Jesuit Iglesia de San Isidoro,
which adjoins a college that
was run by the Jesuits until
1767, when Carlos III banished
them from the city. The church,
featuring a Neo-Classical façade
and Baroque ornamentation
within, was consecrated in
1681. The building has only
one tower; a second, identical
tower was planned but was
never completed.

🏛 Museo Arqueológico Provincial

Calle San Vicente 5. **Tel** 985 20 89 77.
Open 9:30am–8pm Wed–Fri, 9:30am–
2pm & 5–8pm Sat, 9:30am–3pm Sun.
🖥 museoarqueologicode
asturias.com

Since 1952, the
Archaeological and
Ethnographical
Museum has
been housed

A sculpture depicting traders at the market in Oviedo

in the old Benedictine
monastery of San Vicente,
founded in 761. On display are
Palaeolithic tools, Roman finds –
including a mosaic from Vega
del Ciego – pre-Romanesque
treasures, such as an altar from
the Iglesia de Santa María del
Naranco, and Romanesque
and Gothic exhibits. The
permanent exhibitions are
arranged thematically.

🏛 Monasterio de San Pelayo

Calle de San Pelayo 5. Monastery:
Closed to public. Church: **Open** for
mass only.

San Pelayo is a functioning
Benedictine monastery with
a strict monastic rule, and is
closed to visitors except for the
church, which opens to the
public for mass. Its construction
was begun in the 10th century
under the patronage of Teresa
Ansúrez, the widow of Sancho
de León, dubbed El Gordo (The
Fat One). Initially, the church was
to be dedicated to St John the
Baptist, but this was changed in
987 when the reliquary of the
martyr San Pelayo was brought
to Oviedo. Imprisoned by the
Moors, Pelayo refused to
relinquish his faith, for which
he was brutally tortured: his
hands and his feet were cut
off, and he was beheaded in
925. Pelayo's remains were
recovered and taken to León,
from where they were
transferred to Oviedo (see p41).

The First Kings of Asturias

By the time Asturias was annexed by the
kingdom of León in 910, 13 rulers had sat
on the Asturian throne. The first of these
was the legendary Pelayo (718–35). Another
outstanding ruler was Alfonso I (739–51),
who undertook several armed raids in the
Duero river basin. The new state grew
powerful during the reign of Alfonso II
(791–842), whose contemporary was
Charlemagne, with whom he maintained
close contact. Alfonso's successor, Ramiro I
(842–50), was another colourful figure:
an avid art enthusiast, he began the
construction of several pre-Romanesque
churches in the vicinity of Oviedo that
still exist to this day.

A statue of Alfonso II, known as "El Casto"
(the Chaste) (791–842)

Romanesque Churches of Oviedo

Established in the 10th century, the Kingdom of Asturias cultivated Visigothic traditions, creating a local, highly original style of art known as Asturian. Long before the appearance of Romanesque, the Asturian style was characterized by barrel vaults covering entire buildings, the use of buttressing and elongated arches, as well as sculptural decoration in low relief, inspired by Visigothic art. Preserved around Oviedo are several superb examples of this style, such as Santa María del Naranco, San Miguel de Lillo and San Julián de los Prados, which are considered to be the most interesting historic monuments in Asturias.

Santa María del Naranco This aisleless church is illuminated by sunlight entering through the arcaded galleries *(solaria)* – a novel solution in European architecture of the time. The nearby Centro de Recepción e Interpretación Prerrománico has information about the churches in the area.

Arcaded galleries create a light church interior.

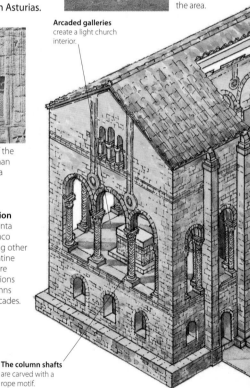

Triple-arched Windows The arches of the arcades are slightly elongated rather than semicircular, which lends the building a certain slenderness.

Byzantine Medallion The interior of Santa María del Naranco features, among other things, a Byzantine medallion. There are also medallions above the columns supporting the arcades.

The column shafts are carved with a rope motif.

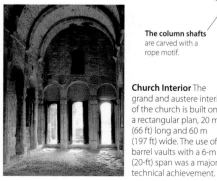

Church Interior The grand and austere interior of the church is built on a rectangular plan, 20 m (66 ft) long and 60 m (197 ft) wide. The use of barrel vaults with a 6-m (20-ft) span was a major technical achievement.

Santa María del Naranco

The church, built in 848, was used as a royal chamber known as the aula regia, *where royal councils of the court of King Ramiro I would be held. It was a two-storey building, with its lower part divided into three sections.*

San Julián de los Prados
Also known as Santullano, this is the oldest pre-Romanesque shrine in Asturias. It was built by Alfonso II in 812–42.

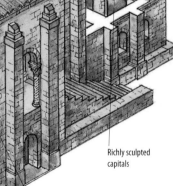

Richly sculpted capitals

Murals The Iglesia de San Julián de los Prados boasts lavish murals with plant and geometrical motifs. The colours are still vibrant today.

The barrel vaulting used in the church did not appear elsewhere in Europe until the 11th century.

San Miguel de Lillo The Church of the Archangel Michael was built in the 9th century by Ramiro I as a royal chapel. Following 18th-century remodelling, it now resembles a Byzantine building. It was made a UNESCO World Heritage Site in 1985.

Columns
The richly carved stone columns feature the spiral rope motif *(soqueado)* – a decorative element typical of the Romanesque style. The capitals are embellished with plant motifs.

Decorative Elements
The Iglesia de San Miguel de Lillo is famous for its decorative motifs, based on geometric and animal themes.

The 12th-century Iglesia de San Pedro in Teverga

⑩ Valle de Teverga

Asturias. **Road Map** D2. ℹ️ Calle San Martín s/n; 985 76 42 93. 📅 Nuestra Señora del Cébrano (15 Aug).
🌐 **tevergaturismo.com**

This area lies to the south of Oviedo. Its main attractions are forests, wild scenery, meandering rivers and foaming waterfalls. Three caves – Cueva Huerta, Cueva de Vistulaz and Vegalonga – have prehistoric wall paintings. The **Parque de la Prehistoria** illustrates the lives and art of the earliest cave dwellers.

The regional capital is **La Plaza**, whose **Iglesia de San Pedro** was built in 1069–76. Just to the west of La Plaza is **Villanueva**, with its equally beautiful Romanesque **Iglesia de Santa María**.

The local culinary delicacies of Teverga are roast mutton and *masera* cheese.

🏛️ Parque de la Prehistoria

San Salvador de Alesga. **Tel** 902 30 66 00. **Open** Mar–Jun & Sep–Nov: 10am–2:30pm & 3:30–6pm Wed–Fri, 10:30am–2:30pm & 4–7pm Sat & Sun; Jul–Aug: 10am–2:30pm & 4–8pm daily; Dec–Feb: 10:30am–2:30pm & 3:30–5:30pm Thu–Sun. 📷 📹 ♿
🌐 **atracciónmilenaria.com**

⑪ Bárzana and Bermiego

Asturias. **Road Map** D1 & D2.
ℹ️ Carretera General, Bárzana; 985 76 81 60 (summer only).

Among the most beautiful mountain villages in Asturias, it was here that the Visigothic aristocracy hid during the Moorish invasion.

Both Bárzana and Bermiego are primarily known for their excellent bread and colourful fiestas. Bermiego, which is surrounded by the Gamonitero and Gamonal hills, features traditional red-roofed houses and characteristic *hórreos* – wooden structures built on stone pillars to prevent rodents from eating the grain stored inside. It's an easy hike to the summit of Gamonitero, from which there are beautiful panoramic views. Next to the church of Santa María stands a locally famous yew tree of impressive dimensions: 14 m (46 ft) high, and with a trunk some 13 m (43 ft) in diameter.

Bárzana is another attractive village. Of greatest interest to the visitor is undoubtedly the **Museo Etnográfico de Quirós**, which opened in 1998 on the site of a former marketplace. The aim of the museum is to present life in the Asturian countryside in times past. On the first floor are a series of reconstructed farm buildings and cattle pens; on the second, a display of tools and craft products. The museum also puts on temporary exhibitions.

🏛️ Museo Etnográfico de Quirós

Barzana. **Tel** 985 76 81 60. **Open** Jul–Sep: 11am–2pm & 3:30–7:30pm Wed–Sun; rest of year: 11am–2pm & 3–6pm Sat, Sun & public hols. **Closed** mid-Dec–Feb. 📷 📹 (call in advance)

A typical red-roofed wooden *hórreo* (granary) in Bárzana

⑫ Parque Natural de Somiedo

Road Map D2. ℹ️ Centro de Recepción, Pola de Somiedo; 958 76 37 58. 🌐 **somiedorural.com**

One of the wildest pieces of wilderness left in western Europe, this large park straddles the Cantabrian mountains, covering an area of 300 sq km (116 sq miles). Somiedo is one of the most representative mountain ecosystems on the Iberian Peninsula, its beech and oak forests providing a sanctuary

The Brown Bear

The brown bear – Europe's largest land predator – is found in the mountain regions of Asturias and in nature reserves such as Somiedo. In the Middle Ages, the brown bear enjoyed great respect, as evidenced by the fact that images of the animal often appeared in coats of arms. Hunting and the destruction of its natural forest habitat caused a rapid decline in numbers. However, things have been improving steadily since the 1990s, and it is estimated that there are now 200 brown bears in Somiedo.

A brown bear in the Parque Nacional de los Picos de Europa

for wolves, brown bears and capercaillies (a large European grouse). The post-glacial Saliencia lakes are remarkable for their breathtaking settings and diverse geology. The largest of them, Lago del Valle, is also the largest lake in Asturias, and is situated at an altitude of 1,550 m (5,085 ft) above sea level. The park is home to several species of wild flowers, which temper the harsh landscape.

Traditional thatched stone cabins, or *teitos*, are the park's most distinguishing feature. Herdsman live in these cabins in spring and summer while their animals graze on the mountain pastures.

Geologically, the landscape of the park is made up of slate, sandstone, quartzite and limestone.

Stone cabins with thatched roofs in the Parque Natural de Somiedo

🅑 **Valdediós**

Asturias. **Road Map** E1. 🅜 150.
🅘 Monastery; 670 24 23 72.
🆆 **monasteriovaldedios.com**

A highlight of this hamlet is the pre-Romanesque **Iglesia de San Salvador**, founded by Alfonso III in 893. It is built on a basilica plan, so the nave is taller than the aisles. The interior painted decoration is very well preserved, assuming in places geometric, Moorish forms. The frescoes on the ceiling are particularly vivid.

Nearby stands a **Cistercian monastery** dating from 1200, with beautiful cloisters from 1522. In 1992, Cistercian monks restored it and established a seminary, but they left in 2009 as they were so few in number. The San Juan Order took over and opened a hostel here to finance the restoration works.

The pre-Romanesque Iglesia de San Salvador in Valdediós

Environs

Approximately 5 km (3 miles) southeast of Valdediós is **Nava**, well known for its July cider festival, with pourings and tastings. The local, four-room **Museo de la Sidra** (Museum of Cider) houses an interesting exhibition on the cider-making process.

🏛 **Museo de la Sidra**
Plaza Principe de Asturias, Nava.
Open mid-Jun–mid-Sep: noon–2pm & 4–8pm Tue, 11am–2pm & 4–8pm Wed–Sat, noon–2pm & 5–8pm Sun; mid-Sep–mid-Jun: 11am–2pm & 4–7pm Tue-Fri, 11am–3pm & 4:30–8pm Sat, 11am–2pm Sun. 🎟 (free Tue). 🅟 ♿

🅒 **Villaviciosa**

Asturias. **Road Map** E1. 🅜 15,000.
🅘 Plaza Obdulio Fernández 51, 985 89 17 59. 🆆 **villaviciosa.es**

The Ría de Villaviciosa, which cuts inland for 8 km (5 miles), is rich in plants and animal life. You can take a fishing boat or kayak trip along the *ría*, which is lined by nice beaches. At the end of the *ría* lies Villaviciosa, a graceful little resort town that attracts visitors, thanks to its well-preserved Romanesque buildings. The most famous of these is the **Iglesia de Santa María de Oliva**, built in the late 13th century. The stonemasons introduced elements of early Gothic style. The side entrances and most of the decorative elements are still Romanesque, but the pointed arches in the main portal and the use of rose windows attest to an interest in new architectural trends.

This mixing of styles and the gradual transition from one style to the next is very much in evidence in **Amandi**, a small but picturesque district of the town. The **Iglesia de San Juan** of 1134, initially designed as a monastery church, is an example of the late Romanesque style. The chancel was entirely dismantled in the 18th century due to subsidence, and was later rebuilt. The highlight of the interior is the sculptural decoration – the religious scenes are infused with plant motifs (fruits, leaves, rosettes), geometric motifs, zigzags and chequered patterns, as well as animal motifs (birds and reptiles).

Villaviciosa is also known as the cider capital of Asturias, and is surrounded by apple orchards, with many traditional *sidrerías* (cider bars) in town.

Romanesque portal of the Iglesia de Santa María de Oliva in Villaviciosa

The richly decorated altar at the church of San Salvador in Llanes

❶ Ribadesella

Asturias. **Road Map** E1. 6,250.
ℹ Paseo Princesa Letizia; 985 86 00 38.
📅 Wed. 🎣 Descent of the Río Sella
(1st Sat in Aug). **W** **ribadesella.es**

The old port straddling the mouth of the Sella river dates from the reign of Alfonso X of Castile, who founded this enchanting seaside town. It has always been of strategic importance for the area.

Today, on one side of the river is the lively seaport full of tapas bars serving fresh fish, while on the other is the more modern part; its beautiful broad beach is the reason why Ribadesella has become a popular holiday resort. A multicoloured flotilla of kayaks arrives here on the first Saturday in August, in an international regatta that is held every year.

On the edge of the town is the **Cueva de Tito Bustillo**, a series of interconnected caves with beautiful prehistoric paintings. Discovered in 1968, the drawings date from the Palaeolithic era – from 22,000 to 10,000 BC – and include superb black and red images of stags' and horses' heads. To protect the paintings, only 15 visitors are allowed on each guided tour. Put on warm clothing when entering the cave, as the temperature is surprisingly cool, and wear sturdy, comfortable walking boots – watch your step, as the cave floors are uneven.

🏛 **Cueva de Tito Bustillo**
Ribadesella. **Tel** 985 18 58 60.
Open mid-Apr–Oct: 10am–5pm
Wed–Sun. 🎟 (free Wed, but it's necessary to reserve in advance by calling the number above).
Children over 7 only.

Environs
Nearby is the charming town of **Llanes**, ever popular for its well-preserved medieval quarter, its busy fishing port and its 30 beautiful sandy beaches. The Asturian coast is the most important Jurassic site in Spain. The interactive and family-oriented **Museo Jurásico**, near the village of Colunga, 46 km (29 miles) east of Villaviciosa (see p99), contains around 20 replica dinosaurs. A great walking trail, which takes in some of the best fossils and dinosaur tracks in the region, begins on nearby Griega beach.

🏛 **Museo Jurásico**
Playa de la Griega, Colunga.
Tel 902 30 66 00. **Open** Feb–Jun &
Sep–Dec: 10am–2:30pm & 3:30–6pm
Wed–Fri; 10:30am–2:30pm & 4–7pm
Sat & Sun; Jul–Aug: 10:30am–8pm
daily. **Closed** Jan. 🎟 (free Wed).
W **museojurasicoasturias.com**

❶ Picos de Europa

See pp104–7.

❶ San Vicente de la Barquera

Cantabria. **Road Map** F1. 4,400.
ℹ Avda del Generalísimo 20; 942 71
07 97. 🎣 La Folía (1st Sun after Easter).

The first mention of this beautiful maritime town dates from Roman times, when a major port already existed here. Alfonso I of Asturias populated the expanding town under his colonization policy, while Alfonso VIII of Castile granted it privileges in 1210.

For centuries, San Vicente was an important stopover for pilgrims travelling to Santiago de Compostela (see pp24–5). Today, it boasts a rich artistic legacy, which includes the **Iglesia de Santa María de los Ángeles**, built between the 13th and 16th centuries. The interior features the beautiful tomb of the Inquisitor Antonio del Corro, who is shown in a reclining pose immersed in the pages of a book.

The 15th-century monastery of **El Santuario de la Barquera** and **El Convento de San Luis** is worth a visit. Now a private property, it is open to the public between April and July, and in mid- to late September.

In the vicinity of San Vicente are broad picturesque beaches – Meron, Tostadero and Oyambre.

Environs
The cave of **El Soplao**, 28 km (17 miles) inland, has brilliant white helictites (like stalactites or stalagmites, but without a stem). These are so dazzling that it has been nicknamed "the subterranean Sistine Chapel". There is a bus service from Santander (see pp114–15) run by ALSA.

🏛 **El Soplao**
Near Rábago. **Tel** 902 82 02 82.
Open call for details. 🎟 🅿
♿ partial. **W** **elsoplao.es**

The picturesque port in San Vicente de la Barquera

Asturian Specialities

Asturian food is hearty, based on flavourful meat (especially bacon and sausage), fresh fish, and very strong cheeses. Trout from mountain streams, as well as salmon and cod caught in the sea, often feature on menus, and the Gijón region is famous for its delicious sardines. Also popular are shellfish, particularly gooseneck barnacles, lobster and shrimps. Fish and shellfish are among the ingredients of *la caldereta* (fish stew). Flavour is further enhanced by the delicious local vegetables, such as peppers, artichokes, lettuce and, above all, beans, which are used to make the traditional Asturian *fabada*. High-quality milk enables the large-scale production of excellent cheeses, of which there are over 40 varieties. But, above all, Asturias is famous for its cider *(sidra)* – a mildly alcoholic drink that is used in many dishes, too.

Cider is stored in wooden casks at the optimum temperature of 9–10ºC (48–50ºF). Too low a temperature will hinder the fermentation process; too high a temperature will overly accelerate it; ideally, the maturation process should take five to six months.

The original labels on the bottles of cider are a guarantee of high quality and traditional production methods; the labels are usually very colourful and bear attractive images of fruit.

During Nava's July Cider Festival, you can sample this drink while enjoying traditional dancing and Asturian folk songs. The cider is poured into a glass from a bottle held high above the head to give it a fizzy head.

Fabada, a tasty, satisfying dish, is made from Asturian beans *(fabes)* and various meats, including local sausage *(chorizo)*, bacon *(tocino)* and ham, which infuse the beans with flavour.

The Asturian village of Llanos de Somerón is famous for its delicious mixed-blossom honey, produced from the nectar of heather and chestnut flowers.

Asturian cheese *(queso asturiano)*, made from cow's, sheep's and goat's milk, has a slightly strong, pungent flavour and smell. The best known are *cabrales* and *taramundi*.

⑯ Parque Nacional de los Picos de Europa

These beautiful mountains were reputedly christened the "Peaks of Europe" by returning sailors for whom this was often the first sight of their homeland. The range straddles three regions – Asturias, Cantabria and Castilla y León – and has diverse terrain. In some parts, deep winding gorges cut through craggy rocks while elsewhere verdant valleys support orchards and dairy farming. The celebrated creamy blue cheese, *cabrales*, is made here. The Picos offer rock climbing and upland hiking as well as a profusion of flora and fauna. Tourism in the park is well organized.

Covadonga
The Neo-Romanesque basilica, built between 1886 and 1901, stands on the site of Pelayo's historic victory.

Lago de la Ercina
Together with the nearby Lago Enol, this lake lies on a wild limestone plateau above Covadonga and below the peak of Peña Santa.

Desfiladero de los Beyos
This deep, narrow gorge with its high limestone cliffs winds spectacularly for 10 km (6 miles) through the mountains. Tracing the course of the Río Sella below, it carries the main road from Cangas de Onís to Riaño.

Ribadesella **Cangas de Onís**
N625
AS114
Covadonga
● **Sames**
Lago Enol
Lago de La Ercina
Desfiladero de los Beyos
N625
Ca
Posada de Valdeón
Oseja de Sajambre
LE244
Puerto de Panderruedas
Puerto de Pontón
Riaño

KEY

① **Bulnes**, one of the remotest villages in Spain, enjoys fine views of Naranjo de Bulnes and can be accessed on foot, and now also by funicular railway up through a tunnel from Puente Poncebos.

② **Naranjo de Bulnes**, with its tooth-like crest, is in the heart of the massif. At 2,519 m (8,264 ft) it is one of the highest summits in the Picos de Europa.

Key

═══ Major road
═══ Minor road
– – Footpath
─── National park boundary

Desfiladero del Río Cares
The Río Cares forms a deep gorge in the heart of the Picos. A dramatic footpath follows the gorge, passing through tunnels and across high bridges up to 1,000 m (3,280 ft) above the river.

A dramatic view of the mountains of the Picos de Europa

VISITORS' CHECKLIST

Practical Information
Road Map E1–2.
ℹ️ Cangas de Onis, 985 84 80 05;
Posada de Valdeón, 987 74 05 49;
Panes; 985 41 42 97.
Fuente Dé cable car: **Tel** 942 73
66 10. **Open** Jul–Sep: 9am–8pm
daily; Oct–Jun: 10am– 6pm daily
(to 8pm May–Jun Sat & Sun).
Closed 1 & 6 Jan; 24, 25 & 31 Dec.

Transport
🚌 From Oviedo to Cangas
de Onis.

The Best Trails

The best walking expeditions in the Picos de Europa can be started from Turieno, Cosgaya and Sotres, where several well-marked trails begin. Free guided expeditions are organized every day in summer from June to September, leaving from the boundary of the park. Hikers who wish to explore the higher areas of the mountains should remember to take the appropriate equipment, boots and warm clothing, as the weather is prone to sudden and dramatic changes.

Statue of a hiker, near Potes

0 kilometres 5

0 miles 5

Fuente Dé Cable Car
The 900-m (2950-ft) ascent from Fuente Dé takes visitors up to a wild rocky plateau pitted with craters. From here there is a spectacular panorama of the Picos' peaks and valleys.

For keys to symbols see back flap

The 18th-century Ermita de Santa Cruz, in Cangas de Onís

Exploring the Picos de Europa

Aside from exploring the mountain trails, it is well worth spending time discovering the towns and villages located within the national park, where many important historic monuments can be found.

Cangas de Onís

Asturias. 6,800. Avenida de Covadonga 1; 985 84 80 05. Sun. Fiesta de San Antonio (13 Jun), Fiesta del Pastor (25 Jul). w cangasdeonis.com

The first capital of the kingdom of Asturias, Cangas de Onís is one of the gateways to the Picos de Europa National Park. Preserved here is the **Ermita de Santa Cruz**, which was built in 733 on the site of an earlier shrine, with a fascinating Bronze Age dolmen by the entrance. The ivy-clad bridge, with its tall arches, dates from the reign of Alfonso XI of Castile (1312–50).

Watersports enthusiasts might wish to attempt the 3-hour canoe trip along the Río Sella.

Covadonga

Asturias.

Set in the northern range of the Picos de Europa, Covadonga is a place of importance for Asturias, and for the whole of Spain. It was here, in 722, that Pelayo, a leader of the Visigothic nobles, won a battle to stop the further advance of the Moors in this part of Asturias. According to Christian tradition, Pelayo's men,

Cave containing Pelayo's tomb in Covadonga

encouraged by the appearance on the battlefield of the Virgin Mary, destroyed the Moorish army. The town remains an important shrine, and crowds of pilgrims come to visit the cave where Pelayo is said to have lived, which is picturesquely set on a hillside. Inside the cave is a chapel containing the warrior's tomb. In 1886–1901, a Neo-Romanesque basilica was built on the spot where Pelayo scored his historic victory. The name of the town derives from *cova longa* (*cueva larga* in Spanish) – the long cave where the warriors prayed to the Virgin before the battle.

Arenas de Cabrales

Asturias. 2,000. Carretera General; 985 84 67 47. San Juan (24 Jun), San Pedro (29 Jun), Fiesta del Queso (last Sun in Aug).

This village, situated 25 km (16 miles) east of Cangas de Onís, is famous as the place where *cabrales*, a pungent blue goat's cheese, is made. On the last Sunday in August, an Asturian cheese festival takes place here, during which the place comes alive with music and dancing.

The village features many beautiful 17th- and 18th-century homesteads, of which the most arresting is the **Casa Palacio de los Mestas**. On the right bank of the Ribelas river rises the small Gothic **Iglesia de Santa María de Llas**, affording fine views of the surrounding area. In the vicinity of Arena de Cabrales are three caves: **Cueva El Bosque**, **Cueva de los Canes** and **Cueva de la Covaciella**. Though quite difficult to get to, the caves are well worth visiting on account of the superb Palaeolithic cave art to be seen inside.

Fuente Dé

Asturias. w cantur.com

The cable car in Fuente Dé takes visitors up to an altitude of 1,900 m (6,234 ft) above sea level. As it ascends 750 m (2,461 ft) up the steep mountain, panoramic views of the

---

Pelayo, Ruler of the Visigoths

Leader of a group of Visigothic nobles, Pelayo encouraged the Asturian villages not to pay dues to the Moors and even to resist them by force of arms. The Moors, in turn, sent troops to the region to quell the rebellion. At the Battle of Covadonga in 722 the scales turned in favour of the Christians, and as the legend of the battle grew, Pelayo became a national hero. It is worth noting, however, that the Asturians did not – as tradition would have it – fight at Covadonga in defence of their faith, but rather in defence of their freedom, just as the barbarian tribes had fought the Romans. It was not until the 11th century that the war against the Moors took on the character of a crusade.

A statue of Pelayo in Covadonga

beautiful, if harsh, surrounding landscape are gradually revealed. From the Mirador del Cable, the observation point at the summit, ambitious walkers can carry on to the peaks of **Pico Tesorero** (2,570 m/8,432 ft) and **Peña Vieja**. Despite the high altitude, the trails are not difficult and your efforts will be rewarded by unforgettable views of the Picos' central massif.

🎬 Potes

Cantabria. 🚶 1,400.
ℹ️ C/Independencia 12; 942 73 07 87.
🏛️ Mon. 🎭 Nuestra Señora de Valmayor (15 Aug), Santísima Cruz (14 Sep).

This small town on the Deva river, picturesquely set amid snowcapped peaks, is the main centre of the eastern Picos de Europa. The narrow winding streets lined with medieval stone houses are full of small shops, and on Mondays a colourful flea market takes place here.

The town's most characteristic monument is a 15th-century defensive tower, the **Torre del**

15th-century Torre del Infantado in Potes, currently the town hall

Infantado. Also worth seeing is the late Gothic 14th-century **Iglesia de San Vicente**, with a beautiful façade and Baroque altars brought here from the Dominican Convento de San Raimundo.

A good way to spend an afternoon in Potes is to hire a bicycle and ride for 9 km (5 miles) to the **Iglesia de Santa María Piasta**. This ideally

proportioned building – pure Romanesque in style – boasts beautiful exterior sculptures.

🎬 Valle de Valdeón

Castilla y León.
The Posada de Valdeón lies on the main tourist trail that runs through the Picos de Europa national park. Huge outcrops of rock dominate the valley, leaving a lasting impression on those who stay in the village of Valdeón.

There is an astonishing variety of flora and fauna, and the valley's meadows provide grazing ground for cattle. Hiking trails to the picturesque ravine of **Garganta del Cares** begin in Valdeón, but shorter walks in the surrounding area are also worthwhile, for every corner of the valley has beautiful views.

Every year on 8 September a festival in honour of the Virgen de Corona (Virgin of the Crown) takes place in the villages of the Valle de Valdeón. Local inhabitants believe that the warrior king Pelayo was crowned here.

Flora and Fauna of Picos de Europa

Foxes, otters and wolves inhabit the lush vegetation in the beech and mixed forests. Eagles, vultures and kestrels circle above the soaring peaks. The flowers that appear in the meadows include Alpine violets, foxgloves and colourful perennials. Visitors are invariably impressed by the richness of the flora and fauna, which include many endemic species.

The steep hillsides, soaring peaks and peaceful valleys and ravines of the Picos form the park's picturesque backdrop.

The pyramidal orchid, with an 8-cm (3-in) long inflorescence and pink or purple flowers, grows in the park's open meadows.

The chamois is one of the larger species to inhabit the park. Herds of these agile animals graze in the mountain meadows.

The owl, with a flat head, short tail, and large bright yellow eyes, is active both during the day and at night; its characteristic soft hoot can often be heard in the park.

Thistles, reaching 1.5 m (5 ft) in height, with blue cone-shaped flowers and broad thorny leaves, are one of many species of plants.

The spring gentian, which flowers between March and August, has short stems with single leaves and often grows on the limestone base of screes.

⑱ Comillas

Cantabria. **Road Map** F1. 🚌 2,500.
ℹ️ Plaza Joaquín del Piélago I; 942 72 25 91. 🚌 Fri. 🎉 San Pedro (29 Jun), El Cristo & Virgen del Carmen (16 Jul). 🌐 comillas.es

This pretty resort is known for its unusual buildings designed by Catalan Modernista architects. Antonio López y López, the first Marquis of Comillas, invited King Alfonso XII here for a holiday; in the early 20th century the town became a haunt of the Spanish aristocracy. López y López hired Joan Martorell to design the **Palacio de Sobrellano** (1881), a huge Neo-Gothic edifice. Comillas' best-known monument is Gaudí's **El Capricho** (open a few days per month; call 942 72 03 65). Built in 1883–5, it is a part-Mudéjar-inspired fantasy with a minaret-like tower with green and yellow tiles. The Modernista **Universidad Pontificia** was designed by Joan Martorell to plans by Domènech i Montaner.

🏠 Palacio de Sobrellano

Comillas. **Tel** 942 72 03 39.
Open Apr–Oct: 10:30am– 6:30pm Tue–Sat (to 1:30pm Sun); Nov–Mar: 10:30am–5:30pm Tue–Sat (to 1:30pm Sun). **Closed** Mon. 🎧 📷 compulsory; book in advance.

The huge, Neo-Gothic Palacio de Sobrellano in Comillas

Environs

Some 11 km (7 miles) from Comillas is the tiny **Cabezón de la Sal**, known already in Roman times as a centre of the salt trade.

One of the villages picturesquely set in the Valle de Cabuérniga

Of note are the magnificent residences, especially the 18th-century **Palacio de la Bodega** with the coat of arms of the de los Cevallos family inlaid in its façade, and the Baroque **Iglesia de San Martín**, dating from the beginning of the 17th century. The best time to visit Cabezón de la Sal is on the second Sunday in August – Regional Cantabria Day – when you can gain an insight into the colourful local traditions.

⑲ Valle de Cabuérniga

Cantabria. **Road Map** F2.
ℹ️ Ayuntamiento, Ruente; 942 70 91 04.

This picturesque valley is home to many interesting *pueblos*. A good place to start is **Bárcena Mayor**, which is

notable for its typical Cantabrian rural architecture. The inhabitants of the village cultivate old craft traditions – in particular carpentry.
Lamiña features a 10th-century hermitage (Ermita de San Fructoso) while **Ucieda** has a beautiful nature reserve with beech and oak forests.

⑳ Alto Campoo

Cantabria. **Road Map** F2. 🚌 1,900.
ℹ️ Estación de Montaña; 942 77 92 23.

High in the Cantabrian mountains, this small but excellent ski resort lies below the three alpine peaks of El Cuchillón, El Chivo and Pico de Tres Mares (2,175 m/7,136 ft). The last of these, the "Peak of the Three Seas", is so called because the rivers rising near it flow into the Mediterranean, the Atlantic and the Bay of Biscay. A chairlift

Gaudí in Cantabria

Antoni Gaudí's El Capricho palace is one of his very few designs to be seen outside Barcelona. This fantasy building owes its name to the minaret-like tower. Typifying his eclectic style, it combines various materials including ceramics, and displays the characteristic freedom of composition, resulting in the stylized "fairytale" appearance.
Gaudí came to work in Comillas through Antonio López y López, who married into the Güell family of industrialists – patrons of the great architect and artist.

Exterior of Gaudí's fairytale-like El Capricho palace in Comillas

reaches the summit of Pico de Tres Mares, from where there is a breathtaking panorama of the Picos de Europa and other mountain chains. The resort has downhill runs totalling 27 km (17 miles) in length and 23 pistes.

㉑ Puente Viesgo

Cantabria. **Road Map** F1. 🏔 2,900.
ℹ️ 942 59 81 05. 🎎 San Miguel (28–29 Sep).

Charmingly situated amid verdant landscape, this village is best known for its two nearby caves with prehistoric paintings. The **Cueva "El Castillo"**, discovered in 1903, has walls that are covered in drawings of horses and bison, but the highlight is the series of hand prints. Experts regard these as the earliest examples of cave art in the Franco-Cantabrian zone, preceding all other geometric and figural images. The prints were made by blowing mineral dyes – probably through a bone pipe – onto the hand while it was pressed against the wall. The colours used to create the images were taken from minerals within the cave.

The **Cueva "Las Monedas"** contains beautiful stalactites and stalagmites, with unusual colouration due to the mixture of minerals and calcium. The paintings in this cave were made with coal and thus look as black; they represent horses, reindeer, goats, bears, bison as well as some signs, dating back 13,000 years.

Fiestas in Asturias and Cantabria

La Folía (Apr) San Vicente de la Barquera. Procession of decorated and illuminated boats.
Fiesta del Pastor (1st Fri in Jul) Castro Urdiales. Shepherds' Festival.
Virgen del Carmen (16 Jul) Comillas. Homage to the Virgin.
Coso Blanco (25 Jul) Cangas de Onís. Night-time parade of carriages.
Battle of the Flowers (last Fri in Aug) Laredo. Flower parade and festivities.
Nuestra Señora de Covadonga (8 Sep) Picos de Europa. Homage to the patron saint of Asturias.

Girls in traditional dress participating in a regional fiesta

Other caves here are "El Pendo", "Covalanas", "Chufín", and "Hornos de la Peña"; check the website for opening hours.

🏠 **Cueva "El Castillo" & Cueva "Las Monedas"**
Puente Viesgo. **Tel** 942 59 84 25. **Open** Apr–mid-Jun & mid-Sep–Oct: 9:30am–2:30pm & 3:30–6:30pm Wed–Sun; mid-Jun–mid-Sep: 9:30am–2:30pm & 3:30–7:30pm Tue–Sun; Nov–Mar: 9:30am–3:30pm Wed–Fri, 9:30am–2:30pm & 3:30–5:30pm Sat, Sun & hols. 🎫 🅿️
🌐 **cuevas.culturadecantabria.com**

㉒ Valle de Besaya

Road Map F1–2.

As early as Roman times, a north–south road linking the Cantabrian coast with the Meseta ran through this long valley. Romanesque buildings are also to be found here, including small churches, which would have been covered initially with wooden roofs. Of special interest are the severe-looking **Iglesia de Barcena de Pie de Concha** and the **Iglesia de Santa María de Yermo**. The latter has an interesting portico comprising five archivolts; below it is a tympanum with a sculpture of a knight fighting a dragon.

Torrelavega, the capital of the Valle de Besaya, boasts several historic monuments, such as the Convento de las Adres, the Iglesia de la Virgen Grande, and the Iglesia de Nuestra Señora de Asunción.

Environs
Retortillo is famous for its excellent therapeutic spa. At **Julióbriga** (modern Campoo de Enmedia) are the remains of a town built by the Romans against the wild tribes of Cantabria. The **Domus de Lulobriga** is a reconstruction of a Roman villa, which has been erected among the ruins of an original Roman dwelling.

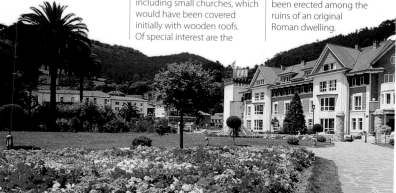

The colourful park in Puente Viesgo planted with flowers and palm trees

㉓ Street-by-Street: Santillana del Mar

In his novel *Nausea*, Jean-Paul Sartre called Santillana del Mar ("Santillana of the Sea") the most beautiful town in Spain. Despite its name, it is actually 3 km (nearly 2 miles) away from the sea. The ensemble of opulent 15th- to 18th-century buildings, attesting to the town's aristocratic legacy, grew up around the collegiate church of Santa Juliana. The church houses the tomb of the martyr Juliana, who is said to have captured the devil – an event depicted in the murals on the walls of the church. The town was laid out along a north–south axis, delineated by its only major street – Calle de Santo Domingo.

Calle Carrera
This cobblestoned street has several houses built by local noblemen, including the 18th-century Casa de Los Bustamante with its characteristic balconies. One of the oldest houses is the Torre de la Villa, which in the 15th century belonged to the Velarde family.

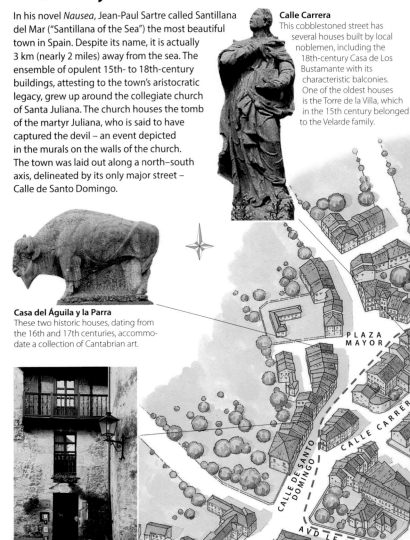

Casa del Águila y la Parra
These two historic houses, dating from the 16th and 17th centuries, accommodate a collection of Cantabrian art.

Houses
The main streets of the town are lined with houses built of a golden-coloured stone, lending it an unforgettable character.

PLAZA MAYOR

CALLE CARRERA

CALLE DE SANTO DOMINGO

AVD LE DORAT

0 metres   50
0 yards   50

★ Museo Diocesano
Housed in the Convento de Regina Coeli (1592), the museum boasts a rich collection of painted figures of saints.

Church Cloisters
The cloister arcades are supported on Romanesque columns with capitals bearing images of animals and hunting scenes.

VISITORS' CHECKLIST

Practical Information
Cantabria. **Road Map** F1.
🚇 4,200. 🛈 C/Jesús Otero;
942 81 88 12. 🎉 Santa Juliana
(28 Jun), San Roque (16 Aug).
🇼 santillanadelmarturismo.
com Museo Diocesano and
cloister: **Tel** 942 84 03 17.
Open Jul–Aug: 10am–1:30pm
& 4–8pm daily; Sep–Jun:
10am–2pm & 4–7pm Tue–Sun.
🅿 🇼 santillanamuseo
diocesano.com

Transport
🚌

★ **Colegiata de Santa Juliana**
An important Cantabrian pilgrimage centre and the most beautiful monument in Santillana, this Romanesque jewel attracts believers and art-lovers alike.

★ **Torre de Don Borja**
This late 14th- to early 15th-century Gothic defensive tower, with its beautiful patio, is now the headquarters of the Fundación Santillana, where exhibitions and conferences are held.

LE CANTÓN

CALLE JESÚS OTERO

APARCA-MIENTO

A car park
enables visitors to leave their car before embarking on a tour of the pedestrianized town centre.

Golden Age of the Nobility

The nobility often placed extravagant mottoes and coats of arms on the façades of their residences. The most beautiful example is the Casa de los Hombrones, which has a family cartouche encircled by two bearded figures; the most unusual is the Casa de Bustamante, which is adorned with the surprising yet eloquent inscription, "The Bustamante daughters are given as wives to kings". On Calle Carrera stands the 18th-century house of the Valdevieso family, whose coat of arms is visible.

A coat of arms on an aristocratic residence in Santillana del Mar

Key
— Suggested route

㉔ Museo de Altamira

In 1985, the Altamira Cave near Santander was added to UNESCO's World Heritage list. The magnificent paintings, the earliest of which date back to 36,000 BC, depict herds of bison, horses, deer and anthropomorphic figures in black contours. The animals are painted with remarkable accuracy that was evidently based on close observation. To protect the works, public entry to the cave is no longer permitted, but the on-site museum contains replicas of the cave and the paintings, with additional exhibitions.

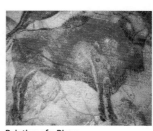

Painting of a Bison
On the ceiling of the cave is a herd of bison painted with amazing realism and expressiveness; some of the bison are standing still, others are running or kneeling, still others have fallen to the ground.

★ Final Gallery
In the final section of the new cave, a replica of part of the original cave, one can admire the lesser-known but still beautiful paintings.

Bears made a lair of the cave once it had been abandoned by humans. The skeleton of a bear that perished in the winter can be seen in a shallow oval cavity on the floor of the new cave.

★ Cave with Paintings
Most of the depictions of animals were painted on the ceiling of a chamber in the main section of the cave, which measures 100 sq m (1,076 sq ft).

Entrance to the new cave

Key

- ☐ New cave
- ☐ Cave with paintings
- ☐ Palaeolithic campsite
- ☐ Archaeological dig
- ☐ Painter's workshop
- ☐ Final Gallery
- ☐ Permanent exhibitions
- ☐ Auditorium
- ☐ Terrace
- ☐ Activities area

Archaeological Dig
In the new cave, fragments of tools used by Palaeolithic hunters can be seen near the dig.

Discovery of the Cave
In 1868 a hunter discovered the entrance to the cave. Marcelino Sanz de Sautuola began to investigate it in 1875, but it was his daughter María who found the paintings in 1879.

Visiting the Museum
Apart from the 20-minute tour, visitors can also take part in workshops entitled "hunting" and "fire", which are designed for both adults and children. The new cave is an impressive replica of part of the original cave, and helps to put the paintings into context for visitors.

★ Daily Life
The museum rooms present the daily life of people in the Palaeolithic era. This exhibit demonstrates fishing and hunting techniques, and the methods by which hides were tanned.

Main entrance

Map of the Cueva de Altamira
The highlight of the cave is the chamber known as the Great Ceiling, situated close to the entrance, which has the greatest number of animals painted on its ceiling. Most impressive is the huge hind, measuring 2.25 m (7 ft) in length. The paintings in this section (marked in green on the diagram) are reproduced in the museum in the new cave.

Entrance

Key
1. Cave with paintings
2. Signs and lines
3. Horses
4. Deer
5. Bison and deer
6. Deer and goat
7. Signs and lines
8. Signs and lines
9. Black quadruped
10. Human figures

0 metres 25
0 yards 25

Hunting Workshop
Here you can learn about the technology used by the Altamira hunters to hunt bison, as well as how to make and handle your own prehistoric weapons.

㉕ Santander

Cantabria. **Road Map** F1. 178,000. ✈ 🚌 🚆 ⛴ ℹ Jardines de Pereda; 942 20 30 00. 🛒 daily. 🎉 Semana Grande (for one week up until 25 Jul), San Emeterio & San Celedonio (31 Aug), Baños de Ola (2nd half of Jul).

Cantabria's capital enjoys a splendid location near the mouth of a deep bay, with the port on one side and mountains on the other. A good place to begin is the **Museo de Arte Moderno y Contemporáneo**, founded in 1907 as the Museo de Bellas Artes. It focuses on modern and contemporary art, but also has some important older pieces. Apart from works by Cantabrian landscape artists, there is a fine portrait of Fernando VII by Goya, interesting canvases by Miró, and paintings by the 17th-century Portuguese artist Josefa de Obidos. Since 1924 the museum has occupied a building designed by Cantabrian architect Leonardo Rucabado, near the main square; on the latter stands

Cloisters at Santander Cathedral

the Iglesia de San Francesco. Just east of the museum is Santander's **market**, with a wide selection of produce, fish and meats. Santander has an array of interesting 19th- to 20th-century architecture. Of note is the **Iglesia de Santa Lucia** (1868) by Antonio de Zabaleta, an artist who introduced Romantic architecture to Spain. A good example of Neo-Gothic architecture is the Jesuit **Iglesia del Sagrado Corazón**. The much-remodelled **cathedral**, whose Romanesque-Gothic crypt (c.1200) was built on the remains of an earlier Roman building, was rebuilt after a fire in 1945. The aisled interior, measuring 31 m (102 ft) long and 18 m (59 ft) wide, is a combination of

Exhibit in the Museo de Prehistoria

Romanesque and Gothic. Found here are the reliquaries of two martyrs – San Emeterio and San Celedonio – who were Roman legionnaires born in León. When the Romans began to persecute Christians, the courageous brothers made a public declaration of their faith, for which they were sentenced to death by beheading; their severed heads were brought by fishing boat to Santander. The city is named after the first of these two martyrs (Portus Sancti Emeterii – Sant'Emter – Santander).

After leaving the cathedral, it is worth paying a visit to the **Museo de Prehistoria**, with its interesting collection of finds from various Cantabrian caves that were inhabited in prehistoric times.

There's no better place to relax than on Santander's beautiful beaches. The 2-km (1.2-mile) long **Playa el Sardinero**, which shares its name with the city's northern suburbs, is one of the eight most unpolluted beaches in the world. It became popular in the mid-19th century, when the Madrid aristocracy began

Santander City Centre

① Museo de Arte Moderno y Contemporáneo
② Market
③ Cathedral
④ Museo de Prehistoria
⑤ Playa el Sardinero
⑥ Palacio de la Magdalena

0 metres 500
0 yards 500

For keys to symbols *see back flap*

to visit. Bordering the beach are gardens, good cafés, and luxury hotels, including the imposing Hotel Real, as well as casinos. Here, too, stands the **Palacio de la Magdalena**, a summer residence of Alfonso XIII. Built in 1911, the palace was designed by two Cantabrian architects – Javier González Riancho and Gonzálo Bringas – and is furnished in the *belle époque* style. In July and August, El Sardinero plays host to a theatre and music festival.

🏛 Museo de Arte Moderno y Contemporáneo

C/Rubio 6. **Tel** 942 20 31 20. **Open** mid-Sep–Jun: 10am–1pm & 5:30–9pm Tue–Sat, 11am–1:30pm Sun; Jul–mid-Sep: 10:30am–1pm & 6–9pm Tue–Sat, 11am–1:30pm Sun.

🏛 Museo de Prehistoria

Mercado del Este, C/Hernán Cortés 4. **Tel** 942 20 99 22. **Open** 10:30am–2pm & 5–8:30pm Wed–Sun (mid-Sep–mid-Jun: 10am–2pm & 5–8pm). 🗾

Exhibits at the Convento de San Francisco museum in Laredo

㉖ Laredo

Cantabria. **Road Map** G1. �‍ 12,000. 🛈 Alameda Miramar s/n; 942 61 10 96. 🎭 Batalla de Flores (last Fri in Aug), Carlos V's last landing (weekend closest to 15 Sep). 🖳 **laredo.es**

Laredo is a historic port and Cantabria's biggest beach resort. In its beautiful old town are remnants of medieval walls and gates. The narrow streets lead up to the 13th-century Gothic **Iglesia de Santa María de la Asunción**, with a 15th-century Flemish reredos of the Virgin Mary of Bethlehem. Worth visiting, too, is the 16th-century **Convento de San Francisco** and its museum, designed in the Herrera style with a Renaissance cloister.

The picturesque Soba valley, location of Soba and Ramales de la Victoria

Environs

On the opposite side of the bay lies the resort of Santoña, the birthplace of Juan de la Cosa, Columbus' mapmaker. This small fishing port has great views from the hilltop Castillo Fuerte de San Carlos. To the west is a huge area of dunes and sea marshes that is home to wetland birds.

㉗ Soba and Ramales de la Victoria

Road Map G1 & G2. 🛈 Calle Barón de Adzaneta 5, Ramales de la Victoria; 942 64 65 04.

These two villages are set in the mountain valley of Asón, once used as a route linking the port of Laredo with the Meseta. Soba offers excellent sightseeing trails with panoramic views. Ramales de la Victoria owes the second part of its name to the victorious battle fought here by the liberals during the first Carlist War *(see p45)*. While in Ramales, be sure to visit the mid-17th century **Iglesia de San Pedro** and the **Iglesia Gibaja**, which was begun in

the mid-16th century. Also worthy of mention is the 17th-century **Palacio de Revillagigedo**, though it is closed to the public. Prehistoric caves can be seen nearby.

㉘ Castro Urdiales

Cantabria. **Road Map** G1. 🚍 32,500. 🛈 Avenida de la Constitución 1; 942 87 15 12. 🎭 Thu. 🎭 Coso Blanco (1st Fri Jul), San Andrés (30 Nov).

Visitors flock to this popular holiday resort for the beautiful beaches: **Playa del Brazomar** and **Playa Ostende**, which can be reached along an attractive trail that skirts the cliffs. There is also a pretty harbourside *paseo*. Rising on a promontory above the town is the imposing **Iglesia de Santa María**, a fascinating example of Cantabrian Gothic. It was built in the 13th century, after which numerous Gothic elements were added. Inside is a tall Gothic sculpture of the seated Mary with the infant Jesus in her lap, and a moving canvas of *The Dying Christ* attributed to Francisco de Zurbarán.

The massive Gothic Iglesia de Santa María in Castro Urdiales

For hotels and restaurants see pp204–5 and pp217–19

The picturesque Las Médulas hills in El Bierzo

㉙ El Bierzo

León. **Road Map** C2–D2.
ℹ Ponferrada; 987 42 42 36.
ⓦ **ponferrada.org**

This northwestern region of León, cut off from the outside world by beautiful mountains, has breathtaking landscapes, pretty villages and picturesque lakes. This is an area with its own identity – the inhabitants speak a dialect of Gallego, and have a unique tradition of folklore and very hearty food.

Since Roman times, the area has also been mined for coal, iron and gold. The ore was extracted from millions of tonnes of alluvium washed from the hills of Las Médulas by a system of canals and sluice gates. It is estimated that the Romans extracted more than 500 tonnes of precious metal from the hills between the 1st and 4th centuries AD.

The impressive landscape, colonized by gnarled chestnut trees, is best appreciated from the viewpoint at Orrelán. Also worth seeing is the **Sierra de Ancares**, a wild region of slate mountains, part of which is a nature reserve – the eastern part of the Reserva Nacional de Os Ancares *(see p79)*. The heathland, dotted with oak and birch copses, is home to wolves and capercaillies.

The area around El Bierzo has much to offer architecture enthusiasts. In the eastern part, along the old road to Santiago de Compostela, are typical pilgrim churches. Several isolated hill villages, such as **Campo del Agua**, contain pre-Roman *pallozas (see p61)*.

㉚ Villafranca del Bierzo

León. **Road Map** C2. 🏔 3,400.
ℹ C/Díez Ovelar 10; 987 54 00 28.
🚌 Tue. 🎉 Fiesta del Cristo (14 Sep).

The tiled-roof houses, hilly surroundings and crystal-clear Burbia river lend this town a special charm. It was here, in the Romanesque **Iglesia de Santiago** (1186), that pilgrims who were too weak to make the final gruelling hike across the hills of Galicia to Santiago de Compostela could obtain dispensation at the Puerta del Perdón (Door of Mercy).

Noteworthy too are the collegiate **Iglesia de Santa María**, housed since 1544 in a former Cluniac monastery, and the **Iglesia de San Francisco** on the Plaza Mayor, founded, according to legend, by St Francis of Assisi during his pilgrimage to Santiago. The interior features a beautiful Mudéjar ceiling. The churches are usually closed, but guided visits can be arranged through the town's tourist office.

Visitors can also sample the local speciality, cherries marinated in *aguardiente*, a strong spirit.

Stained-glass window, Iglesia de Santiago, Villafranca del Bierzo

㉛ Ponferrada

León. **Road Map** C2. 🏔 68,500.
ℹ Calle Gil y Carrasco 4; 987 42 42 36.
🚌 Wed, Sat. 🎉 Virgen de la Encina (8 Sep). ⓦ **ponferrada.org**

Set among hills, this town owes its name to a medieval bridge reinforced with iron *(pons ferrata)*. Rising above a deep valley is its most

---

Chorizo Sausage from León

León is famous for its *chorizo* sausage made from pork and bacon flavoured with paprika, salt, garlic and oregano. There are many variations. The traditional method of making *chorizo* goes back to ancient times. After the ritual slaughter of animals during fiestas, any uneaten meat would be preserved. El Bierzo is also known for *botillo* – a heavy, coarse sausage unique to this region. Today, the places best known for delicious *chorizo* are El Bierzo, Astorga and La Baneza.

A selection of León's famous sausages

interesting building – the majestic **Castillo de los Templarios** (Castle of the Knights Templar), built from 1218 to 1380. This imposing fortress, equipped with towers and battlements, was built to protect pilgrims travelling to Santiago.

Clustered around the foot of the castle is the **old quarter**, whose narrow streets with delightful arcades accommodate most of Ponferrada's monuments. These include the 17th-century Baroque **town hall** on the Plaza Mayor, entered through the Puerta del Reloj (Clock Tower gate), and the 10th-century **Iglesia de Santo Tomás de las Ollas**, a mix of Visigothic and Mozarabic architecture with later Romanesque and Baroque elements. The most impressive feature in the church is its oval chancel, with blind arcades and Moorish arches.

❸❷ Astorga

León. **Road Map** D2. 🗺 12,000. 🚌
🚍 ℹ Glorieta Eduardo de Castro 5;
987 61 82 22. 🏪 Tue. 🎪 Santa Marta (end Aug). 🌐 **turismoastorga.com**

The Roman town of Asturica Augusta was a strategic halt on the Vía de la Plata (Silver Road) linking Andalusia and Galicia. Destroyed by the Moors in the 11th century, the town soon recovered its status as an important stage on the pilgrimage route to Santiago de Compostela.

Its character is influenced by the Maragatos, a people probably descended from Carthaginian and Punic slaves brought here by the Romans to work the mines. Astorga was an important trading centre for them from the 8th century onwards, and until the building of railways in the 19th century, they were the main transporters of goods between Galician ports and Madrid. Among the goods they brought were chocolate and sugar, which is why this inland town is known for producing chocolates and *mantecados* (sweet biscuits).

Gaudí's Palacio Episcopal in Astorga

Aside from the beautiful Gothic **cathedral**, begun in 1471, Astorga's most interesting monument is the fairy-tale **Palacio Episcopal** (1889-93) by Catalan architect Antoni Gaudí. The turreted grey granite block ringed by a moat, with a spacious interior decked out in ceramic tiles – so horrified the diocese that no bishops ever lived in it. Inside is the **Museo de los Caminos**, which is devoted to the pilgrimage to Santiago.

❸❸ Cuevas de Valporquero

León. **Road Map** E2. **Tel** 987 57 64 08.
Open Oct–Apr: 10am–5pm Thu–Sun;
May–Sep: 10am–6pm daily.
Closed mid-Dec–Feb. 🚫
🌐 **cuevadevalporquero.es**

Beneath the village of Valporquero extends a complex of spectacular limestone caves.

Iron and sulphur oxides have tinted the beautiful stalactites and stalagmites with subtle shades of red, grey and black. Skilful lighting picks out the beautiful limestone concretions, creating a memorable effect.

Guided tours take parties through the impressive series of galleries and chambers. They begin with the Pequeñas Maravillas (Small Wonders), which feature fantastic rock formations with imaginative names, such as Las Gemelas (Twins), La Torre de Pisa (Tower of Pisa) and Virgen con Niño (Virgin and Child).

The massive Gran Rotonda, covering an area of 5,600 sq m (60,200 sq ft) and reaching a height of 20 m (66 ft), is the most stunning cave in the system. As the interior is cold and the surfaces uneven, it is advisable to wear warm clothes and sturdy shoes.

Impressive stalactites in one of the Cuevas de Valporquero

㉞ León

León was founded in AD 68 as a camp for the Romans' Seventh Legion. In 914, King Ordoño II transferred the Christian capital here from Oviedo. After repeatedly uniting with, then separating from Castile, the two finally united in the 13th century though Castile, with its capital in Burgos, began to overshadow León as the pre-eminent regional power. León remained strong, however, and the town's most stunning monuments date from this period.

Exploring León

Most of the old quarter (casco viejo) is encircled by walls and pedestrianized. The magnificent cathedral is a good pace to begin a tour of the historic monuments that have survived from the Golden Age of this former regional capital. The city's most important buildings are found in the charming streets around the cathedral.

Arcaded period houses lining the Plaza Mayor

🏛 Cathedral

See pp120–21.

㊟ Plaza Mayor

The square, in the picturesque old quarter, is surrounded by old houses with delightful arcades. The Plaza Mayor is home to León's administrative offices. A good time to visit is on the feast days of St John, in the last week of June, when the square comes alive with fireworks on the riverside, fairs and medieval festivities as well as modern forms of entertainment. More religious in tone are the Semana Santa (Easter Week) celebrations, when the square plays host to processions of monks dressed in special costumes and cone-shaped hats with openings only

for the nose and eyes. The monks carry richly decorated pasos – platforms bearing figures of saints and scenes from the Passion of Christ.

㊟ Palacio de los Guzmanes

One of the most beautiful Renaissance residences in León, built in 1559–66, stands next to the Plaza de Santo Domingo. This three-storey building, currently the seat of the provincial authorities, is centred on an arcaded patio, with gargoyles on the roof, corner towers, and numerous coats of arms on the façade. There are offices on the ground floor, but the upper sections of the building are closed to visitors.

㊟ Casa de Botines

This magnificent building, which resembles a Gothic castle, was designed by Antoni Gaudí in 1892. It was erected in record time – a mere 10 months. Gaudí agreed to take on the task as he was working simultaneously on the Palacio Episcopal in nearby Astorga (see p117), and could oversee both projects at once. The façade sports a figure of St George fighting the dragon, a replica of which later appeared

Part of the Renaissance façade of the Palacio de los Guzmanes

in Gaudí's Sagrada Familia in Barcelona. The building is currently used by a bank.

🏛 Basílica de San Isidoro

Plaza San Isidoro 4. **Tel** 987 87 61 61. **Open** 7am–11pm daily. Museum: **Open** May & Jun: 10am–2pm & 4–7pm Mon–Sat (to 7:30pm Fri & Sat), 10am–2:30pm Sun; Jul–Sep: 9am–9pm Mon–Sat, 9am–2:30pm Sun; Oct–Apr: 10am–2pm & 4–7pm Mon–Sat, 10am–2pm Sun. 🎨 📷

Adjoining the city walls, the basilica was built on the remains of an earlier church destroyed in 998 to house the relics of San Isidoro of Seville. Its construction spanned the 10th to mid-18th centuries. The walls of the royal mausoleum – the final resting place of 23 monarchs, 10 princes, 9 counts and several nobles – are decorated with beautiful 12th-century Romanesque murals. Among them is a cycle devoted to the life of Christ, including a powerful Last Supper, and one surviving sign of the zodiac. The museum contains paintings and frescoes from the royal mausoleum.

The castle-like Casa de Botines, designed by Antoni Gaudí

City Walls

The entire old quarter is encircled by imposing walls. The history of this Roman town is a stormy one; it was not always successful in repelling attacks by the Moors. In 996 AD, for instance, León was plundered by the ruler of the Cordoban Caliphate, Al-Mansur. Later on, however, the walls were strengthened and performed their function well.

Museo de León

Plaza de Santo Domingo 8.
Tel 987 23 64 05. **Open** 10am–2pm & 4–7pm Tue–Sat (Jul–Sep: 5–8pm); 10am–2pm Sun & hols. 🎫 (free Sat & Sun)

This small museum near the Convento de San Marcos has in its collections a famous ivory crucifix, the *Cristo de Carrizo*, dating from the 11th century. The piece originates from the Cistercian Monasterio de Carrizo, which was founded in 1176. Also displayed here are another striking crucifix – the *Cruz de Penalba*, which is encrusted with precious gems – and an altar from the Iglesia de San Marcelo.

Hostal de San Marcos

Plaza de San Marcos 7.
Tel 987 23 73 00. 🌐 **parador.es**

This exclusive parador is one of the real jewels in this state-owned hotel chain. It was built in the 16th century by King Ferdinand as the headquarters of the Knights of Santiago. The order was headed by the monarch himself until the end of the Reconquest *(see pp41–3)*. The richly decorated façade is designed in the characteristic Spanish style of the late Renaissance – known as Plateresque. This name refers to the method of preparing and decorating the stone surfaces, which are meticulously polished all over and bring to mind the techniques of silversmiths (*plateros* in Spanish). All the characteristic features of this exuberant style are evident in the hotel's façade – the arches, panelling, openwork balustrades, turrets, bay windows, and sets of armorial cartouches and medallions bearing images of famous people and various monarchs.

Cristo de Carrizo, Museo de León

VISITORS' CHECKLIST

Practical Information
León. **Road Map** E2. 🚇 132,000. 🛈 Plaza de San Marcelo 1; 987 87 83 27. 📅 Wed, Sat. 🎉 San Juan (24–29 Jun), San Froilán (5 Oct). 🌐 turismoleon.com

Transport
🚃 🚌

MUSAC

Avenida de los Reyes Leoneses 24. **Tel** 987 09 00 00. **Open** 11am–1pm & 5–8pm Tue–Fri, 11am–3pm & 5–9pm Sat, Sun. 🎫 (free 5–9pm Sun). ♿ ♿ ☕ 📷

This striking, contemporary building houses an excellent art gallery with a dynamic, family-friendly programme.

A section of the façade of the Hostal de San Marcos

León City Centre

0 metres 400
0 yards 400

Catedral de León

The master-builders of this Spanish Gothic cathedral par excellence were inspired by French techniques of vaulting and buttressing. The present structure of golden sandstone, built on the site of King Ordoño II's 10th-century palace, was begun in the mid-13th century and completed less than 100 years later. It combines a slender but very tall nave with huge panels of stained glass that are the cathedral's most magnificent feature. Although it has survived for 700 years, there is concern now about air pollution attacking the soft stone.

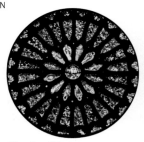

West Rose Window
This largely 14th-century window depicts the Virgin and Child, surrounded by 12 trumpet-blowing angels.

Cathedral Museum
Pedro de Campaña's panel, The Adoration of the Magi, is one of the many magnificent treasures displayed in the museum.

KEY

① **The 13th- to 14th-century**, cloister galleries are decorated with Gothic frescoes by Nicolás Francés.

② **The altarpiece**, includes five original panels created by Gothic master Nicolás Francés.

③ **The choir**, has two tiers of 15th-century stalls. Behind it is the carved and gilded retrochoir, in the shape of a triumphal arch.

Entrance

★ West Front
The three portals are decorated with 13th-century carvings. Those above the Portada del Juicio depict a scene from the Last Judgment, where the Blessed pass into paradise.

Inside the Cathedral
The plan of the building is a Latin cross. The tall nave is slender but long, measuring 90 m (295 ft) by 40 m (130 ft) at its widest. To appreciate the dazzling colours of the stained glass, it is best to visit on a sunny day.

VISITORS' CHECKLIST

Practical Information
Plaza de la Regla. **Tel** 987 87 5770.
Open May–Sep: 9:30am–1:30pm & 4–8pm Mon–Fri, 8:30am–noon & 2–6pm Sat, 9:30–11am & 2–8pm Sun; Oct–Apr: reduced hours, see website. 🕆 daily, see website. ✉ 🅰 Museum: **Open** May–Sep: 9:30am–1:30pm & 4–8pm Mon–Sat; Oct–Apr: reduced hours, see website. 🅰
🆆 catedraldeleon.org

Virgen Blanca
This is a Gothic sculpture of a smiling Virgin. The original is kept in this chapel. A copy stands by the west door.

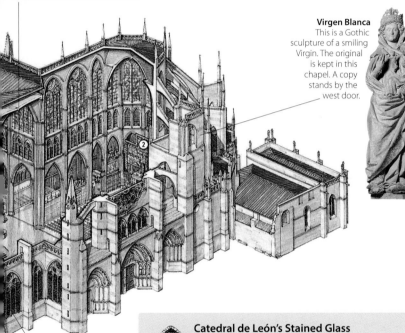

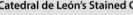

★ Stained Glass
The windows, covering an area of 1,800 sq m (19,350 sq ft), are the outstanding feature of the cathedral.

Catedral de León's Stained Glass

This cathedral's great glory is its magnificent glasswork. The 125 large windows, 57 smaller, circular ones and three rose windows date from the 13th to the 20th centuries. They cover an enormous range of subjects, from fantastical beasts to plants. Many depict saints and characters from biblical stories. Some of the windows reveal fascinating details of medieval life: *La Cacería*, in the north wall, depicts a hunting scene, while the rose window in the Capilla del Nacimiento shows pilgrims at the tomb of St James in Santiago de Compostela in Galicia *(see pp66–7)*.

Window with plant motif

A large window in the south wall

THE BASQUE COUNTRY

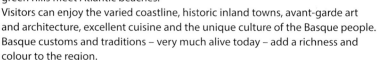

Situated on the Bay of Biscay, and bordering France to the east, the Basque Country is a region where green hills meet Atlantic beaches. Visitors can enjoy the varied coastline, historic inland towns, avant-garde art and architecture, excellent cuisine and the unique culture of the Basque people. Basque customs and traditions – very much alive today – add a richness and colour to the region.

The Basque Country is divided into three provinces – Vizcaya, Álava and Guipúzcoa – with the capital in Vitoria. Little is known about the origins of the Basque people, except that they are the oldest pre-Indo-European ethnic group on the Iberian peninsula.

Secure in their mountain homeland, the Basques lived in isolation from the rest of Spain for centuries, and so retained their distinct traditional language (Euskera) and laws (fueros). When, in the 19th century, Spain started to become more centralized, the Basques felt threatened and began to fight to maintain their privileges. With the onset of industrialization and the influx of thousands of people in search of work, nationalist sentiment took hold. At the end of the century, during the Second Republic, the Basque Country was granted autonomy, though this was later repealed by the Franco regime. In the 1960s, the ETA organization began an armed struggle against Franco's repression, demanding complete Basque independence. When democracy returned to Spain in the 1970s, the Basque Country was again granted autonomy, which was accepted by most moderate Basque nationalists. The ETA continued its armed campaign for independence, but in 2011 a definitive ceasefire was announced.

As a holiday destination, the Atlantic coast offers a tempting variety of sandy beaches, rías and cliffs. In the larger cities, museums give visitors the chance not only to learn about the history of the Basque lands, but also, in Bilbao for instance, to admire fantastic modern art. Those wishing for a more low-key experience can head inland to the region's historic towns, such as the former university town of Oñati.

A typical Basque farmhouse in the countryside near Gernika-Lumo

◄ The flower-covered balcony of Cafe Bizvete in Bilbao

Exploring the Basque Country

The cliffs of the Basque Country are broken by rocky coves, *rías* and wide bays with beaches of fine yellow sand, interspersed with fishing villages. Inland, minor roads wind through wooded hills, valleys and gorges past lonely castles and isolated homesteads. Apart from its beautiful landscapes and numerous historic monuments, the region is world-famous for its cuisine based on fish and seafood, the vibrant street and bar life, and the distinctive cultural life of the Basques, reflected both in cultural festivals and spectacular fiestas.

Colourful houses in the port town of Hondarribia

Sights at a Glance

For hotels and restaurants see pp205–6 and pp219–21

Costa Vasc
Cabo Matxitxako
Bakio
BERMEO **4**
PLENTZIA **2**
Alto del Sollube
340 m (1,115 ft)
Ela
Sopelana
Munc
Algorta
Getxo
Mungia
Cuevas de
Santimamiñ
Santander
Portugalete
Areeta
GERNIKA-
LUMO **3**
RÍA DE BILBAO **2**
Trucios
Larrabetzu
Mercadillo
BILBAO (BILBO) **1**
Basauri
Carranza
Zalla
Galdakao
Amorebiet
Sodupe
AP8
Montes de Ordunte
Balmaseda
Gordexola
N240
N634
Llodio
Igorre
Durang
Castillo-
Elejabeitia
Artziniega
Orozco
Puerto de Urquiola
700 m (2,300 ft)
Amurrio
AP68
Alto de Barazar
604 m (1,980 ft)
Peña Gorbea
1481 m (4,860ft) △
Otxandio
Orduña
Sierra de Gorbed
Izarra
Legutiano
Embalse de
Urrunaga
Murgia
Berberana
Sierra de Arrato
Bóveda
TORRE PALACIO
DE LOS VARONA
Valdegovia
Salinas de
Añana
VITORIA-GA **18**
Espejo **19**
La Puebla de Arganzón
A68
Treviño
A1
Miranda
de Ebro
Berantevilla
Burgos
Zambrana
Peñacerrada
A68
N124
Haro
LAGUARD
N232
A68
Zarac

Getting Around

The A8 (E70) road runs behind the Basque coast and through Bilbao, which also has an international airport. Most towns are linked by national and local bus services. The local rail network is comfortable and has the added advantage of following some unforgettable routes. However, several of the more remote places worth visiting can only be reached by car.

The Guggenheim Museum Bilbao, one of several modern attractions

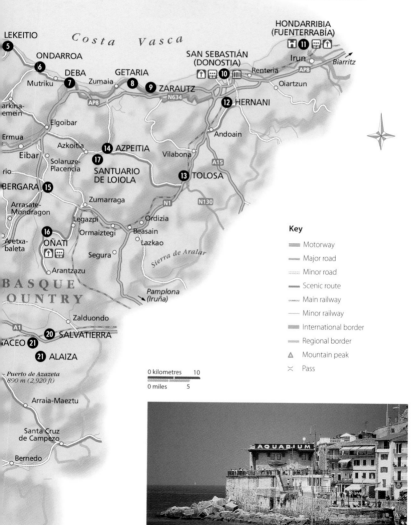

Key

━━ Motorway
━━ Major road
┅┅ Minor road
━━ Scenic route
╌╌ Main railway
── Minor railway
▬▬ International border
▬▬ Regional border
△ Mountain peak
⤬ Pass

A view of the bay and aquarium building in San Sebastián

For keys to symbols *see back flap*

● Street-by-Street: Bilbao (Bilbo)

Bilbao's *casco viejo* – the Old Town – emerged in the 14th century along the banks of the river. Here, amid lively streets, are the Gothic Catedral de Santiago (St James) and other churches and museums. The famous Siete Calles (Seven Streets), from Barrenkale Barrena to Somera, are the focal point, busy with street life, lined with tapas bars serving delicious food, and full of crowds of boisterous locals every weekend. The splendid 19th-century Plaza Nueva is another hub of the Old Town.

Iglesia de San Nicolás de Bari
Built on an octagonal plan, this Baroque church is dedicated to the patron saint of sailors. The interior features a beautiful reredos.

★ Teatro Arriaga
Rich in ornamentation, this early 20th-century building is a symbol of the Plaza de Arriaga (known as El Arenal).

Coat of arms
Visible on the façades of the ancient, often richly decorated, Old Town houses are the imaginative coats of arms of their former owners.

Athletic Bilbao Football Club

Established in 1898, Athletic Bilbao is the oldest football (soccer) club in the Basque Country. It is almost unique in top-flight European football in that only native Basques or players trained in the Basque Country can play for the team. Athletic Bilbao has always been in Spain's top league – it has won the title eight times, the King's Cup 24 times and the Super Cup once. The team, also known as the *rojiblancos* on account of their red and white strips, play at the San Mamés stadium. Supporters queue for hours for tickets.

The badge of Athletic Bilbao football club

| 0 metres | | 50 |
| 0 yards | | 50 |

★ Plaza Nueva
This Neo-Classical arcaded square is lined with attractive pavement cafés. It is also the venue for the Sunday plant, animal and antiques markets.

VISITORS' CHECKLIST

Practical Information
Vizcaya. **Road Map** A4, G1.
🗺 350,000. 🚌 Sun.
📅 Semana Grande (mid-Aug), St. James (25 Jul), San Ignacio de Loiola (31 Jul). 🛈 Plaza Circular 1; 944 79 57 60.
🌐 bilbaoturismo.net

Transport
✈ Loiu. 🚉 Estación de Abando, Plaza Circular 2. 🚌 Termibus, Gurtubay 1; 944 39 50 77.
🚢 in Santurce; 944 83 94 94.

★ Catedral de Santiago
This 14th-century Gothic cathedral, with a small cloister, acquired a Neo-Classical façade and tower in the 19th century. A square with an elegant fountain extends in front of the church.

BRERERIA
LA CRUZ
BANCO DE ESPAÑA
CINTURERIA
TORRE
PL DE SANTIAGO
A. SOTA
CARNICERIA VIEJA
PENKALE
ECHEVARRÍA VIEJA
BELOSTIKALE
CAMARÓN
TENDERIA
ARTEKALE
SOMERA

Museo Vasco
This museum's best-known treasure is the Mikeldi Idol, a wild boar carved from stone, dating from the Iron Age. There are also displays of tools, model ships and Basque gravestones.

Key
— Suggested route

Mercado de la Ribera
This Art Deco building, designed by Pedro Izpizua in 1930, sits on the bank of the Ria de Bilbao. Inside is one of Europe's largest covered food markets.

For keys to symbols see back flap

Guggenheim Museum Bilbao

The Guggenheim Museum Bilbao is the jewel in Bilbao's cultural crown. The building itself is a star attraction: a mind-boggling array of silvery curves by the American architect Frank Gehry, which are alleged to resemble a ship or a flower. The Guggenheim Bilbao's collection represents an intriguingly broad spectrum of modern and contemporary art, and includes works by Abstract Expressionists such as Willem de Kooning and Mark Rothko. The programme also features art on loan from the permanent collections of the other Guggenheim museums (in New York, Venice and Berlin) and fascinating temporary exhibitions.

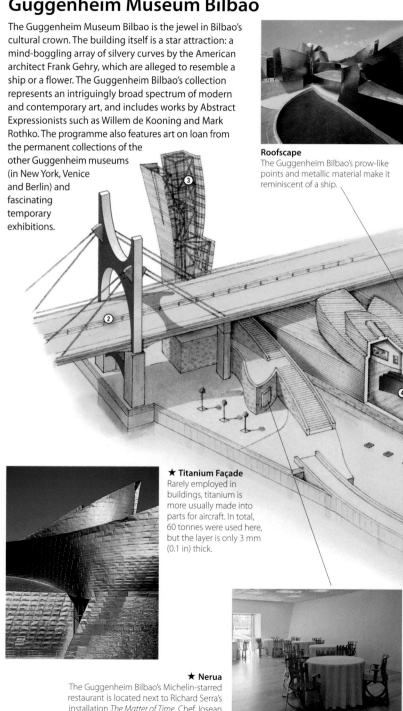

Roofscape
The Guggenheim Bilbao's prow-like points and metallic material make it reminiscent of a ship.

★ **Titanium Façade**
Rarely employed in buildings, titanium is more usually made into parts for aircraft. In total, 60 tonnes were used here, but the layer is only 3 mm (0.1 in) thick.

★ **Nerua**
The Guggenheim Bilbao's Michelin-starred restaurant is located next to Richard Serra's installation *The Matter of Time*. Chef Josean Martínez Alija presents an innovative menu.

★ Atrium
The space in which visitors to the museum first find themselves is the extraordinary 50-m (164-ft) high atrium. It serves as an orientation point and its height makes it a dramatic setting for large pieces.

VISITORS' CHECKLIST

Practical Information
Avenida Abandoibarra 2.
Tel 944 35 90 80.
Open 10am-8pm daily.
Closed Mon (Sep-Jun), 1 Jan,
25 Dec. 🅿 ✉ ♿ 📷 daily.
📷 ✏ 💻
🆆 guggenheim-bilbao.es

Transport
Ⓜ Moyúa. 🚌 1, 10, 11, 13, 18, 27, 38, 48, 71.

Main entrance

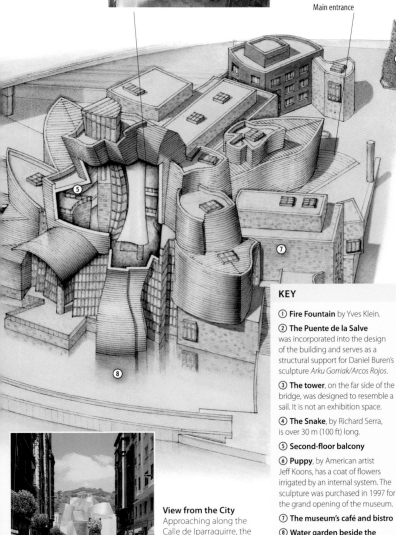

KEY

① **Fire Fountain** by Yves Klein.

② **The Puente de la Salve** was incorporated into the design of the building and serves as a structural support for Daniel Buren's sculpture *Arku Gorriak/Arcos Rojos*.

③ **The tower**, on the far side of the bridge, was designed to resemble a sail. It is not an exhibition space.

④ **The Snake**, by Richard Serra, is over 30 m (100 ft) long.

⑤ **Second-floor balcony**

⑥ **Puppy**, by American artist Jeff Koons, has a coat of flowers irrigated by an internal system. The sculpture was purchased in 1997 for the grand opening of the museum.

⑦ **The museum's café and bistro**

⑧ **Water garden beside the Ria del Nervión**

View from the City
Approaching along the Calle de Iparraguirre, the museum stands out amid traditional buildings.

Exploring Bilbao

Visitors flock to Bilbao to see its museums. By the river is the city's medieval heart, the *casco viejo* (Old Town), built in the 14th century. This area, which can be explored on foot, is home to most of the main sights.

⊡ Catedral de Santiago

Plazuela Santiago 1. **Tel** 944 15 36 27. **Open** noon–1pm & 5–7:30pm Mon–Sat; 10am–1pm Sun & Feast Days.

Dating from the 14th century, the Gothic cathedral has a slender tower rising proudly above the rooftops of the Old Town. The building is dedicated to St James, the patron saint of Bilbao since 1643. The Neo-Gothic façade – the work of Severino de Achúcarro – dates from the 19th century. There is also a Tuscan-style portico and a small cloister.

⊡ Iglesia San Nicolás de Bari

Plazuela de San Nicolás 1. **Tel** 944 16 34 24. **Open** 10:30am–1pm & 5:30–7:30pm Mon–Sat.

This 18th-century Baroque church is dedicated to

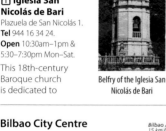

Belfry of the Iglesia San Nicolás de Bari

St Nicholas – San Nicolás de Bari – the patron saint of sailors. Designed on an octagonal plan, the church boasts valuable retables and sculptures by Juan de Mena. The broad façade is adorned with two identical towers and the coat of arms of Bilbao.

⊡ Basílica de Begoña

Calle Virgen de Begoña 38. **Tel** 944 12 70 91 (sacristy). **Open** 10:30am–1:30pm & 5:30–8:30pm Mon–Sat, open on Sun only for mass.

Long revered by the inhabitants of Bilbao, the Madonna of Begoña's shrine is the city's most important church. It stands on a hill where the Madonna is said to have appeared in the 16th century. The style of the basilica is Basque Gothic. The interior has a Neo-Classical reredos with a niche containing a 13th-century sculpture of the Madonna and Child. The portico with the huge triumphal arch dates from the Renaissance; the belfry is a 20th-century addition.

Detail of the high altar in the Basílica de Begoña

⊞ Museo Vasco

Plaza Miguel de Unamuno 4. **Tel** 944 15 54 23. **Open** 10am–7pm Mon & Wed–Fri; 10am–1:30pm & 4–7pm Sat; 10am–2pm Sun. ♿ ▨ (free Thu). ◻ by prior arrangement.

The Museo Vasco occupies the Baroque building of the Jesuit Colegio de San Andrés. The exhibits focus on the history of the Basques. In addition to archaeological finds, there are sections on traditional Basque sports, the Basque maritime legacy, heraldry and weapons. On the top floor there is a model of Vizcaya province,

Bilbao City Centre

① Cathedral
② Iglesia San Nicolás
③ Basílica de Begoña
④ Museo Vasco
⑤ Plaza Moyua
⑥ Ensanche Bilbaíno
⑦ Museo de Bellas Artes

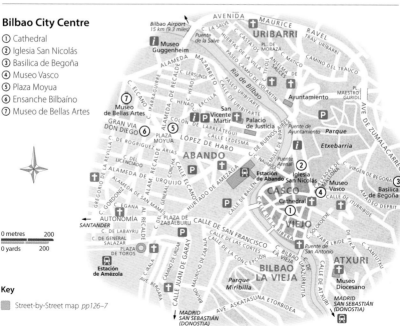

| 0 metres | 200 |
| 0 yards | 200 |

Key

▨ Street-by-Street map *pp126–7*

For keys to symbols *see back flap*

while the ground floor features one of the oldest archaeological finds – the Mikeldi Idol, a sculpture in the shape of the boar from the Iron Age.

🏛 Plaza Moyua

This oval plaza is laid out with formal gardens that are designed around a central fountain. Ernest Hemingway (see p159) once stayed at the Carlton Hotel nearby.

🏛 Ensanche Bilbaíno

The newer part of Bilbao stretches along the Gran Vía de Don Diego López de Haro. Of note here are the Abando and Santander railway stations, the stock exchange building, several churches and the Estadio de San Mamés – home of Athletic Bilbao Football club (see p126). Also worth visiting is the Parque Doña Casilda de Iturrizar.

A sculpture by Eduardo Chillida in front of the Museo de Bellas Artes

🖼 Museo de Bellas Artes

Plaza del Museo 2. **Tel** 944 39 60 60. **Open** 10am–8pm Wed–Mon. ♿ 📷 (free Wed). 📷 📱 museobilbao.com

Set in the Parque Doña Casilda de Iturrizar, in the newer part of town, the large Museum of Fine Art has more than 6,000 exhibits from the 12th century to the present day. Apart from works by artists of international fame, such as Velázquez, Ribera, El Greco and Zurbarán, there are paintings by leading modern Basque artists, including Regoyos, Zuloaga and Echevarría, as well as drawings and sculptures. In the contemporary art section are works by Chillida and Tàpies, among others.

The Ría de Bilbao cut by the Nervión river

❷ Ría de Bilbao and Plentzia

Road Map A4, G1.

The Ría de Bilbao, created by the Nervión river, is known as the "main street of Vizcaya". It stretches 14 km (9 miles) north-west of Bilbao before entering the sea off the working-class town of **Portugalete**, known for its "hanging bridge" (Puente Colgante) across the Nervión. Along the less industrial east bank of the *ría* is the attractive suburb of **Getxo**, with its beaches, marina and waterfront lined with 19th-century villas. At the *ría's* northern end is **Algorta**, a former fishing port that has a beach, pretty old harbour and streets winding up a steep cliff. Beyond there, the *ría* runs up to **Plentzia** – a small port town with an attractive old quarter.

All these places can be reached by metro from Bilbao.

❸ Gernika-Lumo

Vizcaya. **Road Map** A4, G1. 🚊 16,500. 🚌 🚉 ℹ Artekalea 8; 946 25 58 92. 🛒 Mon. 🎭 Anniversary of bombing of Gernika (26 Mar). 📷 organized by the tourist office. 📱 **gernika-lumo.net**

This little town is of great symbolic significance to the Basques as an ancient seat of lawmaking and as the target of the world's first saturation bombing raid, carried out by Nazi aircraft at Franco's request in 1937 (see p47).

The most important place in the town is the Neo-Classical Casa de Juntas, which houses the parliament of the province of Vizcaya.

In the Parque de los Pueblos de Europa are sculptures by Henry Moore and Eduardo Chillida. Also of note are the Gothic Iglesia de Santa María, the Museo de la Paz (Museum of Peace) and Museo Euskal Herria (Museum of the Basque Country).

The Tree of Gernika

For centuries, Basque leaders met in democratic assembly under an oak on a hillside in Gernika-Lumo. In the garden of the Casa de Juntas, inside a pavilion and closely guarded, is the petrified trunk of the *Gernikako Arbola* – the oldest of the oak trees preserved here – symbolizing the ancient roots of the Basque people. It was already over 300 years old when it dried out in 1860. Subsequent oaks at the site have all been grown from acorns taken or descended from the original oak, most recently in February 2005.

The petrified trunk of the *Gernikako Arbola*

The jagged rocks of the inaccessible Matxitxako headland west of Bermeo

❹ Bermeo

Vizcaya. **Road Map** A4, G1. 🚹 17,000.
ℹ️ Parque Lamera s/n; 946 17 91 54.
🎭 Andra Mari Jaiak (7–16 Sep).
🌐 bermeo.org

Bermeo is an important port on the Basque coast, with a busy fishing harbour and excellent seafood restaurants. The town's oldest church is Santa Eufemia (13th–15th century), an aisleless Gothic structure that incorporates Byzantine elements. The Gothic Torre Ercilla accommodates the **Museo del Pescador**, which has an exhibition on the Basques' long heritage of fishing and whaling across the Atlantic.

Several hermitages are located in Bermeo and the surrounding area. The most famous of these is the **Ermita San Juan de Gaztelugatxe**, situated on a rocky island a few kilometres from the town and reached by climbing a flight of 231 steps.

🏛️ **Museo del Pescador**
Torre Ercilla. **Tel** 946 88 11 71.
Open 10am–1:30pm & 4–7:30pm
Tue–Sat, 10am–1:30pm Sun. ♿

Environs
Cabo Matxitxako is a remote headland with two lighthouses. The best beaches are to be found in **Ibarrangelu**, which also has the best surfing in northern Spain. **Elantxobe**, in turn, is a picturesque fishing village that spreads up the precipitous slopes of the highest cliff on the Basque coastline – Monte Ogoño (280 m/918 ft above sea level).

❺ Lekeitio

Vizcaya. **Road Map** A4. 🚹 7,500.
🚌 ℹ️ Independentzia Enparantza;
946 84 40 17. 🎭 San Pedro (29 Jun),
San Antolín (1–8 Sep).
🌐 lekeitio.org

Lekeitio is one of many fishing villages on the Basque coast and its architecture is maritime in style. It also has several historic buildings, including the Gothic **Basílica de la Asunción de Santa María.** Inside is a 16th-century altar. Visible from the town's beautiful beach is the island of **San Nicolás**, which can be reached on foot during low tide.

For years, Lekeitio rivalled San Sebastián as the Basque Country's summer capital, with elegant 19th-century villas lining its pretty seafront. The surrounding area is good for walking.

The town is famous for one of the most raucous of Basque fiestas – the "goose games" of San Antolín (see p36).

Boats in the port of Ondarroa

❻ Ondarroa

Vizcaya. **Road Map** B4. 🚹 9,000.
🚌 ℹ️ Erribera 9; 946 83 19 51.
🎭 organized by the tourist office; book in advance. 🎭 Andra Mari Jaiak (14–17 Aug). 🌐 ondarroa.eu

The road between Lekeitio and Ondarroa is planted with pines. Ondarroa is a small but charming old port on the border with Guipúzcoa province, with an animated harbour and a colourful fishing fleet. It has preserved its medieval town plan, with the names of the streets referring to geographical locations or to traditional Basque sports.

Spanning the Artibai river is the **Puente Viejo**, a Roman bridge that was reconstructed in the 20th century.

Other buildings typical of the area include the 15th-century Gothic **Iglesia de Santa María**, built on a clifftop, and the **Torre de Likona**, a border watchtower from the same period. It was here that the mother of St Ignatius Loyola, founder of the Jesuit order, was born.

The **old town hall** has a façade with Tuscan columns. On a nearby hilltop rises the **Iglesia de Nuestra Señora de la Antigua**, dating from the 12th century but rebuilt in the 17th century. It affords breathtaking views of the surrounding area.

❼ Deba

Guipúzcoa. **Road Map** B4. 5,400. Ifar Kalea 4; 943 19 24 52. San Roque (14–20 Aug). **deba.net**

Deba was a fashionable resort in the 1900s, and so has a line of grand old villas beside its long, wide beach. With crashing surf, it still attracts scores of visitors on summer weekends.

In the town are a few palaces from its 16th-century Golden Age. An important monument is the massive Gothic **Iglesia de Santa María**, with a beautiful cloister and colourfully decorated entrance.

Another well-known site is the shrine in Itziar dedicated to the Virgin Mary. Its interior has a Romanesque sculpture of Mary, patron saint of sailors, and a Plateresque altar. Outside is the bronze sculpture, *La Maternidad* by Jorge Oteiza.

Environs

A clifftop footpath with magnificent coastal views leads through green fields and past huge old farms to **Zumaia**. This popular resort has broad, sandy beaches, including the Playa Santiago. A pleasant afternoon can be spent strolling in the old quarter and visiting the attractive marina.

In the **Espacio Ignacio Zuloaga**, home of a celebrated early 20th-century Basque painter, are displayed Zuloaga's colourful studies of Basque rural and maritime life.

Espacio Ignacio Zuloaga
Santiago Etxea. **Tel** 677 07 84 45. **Open** Mar–Sep: 4–8pm Thu–Sat. **espaciozuloaga.com**

Navigators of the Basque Coast

Juan Sebastián Elcano, born in Getaria, led the first expedition to circumnavigate the globe. Following the death of Magellan, Elcano assumed command on the famous round-the-world voyage. On 6 September 1522, after a voyage of 78,000 km (48,500 miles) lasting three years, Elcano returned to Seville on his ship, the *Victoria*.

Another Basque, Andrés de Urdaneta, led the second Spanish round-the-world voyage in the 1530s. In the 1560s Miguel López de Legazpi conquered the Philippines for Spain. Basque sailors later took part in the exploration of Mexico. In the 1600s navigator Sebastián Vizcaíno explored and mapped the coast of California.

Portrait of the navigator Juan Sebastián Elcano

The octagonal tower of the Iglesia de San Salvador in Getaria

❽ Getaria

Guipúzcoa. **Road Map** B4. 2,600. Parque Aldamar 2; 943 14 09 57. San Antón (17 Jan), San Salvador (6–8 Aug). **getaria.net**

Getaria is a charming trawler port with lively cafés. It is also the centre of Txakolí wine production and known for good food. Just off the coast lies the tiny island of **Monte San Antón**, which is artificially joined to the mainland. It is known as *El Ratón de Getaria* (the Mouse of Getaria) because of its shape. Several archaeological finds have been made near the 14th-century **Iglesia de San Salvador**. The **Museo Cristobal Balenciaga** is a showpiece for the fashion designer who lived here.

Museo Cristobal Balenciaga
Parque Aldamar 6. **Tel** 943 00 88 40. **Open** Mar–May & Oct: 10am–5pm Tue–Fri & Sun, 10am–7pm Sat; Jun & Sep: 10am–8pm Tue–Sun; Jul & Aug: 10am–7pm daily; Nov–Feb: 10am–3pm Tue–Fri & 10am–5pm Sat, Sun.

❾ Zarautz

Guipúzcoa. **Road Map** B4. 23,000. Nafarroa 3; 943 83 09 90. San Pelaio (25–27 Jun), Virgen (14–17 Aug), Fiesta Vasca (9 Sep). **turismozarautz.com**

Like many old towns in the region, Zarautz was traditionally associated with whaling. Nowadays, the mainstay of its economy is tourism. The town boasts the province's longest beach and promenade. The sea here offers excellent conditions for surfing, while the nearby vine-clad hillsides produce the region's famous Txakolí wines. In the old quarter are houses with coats of arms, the Gothic **Torre Luzea**, the medieval **Iglesia de Santa María La Real**, and the Renaissance **Palacio de Narros.** The local cuisine is considered to be among the best in the Basque Country.

The building of the Museo de Ignacio Zuloaga in Zumaia, near Deba

View of the town hall with Monte Urgull in the background, San Sebastián (Donostia) ▶

⑩ Street-by-Street: San Sebastián (Donostia)

San Sebastián was the most fashionable summer resort in Spain at the beginning of the 20th century, and has an elegant traditional promenade all along its curving beach. Today it is delicately old-fashioned. The superb curving bay is closed off by the green hills of Monte Urgull and Monte Igeldo. In the mouth of the bay lies the tortoise-shaped island of Santa Clara. The city is renowned for its summer arts festivals, street life centred in the old town, and unrivalled *pintxos* (the local version of tapas).

★ Monte Urgull
Rising above the Old Town, Monte Urgull is home to the ruined 16th-century fortress of Santa Cruz de la Mota. On the summit stands a statue of Christ – the Sagrado Corazón.

Aquarium and Museo Naval

VIRGEN DEL CORO

PLA DE TRINI

CAMPANARIO

PU

0 metres   50
0 yards   50

Museo Naval
Set in an 18th-century building, the Maritime Museum offers a comprehensive view of the Basques and their connections with the sea.

Santa María del Coro
Although this basilica has earlier origins, its current appearance is 18th-century, combining elements of Gothic, Churrigueresque and Neo-Classicism.

PLA L SA

IGEN

Key

— Suggested route

For hotels and restaurants see pp205–6 and pp219–21

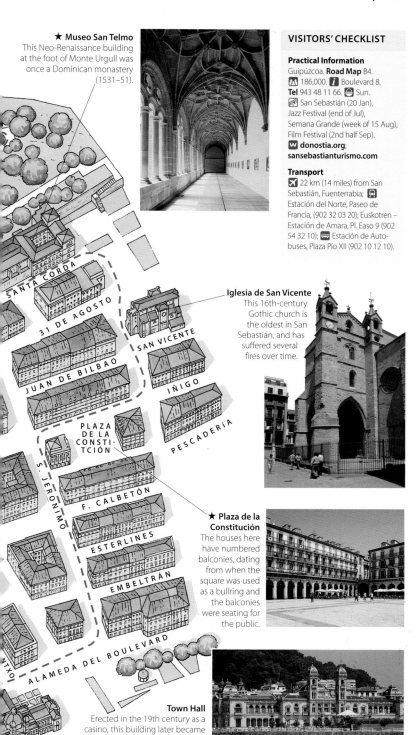

★ **Museo San Telmo**
This Neo-Renaissance building at the foot of Monte Urgull was once a Dominican monastery (1531–51).

VISITORS' CHECKLIST

Practical Information
Guipúzcoa. **Road Map** B4.
186,000. Boulevard 8.
Tel 943 48 11 66. Sun.
San Sebastián (20 Jan),
Jazz Festival (end of Jul),
Semana Grande (week of 15 Aug),
Film Festival (2nd half Sep).
donostia.org;
sansebastianturismo.com

Transport
22 km (14 miles) from San
Sebastián, Fuenterrabia; Estación del Norte, Paseo de
Francia, (902 32 03 20); Euskotren –
Estación de Amara, Pl. Easo 9 (902
54 32 10); Estación de Auto-
buses, Plaza Pío XII (902 10 12 10).

SANTA CORDA
31 DE AGOSTO
SAN VICENTE
JUAN DE BILBAO
ÍÑIGO
PLAZA DE LA CONSTI-TCIÓN
PESCADERÍA
S. JERÓNIMO
F. CALBETÓN
ESTERLINES
EMBELTRÁN
OXIN
ALAMEDA DEL BOULEVARD

Iglesia de San Vicente
This 16th-century Gothic church is the oldest in San Sebastián, and has suffered several fires over time.

★ **Plaza de la Constitución**
The houses here have numbered balconies, dating from when the square was used as a bullring and the balconies were seating for the public.

Town Hall
Erected in the 19th century as a casino, this building later became the town hall when gambling was banned in the city.

The tortoise-shaped island of Santa Clara with the city in the background

Exploring San Sebastián

The most interesting parts of the city are the Old Town and Monte Urgull, the spectacular bay and seafront promenade with its hugely popular beaches of La Concha and Ondarreta, and Monte Igeldo, on top of which stands a lighthouse. All of these sites can be visited on foot. The summits of the two hills are well worth the climb.

🚉 Bahía de la Concha

Between Monte Urgull and Monte Igeldo, along the Paseo de la Concha promenade, extend two beaches – the smaller and more fashionable Playa Ondarreta, and the larger Playa de la Concha. The beaches are divided by a curious rock formation, on which rises the Palacio de Miramar, a palace with carefully maintained gardens. There are excellent views of the bay and the island of Santa Clara from here.

Nearby is Eduardo Chillida's series of sculptures *The Comb of the Winds*. The huge russet-coloured claws complement the grey rock and emerald sea.

🏛 Old Town

Following a fire in 1813, the Old Town was reconstructed in a Neo-Classical style while preserving the medieval street plan. The Parte Vieja is the veritable heart of the old city. Its inhabitants are divided into the *Joshemaritarras* – those born in the vicinity of the Gothic church of San Vicente – and the *Koxkeros* – those born in the vicinity of the church of Santa María. In the latter church is a sculpture of the

city's patron – the Black Madonna and Child, known as the Virgen del Coro.

The main axis of the Old Town is the Calle Mayor. At one end of it stands the church of Santa María, and at the other the cathedral of Buen Pastor.

Another important site is the Plaza de la Constitución, a handsome arcaded square also known as the Consti. Bullfights used to occur here, and today fiestas are held. The Old Town is packed with bars serving delicious *pintxos*.

A street in the Parte Vieja leading to Santa María del Coro

🔼 Monte Urgull

Criss-crossed by parkland paths, Monte Urgull is an ideal place for a stroll. Within its perimeter is the Cementerio de los Ingleses, a cemetery dedicated to the English who perished while trying to capture the city from the French in 1813; today, it is one of the most serene and pleasant spots on the hill. The summit is occupied by the 16th-century fortress of Santa Cruz

de la Mota, which houses a small museum dedicated to the city's history. The building also accommodates three chapels, including one dedicated to the Cristo de la Mota. Above this chapel rises a huge statue of Christ – the Sagrado Corazón.

🏛 Museo Naval & Aquarium

Museum: Paseo del Muelle 24. **Tel** 943 43 00 51. **Open** 10am–2pm & 4–7pm Tue–Sat, 11am–2pm Sun (mid-Jun–mid-Sep: 4–7pm Sun). 🗓 (free Thu) 🅿 🔲 Aquarium: Plaza Carlos Blasco de Imaz. **Tel** 943 44 00 99. **Open** Oct–Mar: 10am–7pm Mon–Fri, 10am–8pm Sat, Sun & hols; Apr–Jun & Sep: 10am–8pm Mon–Fri, 10am–9pm Sat; Jul–Aug: 10am–9pm daily. 🗓 🅿
🌐 aquariumss.com

The Maritime Museum, housed in an 18th-century port building, is devoted to the seafaring life of the Basque people. The display illustrates shipbuilding, the evolution of ports and the development of commerce, and includes a collection of navigational instruments.

In the nearby aquarium visitors can walk through an underwater tunnel while viewing sea creatures in their natural environment.

🔼 Iglesia de Santa María del Coro

Dedicated to the city's patron saint, this church contains a figure of the Black Madonna. According to legend, a certain monk – exhausted by having to climb into the choir to worship the figure – attempted to take it home with him. He hid the figure under his habit and tried to leave, but discovered he was unable to cross the threshold of the church. Only when he returned the figure to its rightful place was he able to leave. Today, it is on the high altar.

The current church dates from the 18th century. Designed by the architects Lizardi and Ibero, it combines elements of Gothic, Churrigueresque and Neo-Classicism. The Baroque façade, with two towers, a clock and a figure of St Sebastián, faces Calle Mayor. Inside is an alabaster cross by Eduardo Chillida and a Cavaillé-Coll organ from 1863. Concerts are held regularly.

The Neo-Gothic Catedral del Buen Pastor

🏛 Museo San Telmo

Plaza Zuloaga 1. **Tel** 943 48 15 80.
Open 10am–8pm Tue–Sun. 🅿 (free Tue). ♿ 🆆 **museosantelmo.com**

One of the most exciting museums in Northern Spain, Museo San Telmo has a fascinating display on Basque culture, mythology and folk traditions. Housed in a Neo-Renaissance building with a modern exhibition hall at the foot of Monte Urgull, its exhibits include ancient discoidal tombstones, magic charms, a reconstruction of a traditional cottage, musical instruments, tools and sports equipment. The ground floor comprises a church, a beautiful cloister accommodating the archaeological section, and rooms for temporary exhibitions.

The impressive permanent art collection includes works by El Greco, Alonso Cano, Rubens, Ribera and Zuloaga.

⛪ Cathedral

Plaza del Buen Pastor. **Tel** 943 46 45 16.
Open 8:30am–12:30pm & 5–8pm Mon–Fri, during services Sat–Sun.

The Neo-Gothic cathedral was designed by Manuel de Echave, while the 75-m (246-ft) high tower is the work of Ramón Cortázar. Its rich ornamentation includes stained-glass windows by Juan Bautista Lázara, gargoyles and pinnacles.

🏘 New Town

Right up until the 19th century, San Sebastián was encircled by walls. When these became defunct, a new solution was needed – especially after 1854, when the city became the provincial capital. The architect Antonio Cortázar put forward a project for the redevelopment of the city: a new district arose with a grid of broad, airy boulevards leading down to the Paseo de la Concha, the beach-side promenade. Key elements of this redevelopment included the cathedral of Buen Pastor, the Palacio Miramar, and the tree-lined Plaza de Guipúzcoa. The most impressive building remains Goiko's Palacio de la Diputación, its façade decorated with the busts of famous Basques.

🎭 Kursaal

Avda. de Zurriola 1. **Tel** 943 00 30 00.
🆆 **kursaal.org**

This spectacular, avant-garde convention centre was designed by architect Rafael Moneo, and opened in 1999. Located next to Gros beach, to the east of the old town, it has helped to revive this once under-used beach. The glass-walled structure hosts the Film Festival, other cultural events and a fashionable café-bar.

🔵 Monte Igueldo

Monte Igueldo, which closes the western end of the bay, looks as if it has toppled over – the layers of rock at the foot of the hill lie vertically. The hill itself, with a funfair and a 19th-century lighthouse, is an ideal spot for rest and recreation. A **funicular railway** takes visitors to the summit.

🚠 Funicular Railway

Tel 943 21 05 64. **Open** Spring & autumn: 11am–8pm Mon–Fri, 10am–9pm Sat, Sun & hols; summer: 10am–10pm daily; winter: 11am–6pm Mon–Tue & Thu–Fri, 11am–7pm Sat & Sun. 🅿

The tower on Monte Igeldo – a good observation point

Festivals in San Sebastián

The International Film Festival, founded in 1953, is one of five leading European annual film festivals. It is held in September and draws more than 100,000 spectators. The special Donostia Prize is awarded as a tribute to the career of an actor or director; winners include the actor Jessica Lange and film director and screen writer Woody Allen. Prizes also go to new films. In addition, the city hosts one of Europe's oldest jazz festivals (July), an international theatre festival, and a classical music festival (August).

Jessica Lange at the Film Festival

View of the town of Hondarribia, with the port in the background

⓫ Hondarribia (Fuenterrabia)

Guipúzcoa. **Road Map** B4. 🚠 16,500.
✈ 🚌 🚆 *i* Arma Plaza 9; 943 64
36 77. 🏠 Wed. 🎊 La Kutxa Eguna
(25 Jul), El Alarde (8 Sep).
w bidasoaturismo.com

The historic quarter of this port town at the mouth of the Río Bidasoa (opposite France) is encircled by 15th-century walls with two gates – the **Puerta de Santa María** and the **Puerta San Nicolás**. Within the quarter are old houses with carved eaves, balconies and coats of arms. The narrow cobbled streets cluster around the church of **Santa María de la Asunción**, a Gothic structure dating from the early 15th century, which incorporates Renaissance and Baroque elements. Aside from the cross-vaulting, the highlight is a remarkable three-faced image of the Holy Trinity, found underneath the choir. In the 16th century, the Church condemned such images, and this is one of very few to have survived in Spain. Also of interest are the Churrigueresque-style retables.

Hondarribia is one of the prettiest of all Basque towns. The lively fishermen's quarter of **La Marina** is famous for its tall, brightly painted houses and seafront cafés. There are also beaches stretching to the north.

Environs
In the historic port-town of **Pasai-Donibane** is the house where the writer Victor Hugo once lived. Regattas are held in the local bay here.

⓬ Hernani

Guipúzcoa. **Road Map** B4. 🚠 19,300.
🚆 🚌 *i* Nafar 18; 943 33 70 28 (Jul & Aug only). 🎊 San Juan (24 Jun).

This small medieval town is located around 8 km (5 miles) south of San Sebastián. Famous for its picturesque streets, Hernani has been awarded the status of Cultural Interest Site. Of particular note are the 19th-century town hall, supported on seven arches, and the Portalondo house, an example of medieval defensive architecture, whose walls are lined with stone facing. Also of interest are the 16th-century church of St John the Baptist and the medieval Gudarien Enparantza, the main square.

The town is surrounded by forests that are scattered with prehistoric remains, including megalithic monuments, dolmens and burial mounds.

One of the charming streets in the small town of Hernani

⓭ Tolosa

Guipúzcoa. **Road Map** B4. 🚠 18,000.
🚆 🚌 *i* Plaza Santa Maria 1; 943 69
74 13. 🏠 Sat. 🎊 San Juan (24 Jun).
w tolosaldea.net

For centuries Tolosa was an important cultural, commercial and industrial centre. In the

Caseríos

The *caserío* (or *baserrí* in Basque), an often huge stone house with a sloping roof, is a typical feature of the Basque landscape. *Caseríos* stand alone in the countryside and are not part of villages; they were originally independent n farms, where many generations of a single family would live, with their animals on the ground floor below. Each *caserío* had its own name, from which the surname of the family who dwelt there was derived.

A typical Basque *caserío*

19th century, it was occupied by the French and was the capital of Guipúzcoa province during the Carlist Wars *(see p45)*. Its renowned carnival was held even during the Franco era, and its November choral music festival is one of the best in the country. Tolosa is also famous for *alubias de Tolosa* – a red bean grown around the town and featured in hearty dishes.

In the Old Town's numerous narrow streets and squares, there are examples of Basque Gothic and Baroque; one such building is the imposing 17th-century Gothic aisled church of Santa María. The church boasts cross-vaulting and a Baroque façade designed by Martín de Carrera. Under the choir is a late-Romanesque portico.

⓮ Azpeitia

Guipúzcoa. **Road Map** B4. 14,500. 🚌 ℹ Santuario de Loiola; 943 02 50 00. 🎭 San Sebastián (19–20 Jan), San Ignacio (30 Jul), Santo Tomás (21 Dec).

As many as 360 *caseríos* are preserved in the vicinity of Azpeitia. The town itself features many beautiful buildings, some in the Mudéjar style; these include, for instance, the Casa Altuna, the magnificent Casa Anchieta – which once belonged to a musician employed by the Catholic Monarchs – and the 14th-century Magdalena hermitage. Also well represented is the Plateresque style, which is evident on the windows of the Casa Plateresca and on the portico of the church of San Sebastián de Soreasu, a Gothic structure whose tower was built by the Knights Templar.

One of the town's oldest buildings is the huge medieval Casa Torre de Enparan, now housing the municipal library. However, Azpeitia is most famous for its shrine to St Ignatius Loyola and other sites associated with the founder of the Jesuit order *(see p142)*.

Colourful houses along the river in Tolosa

⓯ Bergara

Guipúzcoa. **Road Map** B4. 14,900. 🚉 🚌 ℹ Palacio Errekalde. **Tel** 943 77 91 28. 🎭 San Martín de Aguirre (16 Sep). 🔲 bergaraturismo.net

Bergara is one of the most characterful of Basque country towns, with an old centre full of distinguished colleges, churches and mansions built for aristocrats during the town's Golden Age in the 16th and 17th centuries. The first Carlist War ended here in 1839 *(see p45)* – the treaty was signed in the 17th-century **Casa Iritzar**, which features wrought-iron balconies and a coat of arms at the corner of the building.

There are other fine buildings, such as the 16th-century **Casa Arostegi**, which holds exhibitions, and the **Casa Jauregi** (c.1500), which has reliefs depicting plant motifs and figures of royal couples.

Basque Gothic is represented by the aisled church of **Santa Marina de Oxirondo**, built on a square plan. Its tower is Baroque, as is the impressive reredos by Miguel de Irazusta and Luis Salvador Carmona. Also Baroque is the **Iglesia de San Pedro de Ariznoa**, with its squat tower; inside is a canvas with shepherds paying homage to the infant Jesus.

⓰ Oñati

Guipúzcoa. **Road Map** B4. 11,200. 🚌 ℹ San Juan Kale 14; 943 78 34 53. 🎭 San Miguel (29 Sep–4 Oct). 🔲 oinati.eu/turism

A walk through old Oñati is a real treat for architecture enthusiasts. The **Universidad de Sancti Spiritus** – designed by Picart and Gibaja – was the first Basque university, funded by Bishop Zuazola; it operated between 1551 and 1901. The Plateresque façade is adorned with four pilasters and several figures referring to both mythological and religious tradition. A superb courtyard can be found within.

The Monasterio de Bidaurreta, in turn, is a mix of Gothic, Renaissance and Mudéjar. The interior contains aristocratic family tombs and two altars – one Baroque, the other Plateresque in style.

The Plaza de Santa Marina is surrounded by Baroque palaces.

🏛 **Universidad de Sancti Spiritus**
Unibertsitate Etorbidea 8. **Tel** 943 78 34 53. **Open** visits by appointment only; phone ahead to arrange. 🎫 📷 ♿

Environs
From Oñati, a mountain road ascends for 9 km (6 miles) to the **Santuario de Arantzazu**, which lies in the valley at the foot of Alona Hill. In 1469 it is believed a shepherd saw a vision of the Virgin here. This Modernist church, built to replace an earlier one, was designed in the 1950s by Javier Sáiz Oiza and Luis Laorga. It has a tall belfry, huge wooden altar, and doors designed by the sculptor Eduardo Chillida. The Virgin of Arantzazu is the province's patron.

The Universidad de Sancti Spiritus in Oñati

🔟 Santuario de Loiola

Iñigo de Loiola, or St Ignatius (1491–1556), founder of the Jesuit order, was born in the stone manor known as Santa Casa (Holy House). The manor was incorporated in 1681–1738 into a shrine designed by Carlo Fontana, and the rooms where the Loyola family had lived were converted into chapels. The most important of these is the Chapel of the Conversion, the room where Ignatius, as a young soldier, had a profound religious experience while recovering from a battle injury. The Baroque basilica, with a circular nave and a Churrigueresque dome, is the shrine's highlight.

★ Interior of the Basilica
The richly decorated and gilded Churrigueresque interior is covered in grey and pink marble.

Figures by the Santa Casa
The bronze figures, by Juan Flotats, show the return of Ignatius, who had been injured while defending the castle in Pamplona.

★ Santa Casa
In the Holy House – the original home of the Loyola family, around which the Sanctuary was built – is the Chapel of the Conversion, with a beautiful sculpture of Ignatius Loyola.

The Founding of the Jesuit Order

The Jesuit order was founded in Rome in 1539 by St Ignatius, a former soldier, and a group of priests who were dedicated to purifying the Church and resisting Protestantism. Pope Paul III soon approved the order's establishment, with Ignatius as Superior General. The order, which grew wealthy, vowed military obedience to the Pope and became his most powerful weapon against the Reformation. Today, there are nearly 20,000 Jesuits working, mainly in education, in 127 countries.

St Ignatius of Loyola

★ **Museum of Religious Art**
The two rooms of the museum contain rare and valuable exhibits, such as a mahogany reredos, reliquaries, and copies of St Ignatius' *Spiritual Exercises* in many languages.

Coats of Arms
The interior of the dome, 33 m (108 ft) in diameter, is covered in carved royal coats of arms set against a background of pink marble – the work of Gaetano Pace.

Entrance to the Library
The library has 150,000 volumes, of which some 30,000 date from the 15th to 18th centuries. There is also a music archive.

Doors of the Basilica
The doors are made of cedar of Lebanon and mahogany imported from Cuba; in the niche above them is a figure of St Ignatius by Ignacio de Ibero.

⑱ Vitoria-Gasteiz

The inland city of Vitoria is the capital of the Basque Country and the seat of the Basque government. It was founded on a hill – the highest point in the province of Álava and the site of the ancient Basque town of Gasteiz. The city grew rich on the iron and wool trades, and today it is brimming with life. Visitors come to see Vitoria's beautiful architecture and extensive parkland, and to enjoy its excellent restaurants and tapas bars.

Exploring Vitoria

The more impressive historic monuments are concentrated within the relatively small confines of the Old Town; several Renaissance palaces and the most important churches are located here. A good way to end the day is to embark on a *poteo* – a whistle-stop tour of several tapas bars to sample the delicious local cuisine.

🚇 Plaza de la Virgen Blanca

On this large square, named after the White Madonna, patron saint of Vitoria, stands a monument to a battle fought in 1813, when the Duke of

Plaza de la Virgen Blanca in the city centre

Wellington defeated the French during the Peninsular War *(see p45)*. Beethoven wrote a special concerto, *Wellington's Victory*, to commemorate this event. The monument, crowned with the figure of an angel, is the work of Gabriel Borrás. Old houses with glazed balconies surround the vibrant square, but the most important building is the Iglesia de San Miguel.

🏛 Iglesia de San Miguel

This late Gothic aisled church, with Renaissance elements, was built between the 14th and 16th centuries. The high altar, by Gregorio Fernández, is Baroque (1624–32). The church is devoted to the cult of the White Madonna, and a 14th-century statue of her can be found in an outside niche.

🚇 Plaza del Machete

On the wall of the Iglesia de San Miguel facing the Plaza del Machete is a recess that once held an axe on which the city's

rulers swore to uphold the laws or be slain. The square – one of Vitoria's oldest – was also known as the Plazoleta del Juicio (court square), because in former times public executions would take place here.

A figure of the White Madonna in the Iglesia de San Miguel

🏛 Palacio de Escoríaza-Esquivel

Fray Zacarías Martínez 7. **Closed** to the public.

Stone was used in the construction of this 16th-century palace. The façade is Plateresque in style, with chain-like ornamentation running under the roof.

🏛 Catedral de Santa María (Catedral Vieja)

Plaza Burulleria. **Tel** 945 25 51 35. **Open** 11am–2pm, 5–8pm. 🎫 compulsory. Reserve by phone or online. 🅿 ♿ ✉ 🆆 catedralvitoria.com

The 13th-century Gothic Catedral de Santa María de Suso was once part of the city's fortifications. Preserved on the second buttress arch from the northern end is a stone decorated with a rose-like ornament, dating from Visigothic times. The interior is undergoing restoration.

A stained-glass window in the Catedral de Santa María

The Autonomous Basque Government

Since 1979, the Basque Country has enjoyed broad autonomy on the basis of the so-called Statute of Gernika. It has its own parliament and government, while the region's official languages are both Basque (Euskera) and Spanish. Since 2012, the government has been headed by Prime Minister (*lehendakari* in Basque) Iñigo Urkullu of the Basque Nationalist Party (PNV). The Basque prime minister's official seat is the Palacio Ajuria-Enea. Basque politicians have long been putting the case forward for a new statute that would ensure still greater independence from Spain's central government.

The prime ministers of Spain and the Basque Country

The façade of the 15th-century El Portalón

🏛 El Portalón

Calle Correría 147. **Tel** 945 14 27 55 (restaurant).

The famous El Portalón is a rare example of medieval secular architecture of the late 15th century. Originally a merchant's house, with a shop on the ground floor and an apartment above, in the 19th century it became an inn, and today it accommodates an excellent Basque restaurant (see p220).

The name derives from the huge gateway through which carriages would enter.

🏛 Catedral Nueva

Calle Magdalena 1. **Closed** Sat & Sun pm.

When a new diocese covering all three Basque provinces was established in the 19th century, it was agreed that Vitoria needed a new cathedral. Construction lasted several decades. The result – a huge, Neo-Gothic shrine – which has a nave, four aisles and accommodates 15,000 people. Noteworthy are the tall stained-glass windows, the apse, and the stunning gargoyles.

🏛 Museo de Bellas Artes

Paseo Fray Francisco 8. **Tel** 945 18 19 18. **Open** 10am–2pm & 4–6:30pm Tue–Fri, 10am–2pm & 5–8pm Sat, 11am–2pm Sun & hols. 🕮 (free 1st Sat of month). 📷 by prior arrangement.

The Museum of Fine Art is housed in the eclectic Palacio Augusti. The collection of paintings and sculptures includes Classical art and Basque art from 1850 to 1950.

🏛 Museo de la Armería de Álava

Paseo Fray Francisco 3. **Tel** 945 18 19 25. **Open** 10am–2pm & 4–6:30pm Tue–Fri, 10am–2pm Sun. 🕮 (free 1st Sat of month). 📷 by prior arrangement.

The weapons displayed here range from prehistoric axes, through Oriental and Arabic weaponry, to 20th-century pistols. There are also uniforms and other military exhibits. Of particular interest is a section devoted to the Battle of Vitoria in 1813.

VISITORS' CHECKLIST

Practical Information
Álava. **Road Map** A5.
🏠 240,000.
ℹ️ Plaza España 1; 945 16 15 98.
🚇 Thu & Sat.
🎫 San Prudencio (28 Apr), Fiestas de la Virgen Blanca (4–9 Aug).
🌐 vitoria-gasteiz.org/turismo

Transport
✈️ **Tel** 902 40 47 04.
🚉 C/Dato 46; 902 32 03 20.
🚌 Los Herran 70; 945 25 84 00.

Palace housing the Museo de Bellas Artes

🏛 Artium

C/Francia 24. **Tel** 945 20 90 20. **Open** 11am–2pm & 5–8pm Tue–Fri, 11am–8pm Sat & Sun. 🕮 ♿
🌐 artium.org

Opened in 2002, this futuristic contemporary art museum showcases modern Spanish and Basque artists.

Vitoria City Centre

① Plaza de la Virgen Blanca
② Iglesia de San Miguel
③ Plaza del Machete
④ Palacio de Escoríaza-Esquivel
⑤ Catedral de Santa María
⑥ El Portalón
⑦ Catedral Nueva
⑧ Museo de Bellas Artes
⑨ Museo de la Armería de Álava
⑩ Artium

0 metres 200
0 yards 200

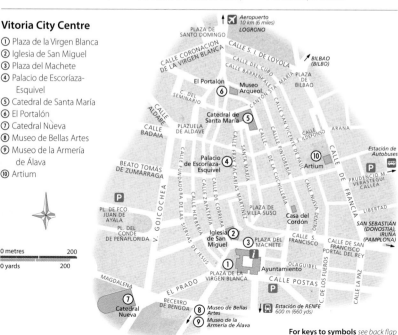

For keys to symbols see back flap

⓳ Torre Palacio de los Varona

Villanañe (Álava). **Road Map** A5.
Tel 945 35 30 40. **Open** Summer:
11am–2pm & 4–7pm Tue–Sat,
11am–2pm Sun; winter: 11am–2pm &
4–7pm Sat, 11am–2pm Sun & public
hols. 🅿 🅲 🅲

The small town of Villanañe
is home to a fine example of
medieval military architecture,
the tower and mansion of the
Varona family. Set on a hill, with
commanding views of the
surrounding countryside, this
imposing structure is the most
well-preserved 14th-century
fortified building in the region.
Its origins date back to the year
680, when the first tower was
built on this site by the Visigoth
admiral Ruy Pérez. Since the
15th century, the mansion
has been home to the Varona
family, and has evolved over
the years with the needs of
its occupants. Nonetheless,
the interior contains a
wealth of interesting
historical detail,
including period
furniture. The
upper rooms
are decorated
with strikingly
colourful
17th- and
18th-century
wallpaper,
which replaced
the tapestries that previously
hung on the walls. Some of the
floors are of wood, while others
are tiled in traditional Manises
porcelain decorated with
scenes from *Don Quixote*.

Torre Palacio de los Varona

⓴ Salvatierra

Álava. **Road Map** B5. 🔼 4,800. 🚉 🚌
🛈 Mayor 8; 945 30 29 31. 🎿 San
Juan Bautista (24 Jun), Nuestra Señora
del Rosario (1st Sun in Oct). 🅲 (see
website) 🅦 **agurain.biz**

Set among green hills and
beech woods is the small town
of Salvatierra. Rising above the
surrounding area is the walled
Old Town. Also worth seeing
are the former hospital of San
Lázaro y la Magdalena and the
Gothic church of Santa María.

The Romanesque Iglesia de San Martin de Tours in Gaceo

㉑ Gaceo and Alaiza

Road Map B5. **Tel** 945 30 29 31. 🅲
by appt. 🅦 **cuadrillasalvatierra.org**

Not far from Vitoria, the villages
of Gaceo and Alaiza conceal
hidden treasure: medieval
murals. In the **Iglesia de San
Martín de Tours** in Gaceo, the
14th-century murals adorn
the crypt and chancel,
presenting the text of
the catechism for the
benefit of non-Latin-
speaking believers.
The murals also
depict the
Holy Trinity,
the Last
Judgement,
scenes from
the Way of the
Cross and the
life of Christ,
and redeemed souls.

In Alaiza is the **Iglesia de
Santa María de la Asunción**,
featuring murals from the same
period but cruder than those at
Gaceo. The depiction is more
schematic and the figures less
complex. The subject matter
relates to conflict, bringing to
mind stark and rather uncom-
promising war reportage.

㉒ Laguardia

Álava. **Road Map** A5. 🔼 1,550. 🚌
🛈 Calle Mayor 52; 945 60 08 45.
🎿 San Juan and San Pedro (24–29
Jun). 🅦 **laguardia-alava.com**

Laguardia is a fascinating old
town encircled by 13th-century
walls, which is closed to traffic.
Underground, at a depth of 6 m

(20 ft), are numerous wine
cellars – *bodegas* or *cuevas*,
which can be visited. Laguardia
is the most important town in
Rioja Alavesa, a district that
has, for centuries, produced
excellent Rioja wines. The land
is extremely fertile, and almost
the entire local population is
involved in vine cultivation.
The town is also celebrated
for its food.

Laguardia is entered through
one of five fortified gateways
incorporated in the ring of walls.
At the centre of Laguardia is the
Plaza Mayor, on which stand
two town halls – the old one,
with the coat of arms of Charles
V, and the current one, which
bears the town's crest. The
Gothic **Iglesia de Santa María
de los Reyes**, of 12th-century
origin, features a richly sculpted,
polychrome interior portal (14th
century), with a delicate statue
of the Virgin and Child dating
from the same period.

One of the fortified gateways leading
to Laguardia

Basque Fiestas and Sports

The Basques are devoted to sports, excelling at conventional games, and inventing many of their own. In football, Basque clubs have always played near the top of their leagues, despite many sticking to a rule of fielding only local, Basque-born players. First among indigenous Basque sports is *pelota*, played between two or four players with bare hands, bats or a long basket. Enormously popular, it's a fast-moving game that's spectacular to watch. The Basques also have a whole range of often outlandish traditional country sports – wagon lifting, sheep fights and tug-of-war – many of which originated as tests of strength and skill between villages, fishermen and mountain farmers. They can be seen at the annual town and village fiestas, together with performances of the equally distinctive Basque poetry, music, dance and folklore.

Bertsolaris are bards who improvise witty songs, whose verses relate current events or legends. They sing, unaccompanied, to gatherings in public places, often in competition.

Estropadak are colourful traditional rowing races held each summer in San Sebastián and all the Basque ports. The long, narrow boats were once used for whale-hunting.

The Tamborrada is a cacophonous festival unique to San Sebastián, in which uniformed drum bands parade around the city during the night of 19 January, giving way to children's drum parades during the next day. Succulent food completes the fiesta.

Harri-jasotzailea (stone lifting), practised by massive-limbed mountain farmers, is one of the best-known Basque sports. Basque lifters regularly exceed the records set by standard, Olympic weightlifters, and legendary champion Iñaki Perureña was long considered the world's strongest man.

Aizkolari competitors have to cut through a row of beech logs in the fastest possible time while standing on top of them, jumping on to the next log as soon as the first one is cut.

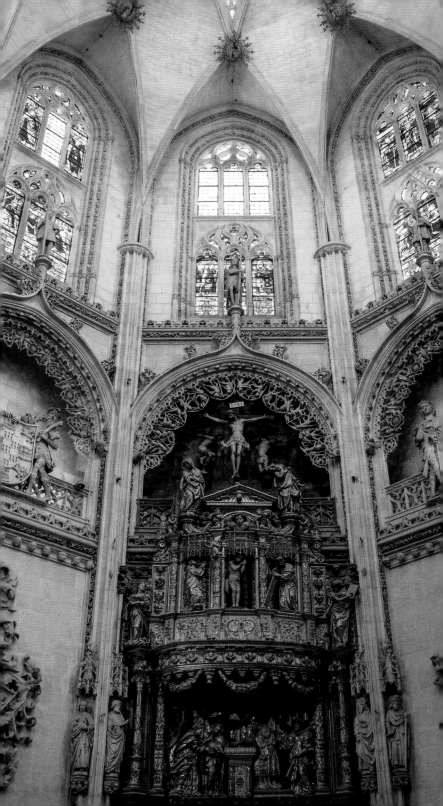

NAVARRA AND LA RIOJA

Navarra, the cradle of the Basques, and La Rioja, famous for its wines, witnessed key events in the Middle Ages, such as the Battle of Roncesvalles against Charlemagne's forces. Both regions were also important stages on the pilgrimage route to Santiago de Compostela. This is evidenced by the many monasteries, churches and bridges that survive, including the 11th-century bridge in Puente la Reina.

Navarra had its Golden Age in the 10th century, when it was a powerful independent kingdom. Its ruler, Sancho III, managed for a brief period to unite nearly all the Christian lands of the Iberian peninsula.

Nowadays, Navarra enjoys a degree of autonomy, with its own parliament and government. It is a small, sparsely populated region, but one that is geographically diverse and with an abundance of flora and fauna. More than 60 per cent of its territory is forested, providing an excellent habitat for the capercaillie and other animal species.

Navarra is divided into three sub-regions: the mountainous Montana, the Zona Media, and Ribera, which enjoys a Mediterranean climate. The region is known not only for captivating land-scapes, but also for the magnificent towns of Olite and Pamplona, which

were founded during Roman times. Northwest Navarra is very strongly Basque, with Euskera an official language. Areas south of Pamplona have far less Basque influence. Medieval Estella and Sangüesa are also historic stopovers on the pilgrimage route of St James.

The first inhabitants of La Rioja – one of the smallest Spanish regions – were dinosaurs, traces of which can be seen around the mountain village of Enciso. Today La Rioja is famous for its excellent wines, produced from grapes that mature slowly on the sunny hillsides. Visitors come here also to attend the wine festival of *Batalla del Vino* (Wine Battle) in Haro. La Rioja, which in the Middle Ages was an important stage on the road to Santiago de Compostela, also boasts superb architecture, such as in Santo Domingo de la Calzada or at the monastery of San Millán de Yuso.

A prehistoric stone hut along the eastern edge of Navarra

◀ The magnificent interior of the Gothic cathedral of Burgos, in the Castilla y León region

Exploring Navarra and La Rioja

These green, mountainous regions have diverse attractions. The Navarrese Pyrenees offer skiing in winter and climbing, caving and canoeing the rest of the year. Minor roads wind through wooded hills, valleys and gorges, passing castles – such as in Olite – Roman towns, and villages. Many of these places, including Roncesvalles, have been immortalized in the region's history. In La Rioja, to the south, the roads cross vineyards, passing towns and villages clustered around ancient churches and monasteries. While in the region, it is well worth venturing slightly further south, into Castilla y León, to visit Burgos, famous for its Gothic cathedral, Frómista with its Romanesque church of San Martín, and the fortified town of Briviesca.

Window in Roncesvalles depicting the Battle of Las Navas de Tolosa

Key

- ▬▬ Motorway
- ▬ Major road
- ▪▪▪ Minor road
- ▪ ▪ Motorway under construction
- ▬ Scenic route
- ▬▬ Railway line
- ▬ National border
- ▬ Regional border
- △ Mountain peak

Beyond the Region

Getting Around

Motorways and minor roads fan out from Pamplona in the direction of Huesca, Zaragoza, Logroño, San Sebastián, Vitoria, and the border with France. Both Navarra and La Rioja have good rail and coach connections with the rest of Spain and further afield. The regions can also be reached by plane. There are airports in Noáin, near Pamplona, and in the vicinity of Logroño.

For hotels and restaurants see pp206–7 and pp221–2

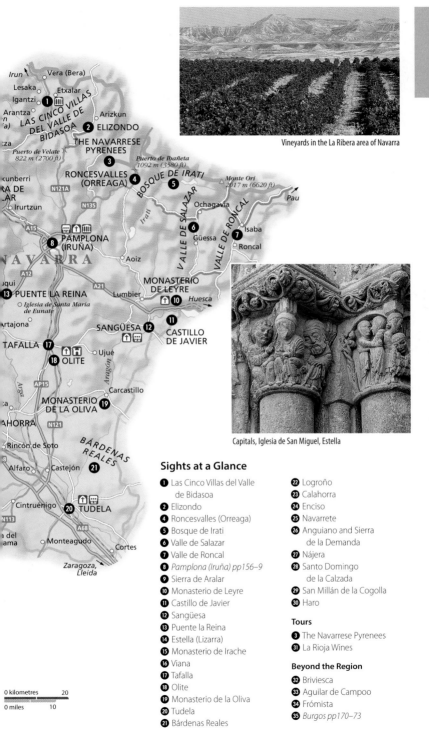

Vineyards in the La Ribera area of Navarra

Capitals, Iglesia de San Miguel, Estella

Sights at a Glance

1. Las Cinco Villas del Valle de Bidasoa
2. Elizondo
4. Roncesvalles (Orreaga)
5. Bosque de Irati
6. Valle de Salazar
7. Valle de Roncal
8. *Pamplona (Iruña) pp156–9*
9. Sierra de Aralar
10. Monasterio de Leyre
11. Castillo de Javier
12. Sangüesa
13. Puente la Reina
14. Estella (Lizarra)
15. Monasterio de Irache
16. Viana
17. Tafalla
18. Olite
19. Monasterio de la Oliva
20. Tudela
21. Bárdenas Reales
22. Logroño
23. Calahorra
24. Enciso
25. Navarrete
26. Anguiano and Sierra de la Demanda
27. Nájera
28. Santo Domingo de la Calzada
29. San Millán de la Cogolla
30. Haro

Tours
3. The Navarrese Pyrenees
31. La Rioja Wines

Beyond the Region
32. Briviesca
33. Aguilar de Campoo
34. Frómista
35. *Burgos pp170–73*

For keys to symbols *see back flap*

0 kilometres 20
0 miles 10

Typical Basque house in the picturesque village of Etxalar

❶ Las Cinco Villas del Valle de Bidasoa

Navarra. **Road Map** B4. 🚍 ℹ️ Bertiz, 948 59 23 86; Bera, 948 63 12 22 (summer only). 🌐 **turismonavarra.es**

In the Bidasoa river valley are five attractive towns that owe their unique character not only to the beautiful forest scenery, but also to the proximity of the border with France and the iron industry that thrived here.

The most northerly is **Bera** (Vera), the largest of the five towns, which has a mix of agriculture and industry. Trade with France has played an important role in this town's history. The celebrated Basque writer Pío Baroja lived here. The highest point in the town is Larun hill, from where there are magnificent views of the forested surroundings.

Heading south to **Lesaka**, the houses here have wooden balconies under deep eaves. The road south continues to pass hills dotted with white farmsteads to reach **Igantzi** (Yanci), the smallest of the towns in the area; the nearby hills conceal several old *caseríos* (Basque farmhouses) as well as a spring with therapeutic powers.

Arantza is the most secluded and remote of the towns. Since the 12th century, pigeons have been caught in huge nets strung across a pass above **Etxalar** (Echalar). From the summit of La Rhune, on the French border above the valley, there are great views of the Pyrenees.

❷ Elizondo

Navarra. **Road Map** B4. 🚗 3,200. 🚍 ℹ️ Museo Jorge Oteiza; 948 58 15 17. 🛒 Sat (every two weeks). 🎉 Santiago (25 Jul).

In the middle of a beautiful valley, straddling the banks of the Baztán river, lies the district capital of Elizondo. In Basque, the name of the town means "beside the church" Traditionally, the inhabitants of Elizondo farmed livestock, but today, despite the infertile soil, agriculture is the mainstay of the economy.

The local architecture features Gothic houses and nobles' residences decorated with coats of arms, testifying to Elizondo's long and splendid past. Reddish stone was used in the construction of most of these buildings.

The town's best-known buildings are the **Palacio de Arizcunenea**, an 18th-century Baroque palace with a façade characteristically set back from the street, and the arcaded **town hall**.

The eclectic **Iglesia de Santiago**, dedicated to the patron saint of Elizondo, was built at the beginning of the 20th century. The towers of the church are imitation Baroque; inside is a Neo-Gothic organ. Two hermitages can be visited in the vicinity of Elizondo – **San Pedro** and **Santa Engracia**.

One of the many houses built for the nobility in Elizondo

Environs

On the northern border of Navarra is **Zugarramurdi**, a town infused with the fragrance of herbs; surrounding it are pastures with grazing cows and hills dotted with large *caseríos* (country houses). Amid the scenery, in striking shades of green, stand ancient houses with coats of arms and the 18th-century **Iglesia de la Asunción**, partially destroyed during the Napoleonic Wars *(see p45)*. More famous, however, are the **Cuevas de Zugarramurdi**, just outside town. The caves are said to have been a meeting place for witches at the end of the 16th century.

🕳️ **Cuevas de Zugarramurdi**
Tel 948 59 93 05. **Open** 11am–6pm Tue–Sun (to 7pm Sat & Sun); summer: 11am–8pm daily (booking advised).
🌐 **turismozugarramurdi.com**

The Witches of Zugarramurdi

In 1609, the Inquisition initiated a trial of 40 women from Zugarramurdi, accusing them of witchcraft; 12 of the women were burnt at the stake. Since that time, the area has been associated with the Cuevas de Zugarramurdi, where witches' sabbaths (*akelarres*) are said to have taken place. *Akelarre* is a Basque word meaning "goat meadow" – it was believed that at these sabbaths the witches would meet with a demon in the form of a goat. A stream known as the Infernal River (*Infernuko Erreka*) flows through the 100-m (32-ft) long caves. Traditionally the witches' legend was commemorated by a summer festival at which roast lamb was eaten.

Cuevas de Zugarramurdi, where witches' sabbaths were supposedly held

❸ The Navarrese Pyrenees

The Navarrese Pyrenees are remarkable for the diversity of their landscape – from idyllic valleys to forbidding mountain peaks. They are a great place for active pursuits, including biking, rafting and paragliding, but also offer a good environment for pleasant walks, rest and relaxation. The towns and villages, whose inhabitants speak Basque, are full of culture and tradition. The megaliths dotted around the region testify to its long history. Wild animals find shelter in the national parks, and sheep graze in the meadows.

Tips for Drivers

Tour route: Approximately 140 km (87 miles).
Stopping-off Places: Accommodation in hotels and *casas rurales (see p202)* is easy to find in the main towns; there are also many places to eat.
Equipment: When hiking in the mountains take warm clothing, as the weather can change suddenly.

⑥ Valle de Baztán
One of the most densely wooded Navarrese valleys, this offers excellent terrain for hiking and climbing.

⑤ Lesaka
This important industrial centre and charming town has *caseríos* and fortified manors (*casas-torre*). Dolmens and other ancient tombs have been discovered nearby.

0 km   10
0 miles   5

④ Oieregi
Most of the village houses here display the valley's emblem – a mermaid with long hair, holding a comb and a mirror.

③ Selva de Irati
This is one of Europe's most extensive deciduous forests, with a preponderance of beech and fir. Deer, wild boar and martens are found here.

② Valle de Salazar
A river rich in trout flows through this beech-covered valley, where typical mountain villages are located; the best-known of these is Ochagavía, with its six stone bridges.

① Valle de Roncal
The most mountainous region of the Navarrese Pyrenees, this alpine area includes the highest peak – Mesa de los Tres Reyes (2,444 m/8,018 ft).

Key

▬▬ Tour route
▬▬ Scenic route
══ Minor road
- - - National border

For keys to symbols *see back flap*

The densely forested countryside around Roncesvalles

❹ Roncesvalles (Orreaga)

Navarra. **Road Map** C4. 🏠 30.
🛈 Antiguo Molino (Old Mill); 948 76
03 01. 🎐 Virgen de Roncesvalles
(8 Sep). 🆆 **roncesvalles.es**

High on a pass through the
Pyrenees – one of the oldest
crossings in the mountains –
is the village of Roncesvalles
(Orreaga in Basque). This old
settlement was built to serve
travellers and pilgrims heading
to Santiago de Compostela (see
pp64–7). Its most important
building is the **Colegiata Real**,
founded by Sancho VII the
Strong, who chose it as his
burial place. Inside the church
is Sancho's white tomb, lit by a
stained-glass window depicting
his great victory at the Battle
of Las Navas de Tolosa in 1212
(see p42). Below a high canopy
is a silver-plated Virgin and

Child (Virgen de Roncesvalles).
The church dates from the
13th century and is one of the
best examples of Navarrese
Gothic, although in the 17th
century it was given a more
Baroque appearance.

The 18th-century **hospital** –
the only one to have survived
to the present day – now
accommodates a youth hostel.

In a slightly out-of-the-way
location is the 12th-
century **Capilla del
Espíritu Santo**, considered
to be the oldest building
in the village. According
to legend, it was
zhere, after the
battle of 778,
that Charlemagne
ordered Roland
and the other fallen
knights to be buried
(see p41).

One of the village's
more modern
buildings is the
presbytery, or Casa
Prioral, which has an
annexe containing a
library and a museum displaying
sculpture, painting, incunabula
and precious jewellery.

A figure of the Virgin
in Roncesvalles

❺ Bosque de Irati

Navarra. **Road Map** C4. 🛈 Ochagavia;
948 89 06 41. 🆆 **irati.org**

In the dampest part of Navarra,
spread across the Salazar and
Aezkoa valleys, is this large
forest, covering an area of

17,000 ha (42,000 acres).
The trees are chiefly beech and
fir, and there are many species
of wild animal, including
red deer, fallow deer, wild
boar and capercaillie.

Hidden deep in the forest
is **Lago Irabia**; there are also
refreshing natural springs and
the fast-flowing Irati river.

At the confluence of the
Urbeltza and Urtxuria rivers
stands the **Ermita de la
Virgen de las Nieves**
(Madonna of the Snows),
while between the villages
of Lumbier, Sangüesa and
Liédena lie the ruins of
a Roman settlement.
Rising high above
the treetops are the
imposing peaks of
Pico de Orhi.

In the district of
Aezkoa are the
ruins of a small
18th-century
weapons factory –
one of the best
examples of
Spanish industrial
architecture of the period.

The Bosque de Irati leaves an
unforgettable impression on
visitors, especially in autumn,
when the beech leaves turn
beautiful colours.

❻ Valle de Salazar

Navarra. **Road Map** C5. 🛈 Ochagavia;
948 89 06 41.

In the eastern part of the
Navarrese Pyrenees extends the
Salazar river valley. Thanks to its
proximity to the sea, it is damper
than other valleys in the region
and is covered in beech woods.

Perched along the banks of
the river are typical mountain
villages featuring stone and
timber houses with thatched
roofs. The prettiest and most
characteristic of these is
Ochagavía. Preserved here
are six stone bridges as well as
the shrine of Santa María de
Muskilda, where a lively fiesta
in honour of the Virgin takes
place in September.

The inhabitants of the Valle
de Salazar earn their living
principally from sheep farming

Roland in Roncesvalles

The 12th-century French epic poem, *The Song of Roland*, describes
how the rearguard of Charlemagne's army – in which Roland led
the Frankish knights – was slaughtered by the Moors. The truth is
somewhat different, however: the victors were not Moors but warlike
Basque highlanders from Navarra,
who wanted to manifest their
independence. Preserved in
Roncesvalles is the stone
upon which Roland tried to
break his sword. A boulder
marks the spot where
Charlemagne is said to
have found the fallen
knight who, according
to legend, was buried
in the Capilla del
Espíritu Santo.

Monument bearing an image of Roland

The mountainous landscape of the Valle de Salazar

Specialities of the Navarrese Pyrenees

The rivers of the Navarrese Pyrenees are flowing with an abundance of trout, which can be caught in the spring and summer. Organized fishing trips are very popular among visitors to the area. Navarra-style trout, or *trucha a la Navarra*, is trout stuffed with *jamón serrano* (thinly sliced cured ham), and then braised in olive oil. Lamb is the most popular meat and *cordero al chilindrón* (lamb stew) features on almost every menu. The Valle de Roncal is known primarily for its local cheese – *queso de Roncal*; it is made between December and July from local sheep's milk and has a distinctive, slightly smoky flavour.

Sheep's cheese from the Valle de Roncal

and forestry. Aside from taking relaxing walks through the idyllic countryside, there is good terrain here for many active sports, including skiing and mountain biking.

❼ Valle de Roncal

Navarra. **Road Map** C5. 🚌 from Pamplona. 🛈 Paseo Julian Gayarre, s/n, Roncal; 948 47 52 56 or 948 47 53 17. 🖵 vallederoncal.es

Situated on the northeastern border of Navarra, the Valle de Roncal is the highest and most mountainous part of the province. Navarra's loftiest peak – Mesa de los Tres Reyes, or Table of the Three Kings – is situated here. Winters in the Roncal Valley are long and snowy; summers are mild.

The village of **Burgui** to the south affords panoramic views of the valley, its contours carved by the Esca river. A medieval bridge can be seen here. **Roncal** (Erronkari), a village with cobbled streets and stone houses, is the geographical heart of the valley.

There are ski runs in the small, post-glacial **Valle de Belagoa**. The district can be toured in a variety of ways: on horseback, by bike, in a four-wheel drive, or on foot.

Environs
Isaba (Izaba), the largest town in the valley, is a ski resort and a popular base for skiers and mountaineers. Situated at the confluence of three rivers, Isaba features fine houses with steep roofs and coats of arms on their façades. The 16th-century

church of San Cipriano contains a painted Plateresque reredos and a Baroque organ.

❽ Pamplona

See pp156–9.

❾ Sierra de Aralar

Navarra. **Road Map** B4. 🛈 Etxarri Aranatz; 608 17 51 90. Lekunberri, Plazaola 21; 948 50 72 04.

The Aralar mountain chain runs along the border between Navarra and the Basque province of Guipúzcoa. This ancient massif, covered in beech, oak and bracken, is criss-crossed by rivers; its highest peak is **Irumugarrieta** at 1,427 m (4,682 ft) above sea level. Some of the mountainsides are so steep that, in order to cut the grass, farmers have to tie themselves to ropes attached to trees. This area is Basque-speaking.

Several megaliths still stand in the area, including the **Albi dolmen**, and a short distance

away are circular shepherds' huts known as *arkuek*.

High in the mountains is the Romanesque **shrine of San Miguel**, with three aisles and apses. The Archangel Michael was traditionally venerated in the area; it was believed he shared some traits with Hermes and was a messenger between heaven and earth. Inside the shrine is a silver-coated figure of him with a crucifix on his head. There is also a superb 12th-century enamelled reredos in the Romanesque-Byzantine style; its centrepiece is an image of the Virgin and Child surrounded by 18 medallions depicting mythological and religious scenes.

Environs
Lekumberri (Lekunberri) is a base for excursions into the valley and mountains. Here are some excellent *caseríos* (Basque farmhouses) bearing coats of arms as well as the aisleless Gothic church of San Juan Bautista, dating from the 13th century. Local crafts can be purchased in the town.

Stone houses with characteristic white chimneys in the Valle de Roncal

❽ Pamplona (Iruña)

In 75 BC, the Roman general Pompey founded the town of Pompaelo on the site of the old Basque settlement of Iruña. Strategically located on the river at the foot of the Pyrenees, Pamplona played the role of a fortified border town. Today, it is the financial, commercial and academic centre of Navarra, offering visitors fine cuisine and pleasant walks along the riverside or through the Old Town. Each July, the world-famous San Fermín festival, with its bull running, totally transforms the city.

Exploring Pamplona

To fully appreciate its charms, Pamplona, with its parks and wide avenues, is best explored on foot. From the old city walls – situated to the north in a loop of the Arga river – you can get a good overview. Going south, the Old Town ends at a massive citadel.

The walls of the city's 16th-century citadel, among parks and gardens

⬆ Ciudadela

Felipe II ordered the construction of Pamplona's citadel in 1571. From the outside, the building looks rather decrepit – grass is yellowed by the sun, and its moats have long been empty – but once you pass through the main entrance, the impression is very different. Encircling the well-kept lawn are the citadel's former buildings, now converted into exhibition rooms. The oldest structure is the powder magazine (Polvorín), dating from 1694. You can climb up the embankment onto one of the surviving bastions for a view of the area.

⬚ Palacio de Navarra

Avenida Carlos III 2; 848 42 71 27. **Open** To large groups only (not individuals), by prior arrangement. ♿

This Neo-Classical palace, designed in 1840 by Juan de Nagusia, is the seat of the provincial government. Set in the tympanum is the Navarra coat of arms flanked by two men – a highlander and an inhabitant of the river basin. Inside is a portrait of Fernando VII by Goya, as well as many other paintings – mostly portraits – from the 19th and 20th centuries. In front of the palace stands a column topped by a symbolic statue of a woman upholding the historic laws (fueros) of Navarra.

⬚ Plaza del Castillo

The square owes its name to a castle raised here in the 14th century. Initially used as a marketplace and place for fiestas, it later became a venue for bullfights, when the balconies of the surrounding houses were used as seating areas. Until the 19th century, the square was enclosed. In 1931, a theatre along one of its sides was destroyed to make way for Avenida Carlos III, an avenue linking the square with the city's new districts.

The colourful façade of one of the city's tenements

⬆ Iglesia San Saturnino

Also known as Iglesia de San Cernín, this Romanesque church (13th century) was built on the site where St Saturninus is said to have baptized some 40,000 pagan townspeople. One of its massive towers is a clock tower, topped by a cockerel – the Gallico de San Cernín, a symbol of the city. In the 18th century, the church's cloister was replaced by the Baroque Capilla della Virgen del Camino. Its beautiful reredos contains a 12th-century wooden robed figure of the Virgin, covered in silver tiles.

⬚ Museo de Navarra

C/Santo Domingo 47; 848 42 64 92. **Open** 9:30am–2pm & 5–7pm Tue–Sat, 11am–2pm Sun and holidays. 🎫 (free Sat pm & Sun). 📷 by prior arrangement. ♿

The Museum of Navarra is located inside the former Hospital de Nuestra Señora

---

The Kingdom of Navarra

Navarra emerged as an independent Christian kingdom in the 9th century, after Sancho I Garcés became king of Pamplona. Sancho III the Great expanded the kingdom, and at his death, in 1035, Navarra stretched from Ribagorza (in Aragón) to Valladolid, but his heirs failed to hold the kingdom together. Sancho VI the Wise (1150–94), recognized the independent rights (fueros) of many towns. In 1234, Navarra passed by marriage to French rulers. In 1512, Fernando II of Castile annexed it as part of a united Spain.

Carlos de Viana, one of the last leaders of independent Navarra

de la Misericordia. Its highlights include Roman mosaics, Gothic and Baroque murals, Romanesque capitals from the cathedral cloister, and an ivory casket that draws inspiration from Islamic decorative motifs.

Richly decorated stalls in the Catedral de Santa María la Real

🏛 Cathedral

C/Dormitalería 1; 948 21 25 94. **Open** 10:30am–6pm Mon–Sat; 10am–2pm, 6:30–9pm Sun (visitor access is through the museum). 🏛 📷

The cathedral of Santa María la Real was built during the 13th–16th centuries, and later remodelled several times. This aisled Gothic shrine has a Rococo sacristy, chapels from various periods, and a Neo-Classical façade designed by Ventura Rodríguez. One of the two towers holds the 12-tonne María bell. Inside, some of the painted decoration on the walls and pillars has been restored. The cloister, with its beautifully carved 14th-century gateways (Puerta Preciosa and Puerta de Amparo) is a masterpiece of European Gothic style.

The Museo Docesano houses a collection of religious art from all over Navarra, including a set of medieval statues of the Virgin.

🎪 Plaza de Toros

Pamplona's bullring, known as the Monumental, holds around 19,500 spectators and is surpassed in size only by the arenas in Madrid and Mexico City. Designed by Francisco Urcola, the Monumental was officially opened in 1922. Several improvements were made in 2005, including the addition of a lift and vehicles for disabled

people, making it one of the most modern bullrings in Spain. The famous July bull run – the *encierro* – ends here.

A square with fountains in the city centre

Pamplona City Centre

① Ciudadela
② Palacio de Navarra
③ Plaza del Castillo
④ Iglesia San Saturnino
⑤ Museo de Navarra
⑥ Cathedral
⑦ Plaza de Toros

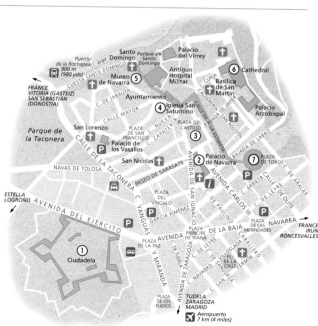

Key

▨ Bull-running route

0 metres 200
0 yards 200

For keys to symbols *see back flap*

San Fermín

This fiesta in honour of Navarra's patron saint, St Fermín (the first bishop of Pamplona), is famous for the *encierro* – a bull run through the Old Town of Pamplona. Starting at the Plaza de Santo Domingo and ending at the bullring, the 840-m (half-mile) bull run occurs daily from 7 to 14 July. However, San Fermín is not just about bulls – this hugely popular fiesta includes parades with orchestras, official state and religious ceremonies, and street dancing and singing. There is also a lot of drinking and good, spontaneous fun.

A statue of St Fermín, Navarra's patron saint, is carried from the town hall to the cathedral in ceremonial procession on 7 July.

Fighting bulls are bred at special ranches and must weigh 460-500 kg (1,014–1,102 lbs) before entering the *corrida*.

The *encierro*, which lasts around four minutes, ends at the Plaza de Toros, where *corridas* are held in the evenings. Although running in front of enraged bulls is dangerous, this does not deter the local young men, keen to display their courage.

Streets and squares filled with colourful, joyous crowds epitomize the fiesta in Pamplona. The various events, especially the hair-raising bull runs, are attended by thousands of onlookers.

The sand in the bullring must be clean and even so that nothing on its surface distracts the bull.

***Encierro* participants** must be physically fit, with good reflexes. Most are dressed in a white shirt and trousers (some wear jeans instead), with a red belt and scarf, and a matching beret.

Bullfights *(Corridas)*

The corrida *begins with a parade set to the spirited music of the* pasodoble. *In the first stage of the bullfight, the mounted* picadores *goad the bull with their steel-pointed lances; in the second, the* banderilleros *provoke the wounded bull by sticking pairs of darts in its back; in the third stage, the matador is left to fight the bull alone.*

The procession of St Fermín includes clergy, town officials and crowds of local people. Dressed in traditional costumes, the men carry pennants displaying the coat of arms of Pamplona and the emblem of Navarra.

Gigantes – huge figures dressed in vivid and often elaborate costumes, participate in the procession in honour of St Fermín. They add colour to the celebrations and are especially popular with children.

The scarlet and yellow cape is used in the second stage of the bullfight. The bull is attracted by the movement of the cape, not by its colour!

The matador wears a *traje de luces* (suit of lights) – a colourful silk outfit embroidered with gold sequins.

The bull's horns are deadly. Only true masters of the art of bullfighting dare to get this close to an angry bull.

The traditional orchestras that take part in the processions and parades are composed of musicians playing *txistu* flutes, clarinets, bagpipes and drums. The parades often have orchestras made up of young boys, who take their role much more seriously than their older counterparts.

Ernest Hemingway

It is thanks to Hemingway and his novel *The Sun Also Rises* that the previously obscure festival of Los Sanfermines was transformed into a riotous international event.

In the 1920s and 1950s, Hemingway visited Pamplona on several occasions, not only to witness the fiesta but also to participate in it. Several of the places he frequented still exist: the Txoko bar, the La Perla hotel, the Iruña café. In 1968, a monument in honour of the Nobel prize-winning author was erected near the arena.

Hemingway – an admirer of the *corrida*

Fun and dancing are an integral part of the fiesta. The *jota* is danced in honour of St Fermín, and people sing for a blessing before the bull run.

A church with three apses near the Monasterio de Leyre

⑩ Monasterio de Leyre

Yesa (Navarra). **Road Map** C5. 🚌 from Yesa. **Tel** 948 88 41 50. **Open** daily. 🅿 **W** monasteriodeleyre.com

The monastery of San Salvador de Leyre is situated high above a reservoir, alone amid breathtaking scenery, backed by limestone cliffs.

The abbey is mentioned in documents dating from the 9th century; in the 10th and 11th centuries, the kings of Navarra found refuge here from the Moors. The abbey experienced its Golden Age in the 11th century, when it was reconstructed by Sancho III the Great, having suffered damage at the hands of the Muslim general Al-Mansur.

In keeping with Cistercian rule, the church is austere in appearance. Of note are the three semicircular apses of equal height. The tower, built on a square base, has triforia (galleries) in each of its walls. Nearby is the entrance to the unusual crypt – underneath its arches rises a forest of squat, completely unadorned columns. The kings of Navarra are buried here.

The façade of the church is decorated with carvings of strange beasts, birds and human figures intertwined with plant motifs. The monks' Gregorian chant during services is wonderful to hear. Part of the monastery now accommodates a hotel.

⑪ Castillo de Javier

Javier (Navarra). **Road Map** C5. 🚌 from Pamplona. **Tel** 948 88 40 24. **Open** 10am–1:30pm & 3:30–6:30pm daily. 🅿 **W** santuariojaviersj.org

In the 10th and 11th centuries, prior to the construction of the castle, a watchtower stood here, to which new buildings were gradually added. In the 16th century, Cardinal Cisneros ordered the castle to be redesigned as a fortress, but in recent times the complex has been restored, including its towers and drawbridge. It now houses a Jesuit college.

St Francis Xavier, a missionary and co-founder of the Jesuit order (and the patron saint of Navarra sportsmen and *pelota* players), was born in the castle in 1506. Preserved here are his bedroom and a chapel with a Gothic walnut crucifix. According to legend, at difficult moments in the saint's life, and on the anniversary of his death, droplets of blood appeared on the crucifix.

The chapel walls are decorated with a macabre mural of grinning skeletons, a depiction of The Dance of Death. Every year from 4 to 12 March, the inhabitants of Navarra make a penitent pilgrimage to the castle chapel.

A crucifix in the Castillo de Javier

⑫ Sangüesa

Navarra. **Road Map** C5. 🏔 5,300. 🚌 ℹ C/Mayor 2; 948 87 14 11. 🚆 Fri. 🎉 San Sebastián (11–17 Sep). **W** sanguesa.es

Set on the pilgrimage route of St James, this town was one of the main trading centres in the region. The **Iglesia de Santa María la Real**, whose construction began in the 12th century, has a splendid Romanesque portal. Preserved in the sacristy is a 15th-century processional monstrance, measuring 1.35 m (4.4 ft) in height. The Romanesque-Gothic **Iglesia de Santiago el Mayor** has a battlemented tower. Inside, it is decorated with motifs of the pilgrimage route – scallop shells (*vieiras*), walking sticks and gourds. A polychrome stone figure of St James was discovered under the church.

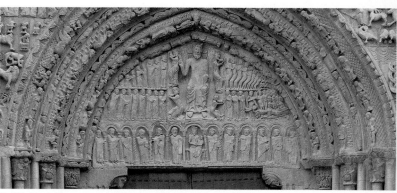

The richly decorated Romanesque portal of the Iglesia de Santa María la Real in Sangüesa

For hotels and restaurants see pp206–7 and pp221–2

The 11th-century bridge in Puente la Reina

⑬ Puente la Reina

Navarra. **Road Map** B5. 🏠 2,900. 🚌
ℹ️ Calle Mayor 105; 948 34 13 01.
🛒 Sat. 🎉 🎊 Santiago (24–30 Jul).

Puente la Reina takes its name from the seven-span, humpbacked bridge built here for pilgrims in the 11th century. On the central section that no longer exists stood a figure of the Virgen del Txori, which was transferred to the church of San Pedro in the 19th century.

On the opposite side of town rises the Romanesque-Gothic **Iglesia del Crucifijo** (13th-century), a church ostensibly built by the Knights Templar. A walkway above the beautifully sculpted entrance connects the church with the pilgrims' hostel. Inside the church is a 14th-century Y-shaped crucifix that was carved from a single tree trunk.

Environs
Isolated in fields about 5 km (3 miles) east of Puente la Reina is the tiny Romanesque **Ermita de Santa María de Eunate**, built in the 12th century. The hermitage's irregular octagonal plan is clearly visible on the Mozarabic-inspired vaulting. Around the church runs a remarkable cloister with many arches; some claim the hermitage is named after the cloister – in Basque *ehun atea* means "one hundred doors".

⑭ Estella (Lizarra)

Navarra. **Road Map** B5. 🏠 14,200. 🚌
ℹ️ C/San Nicolás 1; 948 55 63 01.
🛒 Thu. 🎉 🎊 San Andrés (1st week Aug). 🌐 **estellaturismo.com**

King Sancho Ramírez, who founded Estella in the 11th century, ensured that the pilgrimage route to Santiago passed through the town. Today, Estella is famous for its historic churches, palaces and monasteries, for which it has been dubbed the Toledo of the North. Close to the Ega river stands the **Palacio de los Reyes de Navarra**, the only surviving example of secular Romanesque architecture in the province. Near it, crowning a steep hill, is the **Iglesia de San Pedro de la Rúa**, with an original 13th-century

Coat of arms on a house in Estella

portal and 12th-century cloister. The north portal of the Iglesia de San Miguel (12th- to 14th-century) is adorned with a bas-relief depicting St Michael slaying a dragon. Preserved on Calle Mayor are several houses with coats of arms, including a 17th-century Baroque palace.

⑮ Monasterio de Irache

Ayegui (Navarra). **Road Map** B5.
🚌 Monastery: **Tel** 948 55 44 64.
Open 10am–1:15pm & 4–7pm Wed–Sun (to 6pm in winter). 🎉 book in advance. Museo del Vino: **Tel** 948 55 19 32. **Open** 10am–2pm & 3:30–6pm Sat & Sun (until 7pm in summer). 🎉 book in advance.

The word *iratze* means "fern" in Basque, and there were probably many ferns growing in the vicinity when the Benedictine monks began construction of their monastery in the 11th century. The pilgrims' hostel here was the first to be built in the region. Since the monastery has always been inhabited, the entire complex has been preserved in excellent condition. It comprises a 12th-century church, a cloister in the Plateresque style, a tower, and a Spanish Baroque building that served as a university from 1569 to 1824. The aisleless church features three semicircular apses. The famous Bodegas Irache next to the monastery provides thirsty pilgrims with a free glass of wine.

The Romanesque Palacio de los Reyes de Navarra in Estella

⑯ Viana

Navarra. **Road Map** B5. 🏔 4,000.
ℹ Plaza de los Fueros 1; 948 44 63 02.
🗓 Fri. 🎭 Santa María Magdalena (21–25 Jul).

In the Middle Ages, Viana was an important strategic town, fortified to defend Navarra from Castilian invasions, and a stop on the pilgrimage route of St James. Its massive **town walls** with four gates date from that period, as do the **castle** and churches of Santa María and San Pedro. Viana thrived between the 16th and 18th centuries, when aristocrats built Renaissance and Baroque palaces, decorated with coats of arms, wrought-iron balconies and wooden eaves.

Preserved to this day is the Gothic **Iglesia de Santa María**, with a 16th-century Plateresque façade. Its small windows testify to the building's original defensive purpose. Fine 18th-century paintings by Luis Paret y Alcázar hang in the chapel of San Juan del Ramo.

Near Viana, above the Embalse de las Canas reservoir, is a bird sanctuary.

Detail of a bas-relief on the Iglesia de Santa María in Viana

The monumental Gothic palace in Olite

important defensive role by guarding the Pamplona road. It was first mentioned in a 10th-century Arabic chronicle.

The old quarter, with its cobbled streets, retains a medieval feel. The originally Gothic **Iglesia de Santa María**, rebuilt in the 16th to 18th centuries, is a monumental structure of rather spartan appearance. The **Iglesia de San Pedro** – originally Romanesque – was also remodelled; its Baroque tower is crowned by an octagonal lantern.

Environs

Artajona, situated 11 km (7 miles) northwest of Tafalla, is the only place in Navarra to feature completely preserved medieval walls (13th-century). The main element of the fortifications is the massive Gothic Iglesia de San Saturnino, which has loopholes in its walls and a tower that served as a prison, a belfry and an observation point.

⑱ Olite

Navarra. **Road Map** B5. 🏔 3,900. 🚌
ℹ Plaza Teobaldos 10; 948 74 17 03.
🎭 Virgen del Cólera (26 Aug), Fiestas Medievales (2nd half of Aug), Fiestas Patronales (13–19 Sep). 🌐 olite.es

Olite, once a royal residence of the kings of Navarra, still has fragments of Roman and medieval walls. In the 15th century, Carlos III set about constructing here a monumental eclectic **Palacio Real**, regarded as a gem of Navarrese Gothic style. The palace was meticulously rebuilt in the 19th century after a devastating fire. Next to the complex is a network of medieval underground passageways – remnants of Carlos III's plan to link his residence with the palace in Tafalla. The Gothic **Iglesia de Santa María La Real** features a richly carved portal and a superb Renaissance reredos. The highlights of the 12th-century **Iglesia de San**

Cesare Borgia (1475–1507) in Viana

The son of the corrupt Pope Alexander VI, Cesare Borgia was showered with a series of high church offices, becoming Bishop of Pamplona at 17 and a cardinal at 22, but he left the Church to become his father's chief henchman, and married the sister of Juan III of Navarra. Brutal and single-minded, he was an effective politician and soldier in Renaissance Italy, leading the papal armies in many campaigns. The sudden death of his father in 1503 ended his influence at the papal court. He fled from Italy to Aragón, only to be imprisoned, but escaped to Navarra, where Juan III was fighting against Castilian and French nobles. Cesare died in a siege in 1507, in Viana.

A monument to Cesare Borgia in Viana

⑰ Tafalla

Navarra. **Road Map** B5. 🏔 11,000. 🚌
ℹ C/Túbal 19; 948 70 16 54. 🗓 Fri.
🎭 San Sebastián (20 Jan), Virgen de la Asunción (14–20 Aug).

Legend has it that Tafalla was founded by Tubal, Noah's grandson. What is known for sure is that it performed an

Pedro Apóstol are the Romanesque cloister and the squat Gothic tower topped by a huge spire.

🏛 Palacio Real de Olite
Tel 948 74 00 35. **Open** Oct–Mar: 10am–6pm daily; Apr–Jun & Sep: 10am–7pm Mon–Fri, 10am–8pm Sat, Sun & hols; Jul & Aug: 10am–8pm daily. **Closed** 1 & 6 Jan. 🌐 📷

Environs
To the east of Olite is **Ujué**, one of the better-preserved villages in the lower Pyrenees. It has the medieval atmosphere of a stronghold concentrated around the imposing fortified church of Santa María. It has columns with capitals depicting human and animal figures. The heart of Carlos II is found inside the church.

⑲ Monasterio de la Oliva

Carcastillo (Navarra). **Road Map** C5. 🚌 🚃 from Tafalla. **Tel** 948 72 50 06. **Open** 9am–12:30pm & 3:30–6pm Mon–Sat, 9–11:30am & 4–6pm Sun. 🌐

Visitors are greeted with a serene atmosphere at this Cistercian monastery, whose design is characterized by asceticism and simplicity. The monastery was founded in 1143 by the king of Navarra, García

Window, Monasterio de la Oliva

Ramírez. Its aisled church has five chapels, the largest closed by a semicircular apse. Nearby is the complex's oldest building – the Capilla de San Jesucristo.

Storks' nests on top of the Colegiata de Santa María Magdalena in Tudela

⑳ Tudela

Navarra. **Road Map** B6. 🚁 35,500. 🚌 🚃 ℹ Plaza Fueros 5; 948 84 80 58. 🏛 Sat. 🎿 Santa Ana (24–30 Jul). 🌐 **tudela.es**

In medieval times, Tudela was subject to both Christian and Moorish influence, as is aptly demonstrated by the Romanesque-Gothic **Colegiata de Santa María Magdalena**. The church was built on the ruins of a mosque, and one of its Mudéjar chapels – dating from the 16th century – may have been a synagogue originally. Decorative elements from the former mosque are found in the Romanesque cloister. Next to the cathedral rises the 16th-century **Palacio Decanal**, with a Plateresque façade and arcaded gallery. Bullfights once took place on the busy **Plaza de los Fueros**, the city's main square. The **Judería Vétula** is the old Jewish quarter, with tall, narrow brick houses with broad eaves.

㉑ Bárdenas Reales

Navarra. **Road Map** B5–C5. ℹ 948 83 03 08. Park: **Open** 8am–1 hour before dusk daily. 🌐 **bardenasreales.es**

Between the Ebro and Aragón rivers extends a breathtaking natural park of weathered cliffs and crags. Bárdenas Reales is an uninhabited area almost devoid of vegetation. To the north rises a plateau, El Plano de Bárdenas; in the middle is the Bárdena Blanca, named for its white gypsum cliffs; and to the south is the Bárdena Negra, composed of reddish clay and limestone. Centuries of erosion have given rise to plateaus, plains, rock-needles and river ravines.

In nearby Valtierra, the local caves have been converted into a guesthouse – a good place to stop before setting off on one of the trails through the geological formations.

Colourful rocks worn into fantastic shapes, the remarkable Bárdenas Reales

㉒ Logroño

La Rioja. **Road Map** B5. ⛰ 152,000.
✈ 🚉 🛈 C/ Portales 50; 941 29 12 60.
🚌 Sun. 🎉 San Bernabé (7–11 Jun),
San Mateo (20–27 Sep).
🌐 lariojaturismo.com

Logroño lies on the banks
of the Ebro river, spanned
by the **Puente de Piedra**, a
19th-century stone bridge
designed by Fermín Manso
de Zúniga. It grew over the
centuries, thanks to its location
on the Ebro as well as along the
pilgrimage route of St James.
Today, the city's showpiece is

The stone Puente de Piedra, spanning the Ebro river in Logroño

Baroque high altar in the cathedral of
Santa María de la Redonda

the **Catedral de Santa María de
la Redonda**, with its massive
twin towers and rich Baroque
ornamentation. Of note inside
are the Capilla de Nuestra
Señora de la Paz, containing a
Plateresque reredos, and the
tomb of the cathedral's founder,
Diego Ponce de León.

Near the cathedral stands
the 13th-century **Iglesia de
San Bartolomé**, which might
have formed part of the city's
fortifications. Its impressive
Gothic portal is adorned with
sculpted figures of Christ, the
Virgin, the apostles and saints.
The 16th-century tower shows
Mudéjar influence.

Only a small section of
the **Murallas de Revellín** –
12th-century city walls –
survive, encompassing the
Puerta Revellín, adorned with
the coat of arms of Carlos V.
The monumental 16th-century
Iglesia de Santiago el Real
once housed the archives of
the city council.

The **Iglesia de Santa María
de Palacio** has taken on an
irregular form over the centuries,
and it is difficult to imagine its
original appearance. The most
beautiful element is the
13th-century octagonal tower,
resembling a massive pyramid,
which locals have dubbed
the *aguja* (needle). The Neo-
Classical main portal is adorned
with a figure of the Virgin and
of angels playing instruments.

Logroño City Centre

① Cathedral
② Iglesia de San Bartolomé
③ Murallas de Revellín
④ Iglesia de Santiago el Real
⑤ Iglesia de Santa María
   de Palacio
⑥ Puente de Piedra

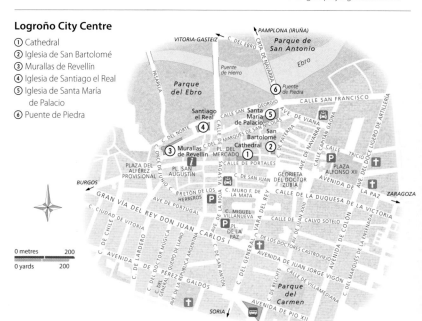

❷❸ Calahorra

La Rioja. **Road Map** B5. 📷 25,000. 🚌
🚉 ℹ️ Plaza del Raso 16; 941 10 50 61.
📅 San Emeterio and San Celedonio
(1–3 Mar). 🌐 **lariojaturismo.com**

Calahorra's history stretches
back almost 2,000
years. Originally
known by its Roman
name of Calagurris, it
was one of the Iberian
peninsula's most
important cities. On
the banks of the
Cidacos river, at
the spot where
its patron saints,
the legionnaires
Emeterio and
Celedonio, are
thought to have
been martyred,
rises a 15th-century
cathedral with a Neo-
Classical façade by
the Raón brothers.
In the cathedral's
chapel of San Pedro
is a Plateresque reredos.

A figure from the
church in Calahorra

The **Iglesia de San Andrés**,
whose construction began in
the 16th century, features a
remarkable tympanum; a crucifix,
with arms of unequal length. On
the door at the main entrance is
a carving that symbolizes the
victory of Christianity over
paganism, the latter represented
by the sun, the moon and a
synagogue. The austere tower is
built of stone and brick. Inside
the church is a magnificent
Rococo altar by Manuel Adán.

The **Monasterio de San José**
was built in the 16th century.
At the high altar are murals
depicting scenes from the life
of St Theresa. To the side of the
altar is a *Flagellation of Christ*,
by Gregorio Hernández.

❷❹ Enciso

La Rioja. **Road Map** B6. 📷 160. 🚌
📅 San Pedro (29 Jun), San Roque y
Virgen de la Estrella (15–16 Aug).

This tiny village of white houses
with red roofs was once a centre
of sheep farming and textiles,
but its best days have long since
passed. Nowadays only one
factory produces the woollen

rugs for which the village was
once renowned. Enciso and the
other villages in the area are
now largely depopulated.

Two important churches
survive here: the 16th-century
Santa María de la Estrella, with
a square tower and a beautiful
15th-century figure of the
Virgin; and the aisleless **San
Pedro**, featuring a 12th-century
battlemented tower. A few
hermitages and the ruins of a
castle are also in the area.

Each year the region
attracts a plethora of
tourists to see the *huellas
de dinosaurios* (dinosaur
footprints), dating from
the Mesozoic period and
spread across several sites.
Visitors can follow the
dinosaur trail from
El Barranco Perdido,
an adventure park that
includes a museum of
palaeontology.

🏛️ **El Barranco Perdido**
Enciso, La Rioja. **Tel** 941 39 60 80.
Open end Mar–mid-Jun & Sep–
mid-Oct: 11am–6:30pm Sat, Sun
& public hols; mid-Jun–mid-Jul:
11am–7pm Tue–Sun; mid-Jul–
end Aug: 11am–8pm daily. 🅿️ 🎫
🌐 **barrancoperdido.com**

❷❺ Navarrete

La Rioja. **Road Map** A5. 📷 2,800. 🚌
ℹ️ Cuesta El Caño; 941 44 10 62.
📅 Wed. 📅 La Virgen y San Roque
(15–16 Aug).

The town of Navarrete, situated
on what was once the border
between Navarra and Castile,

The high altar at Iglesia de la Asunción
in Navarrete

has had many different owners
over the centuries. Today, thanks
to a programme of renovation
the ancient houses with stone
coats of arms (of which there
are more than 50) have
recovered some of their former
splendour. Fine examples can
be seen on **Calle Mayor**.
Running behind the street
is **Cal Nueva**, the former
approach road to the
underground bodegas.

The aisled **Iglesia de la
Asunción**, with a Renaissance
façade and two porticoes, was
begun in the 16th century;
inside is a Baroque reredos.

Not far from Navarrete is a
cemetery whose entrance gate
is the portico of a former pilgrims' hostel. This Romanesque
structure, with elements of early
Gothic, is composed of five
arches, including pointed ones,
decorated with scenes from
the lives of pilgrims and of
St George fighting the dragon.

Dinosaurs from La Rioja

Approximately 100 million years ago, during the Mesozoic period,
La Rioja was a vast river delta – a marshy landscape covered in rich
vegetation. Among the numerous animals living here were dinosaurs,
both carnivorous and
herbivorous, who left their
footprints in the mud.
Over the millennia, due
to geological changes, the
mud turned into rock, and
many of the footprints
have been preserved;
they can be seen on the
marked trails that lead
through the area.

Reconstructed dinosaurs in Valdecevillo

For hotels and restaurants see pp206–7 and pp221–2

㉖ Anguiano and Sierra de la Demanda

La Rioja. **Road Map** A5–6, G3. ⌖ 550. ▦ ⓘ Rioja tourism; 941 29 12 60. ⌖ Santa María Magdalena (22–24 Jul).

With its stone bridge (Puente de la Madre de Dios) that spans the 30-m (98-ft) wide valley of the Najerilla river, Anguiano is famous for the *Danza de los Zancos* that occurs here during the feast of St Mary Magdalene (and on the last weekend in September). The dancers, balanced on stilts, have to negotiate the steep, cobbled street of Cuesta de los Danzadores in time to the music. The dance commemorates a rite of passage that young men had to undergo in the past.

The Sierra de la Demanda is an ancient mountain range that also extends into the province of Burgos. The forested hillsides (inhabited by wild animals) contain many postglacial formations – moraines, cirques and lagoons; San Lorenzo (2,272 m/7,454 ft above sea level) is the highest peak. The mountain chain also conceals archaeological treasures such as medieval hermitages and necropolises. In **Cuyacabras**, there are 166 anthropomorphic tombs and the remnants of a church.

Typical scenery in the Sierra de la Demanda

Mansilla de la Sierra has a 16th-century stone bridge and is located next to the Embalse de Mansilla, a reservoir that is popular for watersports. The Sierra has examples of Romanesque architecture, such as in **Jaramillo de la Fuente**.

Monasterio de Santa María la Real in Nájera

㉗ Nájera

La Rioja. **Road Map** A5, G3. ⌖ 8,500. ▦ ⓘ Plaza de San Miguel 10; 941 36 00 41. ◷ Thu. ⌖ San Prudencio (28 Apr), San Juan and San Pedro (24–29 Jun), San Juan Mártir and Santa María La Real (16–19 Sep). 🚗 🖥 najera.es

At the beginning of the 11th century, when Sancho III of Navarra managed for a time to unite the lands of the Iberian Peninsula, Nájera was capital of this vast empire. A pre-Roman town, Nájera had earlier played host to diverse cultures and communities, from ancient Basque tribes to the Moors. Cut by the Najerilla river, the town has many historic monuments. The most important is the **Monasterio de Santa María la Real**, established in the 11th century on the spot where, according to legend, a statue of the Virgin was found in a cave. The present buildings date from 1422–53, with later elements added until the 16th century. The Gothic aisled church is fortress-like in appearance. At the high altar is a Romanesque sculpture of the Virgin and Child. The beautiful late-Gothic choir is one of the finest examples of this style in Spain. At the back of this is a Renaissance royal pantheon holding the tombs of 12 former rulers of the kingdom of Nájera-Pamplona. Worth seeing too, are the Knights' Cloister (Claustro de los Caballeros), which combines several different architectural styles including ornate filigree Gothic and Plateresque elements, and the Tapa del Sepulcro de Blanca de Navarra, a 12th-century Romanesque tomb lid.

🏛 **Monasterio de Santa María la Real**

Tel 941 36 10 83. **Open** 10am–1pm & 4–7pm (until 5:30pm in winter) Tue–Sat, 10am–12:30pm & 4–6pm (until 5:30pm in winter) Sun & hols. ♿ 🖥 santamarialareal.net

Mountain Villages in the Sierra de la Demanda

Preserved in the Sierra de la Demanda are villages with typical highland homesteads, as well as important historic monuments. Romanesque churches can be seen in Vizcaínos and Jaramillos de la Frontera. The beautiful village of Canales de la Sierra is entirely made up of unchanged, centuries-old stone houses, including grand 16th-century buildings and the 12th-century Santa Catalina hermitage. At the Gothic church in the Valvanera monastery, people worship the patron saint of La Rioja – the Virgen de la Valvanera.

Virgen de la Valvanera, patron saint of La Rioja

㉘ Santo Domingo de la Calzada

La Rioja. **Road Map** A5, G3. 🏔 7,000.
🚌 ℹ Calle Mayor 33; 941 34 12 38.
📅 Sat. 🎭 Fiestas del Santo (10–15
May). 🌐 **lariojaturismo.com**

In the Middle Ages, a hermit
named Domingo established a
hospital and built a bridge over
the Oja river to aid pilgrims on
their journey to Santiago. In
time, a town formed here.

St Dominic's remains are kept
in the 12th-century **cathedral.**
Ornamentation depicting the
Tree of Jesse can be seen on the
pilasters by the entrance to the
chancel. The former high altar,
currently placed in one of the
aisles, is the Renaissance
work of Damià Forment.
The choir, decorated
with figures of saints
and inscriptions
on the stalls, is a
masterpiece of the
Plateresque style.

The most bizarre
element is a cage
set in a wall in
which a live cock-
erel and hen are
kept. The animals
commemorate a
miracle attributed
to St Dominic. It is
said he resurrected a German
pilgrim who had been unjustly
hanged. When the pilgrim's
parents found their son still
alive on the gallows, they
rushed to tell the judge, who
exclaimed, "Nonsense, he's no
more alive than this roast
chicken on my plate!"
Whereupon the chicken stood
up on the plate and crowed.

St Dominic, patron saint of
Santo Domingo de la Calzada

㉙ San Millán de la Cogolla

La Rioja. **Road Map** A5, G3. 🏔 300. 🚌
ℹ Monasterio de Yuso; 941 37 30 49.
Monasterio de Suso: 941 37 30 82
(visits must be booked in advance).
Open Tue–Sun. 🎭 Traslación de las
Reliquias (26 Sep), San Millán y Santa
Gertrudis (12 & 17 Nov). 🎫 🚫 only.
🌐 **monasteriodesanmillan.com**

This village grew up around
two monasteries. On a hillside
above the village is the

Monasterio de San Millán de Yuso, in San
Millán de la Cogolla

**Monasterio de San Millán
de Suso** ("Suso" meaning
upper). It was built in the
10th century on the site of
a community of monks
who lived in caves,
founded by St
Emilian (San
Millán), a shepherd
hermit, in 547. The
church, hollowed
out of pink
sandstone, has
Romanesque and
Mozarabic features.
It contains the
tomb of St Emilian
and the graves of
seven infants of
Lara who, according to legend,
were kidnapped and beheaded
by the Moors.

The **Monasterio de San
Millán de Yuso** ("Yuso" meaning
lower) is in the Cárdenas Valley.
It was built between the 16th
and 18th centuries on the site
of an 11th-century monastery.

The part-Renaissance church
has Baroque golden doors
and a Rococo sacristy, where
17th-century paintings are
hung. The treasury has a
collection of ivory plaques,
once part of two 11th-century
jewelled reliquaries, then plundered by French troops in 1813.

Medieval manuscripts are
also displayed in the treasury.
Among them is a facsimile of
one of the earliest-known texts
in Basque and early Castilian.
It is a commentary by a
10th-century Suso monk on a
work by San Cesáreo de Arles,
the *Glosas Emilianenses.*

㉚ Haro

La Rioja. **Road Map** A5, G2. 🏔 12,000.
🚉 🚌 ℹ Plaza de la Paz; 941 30 35
80. 🎫 📅 Tue, Sat. 🎭 San Pedro
(29 Jun), Virgen de la Vega (8 Sep).
🌐 **haro.org**

Set among extensive vineyards
on the Ebro river, Haro is the
capital of the Rioja Alta region.
The town's main monument is a
Baroque **basilica** devoted to its
patron saint, Nuestra Señora de
la Vega – there's a Gothic figure
of her on the high altar. Of note,
too, is the **Iglesia de Santo
Tomás**, which features star
vaulting and a Baroque tower.
The portal was designed as an
altar and depicts scenes from
the Way of the Cross.

Several bodegas in Haro
offer tours and wine tastings,
and at the end of June the
town's fiesta finishes with a
wine-throwing battle.

The modern architecture of Bodegas Muga, a winery in Haro

㉛ La Rioja Wines

The Rioja wine region, which extends into Navarra and Alava, has been producing wine since the Middle Ages. Vines have taken root extremely well on the sunny hillsides, the soil irrigated by the Ebro river and its tributaries. Atlantic winds blow across the western part, while the eastern part is subject to Mediterranean winds. There are three sub-regions: Rioja Alta, Rioja Baja and Rioja Alavesa. There are over 450 wineries in the region. Typical grape varieties used are *tempranillo* and *garnacha*.

② **Haro**
Haro's limestone-clay soils produce full-bodied wines that are typical of La Rioja. Among the local wineries are the Bodega Cooperativa and Viña Tondonia, with its futuristic pavilion and carafe-shaped wine shop designed by Zaha Hadid.

① **Briñas**
In this tiny village rises a proud 18th-century palace, which has been transformed into the wonderful Hospedería del Señorío de Briñas. The hotel puts on special events that introduce guests to the world of wine.

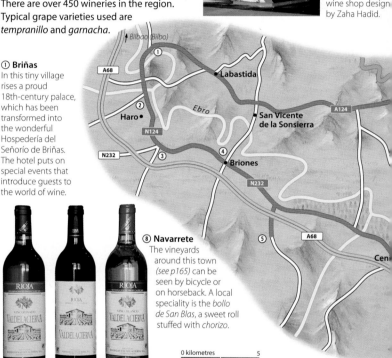

⑧ **Navarrete**
The vineyards around this town *(see p165)* can be seen by bicycle or on horseback. A local speciality is the *bollo de San Blas*, a sweet roll stuffed with *chorizo*.

| 0 kilometres | 5 |
| 0 miles | 5 |

How to Read Wine Labels

The most important information on a label is the name of the producer or *bodega*. Next is the vintage, or *añada*, followed by the type of wine. All wines are classified according to four quality categories: *joven* or *cosecha* (young wine, one or two years old); *crianza* (matured in barrels for at least a year); and *reserva* and *gran reserva* (the best wines that have matured the longest). Each label displays the alcohol content and quality mark.

The producer's name
or *bodega* is the first thing connoisseurs seek. Many labels also list the grape varieties.

Label decoration can be elegant, with illustrations by top graphic designers or painters.

Confirmation of source, or *denominación de origen*, is shortened to DO.

Designation of quality category and vintage

④ Briones
This fortified town is home to the headquarters of Finca Allende, a winery producing celebrated modern wines. The town's Museo de la Cultura del Vino has displays on wine culture.

Tips for Drivers

Tour length: Approximately 94 km (59 miles).
Stopping-off places: Accommodation in hotels and *casas rurales* is easy to find in all the larger places on this route. Many of the bodegas – found in almost every town – offer tours combined with wine tastings.

③ Ollauri
Ollauri produces well-respected red wines. At the beginning of autumn, wine fairs are held here. These involve tastings, visits to the bodegas, and the preparation of wine-based meals.

⑤ San Asensio
This town is known for its high-quality wine. On 25 July it hosts a "wine battle" – the *Batalla del Clarete*, named after the local wine made from grapes cultivated on the light, sandy soils.

⑥ Elciego
The City of Wine, designed by Frank Gehry, is a striking complex that includes a plush hotel, restaurants and wine cellars.

⑦ Fuenmayor
Fuenmayor combines the features of Rioja Alta, Rioja Baja and Rioja Alavesa, which produce different types of wine. Here are major and local producers.

⑨ Logroño
In September, the San Mateo fiesta signals the start of the grape harvest. Events include the treading of grapes and offering of new wines to the Virgen de Valvanera.

Key

▬▬ Motorway
▬▬ Tour route
▬▬ Scenic route
— Minor road

⑩ Laguardia (Biasteri)
Under Laguardia's Old Town are numerous bodegas. Santiago Calatrava's rippling building for the famous Ysios winery attracts thousands of visitors a year.

The eclectic Colegiata de San Miguel in Aguilar de Campoo

❷ Briviesca

Burgos (Castilla y León). **Road Map** G2.
🏛 7,700. 🚉 🚌 ℹ C/Santa Marta
Encimera 1; 947 59 39 39. 🎭 Nuestra
Señora and San Roque (15–16 Aug).
🔳 **turismo-briviesca.com**

Briviesca was originally located in the nearby hills, but in the 14th century it was moved lower down to its present site.

The town's best-known monument is the 16th-century **Convento de Santa Clara**, with a Renaissance walnut reredos carved with scenes depicting the Tree of Jesse and the Way of the Cross. On the Plaza Mayor stands the **Iglesia de San Martín**, with a 16th-century Plateresque façade. Nearby is a 17th-century **Ayuntamiento** (town hall) with a clock tower and three coats of arms. There are also coats of arms on many of the other houses from Briviesca's Golden Age.

❸ Aguilar de Campoo

Palencia (Castilla y León). **Road Map** F2.
🏛 7,500. 🚉 🚌 ℹ Paseo Cascajera
10; 979 12 36 41. 🎭 Tue. 🎭 San Juan
and San Pedro (24–29 Jun).

Aguilar de Campoo is a well-preserved medieval town. Rising above it is an 11th- to 12th-century castle, built on the ruins of a Celtic *castro*.

The houses and palaces in the town, including the **Palacio de Manrique**, are decorated with coats of arms; identical ones can be seen on the massive tower of the **Colegiata de San Miguel**. This eclectic church is mainly Gothic, but with a preserved Romanesque portal and a Spanish Baroque tower. Also worth seeing is the Romanesque **Iglesia de Santa Cecilia**, with its beautiful leaning tower. Its interior has column capitals bearing plaant motifs and scenes of the *Slaughter of the Innocents*. A few medieval bridges also survive in Aguilar.

❹ Frómista

Palencia (Castilla y León). **Road Map** F3.
🏛 850. ℹ Paseo Central; 979 81 01
28. 🎭 Fri. 🎭 San Telmo (1st Sun after
Easter), La Virgen del Otero (8 Sep).
🔳 **fromista.com**

Tiny Frómista features traditional houses built in adobe – sundried brick made from clay and straw – but the village is chiefly famous for its Romanesque **Iglesia de San Martín**, with harmonious proportions and sculptural decoration. Restored to its original appearance, it has three apses, the central one being taller than the others; likewise, the nave is taller than the aisles. An octagonal tower rises above the transept, with two cylindrical towers crowning the façade. The portals are decorated with human and animal figures as well as plant motifs. Similar decoration can be seen on the capitals of the columns inside the church – note how the fable of the Raven and the Fox is presented.

❺ Burgos

Burgos (Castilla y León). **Road Map** F3.
🏛 179,000. 🚉 🚌 ℹ Calle Nuño
Rasura 7; 947 28 88 74. 🎭 Fri, Sat, Sun.
🎭 San Pedro and San Pablo (29 Jun).
🔳 **turismoburgos.org**

Burgos was established in 884 for military reasons. Over the centuries, the city transformed into an important commercial and religious centre, and became the seat of Spanish monarchs and magnates. Burgos experienced its Golden Age in the 16th century when it enjoyed a monopoly on the Castilian wool trade.

Several gateways, including the **Arco de San Esteban**, have survived from the original fortifications. The grandest gateway is the **Arco de Santa María**, built in 1553 in the style of a triumphal arch in honour of Carlos I; its façade, designed by Juan de Vallejo, is carved with statues of dignitaries and contains a figure of the Virgin.

The city's showpiece is the **cathedral** *(see pp172–3)*. The spires crowning its towers are visible from all over Burgos. Inside the Gothic **Iglesia de San Nicolás** is a stone reredos by

Arco de Santa María in Burgos

El Cid (1043–99)

Rodrigo Díaz de Vivar was born of a noble family in Vivar del Cid, north of Burgos. He served Fernando I, but was banished from Castile after becoming embroiled in the fratricidal squabbles of the king's sons, Sancho II and Alfonso VI. He switched allegiance to fight for the Moors, then switched again, capturing Valencia for the Christians in 1094, ruling the city until his death. For his heroism he was named El Cid, from the Arabic *Al-Sidi* (Lord). He was a charismatic man of courage, but it was the poem *El Cantar del Mío Cid* (1180) that immortalized him as a Christian hero.

Statue of El Cid, hero of the Reconquest

Simon of Cologne, depicting the life and miracles of St Nicholas. The **Iglesia de San Esteban** (13th- to 14th-century) accommodates Spain's only museum of altarpieces. Further east stands the **Iglesia de San Lorenzo**, which has superb Baroque vaulting. The **Iglesia de Santa Águeda** is the place where El Cid made Alfonso VI swear that he had nothing to do with the death of his brother, Sancho II.

A magnificent example of 15th-century civic architecture is the **Casa del Cordón** (now a bank), so called on account of the ornamentation in the form of a Franciscan cord motif that surrounds two coats of arms on the façade. The 16th-century palace of the Casa de Miranda houses the **Museo de Burgos**, with exhibits on the archaeology, history and art of the region. Of special interest are the finds from the Roman city of Clunia, the tomb of Juan de Padilla, and an 11th-century Moorish casket.

On the outskirts of town stands the **Monasterio de Santa**

A coat of arms in Burgos Cathedral

María la Real de las Huelgas, a Cistercian convent founded by Alfonso VIII in 1187. The building is Gothic, with Romanesque, Mudéjar and Renaissance elements. South of the Gothic church – the resting place of the convent's founder – is the **Claustro de San Fernando**, cloisters decorated with Moorish designs: geometric patterns, inscriptions, and figures of peacocks and griffins.

To the east of the city is the **Monasterio de la Cartuja de Miraflores**, a Carthusian monastery founded in 1441. This aisleless church has a polygonal apse covered in star vaulting. In front of the high altar, gilded with the first consignment of gold brought back to Spain from the New World, is a star-shaped tomb holding the remains of Juan II and Isabel of Portugal, the parents of Isabel the Catholic Monarch. Both the tomb and the altar are attributed to Gil de Siloé. The hill above the city, on which stands a 9th-century **castle**, offer spectacular views over the city.

🏛 **Museo de Burgos**
C/Miranda 13. **Tel** 947 26 58 75.
Open Oct–Jun: 10am–2pm & 4–7pm Tue– Sat, 10am–2pm Sun; Jul–Sep: 10am–2pm & 5–8pm Tue–Sat, 10am–2pm Sun. 📷 (free Sat & Sun) ♿

🏛 **Monasterio de Santa María la Real de las Huelgas**
C/Compases de Huelga. **Tel** 902 04 44 54. **Open** 10am–2pm & 4–6:30pm Tue–Sat, 10:30am–3pm Sun. 📷 🎫 only (free Wed pm & Thu pm).

🏛 **Monasterio de la Cartuja de Miraflores**
Carratera de la Cartuja. **Tel** 947 25 25 86. **Open** 10:15am–3pm & 4–6pm Mon–Sat; 11am–3pm & 4–6pm Sun.

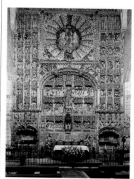

The richly decorated high altar in the Iglesia de San Nicolás

Burgos City Centre

① Arco de Santa María
② Cathedral
③ Iglesia de San Nicolás
④ Iglesia de San Esteban
⑤ Iglesia de San Lorenzo
⑥ Casa del Cordón
⑦ Museo de Burgos
⑧ Monasterio de Santa María la Real de las Huelgas
⑨ Monasterio de la Cartuja de Miraflores

0 metres 200
0 yards 200

For keys to symbols see back flap

Catedral de Burgos

Spain's third-largest cathedral was founded in 1221 by Bishop Don Mauricio under Fernando III. The ground plan – a Latin cross – measures 84 m (92 yds) by 59 m (65 yds). Its construction was carried out in stages over three centuries and involved many of the greatest artists and architects in Europe. The style is almost entirely Gothic, and shows influences from Germany, France, and the Low Countries. First to be built were the nave and cloisters, while the intricate, crocketed spires and the richly decorated side chapels are mostly later work. The architects cleverly adapted the cathedral to its sloping site, incorporating stairways inside and out.

West Front
The lacy, steel-grey spires soar above a sculpted balustrade depicting Castile's early kings.

★ Golden Staircase
This elegant Renaissance staircase by Diego de Siloé (1522) links the nave with the street-level Coronería – a tall Gothic gate also known as one of the Apostles.

Capilla de Santa Ana
The altarpiece (1490) in this chapel is by the sculptor Gil de Siloé. The central panel shows St Anne with St Joachim.

KEY

① **Capilla de la Presentación** (1519–24) is a funerary chapel with a star-shaped, traceried vault.

② **Capilla de Santa Tecla**

③ **Tomb of El Cíd and his wife Doña Jimena**

④ **Lantern**

⑤ **Capilla de San Juan Bautista and museum**

⑥ **Capilla de la Visitación**

⑦ **Capilla del Santísimo Cristo**

Puerta de Santa María (main entrance)

Ambulatory
Several of the reliefs around the chancel were carved by Philippe de Bigarny. This expressive scene, which was completed in 1499, depicts the road to Calvary.

VISITORS' CHECKLIST

Practical Information
Plaza de Santa Maria.
Tel 947 20 47 12. **Open** 9:30am–6pm daily. 🕊 9am–2pm (hourly) & 7:30pm Sun & hols; 9–11am (hourly) & 7:30pm Mon–Fri; 7:30pm Sat. 🔲 ♿ 📷 📹
🌐 catedraldeburgos.es

★ Constable's Chapel
The tomb of the High Constable of Castile and his wife lies beneath the openwork vault of this chapel of 1496.

Sacristy (1765)
The sacristy was rebuilt in Baroque style, with an exuberant plasterwork vault and Rococo altars.

Puerta del Sarmental
The tympanum of this portal of 1240 shows Christ flanked by the Evangelists. Statues of the apostles sit below.

★ Crossing
The magnificent star-ribbed central dome, begun in 1539, rises on four huge pillars. It is decorated with effigies of prophets and saints. Beneath it is the tomb of El Cíd and his wife.

CENTRAL AND EASTERN PYRENEES

The Spanish Pyrenees encompass parts of two regions: Aragón, with the highest, wildest terrain, and Catalonia, where the peaks are more accessible and better developed for tourism. In the mountain villages life proceeds at a slower pace, old traditions are nurtured, and in places such as Broto or Bielsa colourful carnivals are staged.

Stretching 440 km (273 miles) from the Bay of Biscay on the Atlantic Coast to the Cap de Creus on the Mediterranean, the Pyrenean mountain chain forms a natural border between France and Spain. In the 8th century, these inaccessible lands provided excellent refuge from the Moorish invaders, and the Pyrenean valleys were the birthplace of some of Spain's first Christian kingdoms. Later, after their rulers had moved south, the people who remained lived for centuries in isolation from the rest of Spain.

The foothills of the mountains, whose highest peak is Aneto (3,404 m/11,166 ft above sea level), are crossed by the Aragonese variation of the pilgrimage route to Santiago de Compostela, where some of the most interesting Romanesque sites are located. Among them is the Monasterio de San Juan de la Peña,

an architectural gem. Huesca and Jaca, whose history goes back nearly 2,000 years, are the area's main towns.

Well-marked trails run through the mountain valleys, frequented by nature-lovers, who can get a close-up view of the deep ravines, the peaks and the many indigenous species of plants and animals.

The Pyrenees are a paradise for winter-sports enthusiasts. Popular places for winter activities include Formigal, which offers a variety of ski runs, and La Molina – the oldest ski resort in the Eastern Pyrenees.

The principality of Andorra, a tax-free paradise for shoppers, occupies land in the Pyrenees between France and Spain. Its rural charm matches that of the rest of the Pyrenees, and it is also excellent for walkers.

Spanish musher Lopez Cobo competes in the Pirena Advance sled-dog race

◀ The Mallos de Riglos rock formation, near Huesca, Aragón

Exploring the Central and Eastern Pyrenees

The two gateways to the Aragonese high Pyrenees are Huesca and Jaca. This region's most popular sights include the Monasterio de San Juan de la Peña, half-concealed beneath a rock overhang, and the impressively sited Castillo de Loarre. No itinerary would be complete without taking in the beautiful valleys of Ansó, Hecho and Tena, where fiestas are held. In the Catalonian Pyrenees, the main centres are Ripoll, on the route from Barcelona, Puigcerdà, La Seu d'Urgell, the forested Vall d'Aran with its flowery meadows, and the mountain principality of Andorra.

An ornate Romanesque capital in the Iglesia de Santiago in Agüero

Sights at a Glance

A crystal-clear stream in the Parc Nacional d'Aigüestortes

Getting Around

The best way of getting around the Central and Eastern Pyrenees is by car, but take special care on the mountain roads looking out for cattle herds and during winter snowdrifts. The more remote mountain locations are accessible only on foot.

There are train services from Zaragoza and Valencia to Huesca. Jaca can be reached by coach from Huesca and Zaragoza. Minor roads connect Jaca with Pamplona and Aínsa. Buses from Jaca will take you to the entrances to the valleys. The Parque Nacional de Ordesa can be reached from Sabiñánigo.

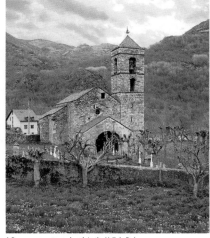

A Romanesque stone church in the Vall de Boí

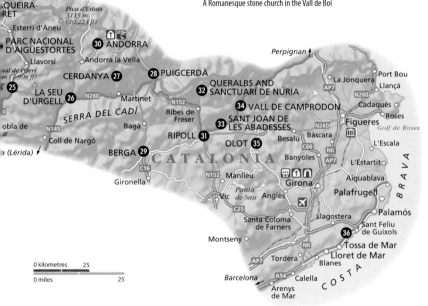

Key

- ▬▬ Motorway
- ▬▬ Dual carriageway
- ▬▬ Major road
- ▭▭ Minor road
- ▪ ▪ Motorway under construction
- ▬▬ Scenic route
- ▬ ▬ Main railway line
- ▬▬ National border
- ▬▬ Regional border
- △ Mountain peak

A field of sunflowers in the Barbastro area

For keys to symbols see back flap

Road through the verdant Valle de Ansó, lined with craggy peaks

❶ Sos del Rey Católico

Zaragoza. **Road Map** C5. 🚌 700.
ℹ️ Plaza de la Hispanidad 1; 948 88 85 24. 🚗 organized by the tourist office. 🗓️ Fri. 🎉 San Esteban (3rd Wed in Aug).

Sos del Rey Católico is one of the Cinco Villas – a group of five picturesque towns granted privileges by Philip V for their loyalty during the War of the Spanish Succession at the beginning of the 18th century, which ended in victory for the Bourbons (see p45).

Coat-of-arms, Sos del Rey Católico town hall

The town owes its name to King Fernando of Aragón, the "Catholic King", who was born here in 1452 (see p44). The **Palacio de Sada**, his reputed birthplace, was built on the ruins of an old castle and features an 18th- century chapel. Also worth a visit are the 15th-century Gothic **town hall** and, at the top of the town, the 11th-century **Iglesia de San Esteban**, with beautiful carved capitals, a Romanesque font, and 13th-century frescoes in two of the crypt apses.

❷ Valle de Ansó

Reached via the A176 motorway from Puente la Reina. **Road Map** C5.
ℹ️ Plaza Domingo Miral 1, Ansó; 974 37 02 25. 🌐 valledeanso.com

Covered in beech, fir and pine, the Valle de Ansó rivals the Valle de Hecho as the loveliest valley in the Pyrenees. Formed by the Veral river, it features an amazing diversity of flora and fauna. Walking between the vertical crags, you might encounter capercaillie, fallow deer and squirrels. When exploring the valley on foot, stop at the village of **Ansó**, 860 m (2,821 ft) above sea level. Because of its location and difficult accessibility, it has always been quite isolated, which has led to the villagers retaining their traditional customs and crafts. On the last Sunday in August, a huge fiesta takes place here, and local people wear traditional costumes resembling medieval attire.

❸ Valle de Hecho

Huesca. **Road Map** C5. 🚌 960.
ℹ️ 974 37 50 02 (winter), 974 37 55 05 (summer). 🌐 valledehecho.net

The stone villages of the green Hecho valley are characterized by red-roofed stone houses, typical of the Pyrenees. The people here speak the local dialect called *cheso*, virtually unchanged since early medieval

Stone houses in the village of Hecho

times. The valley offers good views of the peak of **Castillo de Macher.** Walking trips can be made to **Selva de Oza**, with its striking array of Atlantic flora, as well as to other places amid the mountain landscape.

The largest village in the valley is **Hecho**, which has a sculpture garden left from an open-air festival. Some 2 km (1 miles) north of Hecho lies the bucolic village of **Siresa.** It is home to an interesting Romanesque-Gothic church – San Pedro (1082) – which was once part of a monastery founded in the 9th century by Count Aznar Galíndez. The shrine soon became the region's spiritual capital, and in 922 the monastery was made the see of Aragón.

❹ Puerto de Somport

Huesca. **Road Map** C5. ℹ️ Plaza Ayuntamiento 1 (Canfranc); 974 37 31 41. 🌐 canfranc.es

On the French border, at the head of a long valley (Valle de Canfranc) that runs down to Jaca, the Puerto de Somport (Somport Pass) is one of the most historic crossing points in the Pyrenees. The pass is used by the Romans and medieval pilgrims, and takes its name from the Latin *Summus Portus*.

The pass marks the start of the Aragonese pilgrimage route to Santiago de Compostela, which is older than the more famous route through Navarra. The Aragonese route leads through Canfranc, Villanúa, Jaca, San Juan de la Peña and Santa Cruz de Serós, joining the Navarrese route in Yesa. The pass, on which stands a small chapel with a figure of St James, was a crossing point for the Romans and Moors. Nowadays, the austere scenery is speckled with holiday apartments built for skiing. **Astún** is the best-organized and most modern resort, while **Candanchú** in the Valle de Canfranc is one of Spain's major winter sports centres.

❺ Jaca

Huesca. **Road Map** C5. 🏛 13,000.
ℹ Plaza de San Pedro 11; 974 36
00 98. 🚌 Fri. 🎭 La Victoria (1st Fri in
May), Santa Orosia y San Pedro (25–29
Jun). 🌐 **jaca.es**

This picturesque town, situated in the heart of the Pyrenees, is Roman in origin (2nd century AD). In 795, at the Battle of Las Tiendas, the town repulsed the Moors, mainly due to the bravery of local women. In 1054, Jaca became the first capital of the kingdom of Aragón. This event precipitated the construction of the first Romanesque **cathedral** in Spain, which imitated French designs. Over time, the cathedral itself became a model for churches built on this side of the Pyrenees, and in the 20th century it was declared a World Heritage Site. Built on a basilican plan, the cathedral has a nave, aisles and a transept. The exterior is mostly Romanesque, but inside one can trace the history of church architecture, from Gothic in the star vaulting of the

One of the gates of the citadel in Jaca

aisles, through Renaissance in the chapel of St Michael, to Baroque in the transept pilasters and some of the altars. The central apse has paintings by Manuel de Bayeu, the brother-in-law of Francisco de Goya.

In the cloisters, the **Museo Diocesano** has a fine collection of Romanesque and Gothic frescoes from local churches, including the Iglesia de los Santos Julián y Basilisa. The frescoes from the apse of the Ermita de San Juan Bautista in Ruesta date from the first half of the 12th century – a striking image of the head of Christ Pantocrator was uncovered beneath a layer of paint.

South of the cathedral, on Plaza la Cadena, stands the **Monumento Ramiro I** by Ramón Casadevall Callostro. It commemorates a king who had his court in Jaca and founded a new dynasty. Also worth seeing is the **Torre**

Romanesque capital in the portal of Jaca Cathedral

del Reloj, a 15th-century Gothic clock tower that was built on the site of a former royal palace.

In 1591, Philip II built in Jaca the **Ciudadela** decorated with corner turrets. This is one of only two surviving pentagonal citadels in Europe.

Just west of the town centre lies the **Puente de San Miguel**, a famous medieval bridge on the pilgrimage route.

🏛 **Museo Diocesano**
Plaza de la Catedral. **Tel** 974 35 63 78.
Closed 10am–1:30pm & 4–7pm Tue–Sat (to 8pm Sat, and mid-Jun–mid-Sep), 10am–1:30pm Sun. 📷 ♿ 🛒

Jaca City Centre

① Cathedral
② Museo Diocesano
③ Monumento Ramiro I
④ Torre del Reloj
⑤ Ciudadela

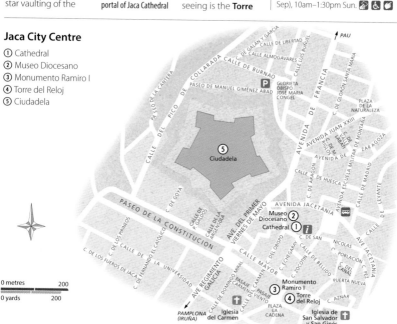

0 metres   200
0 yards   200

❻ Monasterio de San Juan de la Peña

The history of this imposing monastery dates from the Moorish invasion, when hermit-monks, fleeing the Moors, settled here. According to legend it was an early guardian of the Holy Grail. In the 11th century it joined the Benedictine order, and became the first monastery to use the Latin Mass in Spain. The central part of the monastery is on two floors. The lower one is a primitive crypt built in the early 10th century, while the upper floor contains an 11th-century church. After a fire in the 17th century, the building was abandoned in favour of a newer one further up the hillside. This was later sacked by Napoleon's troops, but it has since been restored and now houses an interpretation centre and a hotel.

View of the Monastery
This magnificent Romanesque monastery is half-concealed under a bulging rock overhang (peña).

★ Old Monastery
The oldest part of the complex is the lower Mozarabic church, built in 920 on the site of an earlier rock-hewn shrine dedicated to St John the Baptist.

Holy Grail
According to legend, the chalice used at the Last Supper was hidden in the monastery to prevent its capture by the Moors. A replica is in the central apse of the upper church.

KEY

① **Romanesque church**

② **Museum**

③ **The Lower Church** features 12th-century Romanesque murals. Some of the abbots are also buried here.

④ **7th-century Capilla de San Voto y San Félix**

Royal Pantheon
The 18th-century Neoclassical Pantheon, whose walls are decorated with historical stucco reliefs, contains the stacked tombs of the early Aragonese kings: Ramiro I, Sancho Ramírez and Pedro I.

Lower Mozarabic Church
This church was built by Mozarabs – Christians who lived under Muslim rule, whose architecture and culture were strongly influenced by Islamic styles.

VISITORS' CHECKLIST

Practical Information
Road Map C5. [i] 974 35 51 19.
Open Mar–May, Sep & Oct: 10am–2pm & 3:30–7pm daily; Jun–Aug: 10am–2pm & 3–8pm daily (mid-Jul–Aug: 10am– 8pm); Nov–Feb: 10am–2pm Sun–Fri & 10am–5pm Sat.
[W] monasteriosanjuan.com

★ Capilla de San Victorián
The resting place of the abbots, this Gothic chapel is entered through a beautiful Mozarabic portal.

Capitals

On the 20 Romanesque capitals dating from the 12th century are scenes from the Old and New Testaments in chronological order. They were created by an anonymous artist, referred to as the Master of San Juan de la Peña. The capitals constitute a pictorial Bible, beginning with the Creation and finishing with the Ascension of Christ. The Romanesque style treated sculpture as subordinate to architecture, which is why some of the figures seem out of proportion with each other or awkwardly placed.

A Romanesque capital in the monastery cloister

★ Cloister
The cloistered courtyard was meant to symbolize the New Jerusalem. The capitals of its columns display wonderful carved biblical scenes.

The imposing fortress of the Castillo de Loarre, closely moulded around the contours of the rocky hillside

❼ Agüero

Huesca. **Road Map** C5. 🏔 170.
🛈 San Jaime 1; 974 38 04 89. 🎪 San Roque (15–19 Aug). 🖥 **aytoaguero.es**

The picturesque setting of this attractive village, clustered against a dramatic crag of eroded stone, amply rewards a brief detour from the Huesca–Pamplona road. Rising above the village is the Iglesia de Santiago, whose construction began c.1200. The capitals of the columns in this aisled building are carved with fantastical beasts, as well as scenes from the life of Jesus and Mary. The most beautiful carvings are on the portal, depicting scenes of the Epiphany and Salome dancing. They appear to be made by the Master of San Juan de la Peña *(see p181)*.

❽ Castillo de Loarre

Huesca. **Road Map** C5. 🛈 974 34 21 61. **Open** Nov–Feb: 11am–5:30pm Tue–Sun; Mar–Oct: 10am–7pm daily (until 8pm mid-Jun–mid-Sep). **Closed** 1 Jan, 25 Dec. 🅿 ♿ 🗓 🖥 **castillodeloarre.es**

The ramparts of this sturdy fortress rise majestically above the road approaching from Ayerbe. On a clear day, the hilltop setting is stupendous, with views of the surrounding orchards and reservoirs of the Ebro plain. Inside the curtain walls lies a complex founded in the 11th century on the site of a Roman castle. It was later remodelled under Sancho I (Sancho Ramírez) of Aragón, who established a religious community here, placing the complex under the rule of the Order of Augustine.

Within the castle walls is a Romanesque church containing the remains of St Demetrius.

❾ Biescas and Valle de Tena

Huesca. **Road Map** D5. 🏔 1,700.
🛈 Plaza del Ayuntamiento; 974 48 52 22. 🎪 Fiesta Popular (13 Jun), San Roque (14 Aug), Fiesta de la Virgen (18 Aug). 🖥 **valledetena.com**

The picturesque Valle de Tena is ideal for walkers and hikers; several well-marked trails lead from here to the surrounding peaks, some of which are over 3,000 m (9,842 ft) above sea level. The places most often visited include the **Casita de las Brujas** (Witches' Hut), the **Ermita de Santa Elena**, and the **Parque de Arratiecho.**

Near the entrance to the valley – famous for traditional cheese-making techniques and regional delicacies, such as breadcrumbs with grapes – is the small town of **Biescas**, which spans the Gállego river. The river divides the town into its two districts of El Salvador and San Pedro, to whom the local churches are dedicated.

The Gállego is one of the most spectacular of the fast-flowing Pyrenean rivers, and **Sallent de Gállego** is a centre for whitewater rafting, kayaking, rock climbing, fishing and other adventure sports. The beautiful Panticosa gorge is home to the ski resorts of **Formigal** and **Panticosa**.

❿ Broto

Huesca. **Road Map** D5. 🏔 550. 🚌 from Sabiñánigo or Aínsa. 🛈 Avenida Ordesa 1; 974 48 64 13. 🗓 🎪 San Blas (3 Mar), La Vírgen del Rosario (7 Oct). 🖥 **vallebroto.com**

Situated in the Ordesa valley, Broto is a good base for excursions to the western side of the Parque Nacional de Ordesa *(see pp186–7)*.

A roe deer rests in a village near Broto

The medieval town once played an important strategic role. Its name derives from a Basque word meaning "place covered in blackberry bushes". Broto's inhabitants earn their living from cattle farming and tourism, and they maintain local traditions. On occasion they can be seen performing their dances: the *rapatan*, a shepherds' dance, and *os palateaos*, a war dance.

Rising above the small town is the 16th-century **Iglesia de San Pedro el Apóstol**, from which there are breathtaking views of the valley.

A short walk from Broto leads to two other equally fine views: the 50-m (164-ft) **Sorrosal waterfall** and the **Ermita de Nuestra Señora de Murillo**, some 1,470 m (4,823 ft) above sea level.

Abandoned stone house near Broto

⓫ Torla

Huesca. **Road Map** D5. 🏔 344.
ℹ Calle Fatas 7; 974 48 63 78 (Jul–Sep only).

This village, at the gateway to the Parque Nacional de Ordesa *(see pp186–7)* and huddled beneath the forbidding slopes of Mondarruego, is the main tourist centre in this part of the Pyrenees. Local guides can be hired to take experienced walkers up to the surrounding 3,000-m (9,842-ft) peaks; the most popular of these peaks is **Monte Perdido**, the "Lost Mountain" (3,355 m/11,007 ft above sea level).

Torla is a picturesque town with slate-roofed houses and a church dating from the beginning of the 16th century. Each year in February a carnival is held here, during which all the evil of the past year – personified by a man dressed up as a black beast – is destroyed by a brave hunter. In order to humiliate and overpower it, the beast is dragged through the streets of the town in a colourful procession accompanied by a lively singing crowd.

⓬ Bielsa

Huesca. **Road Map** D5. 🏔 510.
ℹ Plaza Mayor (Ayuntamiento); 974 50 11 27. 🌐 **bielsa.com**

Just 12 km (7.5 miles) from the border with France, the village of Bielsa is a popular base for hikers and mountaineers. It is the main gateway to the eastern side of the Parque Nacional de Ordesa, and especially the Valle de Pineta, one of the park's most beautiful parts. Information about area trails is provided at the local tourist office.

Bielsa was completely destroyed during the Spanish Civil War, so the architecture of the mountain village is relatively new. The principal attraction here is the **Museo Etnológico de Bielsa**, where one can learn about the history of the region and the local carnival. The latter is based on a ritual that was performed in pagan times, in which the participants would say a symbolic farewell to winter and greet the arrival of spring. The participants of this fiesta, known as *Trangas*, have huge rams' horns on their heads, blackened faces and teeth made of potatoes. They are said to represent fertility.

🏛 **Museo Etnológico de Bielsa**
Plaza Mayor. **Open** Jul–Aug, Easter & Christmas: 12:30–1:30pm & 6–7pm Tue–Sun; other times by appt only. 📷

⓭ Aínsa

Huesca. **Road Map** D5. 🏔 2,200.
🚌 Avda. Ordesa 5; 974 50 07 67.
🚃 Tue. 🎉 San Sebastián (20 Jan), Fiestas Mayores (14 Sep).

The history of Aínsa began in 742, when people fleeing the Moors took refuge in the Pyrenees. Having established a small settlement, they decided to repel the Moorish invaders by force. During one such clash, a shining cross reputedly appeared on the battlefield, to which the victory was attributed. The victory is commemorated every other September during the Fiesta de la Morisma.

In the years 1035–38, Aínsa was the short-lived capital of the kingdom of Sobrarbe. The 12th-century **Plaza Mayor**, a broad cobbled square, is surrounded by arcaded houses of brown stone. Also on the plaza stands the belfry of the Romanesque **Iglesia de Santa María**, which was consecrated in 1181. Behind the church, steep narrow streets lead up to the restored **castle** with a preserved citadel, dating from the times of the Reconquest.

Façade detail, Museo Etnológico de Bielsa

Stone houses with arcades on the Plaza Mayor in Aínsa

The Escuain gorge as seen from the Revilla viewpoint ▶

⓮ Parque Nacional de Ordesa

Within its borders, the Parque Nacional de Ordesa y Monte Perdido combines all the most dramatic elements of Spain's Pyrenean scenery. At the heart of the park are four glacial canyons – the Ordesa, Añisclo, Pineta and Escuaín valleys – which carve the great upland limestone massifs into spectacular cliffs and chasms. Most of the park is accessible only on foot: even then, snow during autumn and winter makes it inaccessible to all except those with specialist climbing equipment. In high summer, however, the crowds testify to the park's well-earned reputation as a paradise for walkers and nature-lovers alike.

Valle de Ordesa
The Río Arazas cuts through forested limestone escarpments, providing some of Ordesa's most popular walks.

Torla
This village, at the gateway to the park, huddles beneath the forbidding slopes of Mondarruego. With its core of cobbled streets and slate-roofed houses around the church, Torla is a popular base for visitors to Ordesa.

Broto
Spanning a valley on the banks of the Río Ara, this village has traditional period houses. The extensive valley forms a fantastic backdrop for the fine regional architecture.

For hotels and restaurants see p207 and pp222–3

0 kilometres   3

0 miles   3

Key

═══ Major road

═══ Minor road

– – Mountain trail

▬▬ Spanish–French border

▬▬▬ National park boundary

View from the Parador de Bielsa
The parador at the foot of Monte Perdido looks out at stunning sheer rock faces streaked by waterfalls.

Parador de Bielsa
Valle de Pineta
Bielsa →
Cinca
nte Perdido
5 m (11,008 ft)
efugio de Góriz
Sierra de Las Tucas
Cascada Cola de Caballo
Vellos
de Soaso
Cañón de Añisclo
Garganta de Escuaín
Revilla
Escuaín
Bielsa
Tella
• Nerín
Bestué •
Puértolas •
Vellos
Vellos

Cola de Caballo
The 70-m (230-ft) "Horse's Tail" waterfall is a scenic stopping point near the northern end of the long hike around the Circo Soaso. It provides a taste of the spectacular scenery found along the route.

Hikers in the national park

Tips for Walkers

Several well-marked trails follow the valleys and can be easily tackled by anyone who is reasonably fit, though walking boots are a must. The mountain routes may require climbing gear so check first with the visitors' centre (in Torla) and get a detailed map. Mountain weather changes fast, with snow early or late in the season. High altitude overnight camping is allowed, but only for one night.

Cañon or Garganta de Añisclo
A wide path leads along this beautiful, steep-sided gorge, following the wooded course of the turbulent Río Vellos through dramatic limestone scenery.

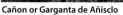

For keys to symbols *see back flap*

Flora and Fauna of Parque Nacional de Ordesa

With some of the most dramatic mountain scenery in Spain, the Parque Nacional de Ordesa makes excellent walking country. The most popular trails through the park are the Camiño del Soaso, Senda de los Cazadores and Faja de las Flores. Some of the animal species encountered here are in danger of becoming extinct but the park offers natural protection for the mountain eagle, capercaillie, chamois, deer, wild boar, marmot and vulture. As well as an abundance of gentians, orchids and belladonna, there are also lush pine and fir forests and many birch, beech and wild cherry trees.

Esparceta (sainfoin), an important honey-yielding and fodder plant, is commonly found in the alpine meadows of the park. This long-lived perennial, reaching a height of 60 cm (24 in), produces clusters of pretty pink or carmine flowers.

The rocky massifs border gentle hills covered in dwarf mountain pines.

The horses grazing in the alpine meadows have vivid colouring.

The meadows are home to many species of flora and fauna.

The viper is a poisonous snake that lives in cold places, avoiding direct sunlight. It hunts for mice, birds and frogs.

Birds of the Parque Nacional de Ordesa

Dunnock
This small bird, also called the hedge sparrow, lives a secretive life among low vegetation. It is found in forests from the lowlands to the Pyrenean dwarf-pine belt, where its rapid flute-like trill can be heard.

Owl
There are several species of owl in the Pyrenees. In the park you'll find the low-flying barn owl, the eagle owl, the brown owl, which eats small rodents, as well as the charming long-eared owl.

Jay
The jay's sharp, screeching call can often be heard in the park. It flies ponderously, due to its slow-flapping wings, which are beautifully coloured and easily recognizable to ornithologists and amateurs alike.

Blue Tit
This graceful bird is also bold, making it easy to spot. It inhabits sparse woodland, making its nest in low hollows. It feeds on berries and seeds, as well as small insects, spiders and snails.

A View of the Park

The stunning mountain peaks and rare species of flora and fauna make Ordesa one of the most frequently visited parks in the Pyrenees. The park can only be visited fully after the snow melts in spring, and even then much of it has to be explored on foot.

The marten is very shy, emerging only at night. A graceful and very agile creature, it is an excellent climber. It feeds on small mammals, birds, insects and berries.

Edelweiss, a symbol of the mountains, is a small flowering plant that grows in grassy alpine areas, usually on inaccessible rocky ledges. It prefers altitudes of 2,000– 2,900 m (6,560–9,515 ft) above sea level.

The breathtakingly steep rock faces are in places cut by waterfalls.

The alpine forest belt (up to 2,400 m/ 7,874 ft above sea level) is composed of fir and beech, or pines.

The mountain ash, with its bright berries, is a member of the olive family and is found up to 1,000 m (3,280 ft) above sea level.

Lush vegetation at lower elevations

The weasel leads a solitary existence, becoming active during daytime and at dusk. It is a good runner and climber, feeding on fledglings, eggs and mice.

The Valle de Bujaruelo was once an important route, with a Romanesque bridge still in place over the Aro river. There are several treks across the valley.

The walls of the Palacio de los Condes de Ribagorza in Benasque

⓯ Benasque

Huesca. **Road Map** E5. 🏔 2,200.
i C/San Sebastián 5; 974 55 12 89.
🚌 Tue. 🎭 San Marcial (30 Jun–6 Jul).
w benasque.com

This village, tucked away in the northeastern corner of Aragón, lies at the head of the Esera valley. Its history stretches back to Roman times; from the 11th century, it belonged to the dukedom of Ribagorza. Its most interesting monuments are the 13th-century **Iglesia de Santa María Mayor** and the Renaissance **Palacio de los Condes de Ribagorza**.

Above the village rises the wild **Maladeta massif** ("Cursed Mountains"), offering ski runs and mountaineering routes, and behind it the two tallest Pyrenean peaks: Aneto (3,404 m/ 11,168 ft above sea level) and Posets (3,371 m/11,060 ft).

The neighbouring resort of **Cerler** has become a popular base for skiing and other winter sports. At **Castejón de Sos**, 15 km (9 miles) south of Benasque, the road passes through **Congosto de Ventamillo**, a scenic rocky gorge.

⓰ Graus

Huesca. **Road Map** D5. 🏔 3,700.
i Plaza Mayor 15; 974 54 08 74.
🎪 organized by the tourist office.
🚌 Mon. 🎭 Santo Cristo y San Vicente Ferrer (12–15 Sep).
w turismograus.com

The famous El Cid *(see p170)* took part in the Battle of Graus (1063), during which the king of Aragón,

Ramiro I, was killed. Concealed in the Old Town lies the unusual **Plaza de España**, surrounded by brick arcades and brightly frescoed half-timbered houses; one of these was home to the infamous Tomás de Torquemada, who in 1483 became Spain's first Inquisitor General.

Also noteworthy is the **Basilica de la Virgen de la Peña**, dating from 1538, with a beautiful Renaissance portal.

Environs
About 20 km (12 miles) to the northeast, at the head of a picturesque valley, lies the hill village of Roda de Isábena, site of the smallest cathedral in Spain, built in 1056–67.

The high altar in the Gothic cathedral in Barbastro

⓱ Barbastro

Huesca. **Road Map** D6. 🏔 17,000.
i Avenida de la Merced 64; 974 30 83 50. 🚌 Sat. 🎭 San Ramón (21 Jun), Natividad de Nuestra Señora (4–8 Sep). **w** turismobarbastro.org

This small town has strikingly beautiful architecture, including the 16th-century Gothic

cathedral and two smaller churches – **San Francisco** and **San Julian**, from the same period. Clearly visible on a hilltop is the **shrine of Santa María del Pueyo**. Originally a Moorish fortress stood here, which was later captured by Pedro II. The Virgin Mary is said to have appeared between the branches of an almond tree, and the site has been a place of pilgrimage ever since.

Barbastro is also the centre of the up-and-coming Somontano wine region.

⓲ Alquézar

Huesca. **Road Map** D6. 🏔 300.
i C/Arrabal s/n; 974 31 89 40.
🎭 San Sebastián (21 Jan). 🎪
w alquezar.org

Some 48 km (30 miles) north-east of Huesca in a spectacular setting, the village of Alquézar was established by the Moors; its name derives from the Arabic *al-qasr*, meaning "the fortress". Indeed, a **castle** was built here by Jalaf ibn-Rasid in the 9th century.

In 1067, the valiant Sancho Ramírez captured the fortress and turned it into a Christian stronghold, the ruins of which can be seen above the village. Slightly later, in 1085, the king founded the **Iglesia de Santa María la Mayor** on the rocks above the Vero river canyon. From this church have survived Romanesque cloisters with carved capitals depicting biblical scenes as well as the free-standing **Capilla del Santo Cristo**. The current, stately collegiate church was built in 1525–32.

The ruins of Alquézar's castle, rising above the Moorish village

Patio of Huesca's Renaissance town hall

⑲ Huesca

Huesca. **Road Map** D6. 🗺 52,000.
🚍 Pl. Luis López Allué; 974 29 21 70.
🚌 🚆 Tue, Thu & Sat. 🎉 San Vicente
(22 Jan), San Lorenzo (9–15 Aug).
🌐 **huescaturismo.com**

Founded under the Roman empire in the 1st century BC, the independent city of Osca had one of the first colleges in Spain. Captured from the Moors in 1096 by Pedro I, Huesca became the capital of Aragón until 1118, when the title passed to Zaragoza. Today, it is the second-largest city in the region.

Be sure to visit the **Palacio Real** and the Romanesque **Iglesia de San Pedro el Viejo**, which was built as a Benedictine monastery; it also served as a royal pantheon, where Alfonso I, Ramiro II, and other Aragonese rulers are buried.

North of the church, in the heart of the city, stands the beautiful Gothic **cathedral** (1274–1515), which was raised on the ruins of a former mosque. Its west front is surmounted by an unusual Mudéjar-style wooden gallery, while the slender-ribbed star vaulting in the nave is studded with golden bosses. The alabaster reredos (1520–33) is considered to be the finest work of the Valencian sculptor Damià Forment; its series of Passion scenes is highlighted by illumination.

Opposite the cathedral is the Renaissance **town hall** (1577 and 1610); inside it hangs *La Campana de Huesca*, a gory 19th-century painting by José

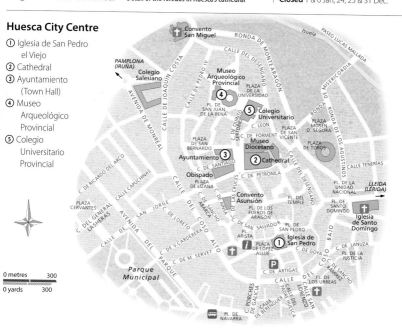

Detail of the reredos in Huesca's cathedral

Casado del Alisal that depicts the beheading of a group of troublesome nobles in the 12th century by order of King Ramiro II. The massacre occurred in the Sala de la Campana, later belonging to the 17th-century university, and now part of the **Museo Arqueológico Provincial.** This museum has excellent archaeological finds and an art collection

Relief, Museo Arqueológico Provincial, Huesca

featuring Gothic frescoes and early Aragonese painting. Among the exhibits is a 15th-century wooden relief from the former Hospital de Nuestra Señora de la Esperanza; the spot where the hospital once stood is now occupied by the **Colegio Universitario** – a university building erected in the 1980s.

🏛 **Museo Arqueológico Provincial**
Plaza de la Universidad 1; 974 22 05 86. **Open** 10am–2pm & 5–8pm Tue–Sat, 10am–2pm Sun and hols. **Closed** 1 & 6 Jan; 24, 25 & 31 Dec.

Huesca City Centre

① Iglesia de San Pedro el Viejo
② Cathedral
③ Ayuntamiento (Town Hall)
④ Museo Arqueológico Provincial
⑤ Colegio Universitario Provincial

0 metres 300
0 yards 300

For keys to symbols see back flap

The lush scenery of the Vall d'Aran

⑳ Vall d'Aran

Lleida. From Pallas on C28; from France via the Pont de Rei on N618. **Road Map** E5. 🗺 7,130. 🛈 973 64 51 97. 🖳 visitvaldaran.com

This Valley of Valleys – *aran* means valley – is a beautiful 600-sq km (230-sq mile) haven of forests and flower-filled meadows on the north side of the Pyrenees, separated from the rest of Spain by towering peaks. The valley was formed by the Riu Garona, which rises in the area and flows out to France as the Garonne.

With only two access routes from Spain – the Vielha tunnel or the road from Esterri d'Aneu over the spectacular Port de la Bonaigua pass – the valley has a more natural connection with France, and locals speak *Aranés*, a variant of Gascon Provençal.

The fact that the Vall d'Aran faces north means that it has a climate similar to that found on the Atlantic coast. Rare wild flowers and butterflies flourish in the perfect conditions created by the damp breezes and shady slopes.

Tiny villages have grown up beside the Riu Garona, often around Romanesque churches, notably at **Bossòst**, **Salardú**, **Escunhau** and **Artíes**.

The valley is ideal for outdoor activities such as skiing and walking. Well-marked trails lead up to the surrounding peaks and glaciers.

㉑ Vielha

Lleida. **Road Map** E5. 🗺 5,500. 🛈 Carrer de Sarriulera 10; 973 64 01 10. 🖴 Thu. 🎪 Fiesta del Valle (17 Jun), Fiesta de Vielha (8 Sep), Feria de Vielha (8 Oct).

Surrounded by alpine peaks, Vielha has experienced some dramatic moments in history. Napoleon's forces entered it in 1810, occupying the entire Vall d'Aran, which was returned to the Spanish crown five years later. Today, Vielha is the capital of the valley and a modern ski resort that attracts visitors due to its picturesque setting and Romanesque **Església de Sant Miguel**. Inside the church is a superb wooden 12th-century crucifix – the *Mig*

Santa María de Mig Aran, in Vielha

㉔ Parc Nacional d'Aigüestortes

Catalonia's only national park is marked by a dazzling string of post-glacial lakes (tarns), waterfalls and towering peaks, including the Agulles d'Amitges that separate the two largest lakes. Chamois, beavers, otters, eagles and grouse all live in the park.

① Church in Taüll
A vibrantly coloured 12th-century mural in the church apse depicts *Christ in Majesty*, a popular motif in Romanesque art.

② Durro
The village of Durro has superb Romanesque churches, including the Església de la Nativitad.

St. Béat
Montrèjeau
Salar
Vielha
Arties
Estanh Tòrt de Rius
Estanys de Colomèrs
Pantà de Senet
Caldes de Boí
Erill la Vall
Boí
La Noguera Ribagorçana
La Noguera de Tor
Vilaller
Benasque Torla
Pont de Suert
Lleida (Lérida)
Lleida (Lérida)
Barcelona

Key

▬ Tour route
▬ Scenic route
= Minor road
-- Trail

The ski resort of Baqueira-Beret, popular with Spanish skiers

Aran Christ. It once formed part of a larger carving, since lost, which represented the *Descent from the Cross.* Also worth visiting is the **Museu Etnológico de Vielha**, in an imposing 17th-century building. The museum is devoted to Aranese history and folklore.

🏛 Museo Etnológico

Carrer Major 26; 973 64 18 15.
Open 10am–1pm & 5–8pm Tue–Sat, 10am–1pm Sun & hols. **Closed** 1 Jan, 17 Jun, 8 Sep, 25 Dec. 🈳 ♿

㉒ Baqueira–Beret

Lleida. **Road Map** E5. 🚠 100.
🛈 902 41 54 15. 🎪 Romería de Nuestra Señora de Montgarri (2 Jul).
🌐 **baqueira.es**

This extensive ski resort, one of the best in Spain, is popular with both the public and the Spanish royal family. Baqueira and Beret were separate mountain villages before skiing became popular, but now form a single resort. There is reliable

winter snow cover, and over 50 km (30 miles) of pistes, serviced by 40 ski-lifts.

㉓ Vall de Boí

Lleida. **Road Map** E5. 🛈 Passeig de San Feliu 43 (Barruera). **Tel** 973 69 40 00. 🌐 **vallboi.com**

This small valley on the edge of the Parc Nacional d'Aigüestortes is dotted with tiny villages, many of which are built around magnificent Catalan Romanesque churches.
Dating from the 11th and 12th centuries, these churches are distinguished by tall belfries, such as the Església de Santa Eulàlia at **Erill-la-Vall**, with six floors. The two churches at **Taüll**, Sant Climent and Santa María, have superb frescoes. The originals are now in the Museu Nacional d'Art de Catalunya in Barcelona and replicas now stand in their place. Other churches worth visiting include those at **Coll**, **Barruera** and **Durro**.

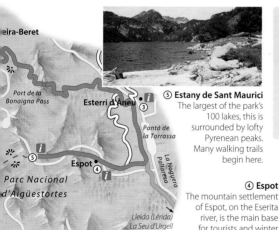

eira-Beret

Port de la Bonaigna Pass

Esterri d'Àneu 🛈
③

Pantà de la Torrassa

🛈
⑤

Espot ④
🛈

Parc Nacional d'Aigüestòrtes

La Noguera Pallaresa

*Lleida (Lérida)
La Seu d'Urgell*

0 kilometres   5
0 miles   5

Tips for Tourists

Tour length: Approximately 110 km (68 miles).
Stopping off points: The larger villages, such as Espot and Esterri d'Àneu, have hotels, restaurants and bars. Arties has an exclusive parador at the edge of the park, and refuges within it. 🛈 973 69 82 32.

⑤ **Estany de Sant Maurici**
The largest of the park's 100 lakes, this is surrounded by lofty Pyrenean peaks. Many walking trails begin here.

④ **Espot**
The mountain settlement of Espot, on the Eserita river, is the main base for tourists and winter sports enthusiasts.

③ **Esterri d'Àneu**
This cultural hub of the Àneu valley features a Romanesque bridge. Here, you can also admire the park's vivid flora, which includes rhododendrons.

㉕ Sort

Lleida. **Road Map** E5. 🏘 2,275. 🛈
Camí de la Cabanera s/n; 973 62 10 02.
🎭 Fiesta Major (1 Aug). 🆆 **sort.cat**

A pretty mountain town, Sort
has a charming historic quarter,
home to the remains of a castle
and the Gothic church of Sant
Feliu. It is a popular destination
for sports' enthusiasts – local
activities include kayaking, white-
water rafting, hiking and skiing
in nearby Port-Ainé (16 km/10
miles). Sort is Catalan for "luck",
and the town is said to boast
more winning lottery tickets
than anywhere else in Spain.

㉖ La Seu d'Urgell

Lleida. **Road Map** E5. 🏘 13,000.
🛈 C/Major 8; 973 35 15 11. 🚌 Tue
and Sat. 🎭 Fiesta Mayor (last week
in Aug). 🆆 **turismeseu.com**

Set in a valley between the
Segre and Valira rivers, this
medieval town contains the
only Romanesque cathedral in
Catalonia, the 12th-century **Santa
María d'Urgell**. Ramón Llambard
worked on the construction of
the church until 1175, but it
remains unfinished to this day.

The town's main thoroughfare
is the **Carrer de Canonges**, lined
with handsome houses, including the **Ca l'Armenter**, a property
of the influential de los Luna family from Aragón, one of whose
members was Pope Benedict XIII.

The town also has ski-lifts and
former Olympic buildings.

㉗ Cerdanya

Road Map F5. 🛈 Puigcerdà; 972 88
05 42.

This large valley on the borders
of Catalonia, France and Andorra
is ringed by peaks over 2,000 m
(6,560 ft) high. Cerdanya is also
bordered in the south by
Catalonia's largest nature park –
Cadí-Moixero. From the popular
observation point at Balcón de
la Cerdanya extend views of the
Cadí-Moixero mountain chain,
La Tossa, and part of the
Pyrenees' northern axis.

Because it is unusually sheltered, the valley has a special

A street in Bellver, located in the verdant Cerdanya valley

microclimate, with balmy
summers and lush countryside
known for its dairy produce.

The border between Spain
and France, agreed in 1659, runs
right across the valley. **Puigcerdà**
is the main town on the Spanish
side, and **Font-Romeu** on the
French side. One village, **Llívia**,
is Spanish but encircled entirely
by French territory. Items from
its historic pharmacy, one of
Europe's oldest, are displayed
at the Museo de Llívia.

Among the sites to be seen
are Neolithic **dolmens** in Eina,
Brangulí, Oren, Talltendre and
Paborde. In **Talló** there is the Via
Ceretana – a Roman road, as
well as a Romanesque cathedral.
There are impressive churches
in several villages, such as Ix,
Planés, Dorres, Guils, Talltorta,
Tarteras, Meránges, Ger, Saga,

All, Olopte, Mosoll and Bastanit.
The village of **Bellver** still has
its 13th-century town walls.

Cerdanya is a major winter
sports area, especially around
La Molina, which is one of the
largest ski resorts in Catalonia.
Other resorts include Masella
and Aransa.

㉘ Puigcerdà

Girona. **Road Map** F5. 🏘 9,120.
🛈 Carrer Querol 1; 972 88 05 42.
🚌 Sun. 🎭 Fiesta del Lago (third
Sunday in Aug). 🆆 **puigcerda.cat**

A popular ski centre in winter,
and a magnet for walkers and
climbers in summer, this is the
main town of the Spanish side
of the Cerdanya. It is set among
hills at an altitude of 1,202 m
(3,944 ft), next to the French
border. The name of the town,
which was established in 1177
by Alfonso II, king of Aragón, is
derived from the Catalan word
puig (hill). Territorial disputes,
involving France and Spain,
were settled by the Peace of
the Pyrenees of 1659, under
which Puigcerdà remained
Spanish, although Cerdanya
was divided by a new border.

In the town centre is a large
man-made **lake** established
in 1310 to channel water from
Querol; it helped to popularize
ice-skating in Spain.

The parish **church** of 1288
suffered damage during a fire;
its present appearance dates
from a partial reconstruction
in 1938, though the interior
contains medieval fragments.

Catalan Romanesque Churches

Simple and beautifully proportioned, the Romanesque style
flourished across western Europe from the 10th to the 13th centuries.
The high valleys of the Catalan
Pyrenees are especially rich in
Romanesque building, with a
distinctive style seen in the great
monasteries of Ripoll and Sant Joan de
les Abadesses or the village churches
of the Vall de Boí or the Cerdanya. The
churches display tall belfries, massive
round apses and an extraordinary
wealth of fresco painting, influenced
by Byzantine art.

The Romanesque church in Taüll

The hilltop sanctuary of Queralt, with the town of Berga in the background

㉙ Berga and Serra del Cadí

C1411/E09. **Road Map** E5–F5 & F6.
🏔 14,200. *i* C/Àngels 7; 938 21
13 84. 🎉 🎭 La Patum (Corpus
Christi). **W** turismeberga.cat

This historic town, at the foot of the majestic Queralt mountain, is famous for La Patum, one of the wildest of Catalan fiestas. Just off the Calle Mayor, a street leads to the **Iglesia de San Joan**, built in 1220 by the Knights Hospitallers. Worth seeing are the former houses of the aristocracy, such as the modernist **Casa Barons** at nos 9–11 Calle Mayor, and opposite the church of San Joan, the **Palacio de los Peguera**. The palace was designed in 1905–8 by Ramon Cot. On its first floor is the Cal Negre café. Also on the main street is an 18th-century windmill – the **Molino de la Sal**.

A spectacular walk leads up from the town to the sanctuary of **Queralt**, high up above Berga, with fabulous views.

The Serra del Cadí has some of the best walking country in the eastern Pyrenees, and contains the lovely, lonely village of **Gosol**, where Picasso painted for several months in 1905.

㉚ Andorra

Principality of Andorra. **Road Map** F5.
🏔 78,000. *i* Plaça de la Rotonda
(Andorra la Vella); 00 376 87 31 03.
W visitandorra.com

Legend has it that Charlemagne established Andorra in 805 to thank local people for their help in fighting the Saracens. For centuries, the principality fought for its independence from the Spanish dukedoms and France, which it gained in 1278. In 1993, it ratified its first-ever constitution.

Situated on the border between France and Spain, the principality occupies an area of 468 sq km (180 sq miles). It is divided into seven districts, characterized by typical mountain scenery and Mediterranean flora. The average altitude is 1,996 m (6,550 ft) above sea level, and the highest peak is Coma Pedrosa (2,946 m/9,665 ft). Winter sports play an important role, with the main ski centres in Arinsal, Pas de la Casa, Grau Roig and Soldeu.

Andorra is theoretically a constitutional monarchy, the ceremonial joint heads of state being the French Count of Foix (a title adopted by the French president) and the Spanish bishop of La Seu d'Urgell. The legislative branch of government is the General Council, comprising 28 elected members. The official language is Catalan, though French and Castilian are also spoken. Andorrans are a minority in their own country, accounting for barely 26 per cent of the population; the remainder is made up of Spanish, Portuguese and French.

For many years Andorra has been a tax-free paradise for shoppers, reflected in the crowded shops of the capital, **Andorra la Vella**. Almost every one of Andorra's 20,000 native residents owns a shop.

Andorra's charm lies not only in its beautiful landscapes, but also its Romanesque architecture. One of the oldest historic monuments is the **Iglesia de Santa Coloma**. It was built in the 9th century in a pre-Romanesque style, then remodelled several times thereafter. Of particular note is the 12th-century belfry with narrow double windows. The **Iglesia de Santa Eulalia** in Encamp, to the east of the capital, is an example of Pyrenean pre-Romanesque religious architecture. The stone **Iglesia de San Juan de Casello** has a typical Lombardy-style belfry.

At fiesta time, the streets of Andorra's towns are filled with people dancing the traditional *sardana*, *marratxa* and *el contrapes*.

A figure of the Virgin Mary, patron of Andorra

The charming 9th-century Iglesia de Santa Coloma in Andorra

The magnificent portal of the monastery in Ripoll

❸❶ Ripoll

Girona. **Road Map** F5. 🏘 11,000. 👤
Plaça Abat Oliba; 972 70 23 51. 🚌 Sat.
🎪 Sant Eudald (second week in May).
📷 check website. 🖥 **ripoll.cat**

Ripoll is known as the "cradle of Catalonia", because it was the first part of Catalonia recovered from the Moors by Guifré El Pelos (Wilfred the Hairy), founder of the 500-year dynasty of the House of Barcelona. He made Ripoll his capital, and in 879 established here the Benedictine **Monestir de Santa María**, an important centre of culture and art. The monastery had a well-stocked library, a scriptorium and a highly regarded monastic school. Abbot Oliba (1008–46) raised a new double-aisled basilica, but this unfortunately suffered extensive damage during an earthquake in 1428. Romanesque cloisters, from the 12th to the 16th centuries, survive. The basilica was reconstructed during the 19th century in a simplified form.

Today, visitors can admire the splendid Romanesque portal, with Christ Pantocrator occupying a central position above the entrance, flanked by angels, apostles and the 24 elders of the Apocalypse. The rich iconography also depicts scenes from the Old Testament, including the Judgement of Solomon and the Dream of Solomon, as well as Old Testament figures such as Moses and David.

❸❷ Queralbs and Sanctuari de Núria

Girona. **Road Map** F5. 🏘 198. 🚂
👤 Estació Vall de Núria; 972 73 20 20.
🖥 **valldenuria.cat**

For a favourite local day out, most people start in the little town of Ribes de Freser, in the Ribes valley. From here the Cremallera (Zipper Train) leads to the pretty village of **Queralbs**, at the halfway point, and Núria at the top. There are great views from the train.

Queralbs is home to the 12th-century Romanesque church of Sant Jaume. Lovely meadows spread across the hillsides around the **Sanctuari de Núria**. Set at an altitude of 1,967 m (6,453 ft), the shrine is an important place of pilgrimage. It was first mentioned in historical documents in 1162. St Gil, who sculpted the altar of the Virgin Mary of Núria, is said to have lived here in the 8th century; the feast of the Virgin is celebrated each year on 8 September.

The shrine was extended in 1449, and again in 1640 and 1648. In 1883, it acquired a Neo-Romanesque church, consecrated in 1913 and completed in 1964. There are some wonderful walks from here.

A colourful stained-glass window in the Sanctuari de Núria

❸❸ Sant Joan de les Abadesses

Girona. **Road Map** F5. 🏘 3,600.
👤 Plaça de l'Abadia 9; 972 72 05 99.
🚌 Sun. 🎪 Fiesta Mayor (second week in Sep). 📷 check website.
🖥 **santjoandelesabadesses.cat**

The beginnings of this pretty market town date back to the establishment in 887 of a **monastery**. It was founded by Guifré el Pelós, first count of Barcelona, as a gift to his daughter, the first abbess.

The Catalan Language

Belonging to the Romance group of Indo-European languages, Catalan emerged as a literary language in the 13th century, although the first Catalan texts appeared as early as the 12th century. After a long period of Castilian (Spanish) dominance, Catalan experienced a renaissance in the mid-19th century. This revival was cut short by the Spanish Civil War; under Franco's dictatorship, the use of Catalan in public places was forbidden. Catalan has now re-emerged from this repression and is in everyday use all over Catalonia, Valencia and the Balearic Islands. It is spoken by around 7 million people.

The emblem of Catalonia

The church in Sant Joan de les Abadesses

The Benedictine monastery was in operation until 1076, when its activities were suspended by a papal bull.

The monastery **church** is unadorned, except for a superb wooden calvary depicting the Descent from the Cross. Made in 1150, it looks modern; part of it (one of the thieves crucified with Christ) was burnt in the Civil War and replaced with great skill. The monastery's **museum** contains a collection of beautiful Renaissance and Baroque altarpieces.

The town, which was encircled by walls with 24 towers and six gates, is approached by the fine 12th-century Gothic bridge that arches over the Ter river.

🔞 Vall de Camprodon

C38, C26. **Road Map** F5. 🚹 Pl. de España 1 (Camprodon); 972 74 00 10. 🆆 valldecamprodon.org

Camprodon is the main town of this long valley, which is home to several charming villages. Nearby is tiny **Llanars**, with its beautiful Romanesque Església de Sant Esteve, tucked away in the old quarter among narrow winding streets. **Setcases**, further up the valley, is a famous beauty spot. Above it is **Vallter**, the easternmost ski resort in the Pyrenees.

🔞 Olot

Girona. **Road Map** G5. 🚹 34,000. 🚹 Calle Hospici 8; 972 26 01 41. 🚍 Mon. 🎉 Corpus Cristi, Fiesta del Tura (8 Sep). 🆆 turismeolot.com

This small market town, set in an odd landscape ringed by stumpy, extinct volcanoes and vast expanses of beech woods, lost most of its historic monuments during an earthquake in 1427. The buildings one sees today date largely from the 18th and 19th centuries. In 1783, a Public School of Drawing was founded in Olot to train local craftsmen. In time, it became an important centre of religious art. Much of the school's work can be seen in the **Museu Comarcal de la Garrotxa**, housed in an 18th-century hospice with a large patio and arcades. The exhibition rooms have exhibits illustrating the development of the provincial economy and crafts.

Detail of *Rainy Taxi*, Teatro-Museu Dalí

🏛 Museu Comarcal de la Garrotxa

Calle Hospici 8. **Tel** 972 27 11 66. **Open** Tue–Sun. **Closed** 1 Jan, 25 Dec. ♿ 📷 (free 1st Sun of month).

🔞 Costa Brava

Girona. **Road Map** G6. ✈ Girona. 🚹 Paseo Maritim s/n, L'Estartit; 972 75 19 10. 🆆 visitestartit.com 🚹 Avda. del Pelegri 25 (Tossa de Mar); 972 34 01 08. 🆆 costabrava.org

The touristy "wild coast", stretching south from the French border for 200 km (124 miles), is a mix of pine-backed sandy coves, golden beaches and crowded resorts. **Lloret de Mar** is the busiest of these.

Trips can be made from **L'Estartit** to the **Illes Medes**, islands that once sheltered pirates and are now a marine reserve with clear waters for snorkelling, while in **Tossa de Mar** the main attraction is the fortified 12th-century Old Town and the golden beach. Inland, but within easy reach of the Costa Brava, is **Figueres**, the hometown of the Surrealist artist Salvador Dalí. The magnificent **Teatro-Museu Dalí**, founded by the artist in 1974, houses works by Dalí. Further south is **Girona**, whose cathedral has a superb silver altar. In the pre-Romanesque Església de Sant Pere de Galligants are fine mermaid sculptures.

🏛 Teatro-Museu Dalí

Pl. Gala-Salvador Dalí. **Tel** 972 67 75 00. **Open** Mar–Jun & Oct: 9:30am–6pm Tue–Sun; Jul–Sep: 9am–8pm daily; Nov–Feb: 10:30am–6pm Tue–Sun. 📷 📷 🆆 salvador-dali.org

View south along the Costa Brava from Tossa de Mar

TRAVELLERS' NEEDS

WHERE TO STAY

Northern Spain offers an exceptional variety of accommodation options. There are places to suit all budgets, and even the most demanding visitor will find something to satisfy them. Those searching for luxury can head straight for the exclusive hotels and paradors, while the family-run *casas rurales* are excellent places to escape the hustle and bustle of the city. There are also mountain refuges with stunning views, and campsites in the coastal areas. Weary pilgrims can find official accommodation and modest meals in towns and villages along the Road to Santiago. Regardless of the standard of accommodation, one thing is certain in Northern Spain: the region's inhabitants will give you a warm welcome and will be ready to help in the event of any problems.

The façade of the Meliá Hotel de la Reconquista, in Oviedo *(see p205)*

Hotel Grading and Facilities

Spacious, comfortable and clean, hotels in Northern Spain are categorized and graded by the regional tourist authorities. Hotels (indicated by an "H" on a blue plaque near the hotel door) are awarded from one to five stars. They usually have ensuite bathrooms or at least a shower in the room. Hostels ("Hs") and pensions ("P") may not have ensuite facilities and they have fewer comforts than hotels, so they are a bit cheaper.

Spain's star-rating system reflects the number and range of facilities available, rather than the quality of service. One star is given to the most modest hotels, and five stars to the most elegant and expensive ones. Two- and three-star hotels are the most popular. The more exclusive hotels have all kinds of amenities, such as on-site parking, Internet access and air-conditioning, as well as facilities for the disabled. All hotels have rooms with a bath or shower unless otherwise specified.

A popular option in all the autonomous regions of Northern Spain are hostels *(hostales)* and guest houses *(pensiones)*, which are cheaper than hotels. These are usually small, family-run places offering just a few beds.

The biggest hotel chains in Northern Spain are the **Grupo Sol-Meliá** and **NH**, with hotels in the main towns. Their facilities are of a high standard and include Internet access. There is also a growing number of small, individually run hotels with a distinctive character and charm, for a memorable stay.

An elegant room at the Gran Hotel Sardinero, Santander *(see p205)*

Paradors

Paradors are government-run hotels, classified from three to five stars. Spain's first parador opened in 1928, and now there is a wide network of thesse hotels spread across the country, so there is never more than a day's drive to the nearest one. The best, such as the Parador de los Reyes Católicos in Santiago de Compostela, are housed in former royal hunting lodges, monasteries, castles and other monuments; some paradors have been purpose-built, often in spectacular scenery or in towns of historic interest.

A parador is not necessarily the best hotel in town, but it can be counted on to deliver a high level of comfort. The bedrooms are usually spacious and comfortable, and furnished to a standard that varies little from parador to parador. Some also offer fine regional cuisine.

If you plan to tour in high season or to stay in the smaller paradors, it is wise to reserve a room. The paradors may be booked online (via the www. parador.es website), through the **Central de Reservas** in Madrid, through representatives outside Spain *(see Directory on p203)* or by calling a parador direct (they have English-speaking staff). Rates can be expensive; it is worth looking for special deals, especially in low season. If you plan to stay at several paradors, check out discount passes on their website, which include five-night stays and lower rates for seniors and youths. Note that the region's most celebrated paradors, particularly those in Santiago de Compostela, must be booked months in advance.

Prices

Spanish law requires all hotels to display their prices at the reception and in every room. Rates for a double room can be as little as €35–40 a night for a cheap one-star hostel; a five-star hotel will cost more than €200 a night, but a room price higher than €350 a night is exceptional.

Prices vary according to room, region and season. High season (*temporada alta*) covers July and August, as well as the major holidays (around Easter and between Christmas and New Year). Note that prices in the main cities drop in July and August, except during festivals. Many of Spain's city hotels charge especially inflated rates for their rooms during fiestas. Prices are slightly lower during the *temporada media* (off-season, from September to October, and May through June), but you'll find the best deals during the low season (*temporada baja*), in November and from February to April, although smaller hotels may be closed during this time. Hotels in the Pyrenees, especially those in the ski resorts, consider winter their high season; those hotels in the mountains that stay open year-round are much cheaper in the summer.

A suite or a very spacious room, or one with a view, a balcony or other special feature, may cost more than average. Rural and suburban hotels are less expensive than those in the city centre.

Most hotels quote prices per room and meal prices per person without including VAT (*IVA*), which is 10 per cent. Traditionally, hotel room rates in Spain have not included breakfast, which has been charged separately. However, a growing number of hotels

The medieval hall of the Parador de Hondarribia *(see p206)*

are now including breakfast. Even so, you will probably find a better and cheaper breakfast at a nearby café.

Booking and Check-In

During the off-season, in rural or small towns, you are unlikely to need to book ahead; however, if you plan to travel in high season or want to stay in a particular hotel, you should reserve a room by phone or email or through a travel agent. You will also need to reserve if you want a special room: one with a double bed (twin beds are the norm); on the ground floor; away from a noisy main road; or with a view.

Resort hotels often close from autumn to spring. Before you travel, it is advisable to check that your preferred hotels will be open at that time of year.

A deposit is not normally required when you book a hotel room unless it is during a peak period or for a stay of more than a few nights. A credit card number is usually enough to hold a reservation. If you have to cancel, do so at least a week before the booking date or you may lose all or some of your deposit.

Most hotels will expect you to arrive by 8pm. If you are delayed, call the hotel to tell them when to expect you.

When checking into a hotel, you will be asked to show your passport or some other form of photographic ID to comply with Spanish police regulations. It will be returned to you as soon as your details have been copied.

At most hotels you will be asked to check out of your room by noon on the last day of your stay, or to pay for another night. Remember to confirm the check-out time when you first check in.

Paying

Most hotels accept all major credit cards, such as VISA and MasterCard. JVC, Diner's Club and American Express are also widely accepted.

Personal cheques, on the other hand, are not accepted – even if they are backed up by a cheque guarantee card or drawn on a Spanish bank.

Cash is always welcome. When tipping hotel staff, the usual amount is €2–3.

The fairy-tale medieval castle housing the Parador de Olite *(see p206)*

The period exterior of Hotel Calle Mayor in Logroño *(see p206)*

Casas Rurales

Hotel accommodation in Northern Spain is supplemented by a large number of family-run *casas rurales*. These country homes make ideal places for those seeking quiet relaxation in a family setting rather than the anonymous atmosphere of a hotel in a bustling city centre. *Casas rurales* usually offer accommodation to a dozen or so visitors. Guests can expect to find clean, well-kept rooms and a friendly atmosphere. In addition, many *casas rurales* provide excellent home cooking and traditional regional cuisine, while others are offered on a self-catering basis.

Another major advantage of *casas rurales* is their affordable price. However, due to their popularity, they are in great demand, particularly in high season, and it is always worth booking ahead by phone, online or through local tourist agencies.

Casas rurales are especially popular in the regions of Asturias, Cantabria and Navarra. In Cantabria they are known as *casonas*, while in Catalonia they are often called *cases de pages*.

Youth Hostels and Mountain Refuges

To use the network of *albergues juveniles* (youth hostels) in Spain, you need to show a YHA (Youth Hostel Association) card from your country or an international card, which you can buy from any hostel. Prices per person are much lower than in hotels or guest houses, but so, too, is the standard of accommodation – basic shared rooms with no private bathrooms. There is no age limit for guests staying in youth hostels. Note that, during term time, many fill up with school groups.

Youth hostels can be booked through the **Red Española de Albergues Juveniles** (Spanish Network of Youth Hostels).

A number of pilgrims' hostels can be found along the Road to Santiago. They vary from basic to quite comfortable.

Mountaineers heading for remote areas may use the *refugios* (refuges). These are shelters with a dormitory, cooking facilities and heating. Some are huts with only about six bunks; others are mountain houses with up to 50 beds. The *refugios* are marked on large-scale maps of mountain areas and national parks, and they are administered by the regional mountaineering associations. The **Federación Española de Montañismo** and the local tourist offices will supply their addresses.

Monasteries and Convents

Some Benedictine and Cistercian monasteries in Northern Spain have rooms available for overnight guests. Many pilgrims on the Road to Santiago choose to stay at monasteries or convents along the way. The rooms are modest, with few amenities.

Guests are expected to tidy their rooms and to help with

A colourful living room in a self-catering holiday flat

the washing-up; they are also expected to observe house rules. Some convents admit only women, and some monasteries only men. Be sure to book well in advance if you plan to stay in a monastery, since many are located in beautiful historic buildings and are consequently very popular.

Self-Catering

In larger Spanish towns, particularly those on the coast, it is possible to rent a holiday flat or villa. These are usually fully furnished lodgings, most commonly studios or flats with one or two bedrooms, a living room, bathroom, kitchen, and balcony or terrace. Some, especially inland, have swimming pools. Check in advance whether you need to bring your own towels and bedding, though these are generally provided at no extra cost. You are expected to keep the flat clean and tidy. A deposit is usually payable at the beginning of your stay and will be returned to you when you leave.

Camp Sites

In Spain, camping is permitted only at official camp sites. Most camp sites have electricity and running water; some also have launderettes, playgrounds, restaurants, shops, a swimming pool and other amenities. The Camping Card International (CCI) can be used instead of a passport to check in at camp sites, and it covers you for third-party insurance; visit www.campingcardinternational.com for more information. Cards are issued in the UK by the AA, RAC and the **Camping and Caravanning Club.**

An invaluable source of information about Spanish camp sites is the *Guía Oficial de Campings*, published each year by Turespaña.

A lot of useful information can also be obtained from the **Federación Española de Clubes Campistas**.

The inviting swimming pool at Hotel Bosque Mar, Reboredo (see p204)

Disabled Travellers

Hotel managers will advise on accessibility for people in wheelchairs, and the staff will always be happy to help, but disabled access is not widespread throughout Northern Spain. Gradually, however, more and more hotels are introducing special facilities for disabled people, such as wheelchair ramps and adapted bathrooms.

COCEMFE (Confederación Coordinadora Estatal de Minusválidos Físicos de España), the Spanish association for the disabled, and **Viajes 2000** travel agency can advise on hotels for guests with special needs.

Travelling with Children

Travelling in Spain with children is a pleasure, since they are welcomed virtually everywhere. Many hotels allow small children to stay for free or at a low rate in their parents' room. Cots or fold-out beds are provided for a small fee. Child-size portions are available in some hotel restaurants, although note that evening opening times may be later than suit many families. It is, however, hard to find restaurants with highchairs.

Recommended Hotels

The hotels featured on the following pages have been carefully selected to give a cross-section of options in every region, covering a range of themes and price categories. You will find everything from sumptuous luxury hotels to friendly seaside resorts and country inns, all listed by area and offering great value within their category.

The entries marked as DK Choice highlight places that offer something truly special. They may be set in beautiful surroundings, or housed in a historic palace or a converted farmhouse where you will be treated like a member of the family. Common to all is a second-to-none quality of service and atmosphere.

DIRECTORY

Hotel Chains

Grupo Sol-Meliá
Tel 902 14 44 40.
W solmelia.com

NH
Tel 902 09 18 57.
W nh-hoteles.com

Hotel Reservations

W centraldereservas.com
W innsofspain.com
W muchoviaje.es
W rusticae.es

Accommodation

Asociación de Empresarios de Hostelería de Asturias
Calle Alonso Quintanilla 3–1,
33002 Oviedo.
Tel 985 22 38 13.
W hotelesdeasturias.org

Asociación de Empresarios de Hostelería de Vizcaya
Calle Gran Vía 38–2,
48009 Bilbao.
Tel 944 35 66 60.
W asociacionhosteleria.com

Paradors

Central de Reservas
Calle José Abascal 2–4,
28003 Madrid.
Tel 902 54 79 79.
W parador.es

IBERTOURS Travel
Unit 5, 20 Commercial Road, Melbourne,
Victoria 3004.
Tel 61 3 9867 8833.
W ibertours.com.au

Keytel International
The Foundry,
156 Blackfriars Road,
London SE1 8EN.
Tel 020 7953 3020.
W keytel.co.uk

PTB Hotels
22960 Calvert St,
Woodland Hills, CA 91367.
Tel 818 884 1984.
37–18 Northern Blvd, Suite 412, Long Island City, NY 11101. Tel 718 897 7272.
W eparadors.com

Casas Rurales

W ecotur.es
W esgalicia.com
W guiarural.com
W toprural.com
W turismerural.com

Youth Hostels

Red Española de Albergues Juveniles
Tel 913 08 46 75.
W reaj.com

Mountain Refuges

Federación Española de Montañismo
Calle Floridablanca 84,
08015 Barcelona.
Tel 934 26 42 67.
W fedme.es

Camping

Camping and Caravanning Club
Greenfields House,
Westwood Way,
Coventry CV4 8JH, UK.
Tel 0845 130 7631 (UK).
W campingandcaravanningclub.co.uk

Federación Española de Clubes Campistas
Calle Quinsá 17,
46113 Moncada.
Tel 961 39 90 09.
W campistasfecc.com

Disabled Travellers

COCEMFE
Calle Luis Cabrera 63,
28002 Madrid.
Tel 917 44 36 00.
W cocemfe.es

Viajes 2000
Tel 902 20 00 11.
W viajes2000.com

Where to Stay

Galicia

DK Choice

BAIONA: Parador de Baiona   €€€
Historic
Ctra de Baiona
Tel 986 35 50 00
🅦 parador.es
This is one of the most beautiful paradors in Spain, located inside an old fortress, with breathtaking views of the Atlantic Ocean. The elegant rooms and apartments are classically furnished. Guests can relax around the outdoor pool or enjoy a game of tennis.

FERROL: Parador de Ferrol   €€
Historic
Rúa Almirante Fernández Martín
Tel 981 35 67 20
🅦 parador.es
Many rooms at this parador enjoy magnificent harbour views. Lovely garden and restaurant.

NOIA: Hotel Pesquería del Tambre   €€
Hotel with character
Santa María de Roo, 15211
Tel 981 05 16 20
🅦 pesqueriadeltambre.com
Ideal for nature lovers, this serene hotel sits on the banks of the Ría Tambre. The rooms boast stone walls and natural textiles.

OURENSE: Carris Cardenal Quevedo   €€
Modern
Rúa Cardenal Quevedo 28, 32004
Tel 988 37 55 23
🅦 carrishoteles.com
A stylish, modern hotel behind a traditional façade. Spacious rooms.

PONTEVEDRA: Parador de Pontevedra   €€
Historic
Rúa Barón 19
Tel 986 85 58 00
🅦 parador.es
Occupying a 16th-century mansion, this parador has antique furnishings and romantic gardens.

REBOREDO: Hotel Bosque Mar   €€
Modern
Rúa Reboredo 93, 36988
Tel 986 73 10 55
🅦 bosquemar.com
Simply furnished apartments and rooms, plus indoor and outdoor pools and a spa.

SANTIAGO DE COMPOSTELA: Costa Vella   €€
Hotel with character
Rúa da Porta da Pena 17, 15704
Tel 981 56 95 30
🅦 costavella.com
Relax under the apple and lemon trees on the terrace or in the glazed gallery overlooking the garden at this charming hotel.

SANTIAGO DE COMPOSTELA: Parador de los Reyes Católicos   €€€
Historic
Praza do Obradoiro 1, 15705
Tel 981 58 22 00
🅦 parador.es
Built in the late 15th century as a pilgrim's hostel, this is now Spain's most luxurious parador, boasting splendid, antique-filled rooms.

SANXENXO: Hotel Rotilio   €
Modern
Avenida del Puerto 7–9, 36960
Tel 986 72 02 00
🅦 hotelrotilio.com
Many of the airy rooms here have private balconies with views of the port. The restaurant is one of the best in town.

VIGO: Hotel Pazo Los Escudos Spa & Beach   €€
Luxury
Avenida Atlántida 106, 36208
Tel 986 82 08 20
🅦 pazolosescudos.com
Right on the Playa de Carril beach, this historic mansion features contemporary rooms, an outstanding spa and a great restaurant.

A path through the delightful gardens at the Hotel Bosque Mar, in Reboredo

Asturias and Cantabria

CASTRO URDIALES: Las Rocas   €€
Modern
Flaviobriga 1, 39700
Tel 942 86 04 00
🅦 lasrocashotel.com
Most of the airy, spacious rooms at this beachfront hotel have wonderful sea views. The restaurant has an excellent reputation for its seafood.

COMILLAS: La Solana Montañesa   €
Hotel with character
La Campa 22, 39520
Tel 942 72 10 26
🅦 lasolanamontanesa.com
Rustically decorated cosy rooms, views over the Old Town, a garden with a children's play area and a barbecue are some of the features that make this a great option in Comillas.

CUDILLERO: La Casona del Pío   €
Hotel with character
Calle Riofrío 3, 33150
Tel 985 59 15 12
🅦 lacasonadepio.com
The rooms at this hotel housed in a former fish-salting factory in the Old Town have stone walls and antique-style furniture. The bathrooms come with Jacuzzis.

FUENTE DÉ: Hotel El Rebeco   €
Hotel with character
Ctra Fuente Dé
Tel 942 73 66 00
🅦 hotelrebeco.com
Located next to the cable car, this stone-built hotel is popular with climbers and hikers. Its rustically decorated rooms offer sublime mountain views.

GIJÓN: Hotel Central   €
Hotel with character
Plaza del Humedal, 33207
Tel 985 09 86 51
🅦 hotelcentrogijon.es
Overlooking a pretty square, this stylish family-run hotel offers quiet rooms decorated in pale colours, plus a lobby bar with an open fire.

DK Choice

GIJÓN: La Ermita de Deva €€
Hotel with character
Camino de Valliquín 432, 33394
Tel *985 33 34 22*
 laermitadedeva.es
This enchanting family-run hotel is set in an early 18th-century stone house on the edge of Gijón. Its inviting rooms preserve the original features but are equipped with modern conveniences. The tranquil gardens contain a pretty 16th-century chapel. The delightful owners go out of their way to ensure their guests feel at home.

LEÓN: La Posada Regia €€
Historic
Calle Regidores 9–11, 24003
Tel *987 21 31 73*
regialeon.com
Occupying a pair of traditional buildings, this hotel has attractive rooms with exposed brick walls and wooden furnishings.

LEÓN: Parador Hostal de San Marcos €€€
Luxury
Plaza de San Marcos 7, 24001
Tel *987 23 73 00*
parador.es
This parador is housed in a fine Renaissance building with a superb Plateresque façade. The rooms feature antique furniture.

LLANES: Hotel Don Paco €
Hotel with character
Colegio de la Encarnación 1, 33500
Tel *985 40 01 50*
hoteldonpacollanes.com
A former Baroque convent houses this small hotel with modern rooms, a pretty garden terrace and a good restaurant.

LUARCA: Hotel Villa de Luarca €
Hotel with character
Calle Álvaro de Albornoz 6, 33700
Tel *985 47 07 03*
hotelvilladeluarca.com
Featuring warmly furnished rooms, this friendly hotel in a traditional townhouse in the heart of Luarca is only a stone's throw from the beach.

OVIEDO: Hotel Rosal €
Modern
Calle Cabo Noval 2, 33007
Tel *985 20 29 84*
hotelrosal.es
This small hotel in the historic town centre offers tastefully decorated, minimalist rooms, many with wonderful views over the city. Excellent service.

The sleek reception area at the Gran Hotel Sardinero, Santander

OVIEDO: Meliá Hotel de la Reconquista €€€
Luxury
Calle Gil de Jaz 16, 33004
Tel *985 24 11 00*
hoteldelareconquista.com
The finest address in town, this sumptuous hotel boasts huge designer rooms in a magnificent 18th-century palace. Former guests have included the Spanish royal family and Woody Allen.

RIBADESELLA: Don Pepe €
Modern
Dionisio Ruisanchez 12, 33560
Tel *985 85 78 81*
hoteldonpepe.com
Most of the bright rooms at this hotel overlooking the beach enjoy sea views from their private balconies.

SAN VICENTE DE LA BARQUERA: Posada Punta Liñera €
Hotel with character
Calle Boria 12, 39540
Tel *942 71 22 25*
puntalinera.com
A short drive from the town centre, this welcoming rural hotel has rustically furnished rooms and a garden with wonderful sea views.

DK Choice

SANTANDER: Hostal Jardin Secreto €
Guest house
Calle del Cardenal Cisneros 37, 39007
Tel *942 07 07 14*
jardinsecretosantander.com
Simple yet stylish, this delightful place offers a range of services, including a pillow menu, but keeps the intimacy of a bed-and-breakfast. Guests can relax on the pretty garden terrace, tuck into local pastries at breakfast, and enjoy discounted entry to a neighbouring spa.

SANTANDER: Gran Hotel Sardinero €€€
Luxury
Plaza de Italia 1, 39005
Tel *942 27 11 00*
hotelsardinero.es
Overlooking the city's most famous beach, this elegant hotel has large, modern rooms, many with sea views, and a splendid restaurant.

SANTILLANA DEL MAR: Posada Araceli €
Guest house
Calle la Robleda 20, 39330
Tel *942 84 01 94*
posadaraceli.com
Each room has been individually decorated with locally made furnishings at this attractive rural guest house, which is set in tranquil gardens near the historic centre.

SANTILLANA DEL MAR: Hotel Casa de Marqués €€€
Luxury
Calle Cantón 24, 39330
Tel *942 81 88 88*
hotelcasadelmarques.com
Housed in a magnificent 15th-century palace, this hotel has sumptuous rooms that overlook a romantic garden. Don't miss the splendid staircase made out of a 700-year-old oak tree. There is also an excellent restaurant.

The Basque Country

BILBAO: Arriaga Suites €
Modern
Bidebarrieta 3, 48005
Tel *635 70 72 47*
arriagasuites.com
Situated in Bilbao's historic quarter, these simple, yet stylish, rooms boast amenities such as a microwave and fridge. A good option for families.

For more information on types of hotels *see page 203*

BILBAO: Hotel Miró €€€
Design
Calle Alameda Mazarredo 77, 48009
Tel 946 61 18 80
w mirohotelbilbao.com
A contemporary, boutique
hotel with personal service, an
honesty bar and immaculate,
minimalist rooms.

**BILBAO: Silken Gran Hotel
Domine Bilbao** €€€
Design
Calle Alameda Mazarredo 61, 48009
Tel 944 25 33 00
w hoteles-silken.com
A spectacular interior designed
by Javier Mariscal, a great
restaurant, a spa and stunning
views of the Guggenheim.

GETARIA: Hotel Iturregi €€€
Hotel with character
Barrio Azkizu, 20808
Tel 943 89 61 34
w hoteliturregi.com
This beautiful, small, luxury hotel
set in a traditional country house
has wonderful views over the
vineyards and romantic rooms.
There is also a pool and a garden.

DK Choice

HONDARRIBIA: Obispo €€
Hotel with character
Plaza del Obispo s/n, 20280
Tel 943 64 54 00
w hotelobispo.com
A 14th-century palace in the
historic quarter houses this
enchanting hotel. Individually
decorated rooms preserve lots
of original details. In summer,
you can relax on the terrace;
in winter, get cosy in front of
the open fire. Superb service.
Bikes are available.

**HONDARRIBIA: Parador
de Hondarribia** €€€
Historic
Plaza de Armas 14, 20280
Tel 943 64 55 00
w parador.es
Housed in a 10th-century castle,
this parador offers stunning
views of the bay from its terrace
and an excellent restaurant.

**LAGUARDIA: Posada
Mayor de Migueloa** €€
Hotel with character
Mayor de Migueloa 20, 01300
Tel 945 60 01 87
w mayordemigueloa.com
Housed in the Palacio de Viana,
which dates back to the 17th-
century, this friendly hotel has
traditionally decorated rooms
and a restaurant serving the
area's fine wines.

LEKEITIO: Zubieta €€
Hotel with character
Calle Portal de Atea, 48280
Tel 946 84 30 30
w hotelzubieta.com
Oozing charm, this hotel is
surrounded by a garden. Rooms
are classically decorated, and
there is an atmospheric tapas bar.

MUNDAKA: El Puerto €
Hotel with character
Portu Kalea 1, 48360
Tel 946 87 67 25
w hotelelpuerto.com
A pretty, traditional hotel sitting
right on the harbour. Some
rooms have balconies with sea
views. Watch the sun set over the
old fishing port from the bar.

SAN SEBASTIÁN: Aida €
Guest house
Calle Iztueta 9, 20001
Tel 943 32 78 00
w pensionesconencanto.com
Immaculate, modern rooms just
a 10-minute walk from the Old
Town and the beach.

**SAN SEBASTIÁN: Hotel de
Londres y de Inglaterra** €€€
Luxury
Calle Zubieta 2, 20007
Tel 943 44 07 70
w hlondres.com
Old-fashioned charm and
contemporary comforts meet
at this hotel overlooking the
Bay of La Concha. Many rooms
boast unbeatable sea views.

**SAN SEBASTIÁN:
María Cristina** €€€
Luxury
Paseo Republica Argentina 4, 20004
Tel 943 43 76 00
w hotel-mariacristina.com
A glorious *belle époque* hotel
that retains many of its original
details, the María Cristina remains
the city's premier address thanks
to its palatial suites, gardens and
spectacular restaurant.

**VITORIA: La Casa de los
Arquillos** €
Hotel with character
Paseo de los Arquillos 1–2, 01001
Tel 945 15 12 59
w lacasadelosarquillos.com
This city-centre hotel has stylish,
white-on-white rooms, each
featuring the works of local artists.

ZARAUTZ: Hotel Olatu €
Modern
Ipar Kalea, 10, 20800
Tel 943 00 55 22
w olatuhotela.com
In the historic centre, but close
to the beach, this friendly hotel
has attractive rooms.

Occasional colourful touches offsetting a
white room at the Hotel Mirò, in Bilbao

Navarra and La Rioja

**ÁBALOS: Hotel Villa
de Ábalos** €€
Historic
Plaza Fermín Gurbindo 2, 26339
Tel 941 33 43 02
w hotelvilladeabalos.com
Set amid vineyards, this hotel
occupies a traditional stone
house, and its restaurant serves
vegetables from its own garden.

BURGOS: Hotel Landa €€€
Luxury
Carretera Madrid–Irún, Km 235, 09001
Tel 947 25 77 77
w landa.as
This elegant hotel on the outskirts
of Burgos has sumptuous rooms
designed by Pascual Ortega, and
lovely gardens.

**ELCIEGO: Hotel Marqués
de Riscal** €€€
Luxury
Torrea 1, 01340 Elciego
Tel 945 18 08 80
w hotel-marquesderiscal.com
Stunning architecture by Frank
Gehry, spectacular interiors and
an award-winning restaurant.

LOGROÑO: Hotel Calle Mayor €€
Design
Marqués de San Nicolás 71, 26001
Tel 941 23 23 68
w hotelcallemayor.com
Stay in chic, contemporary rooms
at this hotel in a beautifully
restored 16th-century palace.

OLITE: Parador de Olite €€
Historic
Plaza Teobaldos 2, 31390
Tel 948 74 00 00
w parador.es
Set in a medieval castle with
fairy-tale spires, this parador
has elegantly furnished rooms.

PAMPLONA: Navarra €
Guest house
Calle Tudela 9, 31002
Tel 948 22 51 64
w hostalnavarra.com

Friendly and family-run, this city-centre option offers a number of attractive rooms complete with small fridges.

DK Choice

PAMPLONA: Gran Hotel La Perla €€€
Luxury
Plaza del Castillo 1, 31001
Tel *948 22 30 00*
W granhotellaperla.com
Illustrious guests at this 19th-century hotel, now an ultra-chic urban hideaway, have included Charlie Chaplin and three kings. The sumptuous designer furnishings are beautifully paired with antiques, and amenities include a fine restaurant.

SAN MILLÁN DE LA COGOLLA: La Posada de San Millán €
Hotel with character
Calle Prestiño 5, 26326
Tel *941 37 31 61*
W lapoasadadesanmillan.es
With rustic rooms decorated in warm colours, this place also has views over the San Millán valley.

SANTO DOMINGO DE LA CALZADA: Parador de Santo Domingo €€
Historic
Plaza del Santo 3, 26250
Tel *941 34 03 00*
W parador.es
A 13th-century hostel for pilgrims houses this comfortable parador, which boasts a fine restaurant and magnificent country views.

VERA DE BIDASOA: Churrut €€
Hotel with character
Plaza de los Fueros 2, 31780
Tel *948 62 55 40*
W hotelchurrut.com
The traditionally furnished rooms in this 18th-century farmhouse feature beamed ceilings.

VILLABUENA DE ÁLAVA: Hotel Viura €€€
Design
Calle Mayor s/n, 01307
Tel *945 60 90 00*
W hotelviura.com
Featuring daring architecture and bold interiors, the Viura also has a spectacular wine cellar.

Central and Eastern Pyrenees

DK Choice

AINSA: Los Siete Reyes €€
Historic
Plaza Mayor s/n, 22330
Tel *974 50 06 81*
W lossietereyes.com
Overlooking the medieval square in the town centre, this charming hotel occupies a 16th-century building with porticoes. The exquisite rooms pair contemporary design with stone walls and wooden beams. Tranquil and relaxing, it's ideal for exploring the Ordesa National Park.

ANDORRA LA VELLA: Andorra Park Hotel €€€
Modern
Les Canals 24, AD500
Tel *376 877 777*
W andorraparkhotel.com
The rooms at this contemporary hotel are spacious and feature Jacuzzis. There are also a spa, an outdoor pool and sports facilities.

ARTIES: Parador de Arties €€€
Hotel with character
Ctra Baqueira-Beret, 25599
Tel *973 64 08 01*
W parador.es
A modern parador built with traditional materials, this offers stylish rooms, an outdoor pool and fabulous mountain views.

BAQUEIRA-BERET: Meliá Royal Tanau Hotel €€€
Modern
Carretera de Beret s/n, 25598
Tel *902 14 44 40*
W melia.com
A stunning boutique hotel, with a pool and a spa, at the foot of the slopes in Spain's finest ski resort.

BENASQUE: Hotel Selba d'Ansils €
Modern
Ctra de Anciles, Km 1.5, 22440
Tel *974 55 20 54*
W hotelselbadanils.com
This beautiful mountain hotel has incredible views, a huge fireplace and elegant rooms.

BIELSA: Hotel Valle de Pineta €
Hotel with character
Ctra Baja s/n, 22350
Tel *974 50 10 10*
W hotelvalledepineta.com
Many of the pretty rooms at this rural hotel have balconies for soaking up the mountain views.

CANDANCHÚ: Edelweiss €
Modern
Ctra Francia, Km 189, 22889
Tel *974 37 32 00*
W edelweisscandanchu.com
You can see the slopes from this inviting hotel, which also boasts an excellent restaurant.

HUESCA: Posada de la Luna €
Hotel with character
Carrer Joaquin Costa 10, 22003
Tel *974 24 17 38*
W posadadelaluna.com
Original artwork with a planetary theme is the hallmark of this modern hotel in the old quarter.

HUESCA: Hotel Sancho Abarca €€
Design
C/Coso Alto 52, 22002
Tel *974 22 06 50*
W hotelsanchoabarca.com
Chic designer rooms, a spa and an outdoor pool are on offer at this glamorous hotel.

DK Choice

JACA: Barosse €€
Hotel with character
Carrer Estiras 4, Barós 22712
Tel *974 36 05 82*
W barosse.com
An exquisite design hotel in a tiny village outside Jaca, this has just a handful of romantic, beautifully furnished rooms. An adult-only space, it has a Jacuzzi in the gardens. Massages can be arranged, as well as wonderful candle-lit dinners.

Beamed ceilings and contemporary furniture at the Hotel Calle Mayor, Logroño *(see p206)*

For more information on types of hotels *see page 203*

WHERE TO EAT AND DRINK

Every region of Northern Spain has its own cuisine and its own distinctive dishes. Eating establishments range from simple tapas bars – found in even the smallest villages – where you can drop in for a quick meal or a drink, to top-quality gourmet restaurants where you can linger for hours. The Basque Country, in particular, is justifiably renowned for its outstanding culinary tradition. Bodegas are good places to sample local wines, while in Asturias you'll find *sidrerías* serving, among other things, excellent cider.

Some of the delicious fare on offer at Las Termas, in Astorga *(see p217)*

Restaurants and Bars

After a long day's sightseeing, there's no better place to visit than a tapas bar. Tapas are considered an art form in this region of Spain, and as well as traditional taverns, you will find a large number of gourmet taverns serving particularly creative concoctions. Some bars, however, especially pubs (late-opening bars for socializing), serve no food.

If sand and sea are your aim, then *chiringuitos* are a good option. These beachside bars serve food and drinks. For an inexpensive sit-down meal, try one of the family-run *ventas*, *posadas*, *mesones* or *fondas*, which offer simple but tasty food.

For something more substantial, choose from the wide array of restaurants across the price spectrum.

Eating Hours

The Spanish breakfast *(desayuno)* is a light meal usually consisting of milky coffee *(café con leche)* and a pastry, biscuits or toast.

Many office workers step out to a café or tapas bar for a quick mid-morning snack between 10 and 11am. The Spanish eat their main meal of the day at around 2pm. Sunday lunch is a very busy time in restaurants, particularly in the countryside and on the coast.

Visitors looking for an earlier or lighter lunch can go to a tapas bar and order a few tapas *(see pp212–13)* – small savoury snacks that range from cold meats and cheeses to hot dishes. Tapas are often accompanied by a beer *(cerveza)*, a glass of red wine *(vino tinto)* or a soft drink.

Cafés, tea rooms *(salones de té)* and pastry shops *(pastelerías)*

Begoña in Posada de Valdeleón *(see p218)*

fill up between 5 and 7pm for afternoon snacks *(la merienda)*. By 8pm, the bars are crowded again with people having tapas accompanied by sherry, wine or beer.

Dinner *(la cena)* is eaten late in Spain – at 9pm or 10pm, especially on Friday and Saturday nights. In the summer, people tend to eat their meal even later. Spanish restaurants will rarely serve meals earlier in the evening.

Most restaurants have a break between 4 and 8pm. They also usually close one day a week, often Monday, and most also close on Sunday evening, too, as well as on some public holidays. In big cities, many close for an annual holiday, usually in August.

Reading the Menu

The Spanish term for menu is *la carta*. It usually features *sopas* (soups), *ensaladas* (salads), *entremeses* (starters or hors d'oeuvres), *revueltos y tortillas* (eggs scrambled with different ingredients such as prawns or asparagus, and potato omelettes), *verduras y legumbres* (vegetable dishes), *pescados y mariscos* (fish and shellfish), *carnes y aves* (meat and poultry) and *postres* (desserts). Most restaurants offer a *menú del día*, or menu of the day, costing from around €10 and consisting of a starter *(entrada)*, bread *(pan)*, main course *(plato principal)*, dessert *(postre)* and something to drink *(bebida)*, usually water or wine; coffee may cost extra. This is by far the best-value way to eat, and much cheaper than ordering off the full menu. However, most restaurants offer set menus only for lunch and only during the week. It's nearly always cheaper to eat lunch in restaurants than it is to eat dinner.

Another type of set menu is the *menú de degustación*, a gourmet or tasting menu that is usually found only in upscale restaurants. It is a great deal more expensive than a *menú del día*, consisting of a selection of the chef's special dishes in smaller portions.

Booking

For popular and acclaimed restaurants, as well as all upscale dining establishments, it's wise to book ahead for Friday and Saturday evenings and for Sunday lunch. The rest of the week, restaurants are less busy, and you can usually get a table. It's also worth booking ahead for any restaurant that has a particular regional speciality – and ordering that dish at the same time, as some specialities are available only with advance notice. Reservations can usually be made by phone.

Cafés

Cafés and pastry shops in Northern Spain enjoy a good reputation. Some make their own chocolate, which can include almonds (*almendras*), hazelnuts (*avellanas*), walnuts (*nueces*) or orange peel (*cáscara de naranja*). Coffee is invariably excellent and aromatic. The most popular types are espresso (*café solo*), espresso with a splash of milk (*cortado*) and milky coffee (*café con leche*). Also popular are combinations, such as espresso with a dash of brandy (*carajillo*).

Prices and Tipping

VAT (*IVA*) of 10 per cent is added to the bill. Some Spanish restaurants may add a service charge, too (*servicio incluído*), but in others it's normal for tourists to tip the staff, especially if they've been particularly helpful. There's no expectation of a set percentage, though, and locals tip very little. It's reasonable to leave around 5–10 per cent of your bill.

Outdoor dining in the Basque town of Hondarribia

Major debit and credit cards are accepted in most restaurants, but it is wise to have cash with you when visiting small cafés, bars or country taverns.

Prices depend on the category of restaurant and on what you order. The *menú del día* in a small restaurant will be priced at around €10. For an evening meal in a comfortable mid- to upper-range restaurant, you can eat well for €40. In an elegant city restaurant, you should expect to pay more than €40.

Children and Vegetarians

Most eating places welcome children and will serve small portions if requested.

The choices for vegetarians are limited in Spanish cuisine, which relies heavily on fish, seafood and meat. Tapas can be a good choice for vegetarians, however, with a selection of salads, cheeses, potato, egg and vegetable dishes available.

Disabled Access

Few restaurants, especially those located inside historic buildings, are wheelchair-friendly. It is worth phoning in advance to check on access to tables and toilets.

Dress

Casual wear is acceptable in all but the very smartest city restaurants.

Recommended Restaurants

The restaurants featured on the following pages have been carefully selected to give a cross-section of options in every region: you will find everything from Michelin-starred fine dining and traditional restaurants, to beachfront bars with barbecued seafood and gastrotaverns serving original tapas. Places serving Modern Spanish food offer contemporary versions of traditional classics, whereas places described as Traditional Spanish serve more conventional fare, such as stews and grilled meat or fish dishes.

Entries labelled as DK Choice highlight exceptional establishments that offer more than just excellent food, be it a celebrity chef, an unusual location or a unique menu.

The charming interior of the Casa Conrado in Oviedo (*see p218*)

The Flavours of Northern Spain

The wild, wet north of Spain is as famous for its rain as it is for its culinary excellence. The rain keeps the pastures lush and green – perfect dairy farming terrain – and the Atlantic provides a wonderful variety of seafood. The Basques, in particular, are celebrated chefs, and the region boasts some of the finest restaurants in Europe, along with gastronomic societies (called *txokos*) in every village. Inland and in the remoter regions you'll find old-fashioned country cooking – roast lamb and tender young beef, slow-cooked stews – and traditionally made cheeses.

Idiazábal cheese

Pulpo a la gallega, one of Galicia's signature dishes

Galicia

The westernmost tip of Spain is famous for its extraordinary seafood – from staples like cod (*bacalao*) to delicacies like barnacles (*percebes*), which look like tiny dinosaur feet. Every bar will serve up a plate of *pulpo a la gallega* (octopus with paprika and olive oil) or *pimientos de padrón* (small spicy green peppers). Inland, you'll find tender veal, free-range chicken and delicate soft cheeses such as *tetilla*.

Asturias and Cantabria

The bay-pocked coastline provides delicious fresh fish, often served simply grilled or simmered in casseroles. Inland, the lush pastures form Spain's dairy country – most Spanish milk, cream and some of its finest cheeses come from this region. Try Asturian *cabrales*, a pungent blue cheese, accompanied by local cider. The mountains provide succulent meat and game, often stewed with beans, as in Asturian *fabada*.

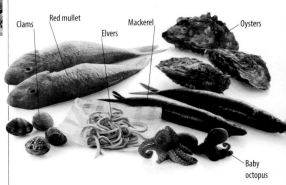

Clams   Red mullet   Elvers   Mackerel   Oysters   Baby octopus

Fish and seafood from the waters of Northern Spain

Regional Dishes and Specialities

Cherries

Unsurprisingly, seafood rules supreme along the coastline, from the ubiquitous octopus in a piquant sauce served in Galicia to the extraordinary spider crabs which are a sought-after delicacy in the Basque lands. The verdant pastures and rich farmland provide a wealth of fresh vegetables, including Navarra's justly famous asparagus, along with all kinds of wonderful cheeses. Slow-cooked stews, an Asturian speciality, are particularly good in the mountains, along with tender lamb and outstanding game in season. The renowned wines from La Rioja are excellent, but those of adjoining Navarra are less expensive and often equally interesting. The crisp whites of Galicia and the Basque lands are the perfect accompaniment to the fresh seafood, and throughout the North you'll find powerful liqueurs flavoured with local herbs.

Bacalao al Pil Pil Salted cod is cooked slowly with olive oil, chilli and garlic to create this classic Basque dish.

Array of *pintxos* laid out in a bar in the Basque Country

Basque Country

The Basque Country is a para-dise for gourmets, renowned throughout Spain for the excellence of its produce and the creative brilliance of its chefs. Basque cuisine leans towards seafood, of which there is a dazzling variety: humble salted cod and hake (elevated to new heights with delicious sauces) are most common, but sought-after delicacies include elvers (baby eels) and spider crab. Basque wines, drunk young and tart, offer the perfect balance. Bar counters groan with platters of *pintxos* – the Basque variant of tapas, and the Basques also make wonderful cheeses, including delicate, smoky Idiazábal.

Navarra and La Rioja

The fertile farmland of land-locked Navarra produces a spectacular array of fruit and vegetables such as asparagus, artichokes, cherries, chestnuts and peppers. In the Navarrese mountains, lamb is the most popular meat, as well as richly flavoured game in season, such as partridge and hare. *Trucha a la navarra* is the region's famous fish dish.

Tiny La Rioja is Spain's most famous wine region,

Red peppers – a speciality of La Rioja and popular in many dishes

producing rich, oaky reds and whites. The cuisine of La Rioja borrows from the neighbouring Basque Country and Navarra, with lamb a big feature, along with seafood and top-quality vegetables.

Central and Eastern Pyrenees

Hearty dishes with mountain-fresh ingredients typify Pyrenean cuisine, with a great variety of pork and poultry dishes such as *pollo al chilindrón* – chicken with onion, tomato, pepper and ham. For those who prefer fish, a good option is *bacalao al ajoarriero*, cod with potatoes and onions.

On the Menu

Trucha a la Navarra Trout, stuffed with ham and quickly grilled or fried.

Lacón con grelos Smoked pork shoulder joint with turnip leaves and potatoes.

Filloas queimadas Pancakes flambéed with *aguardiente*, cognac or whisky.

Sobaos, carajitos, casadielles Sponge cakes filled with nuts.

Angulas a la Bilbaína Baby eels cooked in olive oil with garlic, a seasonal Basque treat.

Pimientos rellenos Peppers stuffed with meat or fish.

Vieiras Baked scallops.

Empanada Gallega These golden pastries are stuffed with tuna and a wide choice of other fillings.

Chilindrón de Cordero Made with succulent lamb, this is a rich, hearty stew from the mountains of Navarra.

Leche Frita "Fried milk" is a delicious, custardy dessert from Cantabria. Simple but utterly delicious.

Choosing Tapas

Tapas are small snacks that originated in Andalusia to accompany sherry. Stemming from a bartender's practice of covering a glass with a saucer or *tapa* (cover) to keep out flies, the custom progressed to using a chunk of cheese or bread, and then to a few olives placed on a platter to accompany a drink. Choose from a range of appetizing varieties, from cold meats to elaborately prepared hot dishes of meat, seafood or vegetables. The Basque variant – *pintxos* – are like an open sandwich. Many bars also serve *raciónes*, which are larger portions.

Mixed green olives

Patatas bravas is a piquant dish of fried potatoes spiced with chilli and paprika.

Albondigas (meatballs) are a hearty tapa, often served with a spicy tomato sauce.

Almendras fritas are fried, salted almonds.

Banderillas are canapés skewered on toothpicks. The entire canapé should be eaten at once.

Calamares fritos are squid rings and tentacles which have been dusted with flour before being deep fried in olive oil. They are usually served garnished with a piece of lemon.

Jamón serrano is salt-cured ham dried in mountain (serrano) air.

On the Tapas Bar

Alcachofas rellenas de carne Meat-stuffed artichokes seasoned with onion, tomato, garlic, cheese and parsley.

Almejas a la marinera Clams sautéed in a wine, onion and garlic broth, garnished with parsley.

Anchoas rellenas Anchovies stuffed with onion and red or green pepper.

Bacalao a la vizcaína Salt cod served in a tomato sauce seasoned with paprika, onion, fried bread, garlic and almonds.

Berenjenas gratinadas Baked aubergine (eggplant) stuffed

with *jamón serrano* and cheese, served in an oregano-seasoned tomato sauce.

Boquerones en vinagre Small sardines in a vinaigrette.

Brochetas de marisco Seafood skewers of lobster or mussels with mushrooms and green pepper.

Brochetas de verduras Vegetable skewers, usually consisting of marrow, aubergine (eggplant), red peppers and tomatoes.

Buñuelos de bacalao Fried salt cod balls coated in breadcumbs and beer.

Calamares a la romana Fried squid rings.

Callos A serving of tripe.

Champiñones rellenos Mushrooms stuffed with onion, garlic, red pepper and *chorizo* (sausage).

Chuletitas de cordero con alcaparras Fried, breaded veal served in a caper-flavoured tomato sauce.

Empanada gallega Crispy pastry filled with fish, seafood or meat.

Endivias al queso de Cabrales Chicory leaves finished with a cheese and sour cream dressing.

Tapas Bars

Even a small village will have at least one bar where the locals go to enjoy drinks, tapas and conversation with friends. On Sundays and holidays, favourite places are packed with whole families enjoying the fare. In the Basque Country and Asturias it is customary to move from bar to bar, sampling the specialities of each. A *tapa* is a single serving, whereas a *ración* is more substantial. Tapas are usually eaten standing or perching on a stool at the bar rather that sitting at a table, for which a surcharge is usually made.

Diners make their choice at a busy tapas bar

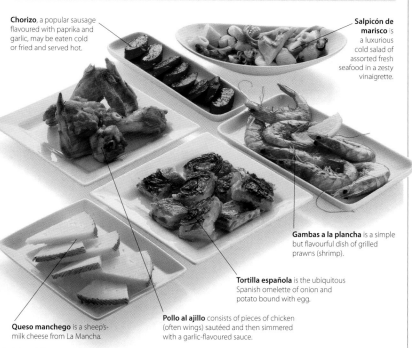

Chorizo, a popular sausage flavoured with paprika and garlic, may be eaten cold or fried and served hot.

Salpicón de marisco is a luxurious cold salad of assorted fresh seafood in a zesty vinaigrette.

Gambas a la plancha is a simple but flavourful dish of grilled prawns (shrimp).

Tortilla española is the ubiquitous Spanish omelette of onion and potato bound with egg.

Queso manchego is a sheep's-milk cheese from La Mancha.

Pollo al ajillo consists of pieces of chicken (often wings) sautéed and then simmered with a garlic-flavoured sauce.

Escalopines al queso de Cabrales Beef escalopes served with a Cabrales or some other blue cheese sauce.

Espárragos rellenos de salmón White asparagus stuffed with smoked salmon.

Espárragos verdes con jamón Green asparagus and ham, baked in a cheese sauce.

Gambas al ajillo Garlic prawns.

Mejillones a la vinagreta Mussels in a vinaigrette with onion, hard-boiled egg and parsley.

Patatas alioli Fried, cubed potates in a garlic mayonnaise sauce.

Pimientos rellenos de bacalao Red peppers stuffed with cod and seasoned with onion, salt and pepper.

Pimientos rellenos de chipirones Red peppers stuffed with seafood.

Pulpo a feira Octopus seasoned with hot and sweet paprika, bay leaves, olive oil and salt – a Galician speciality.

Revuelto de oricios Scrambled egg with sea urchins.

Riñones al jerez Kidneys served in dry sherry and seasoned with olive oil, onion and garlic.

Salpicón de marisco A seafood salad, prepared mainly with shellfish such as mussels, but which may also contain squid, octopus and other seafood.

Sardinas asadas Roasted sardines.

Tortilla de patatas Traditional Spanish potato omelette, seasoned with salt, pepper and a little bit of cheese.

Vieiras gratinadas Fresh scallops served in a tasty béchamel sauce.

What to Drink in Northern Spain

Northern Spain is renowned as a wine-producing region. The best-known reds are from La Rioja, while the finest white wines are produced in Galicia and the sub-regions of Rías Baixas and Ribeira Sacra. When in Asturias, be sure to try the excellent cider, which can be sampled in special establishments known as *sidrerías*. Many other beverages – alcoholic and non-alcoholic – are served in bars and cafés, which provide an important focus for life in Spain. The Spanish are also great coffee drinkers. In summer a tempting range of cooling drinks is on offer, in addition to beer, which is always available.

Customers enjoying a drink at a café terrace in Haro

Café solo

Café con leche

Camomile   Lime flower

Hot Drinks

Hot chocolate

A plate of *churros* (batter sticks)

The most popular hot drink is coffee (*café*), which is drunk at all times of the day and served in a variety of ways. In the morning it is customary to drink *café con leche* – a large half-and-half measure of milk (warm or cold) and coffee. In the afternoon and evening, most common is *café cortado* – an espresso with a splash of milk. Strong plain espresso (*café solo*) is also popular. The Spanish have a taste for hot chocolate, which is served with batter sticks (*churros*). Herbal teas include camomile (*manzanilla*) and lime flower (*tila*).

Cold Drinks

Spanish tap water is safe to drink, and many cities have convenient street-side water dispensers. Bottled mineral water, either still (*sin gas*) or sparkling (*con gas*), is available from shops. A popular thirst-quenching drink is *horchata*, a non-alcoholic, sweet milky beverage made from ground tiger nuts (*chufas*). *Zumo* is juice, sometimes from freshly squeezed fruit.

Sparkling mineral water

Horchata, made from *chufas*

Zumo, freshly squeezed juice

Mixed Drinks

Sangria is a refreshing mixture of red wine, *gaseosa* (lemonade) and other ingredients including chopped fruit and sugar. Wine diluted with lemonade is called *vino con gaseosa*. Another favourite drink is Agua de Valencia, a refreshing blend of *cava* (sparkling wine) and orange juice. Young people will often order the popular *cuba libre*, cola with white rum.

Sangria

The popular *cuba libre*

Vino con gaseosa

Spirits and Liqueurs

The most common spirits drunk in Northern Spain are liqueurs. *Anís*, flavoured with aniseed, is popular; so, too, is *pacharán*, a richly coloured liqueur made from sloes and produced mainly in Navarra. The somewhat stronger *orujo* originates from Galicia; it is usually colourless, but there are also flavoured varieties: coffee, cherry or herb, with colours appropriate to the content.

Anís

Pacharán

Orujo

Herb liqueur

Wine

No visit to Northern Spain is complete without sampling the local wines. The key standard for the industry is the Denominacíon de Origen (DO) classification, which guarantees the wine's origin and quality. The most renowned wine-producing region is La Rioja, where many vineyards established in the 19th century by émigrés from Bordeaux are still operating today. The best wines from this region are the dry red *tinto*. In Galicia, the most popular wines are *albariño*, *loureira* and *treixadura* from the sub-regions of Rías Baixas, Ribeiro, Valdeorras, Ribeira Sacra and Monterrei. In the Basque Country, it is well worth trying *txakolí*, a refreshing and slightly prickly white wine.

Montesierra white wine

Tempranillo red wine

Galician *albariño*

Jarrero from La Rioja

Cider

Sidra, or cider, has been produced in Northern Spain since medieval times. There are several varieties of cider, including *colunga*, *porico* and *panquerina*. It is usually drunk in establishments known as *sidrerías*, or *chigres*. Traditionally, a thin stream of cider is poured into the glass from a great height; masters of this art manage not to spill a single drop.

Bottles of cider

Queimada being served

Queimada

Queimada is a traditional Galician drink based on *orujo* – a fiery spirit made from grapes. The alcohol is poured into a special clay pot, to which sugar, coffee beans and slices of lemon or orange are added, and the mixture is then heated up over a fire. According to tradition, witches (*meigas*) would stay well away from anyone who had been drinking *queimada*.

Beer

As a rival of wine, beer is becoming increasingly popular in Spain, even in regions where there is no beer-drinking tradition. Most Spanish beer (*cerveza*) is bottled lager, but you can also find it on draught. Popular brands include San Miguel and Mahou, and in Galicia – Estrella. To order a bottled beer in a bar, ask for *"una cerveza"*; if you want a draught beer, ask for *"una caña"*.

Galician *Estrella*

Where to Eat and Drink

Galicia

A CORUÑA:
Adega O Bebedeiro   €€
Traditional Spanish
C/Ángel Rebollo 34, 15002
Tel *981 21 06 09* **Closed** *Sun dinner; Mon*
With stone walls covered in old tools and pots, this welcoming, rustically furnished restaurant serves beautifully fresh seafood and succulent roast meats, paired with local wines.

A CORUÑA: Domus   €€
Seafood
C/Ángel Rebollo s/n, 15002
Tel *981 20 11 36* **Closed** *Tue, Wed & Sun dinner; Mon*
Set in the surroundings of the Domus science museum, this place enjoys spectacular views from huge windows. On the menu is elegantly prepared and beautifully presented seafood.

DK Choice

A CORUÑA: Pablo Gallego €€€
Contemporary Spanish
C/Capitán Troncoso 4, 15001
Tel *981 20 88 88* **Closed** *Sun dinner*
The elegant contemporary interior, which features curving wooden screens and stone walls, provides the perfect setting for the award-winning cuisine. Exquisite traditional dishes such as *pulpo a la gallega* (octopus cooked with paprika) share the menu with more imaginative fare such as red mullet with rice cooked in squid ink and a sea anemone foam.

BAIONA: Pazo de Mendoza €€
Traditional Spanish
C/Elduayen 1, 36300
Tel *986 35 72 79*
This hotel restaurant, set in an elegant 18th-century building, offers a wide choice of meat and seafood dishes. Dine on the delightful terrace on fine days.

CAMBADOS: María José   €
Seafood
C/San Gregorio 2, 36630
Tel *986 54 22 81* **Closed** *Mon & Sun dinner*
A pretty restaurant with a large terrace, María José offers charming views to go with its wonderful seafood. Try the oven-baked scallops, or the rice and shellfish in a rich broth.

FERROL: Mesón O Carabel   €
Tapas
C/San Sol 69, 15402
Tel *981 35 78 74* **Closed** *Mon*
This friendly inn in the heart of Ferrol serves a fantastic range of tapas, perfectly accompanied by Galician wines. Local charcuterie and seafood (including the popular Galician-style octopus) are also on the menu.

LUGO: España   €€
Contemporary Spanish
C/del Teatro 10, 27001
Tel *982 24 27 17* **Closed** *Sun dinner; Mon*
Light and bright, with modern art on the walls, España serves imaginative dishes such as turbot with pil-pil sauce and pea purée, or cod brandade with tomato foam. The adjoining gastrobar serves equally creative tapas.

LUGO: Mesón de Alberto €€
Traditional Spanish
Rúa Cruz, 4, 27001
Tel *982 22 83 10* **Closed** *Tue dinner; Sun*
Dine leisurely in the elegant, modern restaurant, which serves a wide choice of seafood and meat dishes, or grab a stool at the lively tapas bar.

NOIA: Albores   €
Traditional Spanish
C/Escultor Ferreiro 28, 15200
Tel *981 82 01 52* **Closed** *Mon (except Jul & Aug)*
A simple, cosy restaurant in the Old Town, Albores offers great-value traditional cuisine, plus some delicious tapas, including their famous *empanadas* (small pies with different fillings).

The entrance to A Casa dos Martínez, a traditional restaurant in Padrón

Price Guide
Prices are based on a three-course meal for one, including a half-bottle of house wine, tax and service.

€	up to €35
€€	€35 to €50
€€€	over €50

DK Choice

O GROVE: Culler de Pau €€€
Contemporary Spanish
C/Reboredo 73, 36980
Tel *986 73 22 75* **Closed** *Mon & Thu dinner; Tue*
One of the most exciting chefs in Galicia, Javier Olleros, is at the helm of this stylish, minimalist restaurant, which has huge windows offering spectacular views of the Ría de Arousa. His creations might include lamb with a spiced anchovy butter, or sea anemones with local clams and leeks.

OURENSE: A Taberna   €€
Seafood
Rúa Julio Prieto Nespereira 32, 32005
Tel *988 24 33 32* **Closed** *Mon*
Featuring beamed ceilings and dressers filled with china, this charming restaurant serves delicious traditional cuisine, including fabulous seafood and succulent grilled local meats.

PADRÓN: A Casa dos Martínez €
Traditional Spanish
Rúa Longa 7, 15900
Tel *981 81 05 77*
In the historic centre of Padrón, this family-run restaurant offers local specialities prepared with a modern touch. Try the sardines with the famous local peppers.

PONTEVEDRA: Santa Clara   €
Traditional Spanish
C/Santa Clara 33, 36001
Tel *986 10 42 44* **Closed** *Sun–Wed dinner*
In an 18th-century building, this cosy spot offers a wide selection of salads, seafood, paellas and risottos. Great-value set menus and tapas are also available.

RIBADAVIA: Gastrobar O Birrán €
Tapas
Praza da Madalena 8, 32400
Tel *988 47 23 17* **Closed** *Sun*
This tiny, appealing gastrobar offers traditional and contemporary tapas and *raciones*. Go for fresh razor clams or mussels, melted Arzúa cheese with a spicy marmalade, or *croquetas* with ham and wild mushrooms.

SANTIAGO DE COMPOSTELA:
Casa Marcelo €
International Cuisine
Rúa das Hortas 1, 15705
Tel *981 55 85 80* **Closed** *Sun dinner; Mon*
Chef Marcelo Tejado's restaurant is a trendy, informal gastrobar serving original and creative dishes from Spain and around the world.

SANTIAGO DE COMPOSTELA:
O Beiro €
Tapas
Rúa da Raiña 3, 15704
Tel *981 58 13 70* **Closed** *Mon*
This wine shop-cum-bar pairs its extensive wine selection with simple tapas, including local hams and charcuterie, cheeses and *tarta de Santiago* (almond tart).

SANTIAGO DE COMPOSTELA:
O Curro da Parra €
Contemporary Spanish
Rúa Travesa 20, 15704
Tel *981 55 60 59* **Closed** *Mon*
With exposed stone walls and modern furnishings, this place serves market-fresh tapas and dishes such as pork with spinach and apple purée, or oven-baked cod with vegetable tempura.

SANXENXO: La Taberna del Rotilio
€€
Seafood
Avenida Porto 7–9, 36960
Tel *986 72 02 00* **Closed** *Sun dinner; Mon (except summer)*
This hotel restaurant on the seafront serves traditional seafood dishes with a twist. Try the grilled *zamburiñas* (scallops), rice with monkfish, or the scrambled eggs with cockles and seaweed.

SANXENXO: Pepe Viera
€€€
Contemporary Spanish
Camiño de Serpe, Raxó 36992
Tel *986 74 13 78* **Closed** *Tue–Thu dinner, Sun dinner (except summer); Mon*
Enjoy Michelin-starred cuisine in this chic restaurant on the outskirts of Sanxenxo. Dishes on the set menus (€29–78) might include avocado cannelloni with salmon ceviche, or marinated turbot with lemon and sesame.

VIGO: Casa Marco
€€
Seafood
Avenida de García Barbón 123, 36201
Tel *986 22 51 10* **Closed** *Sun*
This is an elegant restaurant serving excellent Galician cuisine with an emphasis on seafood. Try the fish of the day, or the monkfish and prawn *brocheta*. Leave room for dessert.

The warm ambience in the dining room at Las Termas, Astorga

VIGO: Mesón O Porton
€€
Seafood
Pescadería 1, 36202
Tel *986 43 81 08* **Closed** *Tue*
A friendly, rustic restaurant in the historic quarter, O Porton specializes in classic local rice dishes and seafood. Don't miss the platters featuring a dazzling range of shellfish, and be sure to try the home-made desserts.

VIGO: Maruja Limón
€€€
Contemporary Spanish
Av de Galicia 103, 36216
Tel *986 47 34 06* **Closed** *Tue, Wed & Sun dinner; Mon*
Award-winning chef Rafa Centeno presents superb Galician cuisine at this minimalist restaurant. Fresh seasonal produce is key to such dishes as marinated clams with cucumber or tender beef stewed with cherries.

Asturias and Cantabria

ASTORGA: Las Termas
€
Traditional Spanish
C/Santiago 1, 24700
Tel *987 60 22 12* **Closed** *Mon (except summer)*
This is a great place to try traditional favourites such as wild mushrooms with local cheese, *cocido maragato* (a rich pork and chickpea stew) and grilled meats from the nearby mountains.

AVILÉS: Don Pascuale
€
Italian
C/de la Ferrería 26, 33402
Tel *985 51 20 94* **Closed** *Tue & Wed*
Pasta dishes, pizzas and calzones baked in a brick oven are on offer at this friendly and relaxed restaurant, which is popular with local families. Be sure to leave enough room for the delicious tiramisú.

DK Choice

AVILÉS: Llamber
€€
Contemporary Spanish
C/Galiana 30, 33402
Tel *984 83 23 48* **Closed** *Mon, Tue*
The Asturian chef at this stylish gastronomic tavern works magic with fresh, seasonal produce. Choose from a constantly changing menu of dishes that might include rice in squid ink with aioli, or a platter of grilled local meats and sausages. A selection of home-made breads and a carefully chosen wine list complement the menu.

CANGAS DE ONÍS: El Molín de la Pedrera
€
Traditional Spanish
C/Río Güeña 2, 33550
Tel *985 84 91 09* **Closed** *Wed; Jan*
This inviting stone-and-wood restaurant offers dishes such as Asturian *fabada* (pork and bean stew) or fresh hake with almonds. Wash them down with local cider.

CANGAS DE ONÍS: El Cenador de los Canónigos
€€
Contemporary Spanish
Av Contraquíl, 33550
Tel *985 84 94 45* **Closed** *Sun dinner; Mon & Tue*
This elegant hotel restaurant has huge windows with great views. Grilled cod with onion confit and beef stew with potatoes feature on the Asturian menu.

CASTRO URDIALES: Sidrería Marcelo
€
Traditional Spanish
C/Ardigales 12, 39700
Tel *942 86 70 58* **Closed** *Mon (except summer)*
Cosy and popular, this family-run place serves solid local fare. Try the *chuletón*, succulent grilled beef, or the cod tortilla. There is a good set lunch menu, too.

For more information on types of restaurants *see page 208*

GIJÓN: Ciudadela €€
Tapas
C/Capua 7, 33202
Tel *985 34 77 32* **Closed** *Sun dinner; Mon*
The gourmet tapas and daily specials here are prepared with whatever is in season. Try creative variations of *pote Asturiana* (a hearty stew), or the steak with foie gras and Port wine.

GIJÓN: Los Nogales €€€
Seafood
Camino de la Matona 118, Santurio, 33394
Tel *985 33 63 34* **Closed** *Tue*
A family favourite on Sunday lunchtimes, Los Nogales serves dishes such as seafood paella, rice with prawns, and platters of freshly grilled shellfish and fish.

LAREDO: Casa Felipe €
Traditional Spanish
C/Corregimiento de Laredo 5, 39770
Tel *942 60 32 12* **Closed** *Mon*
This long-established restaurant has a tapas bar serving traditional favourites such as *croquetas* and tortilla, as well as a dining room where you can tuck into stews, grilled meat and seafood.

LEÓN: La Poveda €
Traditional Spanish
Ramiro Valbuena 9, 24002
Tel *987 22 71 55*
This friendly and family-run restaurant prides itself on using the freshest local produce. Try the plump asparagus, followed by grilled lamb chops with fried potatoes, and cheesecake.

LEÓN: Bodega Regia €€
Traditional Spanish
C/Regidores 9, 24003
Tel *987 21 31 73* **Closed** *Sun*
Set in a charming 14th-century building, this warmly decorated restaurant serves classic Leonesa dishes: roast suckling pig, local black pudding and baked trout.

LEÓN: Restaurante Pablo €€
Contemporary Spanish
Avenida los Cubos 8, 24007
Tel *987 21 65 62*
This restaurant near the cathedral is the best bet in the city for innovative cuisine. Prawns with pistachio and tofu, and grouper ceviche with mango are just some of the treats on offer.

LLANES: El Jornu €€
Seafood
Carretera Pancar s/n, Pancar, 33500
Tel *985 40 16 15* **Closed** *Sun dinner; Mon*
Find a fabulous choice of seafood and shellfish at El Jornu. Don't miss the delicious signature dish of rice with clams, onions and parsley. The pick of the starters are the fresh prawns with aioli.

LUANCO: Casa Nestor €€
Traditional Spanish
C/Conde del Real Agrado 6, 33440
Tel *985 88 03 15* **Closed** *Mon*
Established in 1932, this warmly decorated restaurant offers a tasty and wide-ranging menu of seafood and rice dishes, along with a selection of grilled meats.

OVIEDO: Casa Conrado €€
Traditional Spanish
C/Argüelles 1, 33003
Tel *985 22 39 19* **Closed** *Sun*
Classically decorated, this is the ideal spot to tuck into traditional dishes such as gazpacho, cod tortilla, baked clams with local beans, or octopus with caramelized onions and aioli.

OVIEDO: Casa Fermín €€€
Traditional Spanish
C/San Francisco 8, 33003
Tel *985 21 64 52* **Closed** *Sun*
Dating back to 1924, this elegant place serves modern versions of classic recipes. On the menu are such delicacies as marinated clams with guacamole, and crayfish in broth with bacon.

POSADA DE VALDEÓN:
Begoña €
Traditional Spanish
Plaza La Cortina Concejo s/n, 24915
Tel *987 74 05 16*
A charming country restaurant serving large portions of home-cooked food. Chickpea stew, rice with clams, and roast kid or lamb all appear on the menu, with crème caramel for dessert.

POTES: Casa Cayo €
Traditional Spanish
C/Cantabra 6, 39570
Tel *942 73 01 50*
The exposed brick walls and wooden furnishings create a perfect setting for the rustic fare on offer – grilled lamb chops, stews and hearty soups.

PUENTE VIESGO: El Marqués €€
Seafood
C/Manuel Pérez Mazo, 39670
Tel *942 59 86 94*
Grab a table with views of the *ría* at this restaurant specializing in local seafood. The menu features spider crab, lobster, clams and more. The adjoining tapas bar is always lively.

RIBADESELLA: La Parrilla €€
Seafood
Av Palacio Valdés 27, 33560
Tel *985 86 02 88* **Closed** *Sun dinner; Mon*
This roadside eatery doesn't look like much from the outside, but it always draws a big crowd for its heaped plates of fresh local seafood. They also serve meat cooked on a charcoal grill. There are no prices on the menu, so ask before ordering.

SALINAS (AVILÉS):
Real Balneario de Salinas €€€
Seafood
Avenida de Juan Sitges 3, 33405
Tel *985 51 86 13* **Closed** *Sun dinner; Mon*
Perfect for a special occasion, this restaurant earned a Michelin star for its updated versions of classic local recipes. Try the whole baked lobster with orange and saffron, or the confit of suckling pig.

SAN VICENTE DE LA
BARQUERA: Annua €€€
Contemporary Spanish
Paseo de la Barquera, 39540
Tel *942 71 50 50* **Closed** *Tue, Wed & Sun dinner; Mon; Nov–Mar*
With a stunning waterfront setting, this Michelin-starred restaurant offers a magnificent menu of contemporary creations such as the distinctive "Message in a Bottle", a seafood concoction presented in a bottle.

Enjoying an alfresco lunch in the centre of Oviedo

Key to Price Guide *see page 216*

Stark styling and fabulous views at Nerua, in the Guggenheim Museum, Bilbao

SANTANDER: La Bombi €€
Seafood
C/Casimiro Sáinz 15, 39003
Tel *942 21 30 28*
In the Puertochico area, this charming restaurant serves seafood fresh from the harbour. Try the scrambled eggs with sea anemones and wild turbot.

SANTANDER: Posada del Mar €€
Traditional Spanish
C/Castelar 19, 39004
Tel *942 21 30 23* **Closed** *Sun (Jun–Sep)*
Pick your dinner from the choice of seafood displayed on ice. Try the gratinéed spider crab or go for the classic fried calamari.

SANTANDER: El Serbal €€€
Contemporary Spanish
C/Andrés del Río 7, 39004
Tel *942 22 25 15* **Closed** *Sun dinner; Mon*
Come here for superb Cantabrian cuisine with a modern touch. Only the freshest seafood, caught on the day, is served. The chef here has earned a Michelin star.

SANTILLANA DEL MAR: Casa Uzquiza €
Traditional Spanish
C/Escultor Jesús Otero 5, 39330
Tel *942 84 03 56* **Closed** *Mon*
Simple and charming, this restaurant serves a great-value set lunch and a choice of local stews, grilled meats and seafood.

SANTILLANA DEL MAR: Restaurante Gran Duque €
Traditional Spanish
C/Escultor Jesús Otero 7, 39330
Tel *942 84 03 86* **Closed** *Mon*
This stone-walled restaurant has a menu of regional specialities. Tuck into big platefuls of grilled meats or seafood, accompanied by stuffed peppers or artichokes.

DK Choice
VILLAVICIOSA: El Verano €
Seafood
Lugar Cabriton, Argüero, 33300
Tel *985 99 91 09* **Closed** *Mon dinner; Tue*
Although a little off the beaten track, this simple family-run restaurant is well worth the effort. It has a reputation for its beautifully fresh seafood. Ask the friendly staff for recommendations, or go for the superb octopus and potato stew.

The Basque Country

ALAIZA: Señorío de Alaiza €
Traditional Spanish
C/Alaiza 1, 2 km de Salvatierra–Agurain, 01207
Tel *945 31 26 28* **Closed** *Tue–Thu dinner; Mon*
Basque classics like *marmitako* (fish stew) and cod *al pil-pil* (with a herb sauce) are served in a 19th-century stone house that also doubles as a wine museum. Book ahead.

AZPEITIA: Jai Alai €
Traditional Spanish
Elosiaga Auzoa 393, 20730
Tel *943 81 22 71* **Closed** *Sun–Wed dinner; Aug*
This country eatery serves grilled fish and meat in a rustic dining room that is always packed with locals. Good set lunch menu.

BILBAO: Victor €€
Traditional Spanish
Nueva Plaza 2, 48005
Tel *944 15 16 78* **Closed** *Sun*
Established in 1940, Victor is famous for its oxtail ragout stewed in red wine. Also good is the hake stuffed with baby squid.

BILBAO: Etxanobe €€€
Contemporary Spanish
Palacio Euskalduna, Avenida Abandoibarra 4, 48001
Tel *944 42 10 71* **Closed** *Sun; 1–15 Aug*
This Michelin-starred restaurant has huge windows overlooking the river. On the menu are dishes such as grilled scallop ragout with basil, vegetable tempura, and hake with clams.

BILBAO: Guria €€€
Traditional Spanish
Gran Vía de Don Diego López de Haro 66, 48011
Tel *944 41 57 80*
This place has a restaurant and a more casual bistro. Dishes are prepared with fresh seasonal produce. Try the crab salad, or the roast pigeon with foie gras.

BILBAO: Mina €€€
Contemporary Spanish
Muelle Marzana, 48003
Tel *944 795 938* **Closed** *Mon, Tue & Sun dinner*
A light and airy modern restaurant by the river, Mina offers creative cuisine prepared with fresh seasonal produce. Dishes might include aubergine with red tea, or Cantabrian hake roasted with langoustines.

BILBAO: Nerua (Restaurante Guggenheim Bilbao) €€€
Contemporary Spanish
C/Abandoibarra 2, 48001
Tel *944 00 04 30* **Closed** *Sun dinner; Mon*
With its own separate entrance in the Guggenheim, this beautiful restaurant offers imaginative, award-winning dishes such as aubergine with miso and white bean broth, or foie gras with artichokes and black olives.

GERNIKA-LUMO: Boliño El Viejo €
Traditional Spanish
C/Adolfo Urioste 1, 48300
Tel *946 25 10 15* **Closed** *Tue & Sun dinner*
Classic country cooking is available at this family-run tavern. Try the white beans, a popular local dish, and the fish soup, or the meatballs. Finish up with the *flan* (crème caramel).

GERNIKA-LUMO: Zallo Barrí €€€
Traditional Spanish
Juan Calzada Kalea 79, 48300
Tel *946 25 18 00* **Closed** *Sun–Thu dinner*
This elegant restaurant serves a range of creative local dishes. The puff-pastry parcel with foie gras and wild mushrooms is delicious, as is the hake with a parsley sauce.

DK Choice
GETARIA: Kaia-Kaipe €€€
Seafood
C/General Arnao 4, 20808
Tel *943 14 05 00* **Closed** *Mon dinner*
Kaia-Kaipe serves superb fresh seafood from its own hatchery, with simpler dishes in the bistro and more elaborate fare upstairs. Try the velvety anchovies, the clams in marinara sauce, or the turbot; if you eat on the harbourfront terrace, you can watch your fish being grilled.

HONDARRIBIA: El Curry Verde €
Vegetarian
Santiago Kalea 67, 20280
Tel *943 53 77 79* **Closed** *Mon–Thu &*
Sun dinner; Wed
This tranquil spot is an oasis for
vegetarians. The speciality is curry,
but they serve great soups, stir
fries and stews, too. It's also worth
visiting for the home-made cakes.

HONDARRIBIA: Alameda €€
Contemporary Spanish
Minasoroeta Kalea 1, 20280
Tel *943 64 27 89* **Closed** *Sun & Tue*
dinner; Mon
Spider-crab cannelloni and fresh
fish of the day with seaweed
and lemon are just two of the
dishes at this chic, modern
restaurant. Wine pairings are
available with the set menus.

HONDARRIBIA: Sebastián €€
Traditional Spanish
C/Mayor 11, 20280
Tel *943 64 01 67* **Closed** *Tue lunch;*
Mon
Set in the enchanting historic
quarter, this romantic restaurant
prepares delicacies such as
monkfish medallions with
langoustine and crab, or sirloin
steak with foie gras.

**LASARTE: Martín
Berasategui** €€€
Contemporary Spanish
C/Loidi 4, 20160
Tel *943 36 64 71* **Closed** *Sun dinner;*
Mon & Tue
Tuck into oysters with cucumber,
fruit, kafir and coconut, or roast
red mullet with crystals of
edible scales and cuttlefish at
Berasategui's beautiful flagship
restaurant, which has three
Michelin stars.

**PASAI DONABANE:
Casa Cámara** €€€
Contemporary Spanish
C/San Juan 79, 20110
Tel *943 52 36 99* **Closed** *Sun dinner;*
Mon
Established in 1882, this beautiful
restaurant occupies an 18th-
century building on the seafront.
Exquisite dishes include scallops
with saffron and pineapple
sauce, and a magnificent
platter of shellfish and fish.

San Sebastián: La Muralla €€
Traditional Spanish
C/Embeltrán 3, 20003
Tel *943 43 35 08* **Closed** *Sun dinner*
Relaxed and intimate, this
charming restaurant specializes
in traditional Basque cuisine with
a modern twist. They offer a
range of great-value set menus,
plus a well-chosen wine list.

SAN SEBASTIÁN: La Perla €€
Traditional Spanish
Paseo de La Concha s/n, 20007
Tel *943 45 88 56* **Closed** *Tue (Oct–*
Mar)
With big windows overlooking
the bay, this restaurant serves
updated versions of traditional
local dishes. Try the rice and
clams, and the octopus salad
with sweet paprika vinaigrette.

SAN SEBASTIÁN: Akelarre €€€
Contemporary Spanish
Paseo Padre Orcolaga 56, 20008
Tel *943 31 12 09* **Closed** *Sun dinner;*
Mon (also Tue Jan–Jun); Feb, 15–30 Oct
Chef Pedro Subijana boasts three
Michelin stars. His signature
dishes include essence of spider
crab with its caviar on blini, and
infusion of green broth with
crayfish or smoked monkfish.

SAN SEBASTIÁN: Arzak €€€
Contemporary Spanish
Avenida del Alcalde José Elosegi 273,
20015
Tel *943 27 84 65* **Closed** *Sun & Mon;*
14 Jun–1 Jul & 2–26 Nov
Credited with kickstarting the
revolution in Spanish cuisine in
the 1970s, Juan Mari Arzak is now
aided by his equally talented
daughter Elena. His restaurant
has three Michelin stars.

SAN SEBASTIÁN: Mugaritz €€€
Contemporary Spanish
Aldura Aldea 20, Errentería, 20100
Tel *943 52 24 55* **Closed** *Tue lunch,*
Sun dinner; Mon
Beautifully set in an oak forest
on a hillside, this enchanting
restaurant offers Michelin-starred
cuisine. Signature dishes include
edible "stones" (actually potatoes)
with aioli, and veal with vine
cutting embers and thyme.

The shaded terrace at Martín Berasategui's
three-Michelin-starred restaurant, Lasarte

SAN SEBASTIÁN: Rekondo €€€
Contemporary Spanish
Igeldo Pasealekua 57, 20008
Tel *943 21 29 07* **Closed** *Sun*
Boasting a world-class wine
cellar, this panoramic restaurant
on top of Mount Igueldo serves
fresh Basque specialities such
as clams with lemon, grilled
sole, and scrambled eggs with
wild mushrooms.

TOLOSA: Frontón €€€
Traditional Spanish
Paseo de San Francisco 4, 20400
Tel *943 65 29 41* **Closed** *Sun dinner;*
Mon
Modern regional cuisine
prepared with the finest seasonal
produce is on offer at this elegant
restaurant, which serves dishes
such as hake "cheeks" with
piquillo peppers, and roast
pigeon with dates and pistachios.

VITORIA: Tximiso Taberna €
Traditional Spanish
C/Manuel Iradier 8, 01005
Tel *945 14 83 38* **Closed** *Sun dinner*
There are so many fabulous
tapas lining the bar of this
welcoming tavern that it's hard
to choose. The local black
pudding *(morcilla)* and the
scrambled eggs with wild
mushrooms are good options.

VITORIA: Araba €€
Traditional Spanish
Av de Los Huetos 17, 01010
Tel *945 22 26 69* **Closed** *Mon*
A very chic, modern restaurant
(part of a boutique hotel),
Araba has a short, simple
menu that includes grilled
salmon, lamb chops and
home-made rice pudding.
The set lunch is a bargain.

VITORIA: El Portalón €€
Traditional Spanish
C/Correría 147–151, 01001
Tel *945 14 27 55* **Closed** *Sun dinner*
Set in a beautiful 15th-century
building, El Portalón offers a wide
choice of meat, fish and rice
dishes. Try the *chuléton*, a juicy
slab of beef, or the rice with
prawns and baby squid.

ZARAUTZ: Karlos Arguiñano €€
Traditional Spanish
C/Mendilauta 13, 20800
Tel *943 13 00 00* **Closed** *Wed; Jan.*
Also: Jun–Oct: Sun dinner; Nov–May:
Sun–Tue & Thu dinner
A beachfront restaurant and
hotel run by the eponymous chef
(a TV personality in Spain), this
place offers delicious modern
cuisine. Highlights include
squid ravioli and roast cod
with a mushroom purée.

ZARAUTZ: Otzarreta €€€
Contemporary Spanish
C/Santa Clara 5, 20800
Tel 943 13 12 43 **Closed** Sun dinner; Mon
With a beautiful terrace overlooking an enchanting garden, this restaurant offers a wide selection of local seafood and meat dishes. Splash out on the fabulous shellfish platter.

Navarra and La Rioja

BURGOS: Cerveceria Morito €
Tapas
Sombrereria 27, 09003
Tel 947 26 75 55
This rustically decorated spot is always packed with locals enjoying treats such as country bread topped with goat's cheese and raspberry marmalade, or *patatas bravas* (fried cubes of potato).

BURGOS: Casa Ojeda €€
Traditional Spanish
C/Vitoria 5, 09004
Tel 947 20 90 52 **Closed** Sun dinner
In a handsome historic building with a wooden gallery, this place is traditionally decorated. Come here for tasty delicacies such as roast suckling pig, or Santoña anchovies with red peppers.

BURGOS: El 24 de Paloma €€
Traditional Spanish
C/Paloma 24, 09003
Tel 947 20 86 08 **Closed** Sun dinner; Mon
Tender roast lamb and duck in three textures with raspberries are the highlights at this stylish place, which prides itself on using the finest local ingredients.

ELIZONDO: Eskisaroi €
Traditional Spanish
C/Jaime Urrutia 40, 31700
Tel 948 58 00 13 **Closed** Thu (except summer)
Delicious home-cooked fare – mainly grilled meat and fish dishes – and well-chosen wines make this restaurant in an old stone house a great place to stop in Elizondo. Reasonable prices.

ESTELLA: La Cepa €
Traditional Spanish
Plaza de los Fueros 15, 31200
Tel 948 55 00 32 **Closed** Sun dinner
This has a smart, black-and-white dining room and a menu featuring seasonal specialities prepared with a creative touch. Try a salad of marinated sardines with raspberry and ginger dressing, or a pheasant risotto with mushrooms and truffles.

An elegantly presented dessert at Mesón Egües, Logroño

ESTELLA: Navarra €
Traditional Spanish
C/Gustavo de Maeztu 16, 31200
Tel 948 55 00 40 **Closed** Mon
Tuck into the famous Navarran asparagus and artichokes, along with grilled meat and seafood, at this restaurant in an attractive townhouse. The rustic café-bar is a great option for families.

EZCARAY: El Rincón del Vino €€
Traditional Spanish
C/Jesus Nazareno 2, 26280
Tel 941 35 43 75 **Closed** Sun–Thu dinner; Tue
Try the *parillada Riojana* – a platter of grilled lamb and pork – at this restaurant, which has a roaring fire in winter. The roasted artichokes and fish dishes are also good, as is the wine list.

EZCARAY: El Portal €€€
Contemporary Spanish
Padre José García 19, 26280
Tel 941 35 40 47 **Closed** Sun dinner (except summer); Mon
With two Michelin stars, this enchanting hotel restaurant presents exquisitely made cuisine. Signature dishes include the "Spiral of Basil and Mozzarella" and the venison on red onion and chestnut cream.

DK Choice

HARO: Madrid Jamonero €
Tapas
Plaza de la Paz 25, 26200
Tel 941 31 00 00 **Closed** Mon
This bustling tapas bar in the heart of the town has a wonderful terrace on the square and a bar heaped with a dazzling display of *pintxos* (Basque-style tapas). The wafer-thin Iberian ham (the house speciality) is excellent, as are the Cantabrian anchovies and croquetas.

HARO: Terete €€
Traditional Spanish
C/Lucrecia Arana 17, 26200
Tel 941 31 00 23 **Closed** Sun dinner; Mon (except Aug); 1–15 Jul & 15–30 Nov
The classic country dish *cordero asado* – roast lamb – is the undisputed highlight at this delightfully old-fashioned restaurant. Established in 1877, Terete specializes in roast meats baked in a traditional brick oven.

LOGROÑO: Bar Soriano €
Tapas
C/Laurel 2, 26001
Tel 941 22 88 07 **Closed** Sun dinner
Each of the tapas bars lining this street in Logroño has a different speciality. *Champis* (mushrooms) are the main draw at Soriano (even the sign is mushroom-shaped). Try them grilled and piled on a slice of baguette.

LOGROÑO: El Cachetero €
Traditional Spanish
C/Laurel 3, 26001
Tel 941 22 84 63 **Closed** Sun dinner
There's a century of tradition behind this restaurant, where the famous local vegetables are the main highlight, along with traditional roast meats, as well as modern dishes such as warm salad of baby squid and langoustines.

LOGROÑO: Mesón Egües €€€
Traditional Spanish
C/Campa 3, 26005
Tel 941 22 86 03 **Closed** Sun
A traditional *asador* (roast house), Mesón Egües has earned a top reputation for the impeccable quality of its lamb, kid, beef and seafood, which can be served grilled at the table, accompanied by a range of fresh seasonal vegetables.

For more information on types of restaurants see page 208

OLITE: Casa Zenito €€
Traditional Spanish
C/Mayor 16, 31390
Tel *948 74 00 02* **Closed** *Sun dinner; Mon*
In the medieval heart of Olite, this welcoming hotel restaurant has a menu of refined regional classics, such as *pulpo a la gallega* (boiled octopus with paprika), grilled scallops and local venison.

PAMPLONA: Bar Gaucho €
Tapas
C/Espoz y Mina 7, 31002
Tel *948 22 50 73* **Closed** *Sun dinner*
The elaborate *pintxos* (Basque-style tapas) at this attractive, wood-panelled bar have won awards. Tasty morsels include smoked eel with tomato jelly, sea anemone and truffled egg.

PAMPLONA: Enekorri €€
Contemporary Spanish
C/Tudela 14, 31003
Tel *948 23 07 98* **Closed** *Sun*
Sleek and contemporary, this restaurant creates dishes such as artichokes with lobster and a mandarin reduction, followed by coconut and white chocolate cream with beetroot sorbet.

PAMPLONA: Europa €€
Contemporary Spanish
C/Espoz y Mina 11, 31002
Tel *948 22 18 00* **Closed** *Sun*
The Michelin-starred chef at this classic restaurant incorporates the finest local produce into dishes such as rice with vegetables, mushrooms and baby squid, or a cheese *bonbon* with rhubarb and ginger marmalade.

DK Choice

PAMPLONA: Rodero €€€
Contemporary Spanish
C/Emilio Arrieta 3, 31002
Tel *948 22 80 35* **Closed** *Mon & Tue dinner; Sun*
Go for the *menú degustación* (tasting menu) at this outstanding family-run restaurant, which has a charming dining room decorated in warm colours. Each dish is a work of art. Opt for the mushrooms and truffles with a golden veil, or the rice cooked in squid ink with scallop, coconut and coriander (*cilantro*).

PUENTE LA REINA: La Conrada €
Traditional Spanish
Paseo de los Fueros 17, 31100
Tel *948 34 00 52*
A friendly, old-fashioned tavern, that offers a tasty menu of grilled meats, local vegetables, and stews (the house speciality). Tapas and burgers are also available, as is a fixed-price menu.

RONCAL: Taberna Suargi €
Traditional Spanish
Barrio Iriondoa 36, 31415
Tel *948 47 51 95* **Closed** *Sun dinner*
This friendly tavern in the Navarran Pyrenees offers a choice of tapas and an affordable set lunch. The *migas*, a traditional country dish of sausage, garlic and bread fried up in olive oil, are particularly good.

SANTO DOMINGO DE LA CALZADA: El Rincón de Emilio €
Traditional Spanish
Plaza de Bonifacio Gil 7, 26250
Tel *941 34 09 90* **Closed** *Tue dinner; Feb*
This delightful country restaurant with a pretty garden specializes in the region's fine local produce, prepared in classic recipes such as *menestra* (stewed vegetables with lemon and olive oil).

TUDELA: Restaurante 33 €
Traditional Spanish
C/Pablo Sarasate 7, 31500
Tel *948 82 76 06* **Closed** *Sun–Wed dinner*
Vegetables, grown in the restaurant's own garden, are the speciality here. Enjoy a pastry with leek and prawn, artichokes with foie gras, or a creamy soup with wild borage.

VIANA: Borgia €€
Traditional Spanish
C/Serapio Urra 1, 31230
Tel *948 64 57 81* **Closed** *Sun–Thu dinner*
In an attractive dining room featuring original beamed ceilings and contemporary furnishings, Borgia serves updated versions of local classics like artichokes with ham or oven-baked cod.

Central and Eastern Pyrenees

DK Choice

AINSA: Bodega de Sobrarbe €
Traditional Spanish
Plaza Mayor 2, 22330
Tel *974 50 02 37* **Closed** *Sun*
A good choice on Ainsa's main square, this restaurant is located in a medieval wine cellar. Rustic mountain dishes such as hearty stews, wild boar and venison (in autumn) are the highlights.

The cosy dining room at Andria, in La Seu d'Urgell (*see p223*)

AINSA: Bodegón de Mallacan €
Traditional Spanish
Plaza Mayor 6, 22330
Tel *974 50 09 77* **Closed** *Mon (in winter)*
Set in a 12th-century building on the main square, this hotel restaurant features medieval-style decor and serves local favourites such as roast lamb, plus wild mushrooms and game in season.

DK Choice

AINSA: Callizo €€
Contemporary Spanish
Plaza Mayor s/n, 22330
Tel *974 50 03 85* **Closed** *Sun dinner; Mon*
Original, beautifully presented dishes at this charming restaurant in the heart of Ainsa include confit of cod with lilac, raisins and pine nuts, and lamb with potatoes and truffles. Finish up with some local cheeses or a delicious *torrija* (bread pudding) for dessert. The tasting menus are packed with dishes, so be prepared to spend at least three hours here if you choose this option. There are also superb panoramic views.

ANDORRA LA VELLA: Borda Estevet €€
Traditional Spanish
Carretera de la Comella 2, AD500
Tel *(376) 874 920*
Delicious Pyrenean dishes are served at this rustically decorated mountain restaurant. One of the highlights on the menu is the platter of grilled beef and veal. Other options include a salt cod and langoustine salad.

ARTIES: Casa Irene €€€
Contemporary Spanish
C/Major 3, 25599
Tel *973 64 43 64* **Closed** *Mon*
This stylish spot offers a modern
take on classic Spanish cuisine.
Try the *coca* (flatbread) topped
with aubergine caviar, roast
tomatoes and sardines, and save
room for the fabulous desserts.

BARBASTRO: Flor €
Traditional Spanish
C/Goya 3, 22300
Tel *974 31 10 56* **Closed** *Sun dinner;
Mon*
This award-winning restaurant
is spacious and modern, and it
serves fresh, inventive cuisine.
Traditional roast suckling pig
is paired with spicy couscous,
and the creamy rice with
seafood is delectable.

BENASQUE: El Fogaril €€
Traditional Spanish
Av los Tilos, 22440
Tel *974 55 16 12* **Closed** *15–30 Oct*
At this cosy hotel restaurant,
the menu focuses on traditional
local dishes, including mountain
stews, fresh game and wild
mushrooms (in season), all
accompanied by a choice of
Somantano wines.

BERGA: Sala €€€
Traditional Spanish
Passeig de la Pau 27, 08600
Tel *938 21 11 85* **Closed** *Sun dinner;
Mon*
A spacious, cosily decorated
restaurant, Sala specializes
in classic Catalan mountain
dishes with a modern update.
The house speciality is wild
mushrooms, which are prepared
in myriad delicious ways.

HUESCA: Las Torres €€
Contemporary Spanish
C/María Auxiliadora 3, 22003
Tel *974 22 82 13* **Closed** *Mon
dinner; Sun*
An eclectically decorated dining
room with crystal chandeliers
and copies of famous artworks is
the theatrical setting for creative
dishes such as foie gras and
Iberian ham sushi with melon.

HUESCA: Lillas Pastia €€€
Contemporary Spanish
Plaza de Navarra 4, 22002
Tel *974 21 16 91* **Closed** *Sun dinner;
Mon*
The constantly changing
menu at this contemporary
restaurant makes the most of
fresh seasonal produce. They
also offer a fabulous menu
featuring the house speciality,
truffles, in every course.

JACA: Lilium €
Traditional Spanish
Av del Primer Viernes de Mayo, 22700
Tel *974 35 53 56* **Closed** *Mon*
This traditionally decorated
restaurant offers both classic and
contemporary local dishes. Its
inspired tapas (available as part
of a set menu) have won awards.

JACA: La Cocina Aragonesa €€
Traditional Spanish
Cervantes 5, 22700
Tel *974 36 10 50*
Delicious game, rice cooked with
squid ink, lobster and fabulous
desserts are on offer at this
charming place, which has a
roaring fire and traditional decor.

LA SEU D'URGELL: Andria €
Traditional Spanish
Passeig Joan Brudieu 24, 25700
Tel *973 35 03 00* **Closed** *Sun dinner;
Mon*
Choose a table on the leafy
terrace of this restaurant, and
dine on tasty specialities such
as stuffed guinea fowl with
cranberries and pine nuts, or a
refreshing vichysoisse with apple.

DK Choice

OLOT: Umami €€
Tapas
Avinguda Reis Catòlics 31, 17800
Tel *972 27 65 71* **Closed** *lunch;
Mon*
This stylish, informal gastrobar
specializes in unusual, creative
tapas including sweet potato
timbale with wild mushrooms,
tuna tataki and slivers of pork
fillet with lemon. You'll also find
classics like fried calamari and a
choice of hams and charcuterie.
The wine list has a well-chosen
selection of Catalan wines.

OLOT: Les Cols €€€
Contemporary Spanish
*Mas Les Cols 2, Ctra de la Canya s/n,
17800*
Tel *972 26 92 09* **Closed** *Tue & Sun
dinner; Mon*
This restaurant (with two
Michelin stars) is at the vanguard
of contemporary Catalan cuisine.
Tasting plates might include cod
brandade with muscat grapes and
hot pepper oil, or duck terrine.

PUIGCERDÀ: El Caliu €
Traditional Spanish
Carrer d'Alfons I 1, 17520
Tel *972 14 08 25* **Closed** *Wed*
A cosy, traditionally decorated
restaurant, this is a great place to
try specialities of the Cerdanya
region, such as *trinxat* (a kind
of bubble-and-squeak topped
with bacon) or a pastry filled
with wild mushrooms.

**PUIGCERDÀ: Torre
del Remei** €€€
Traditional Spanish
*C/El Remei 3, Bolvir de la Cerdanya,
17539*
Tel *972 14 01 82*
Part of a luxury hotel, this
restaurant serves Catalan cuisine
with a contemporary twist. Try
the vichyssoise over shellfish
cannelloni, or the superb
Mediterranean rice dishes.
The wine list is outstanding.

**SANT JOAN DE LES
ABADESSES: Casa Rudes** €
Traditional Spanish
Carrer Major 10, 17860
Tel *972 72 01 15* **Closed** *Sun dinner*
Classic Catalan country cooking
is the draw at this delightful
restaurant, which opened in 1893.
Choose local sausage and beans
or a stew, and finish up with
crema catalana (crème brûlée).

Understated elegance at Torre del Remei, Puigcerdà

For more information on types of restaurants *see page 208*

SHOPPING IN NORTHERN SPAIN

Spain has a thriving shopping culture, with many unique, family-run boutiques as well as a few reliable chain stores and big department stores. Staff are usually friendly and patient, and there is a vast selection of goods on offer. In the main shopping areas you'll find designer boutiques with high-end merchandise, though many offer seasonal discounts. Spanish shoes and clothes are elegant and, compared to France or Italy, good value for money. Food products, especially fish and seafood, are best bought at markets, where the quality is higher than in shops. Cider and wine are popular purchases with visitors to Northern Spain. Also popular are religious souvenirs connected with the pilgrimage route of St James, as well as local crafts including wicker baskets, hand-made lace and clogs.

A wide array of nuts for sale

Opening Hours

Supermarkets, hypermarkets and department stores are usually open from 10am to 9 or 10pm (also on Saturdays), and in larger cities they are sometimes open even longer.

Most small shops in Northern Spain open Monday to Saturday from 10am to 8 or 9pm, but they close for a long lunch break from 2 to 4:30 or 5pm. Service-related shops such as dry cleaners usually open an hour earlier and close an hour later. Bakeries open at 7:30 or 8am.

Traditionally, the only shops open on Sundays and holidays have been bakeries, *pastelerías* and newsstands, and most other small shops still close on Sundays, except in the run-up to Christmas. However, larger stores are allowed to open on a few Sundays each year, and a growing number of shops are open in resort towns.

Payment Methods

Cash is quicker to use for small purchases, and may be preferred in some small shops.

Credit cards are widely accepted, but cheques are not.

VAT

Value added tax (VAT), known as *IVA* in Spanish, is included in the price of nearly everything in Spain. Look for the words *IVA incluido* or *con IVA* (VAT included) and *sin IVA* (VAT not included) to see if tax is included on your hotel or restaurant bill.

Rates vary, depending on the type of purchase. For some basics, such as children's clothes, it's 4 per cent. For most services, including restaurant and hotel bills, it's 10 per cent. For everything else, including most clothing and luxury and gift items, it's 21 per cent.

Non-EU residents are eligible for a VAT refund if purchases exceed €91 worth of goods. These do not have to be one-off purchases. For example, during your stay in Northern Spain you can collect receipts for purchases made from the same shop and then ask the sales assistant for one tax-free invoice at the end, detailing your transactions. You'll need to show your passport to receive a form. You must have the VAT refund form stamped at a Spanish customs office. Present the stamped form at a Spanish bank at the airport for a same-day refund, or mail it for the refund to be credited to your credit card.

Sales

Spain's twice-annual *rebajas* (sales) are a fantastic opportunity to find good deals on everything from shoes and clothes to linens, electronics and household goods. Some stores offer a reduction of 50 per cent or more.

The first *rebajas* of the year begin on 7 January (the day after Epiphany) and continue until mid-February. Summer *rebajas*

Colourful stalls on the promenade in Oviedo

start in early July and continue until early August. Although January and August are the traditional sales periods, many shops now also have sales at other times of the year, offering goods at very attractive prices.

In large department stores, discounted goods are usually found on the top floor and less frequently in the basement.

Large Stores and Supermarkets

Spain's leading department store is El Corte Inglés, with its characteristic triangular green, black and white logo. This mega-store, with a branch in every major city, sells internationally recognized brands of shoes, clothing, sports goods, furniture, accessories and cosmetics. There is usually also a well-stocked electronic goods department, selling everything from CDs, DVDs, televisions and audio devices to cameras. Various customer services, such as hairdressers and travel agents, can be found in every El Corte Inglés store. In the basement there is usually a large self-service grocery store – Hipercor.

Alcampo and Carrefour sell everything from groceries to clothing to household goods and appliances, and are usually located out of town, so are accessible only by car. FNAC stores have a wide range of music and books.

Entrance to a shop selling wine and liqueurs

Shopping Arcades and Malls

Spanish shopping arcades are elegant, brightly lit and tastefully designed; their displays change on a regular basis. The arcades are usually filled with designer boutiques, and the choice is truly vast. Although items are usually on the expensive side, you can often find goods at reduced prices as well as seasonal discounts in summer and winter.

Aside from clothes and shoe shops, every arcade has cafés, bars and restaurants, where you can enjoy a welcome break after a burst of shopping.

American-style malls, called *centros comerciales* in Spain, are gaining popularity and can be found on the outskirts of most large cities.

Markets

Every large town in Northern Spain has a daily food market, where you can buy bread, cheese, fruit, vegetables, meat, sausage, fish, seafood, as well as *frutos secos* (a variety of nuts, almonds and dried fruits) and honey. The smaller towns have designated market days, where stalls are set up, often on the town square. Most markets have a few cafés where you can grab a quick coffee or a snack. It's best to visit markets in the mornings, from 8am to 1pm. Most close around 2 to 3pm, and even if they re-open after

A local woven wicker basket

4pm, many stalls remain shut. The earlier you arrive, the better chance you'll have of picking up the freshest, cheapest, and most attractive products.

Northern Spain has a strong crafts heritage, and the best places to buy authentic items are the artisan markets. The items on sale include basketware and leather goods – reasonably priced shoes, wallets and accessories. In Galicia you will find the popular bobbin lace and pottery, in La Rioja the region's famous wine, in Asturias clogs, and in the Pyrenees a range of wood products.

Bookstalls are also popular, selling cheap second-hand books. It's worth taking a look, as you can sometimes find rare books at bargain prices.

A fruit and vegetable market in Santiago de Compostela

A range of goods outside the entrance to a souvenir shop

What to Buy in Northern Spain

Whether it's Basque berets or Galician pottery, each region of Northern Spain has its own unique handicrafts and souvenirs for sale, making shopping an enjoyable experience. Every town has a selection of souvenir shops and markets selling craft products and delicious foodstuffs. Especially popular are handmade goods such as wooden clogs, wicker baskets and Galician bobbin lace, as well as items connected with the pilgrimage route of St James. The region produces delicious wines and other alcoholic beverages – La Rioja wines, Galician *orujo* and *queimada*, and Asturian cider, are all good choices for gifts to take home.

Souvenirs in an antique shop in Santillana del Mar

Souvenirs of the Pilgrimage Route of St James

Northern Spain, and Galicia in particular, is strongly associated with the pilgrimage route to Santiago de Compostela, along which thousands of pilgrims travel each year. Religious artifacts, such as figures and paintings of St James, miniature models of Santiago Cathedral, and scallop shells, are available.

Scallop Shell
This white shell is a symbol of the route of St James — pilgrims would use these shells as spoons or cups.

A figure of St James
Figures of St James in various poses – sitting, standing, usually with a staff in hand – can be bought in practically every place along the pilgrimage route.

Pilgrim's Walking Stick
Wooden walking sticks and gourds for water were once indispensable items carried by every pilgrim. They are now popular souvenirs.

Regional Souvenirs

Every region has its own typical souvenirs. Especially popular are ceramic plates decorated with images of important regional buildings. In Galicia, you can buy ceramic figures and utensils, as well as *azabache* – jet – jewellery. The Basque Country is famous for its berets and figures of the patron saints of Basque towns, while in Asturias you can buy tiny granaries and figures of the Virgen de Covadonga.

Dancing Basque
Dressed in a characteristic white outfit, with a red sash around his waist, the Dancing Basque model is a popular purchase.

Basque Beret Typical black berets (*txapela* or *boina de Tolosa*) are often adorned with the emblems of football clubs or the Basque national flag.

Tower of Hercules
A blue-and-white ceramic Tower of Hercules, a symbol of A Coruña, is a typical souvenir. In many towns you can buy ceramic miniatures of famous buildings.

Cantabrian candle holder, with windable wick

Ceramic plate from Santillana del Mar

Crafts

Every region has its own unique hand-made products. Galicia is famous for its bobbin lace; the Pyrenees region for its wooden spoons; and in Asturias you can buy clogs (*almadreñas* or *madrenyes*) with three heels – one at the front and two at the back – made from a single piece of willow or chestnut wood.

Wicker Baskets

Hand-woven wicker baskets, bread trays and wicker furniture can be bought all over Northern Spain.

Asturian clog

Bobbin Lace Galician lace is called *encaixes de Camariñas*. The designs were originally brought to Galicia from Flanders and were used at the royal court.

Pottery

Northern Spain is renowned for its beautiful pottery. Aside from ceramic figures and *olas* (typical earthenware containers, produced in three sizes), souvenir shops sell ceramic reproductions of bas-reliefs from Spanish churches.

Ceramic piggy bank

Bas-relief reproduction of the Last Supper

Vases from Buño

Beautiful earthenware containers are produced in many places in Galicia. Those from Buño are simple in form and are painted brown, blue and white.

Food

Natural produce reigns supreme at Spanish markets. In Galicia you can buy mixed-blossom honey and *pimientos de Padrón* (small spicy peppers), while markets in the Basque Country offer a magnificent variety of seafood and dried fish.

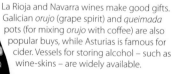

Cheeses

Northern Spain is known for its cheeses. In Cantabria you'll find *Cabrales* and *Picón*; in Galicia the mild *Tetilla* and *San Simón*; and in the Basque Country *Idiazábal*.

Jar of Galician honey

Spirits and Liqueurs

La Rioja and Navarra wines make good gifts. Galician *orujo* (grape spirit) and *queimada* pots (for mixing *orujo* with coffee) are also popular buys, while Asturias is famous for cider. Vessels for storing alcohol – such as wine-skins – are widely available.

A bottle of Viña Costeira

A bottle of white wine

A bottle of red wine

Wine-skin

Vessel for serving *queimada*

ENTERTAINMENT IN NORTHERN SPAIN

At the forefront of Northern Spain's diverse cultural life are the vibrant fiestas. Each town stages celebrations to honour its patron saint. Some events are small-scale and local in character; others, such as the *Los Sanfermines* festival in Pamplona, attract great crowds.

In summer there are festivals of jazz, film, theatre and folklore; many enjoy international status. All religious holidays are celebrated with great pomp and ceremony – Easter Week festivities include colourful processions, while at Corpus Christi the streets of towns and cities are carpeted with intricate designs made from brightly coloured flower petals. There is also a full calendar of entertainment options, from theatre and cinema to sport.

The magnificent lobby of the Teatro Arriaga in Bilbao

Theatre, Ballet and Concerts

One of the most beautiful theatre buildings is the eclectic **Teatro Arriaga** in Bilbao. Here you can see productions from around the world, as well as ballet performances and concerts. Bilbao is also home to the modern **Palacio Euskalduna**, where concerts, ballet, theatre and conventions are held. The **Kursaal**, a major music, dance and theatre venue, is located in San Sebastián.

Oviedo's showpiece is the historic **Teatro Campoamor**, which was established in 1892. Top Spanish and foreign productions are staged here, as are classical music concerts and ballet productions.

The best-known theatre in Galicia is the **Teatro Rosalía de Castro** in A Coruña. In Asturias, the cultural hub of Gijón is the **Teatro Jovellanos**. This late 19th-century building hosts drama productions and symphony concerts, as well as rock and pop concerts. It is also the setting of the International Film Festival of Gijón.

Cinema

Northern Spain is home to some of the biggest names in Spanish cinema and hosts several exciting film festivals.

The great film director Carlos Saura was born in Huesca and Bilbao is the home of director Álex de la Iglesia; Imanol Uribe lived here, too.

Every September, the acclaimed **Festival Internacional de Cine de San Sebastián** takes place in the Basque city of San Sebastián. Stars of the silver screen converge on the **Kursaal arts centre** to attend the festival.

Other regions of Northern Spain also host important events. The **Independent Film Festival** takes place in Ourense, and Spanish-American films are shown at the **Festival de Cine de Huesca**. In Gijón, films from around the world can be seen at the **Festival Internacional de Cine de Gijón**. Towns and cities in Northern Spain have both small arts cinemas and large multiplexes. The leading major cinemas belong to the Yelmocineplex network – **Ocimax** in Gijón, **Yelmo Los Rosales** in Coruña, and **Yelmo Los Prados** in Oviedo.

Foreign films are usually shown dubbed into Spanish or sometimes a local language, but an increasing number of cinemas, especially in cities, show films in their original language – most often English – with subtitles. This is indicated by the letters VO (for *versión original*) on cinema advertising and newspaper listings.

Nightlife

Spain's prodigious nightlife starts later than in most other countries, with 11pm considered an early start for most revellers. At weekends, in particular, the towns and cities of Northern Spain are buzzing with life late into the night. Social activities and entertainment are concentrated in the bars and clubs located primarily on the cities' main

Classic cars during the Santiago pilgrimage

The exciting August regatta on the Sella river

division clubs, are Anoeta in San Sebastián (Real Sociedad club), **Estadio de Fútbol de San Mamés** in Bilbao (Athletic Bilbao), El Sadar in Pamplona (Osasuna), El Sardinero in Santander (Racing de Santander), **Estadio Municipal del Riazor** in A Coruña (Deportivo) and Balaídos in Vigo (Celta Vigo). Other popular spectator sports are cycling, tennis and Basque sports, such as *pelota*.

Fiestas

Regardless of when you visit Northern Spain, you're bound to encounter some local festivities. The Spanish love fiestas, of which there are several kinds: religious, folkloric, or those held in honour of a patron saint or to commemorate a particular event. Every town celebrates the feast day of its patron saint by staging a colourful fiesta, comprising bands, parades, fireworks and other attractions.

Religious holidays are celebrated on a grand scale, with processions, fairs and other commemorative events. The biggest fiesta in Galicia is held on St James's Day (25 July), while in Asturias the main event is *La Santina* procession in Covadonga (8 September).

The most important religious holiday is Easter. During Easter Week, city streets throughout the region are filled with processions of monks carrying platforms bearing figures of saints and Passion scenes.

streets and squares – the Old Town in Bilbao, in Cañadío, the city center of Santander, along the Calle Mon in the university town of Oviedo, the old town of San Sebastián, which is known for bar-hopping, and at Orzán beach in A Coruña.

Sport

Football is practically a religion for many Spanish men, and the top clubs attract thousands of spectators. The chief stadiums in the north, home to the first-

Traditional parade during Easter Week (Semana Santa) in Bilbao

DIRECTORY

Theatre, Ballet and Concerts

Kursaal
Avenida De Zurriola 1
20002 San Sebastián.
Tel 943 00 30 00.
W kursaal.org

Palacio Euskalduna
Abandoibarra 4,
Bilbao. **Tel** 944 03 50 00.
W euskalduna.net

Teatro Arriaga
Plaza Arriaga 1,
Bilbao.
Tel 944 79 20 36.
W teatroarriaga.com

Teatro Campoamor
C/ Diecinueve de Julio 1,
Oviedo.
Tel 985 20 75 90.
W teatrocampoamor.es

Teatro Jovellanos
Paseo de Begoña 11
33201 Gijón.
Tel 985 18 29 29.
W teatrojovellanos.com

Teatro Rosalía de Castro
Rúa Riego de Agua 37
15001 A Coruña.
Tel 981 18 43 49.

Festivals

Festival de Cine de Huesca
Avenida Parque 1, 2nd floor 22002 Huesca.
Tel 974 21 13 62.
W huesca-filmfestival.com

Festival Internacional de Cine de Gijón
C/ Cabrales 82 33201
Gijón. **Tel** 985 18 29 40.
W gijonfilmfestival.com

Festival Internacional de Cine de San Sebastián
Plaza Okendo 1, 20004
San Sebastián.
Tel 943 48 12 12
W sansebastian festival.com

International Independent Film Festival
C/ Canle 2 32004
Ourense. **Tel** 988 39 12 90.
W ouff.org

Cinema

Kursaal
see Theatre, Ballet and Concerts (left).

Ocimax Gijón
Maestro Amado Morán
33212 Gijón.
Tel 985 30 80 27.

Yelmo Los Prados
Calle Fernandez Ladreda
33010 Oviedo.
Tel 985 11 99 20.
W yelmocines.es

Yelmo Los Rosales
Ronda de Outeiro 419
15011 A Coruña.
Tel 981 12 80 92.
W yelmocines.es

Sport

Estadio de Fútbol de San Mamés
Alameda Mazarredo 23
48009 Bilbao.
Tel 944 24 08 77.
W athletic-club.net

Estadio Municipal de Riazor
Calle Manuel Murguía
15011 A Coruña.
Tel 981 22 94 10.

SPORTS AND OUTDOOR ACTIVITIES

Thanks to its diverse geography and temperate climate, Northern Spain is an ideal destination for outdoor enthusiasts. The Atlantic coast offers excellent opportunities for water sports, especially windsurfing, while inland, rafting and canoeing trips are organized along fast-flowing highland rivers. In the Pyrenees, spanning Navarra, Aragón, Andorra and Catalonia, outdoor activities are possible all year round. Hiking and climbing are popular in summer, while in winter skiers can take advantage of the numerous well-maintained pistes. Northern Spain's verdant landscapes can also be explored on horseback or by bicycle, thanks to an extensive network of trails.

A trail through the Parc Nacional d'Aigüestortes in the Pyrenees

Walking and Trekking

The most accessible form of leisure activity in Northern Spain is walking, particularly mountain-walking. Its increasing popularity is due largely to the preponderance of well-marked trails, good accommodation and excellent guides. There are scenic trails throughout the mountains of Northern Spain, particularly in the Pyrenees, as well as in the Cantabrian Mountains, from the Ancares range on the border of Galicia, León and Asturias, through the Picos de Europa in the northern reaches of the Iberian Mountains.

The principal network of marked trails includes Major Trails (*Grandes Rutas* or *GR*, marked by red-and-white signs) and Minor Trails (*Pequeñas Rutas* or *PR*, marked by white-and-yellow signs). One of the most famous trails is GR 1, also known as the "Historical Trail", which starts at the ruins of Empúries, on the Mediterranean coast near Girona, and proceeds to Cabo Fisterra (Cape Finisterre) in Galicia, via the Pyrenees, the Basque Country, the northern part of Burgos province and the Pilgrims' Road to Santiago. The GR 1 reflects the philosophy behind the planning of hiking trails in Spain, which is based on linking active leisure with culture and sightseeing. This philosophy is visible, too, in the GR 12 Euskal Herria (Basque Country) trail, which incorporates the most important places associated with Basque culture. Another trail well worth taking is the GR 11 (Pyrenean Trail), which goes from Hondarribia, through Elizondo, Roncesvalles, Ochagavía and Isaba in Navarra, the Ordesa valley, Andorra and Puigcerdà to Cap de Creus in Catalonia.

Aerial Sports

The best way to take in Northern Spain's landscape is to view it from above, and this part of the country provides an excellent environment for aerial sports enthusiasts. For those who have forever been fascinated by birds' ability to fly, paragliding and hang-gliding are two excellent options. Paragliding is especially popular on account of the beautiful mountain scenery.

The **Real Federación Aeronáutica Española** will send information about Spanish airfields and clubs where visitors can practise flying, gliding and parachuting. The organization also provides information on the best locations for ballooning, hang-gliding and paragliding.

A foreign private pilot's licence is valid in Spain for a maximum of six months.

Paragliding above the Vall d'Aran in the eastern Pyrenees

Surfers in the Basque resort of Mundaka

Water Sports

The Atlantic coast is great for both sunbathing and water sports, including windsurfing. In Galicia, windsurfers head for Pantin beach; in Asturias, the beaches in Salinas are popular; the Basque Country is home to the best surfing spots, such as the towns of Mundaka and Zarautz.

Many more beaches offer kitesurfing and bodyboarding all year round; kayaks and catamarans are also available. Sailing is popular, too, and you can rent a yacht by the day or week, or sign up for a half- or full-day sailing excursion. Tourist offices at the coastal resorts provide information about local hire of boats and sailboards. Sailing information is also provided by the **Real Federación Española de Vela**.

The Galician coast is also excellent for snorkelling and diving. A wonderful experience can be had exploring old ship-wrecks on the ocean floor.

Speciality centres offer canoeing and white-water rafting in the mountains of Northern Spain. In Galicia, such centres can be found in the upper reaches of the Miño and Ulloa rivers; in Asturias on the Sella river; and in Cantabria on the Ebro and Asón. Pyrenean rivers, such as the Ara, Esera and Gállego, offer some of the best rafting.

Naturism

Naturism is legal in Spain and is popular among local people and visitors alike. Specially designed nudist, or naturist beaches, are not hard to find.

The beautiful beaches of the Atlantic coast, often concealed by bays, offer an ideal environment for nudists. The website of the **Federación Española de Naturismo** has descriptions of nudist beaches in various regions of Northern Spain and provides information on their location and facilities.

Hunting and Fishing

The Atlantic coast, as well as the hundreds of mountain streams, rivers and reservoirs, provide an attractive environment for fishing, particularly fly-fishing. The most common species caught are brown and rainbow trout, sea trout, and Atlantic salmon. In Galicia, the best fishing spots are located in the Eume, Tambre and Miño river basins. In Asturias, fishing is popular on the Sella, Narcea and Esva rivers. The Saja river basin is the best fishing ground in Cantabria. In the Basque Country, anglers head for Bayas and Zadorra, while in La Rioja, the Iregua river is considered

to be the top spot. In the Catalonian Pyrenees, the Noguera and Alto Segre rivers are excellent for fishing.

Each region of Northern Spain has its own strict fishing regulations. All the fishing grounds (for instance, the so-called "catch and release" grounds) are clearly marked. Permits for river or sea fishing from one day to one year, and for fishing competitions, are issued by the *comunidades* (regional governments).

Fishing – a popular activity in the rivers of Northern Spain

The **Federación Española de Pesca** gives information on licences, locations where fishing is permitted and the dates of open seasons. Fishing centres and many hotels in fishing areas will advise on permits, and will often obtain one for you.

If you want to hunt or shoot in Spain you must be licensed and insured. To obtain a licence, apply to the local *Consejería de Medio Ambiente*. Information about hunting and shooting is provided by the **Real Federación Española de Caza**.

Canoeists playing water football

A ski resort in Andorra

Winter Sports

Spain's mountainous terrain makes it an excellent place for skiing, and resorts here are often cheaper than those in the Alps or other places in Europe. There are numerous winter resorts in Northern Spain, particularly in the Pyrenees. Especially popular is the huge ski resort of **Baqueira-Beret**, one of the largest in Spain. Skiers have at their disposal 71 pistes and 32 ski lifts, which ascend to between 1,500 m (5,000 ft) and 2,500 m (7,600 ft) above sea level. After a hard day's skiing, you can relax in nearby Arties' thermal springs.

Other popular Pyrenean resorts include Candanchú and Panticosa, in Huesca province, and Masella, in the province of Girona. There are also good resorts in the Cantabrian Mountains, such as **Manzaneda** in Galicia, San Isidro and Leitariegos in León, and **Alto Campoo** in Asturias. Here, skiers can enjoy several well-maintained and often picturesque runs, of varying length and difficulty. Andorra is another big destination for skiing and winter sports.

Nowadays, an increasing number of people don their snowshoes to explore the snow-covered mountainsides and valleys on foot.

Aside from snowboarding, downhill and cross-country skiing, Pyrenean spas offer numerous other attractions to keep visitors entertained. Most of the resorts have swimming pools, ice rinks, and a choice of restaurants, bars and nightclubs.

Every region of Northern Spain has its own winter sports association. The **Federación Española de Deportes de Montaña y Escalada** can supply details about mountain sports and mountain conditions. Ski resorts themselves usually have good websites with up-to-date information.

Cycling and Horse Riding

Cycling and horse riding are both very popular activities in Northern Spain. The coastal areas, mountain valleys and picturesque inland trails provide terrain that is ideally suited to horse riding.

It is fairly easy to hire a horse, and many tour operators now specialize in equestrian holidays. The **Real Federación Hípica Española** can provide additional information on horse riding and pony trekking.

Information about cycle routes is provided by the **Real Federación Española de Ciclismo**.

Bicycles can be rented in almost every town in Northern Spain. The region can be toured on picturesque minor roads or special **Vías Verdes** routes (see box).

The La Toja golf course on an island in Galicia

Golf and Tennis

The success of golfers such as Ballesteros, Olazábal, Jiménez and Sergio García is thanks in no small part to the excellent standard of Spanish golf courses. The number of golf courses is steadily increasing, too. From Galicia to northern Catalonia, visitors will find golf courses to suit all types of

---

Vías Verdes

The Vías Verdes (Green Routes) programme was established in 1993 and enjoys huge popularity among both visitors and Spaniards alike. Its aim is to adapt old, disused railway lines so that they can be used for walking, cycling and horse riding. Many of the converted railway lines are also wheelchair-friendly. The picturesque routes lead through hills and lush meadows, passing historic towns and ancient monasteries. Among the best routes in Northern Spain are the Vía Verde del Plazaola in Navarra (40 km/ 25 miles) and the Vía Verde del Río Oja in La Rioja (28 km/ 17 miles).

Cyclists on the Vía Verde del Río Oja route in La Rioja

player – beginners, big hitters, technical masters. The majority of courses are 9-hole, but 18-hole ones are not uncommon. Apart from their purely sport-related qualities, golf courses in Northern Spain are also often set in beautiful landscapes. In this regard, the leading courses are in Galicia – the Ría de Vigo in the province of Pontevedra and La Toja in an island spa. A remarkable combination of sea and mountains can be found in Asturias and Cantabria; here, the best courses are La Rasa de Berbes in Ribadesella, La Cuesta in Llanes, Santa Marina in San Vicente de la Barquera (designed by Severiano Ballesteros) and Pedreña near Santander. In the province of Álava, the excellent Álava Izki Golf course in Urturi was also designed by Ballesteros.

Many admire Navarra's Zuasti course in Zuasti de Iza, designed by José María Olazábal, while in Catalonia the Aravell Golf Andorra is not to be missed. Most golf courses have their own websites where you can learn more about course specifications and the rules of various clubs.

Ponies for hire

Information is also provided by the **Real Federación Española de Golf** or by www.golfspain.com.

Tennis is also a popular sport. In most tourist areas there are tennis courts for hire. The local tourist information office can advise on the nearest court. Many travel agents arrange tennis holidays for enthusiasts. For more information, contact the **Real Federación Española de Tenis**.

Activities for Children

Northern Spain has many facilities that cater for children, and children can accompany their parents on outdoor holidays. Many beaches have special play areas with slides and paddling pools. Rental shops offer children's bicycles as well as bicycles with special chairs for carrying children. Stables often have ponies as well as horses for hire.

Skiing holidays are also suitable for children. All ski resorts have ski schools for children, with various events and competitions.

An excellent time can be had at aquariums, where children and parents alike can admire the Atlantic's many colourful species of fish.

DIRECTORY

Aerial Sports

Real Federación Aeronáutica Española
Carretera de la Fortuna
28044 Madrid.
Tel 915 08 29 50.
🔲 rfae.org

Water Sports

Real Federación Española de Vela
Luis de Salazar 9 28002
Madrid. **Tel** 915 19 50 08.
🔲 rfev.es

Naturism

Federación Española de Naturismo
🔲 naturismo.org

Hunting and Fishing

Federación Española de Pesca
Navas de Tolosa 3 28013
Madrid. **Tel** 91 532 83 52.
🔲 fepyc.es

Real Federación Española de Caza
C/ Francos Rodríguez 70
28039 Madrid.
Tel 91 311 14 11.
🔲 fecaza.com

Winter Sports

Alto Campoo
Zona Valle Campoo 39200
Reinosa (Cantabria).
Tel 942 77 92 22 (pistes).
Tel 902 21 01 12 (info).
🔲 altocampoo.com

Baqueira-Beret
Tel 973 63 90 25 (pistes).
Tel 902 41 54 15 (info).
🔲 baqueira.es

Manzaneda
Estación de Manzaneda
32780 Puebla de Trives.
Tel 988 30 90 80.
🔲 manzaneda.com

Federación Española de Deportes de Montaña y Escalada
Floridablanca 84
08015 Barcelona.
Tel 93 426 42 67.
🔲 fedme.es

Cycling and Horse Riding

Real Federación Española de Ciclismo
Ferraz 16 28008 Madrid.
Tel 915 40 08 41.
🔲 rfec.com

Real Federación Hípica Española
Calle Monte Esquinza 28
28010 Madrid.
Tel 914 36 42 00.
🔲 rfhe.com

Vías Verdes
🔲 viasverdes.com

Golf and Tennis

Real Federación Española de Golf
Paseo Joaquín Rodrigo 4
28224 Pozuelo de
Alarcón, Madrid.
Tel 902 20 00 52.
🔲 golfspainfederacion.com

Real Federación Española de Tenis
Passeig Olímpic 17 (Estadi
Olímpic), 08038 Barcelona.
Tel 93 200 53 55.
🔲 rfet.es

SURVIVAL GUIDE

PRACTICAL INFORMATION

Northern Spain has a solid tourist infrastructure, beyond the attractions of its coastline, bullfights and flamenco. Each of its regions has its own tourist information service, and there are tourist information offices in every city, and local offices in many smaller towns, especially on the coast. All offer help with finding accommodation, restaurants and activities in their area. In the last few years, the Spanish tourist

authorities have intensively promoted "Green Spain" – the regions of Galicia, Asturias, Cantabria and the Basque Country that border the Cantabrian Sea. The Spanish themselves come here for their holidays to escape the busy and overcrowded south. August is Spain's main holiday month. Many businesses close for the month, and roads are busy at the beginning and end of this period.

ERRESERBATUA

BIZKAIKO FORU ALDUNDIA

RESERVADO
DIPUTACION FORAL
DE BIZKAIA

A bilingual parking sign in Basque and Castilian

Language

The main language of Spain is *castellano* (Castilian), which is spoken by almost everyone. In addition, there are three main regional languages: *gallego* (Galician), which is spoken in Galicia, *euskera* (Basque), spoken in the Basque Country and part of Navarra, and *catalá* (Catalan), spoken in Catalonia. Galician, Basque and Catalan are not dialects

of Castilian. They are wholly independent languages, and the Galicians, Basques and Catalans are very sensitive on this issue.

Visitors with a knowledge of Spanish or Portuguese will not have any difficulty understanding Galician. Knowledge of Spanish or French is useful for understanding Catalan. Workers who speak English are often employed in places that deal with tourists.

When to Visit

The best time to visit Northern Spain depends on what you plan to do here. If your aim is a beach holiday on the Atlantic coast, then July and August are the best months. May, June and September are all good months to explore the historic sites of Northern Spain in relative peace and quiet. Galicia, Asturias, Cantabria and the Basque Country all have higher rainfall than other regions of Spain. Summer in Northern Spain is warm without being oppressively hot. Temperatures rarely exceed 30°C (86°F).

Visas and Passports

Visas are not required for citizens of EU countries, Switzerland, Norway or Iceland. A list of entry requirements, which is available

from Spanish embassies, specifies many other countries, including New Zealand, Canada, the USA and Australia, whose nationals do not need to apply for a visa if visiting Spain for less than 90 days. Thereafter they may apply to the *Gobierno Civil* (a local government office) for an extension. You need proof of employment or of sufficient funds to support yourself during a long stay. Visitors from other countries must obtain a visa before travelling.

If you know in advance that you will be staying longer than 90 days, you should apply to your nearest Spanish embassy for a visa. The process of issuing a visa can take from one to four months.

oficina de turismo

A Spanish tourist information office sign

Tax-Free Goods

Non-EU residents can reclaim VAT (value-added tax) on purchases worth over €91 (*see p224*). At certain airports, such as in Madrid and Barcelona, you can get a cash refund on the spot.

Tourist Information

All major towns and cities have a tourist information office (*oficina de turismo*), which will provide you with maps, lists of hotels and restaurants, and information about the locality.

A café in Pamplona

◀ The harbour at San Sebastian (Donostia)

Tourists on a sunny street in San Sebastián

Weights, Measures and Electricity

Spain uses the metric system for weights and measures, including distances marked on road signs.

The electricity supply in Spain is 220 volts. Plugs have two round pins. A standard travel converter enables you to use appliances you have brought from home while on holiday in Spain. If you need to buy one after you arrive, they are available in department stores in most major towns and cities.

Opening Hours

In Northern Spain, most museums, galleries and monuments close on Mondays. On other days they generally open from 10am to 2pm and from 5 to 8pm, although in some cases they are open all day. Admission is charged for most museums and monuments, as well as some cathedrals and churches. Admission for many museums is free on Sundays.

Spanish Time

In winter, Spain is one hour ahead of Greenwich Mean Time (GMT) and in summer one hour ahead of British Summer Time (BST), ie GMT + 2. Spain uses the 24-hour clock, so 1pm = 13:00.

Facilities for the Disabled

Spain's National Association for the Disabled, COCEMFE (*Confederación Coordinadora Estatal de Minusválidos Físicos de España*), publishes guides to facilities in Spain and will help plan a holiday to suit individual requirements. **Viajes 2000** travel agency specializes in holidays for disabled people *(see p203)*.

In the UK, Tourism for All (www.tourismforall.org.uk)

offers information on facilities for the disabled in Spain.

Student Information

Holders of the International Student Identity Card (ISIC) are entitled to benefits, such as discounts on travel and reduced entrance fees to museums and galleries.

The ISIC website lists travel agencies in Spain specializing in young and student travellers (www.isic.org).

In Spain, you can obtain additional information from youth information centres (Centros de Información Juvenil – CIJ) in large towns (www.euro26.org).

Travelling with Children

Spain is a child-friendly country for the most part, and it's usual for children to accompany parents wherever they go. In the evenings, it's not uncommon to see children with their families in restaurants, even at midnight. By law, children travelling in a car must always sit on the back seat and wear a seatbelt; babies and small children should be secured in approved children's car seats. Nowadays, many airports, stations and restaurants have washing and nappy-changing facilities.

A disabled-access sign

Personal Security and Health

In Spain, as in most European countries, rural areas are generally safe, but certain parts of cities are subject to petty crime. Carry cards and money in a belt and never leave anything visible in your car when you park it. Taking out medical insurance cover is advisable, but for minor health problems pharmacists are a good source of assistance. Northern Spain is well supplied with pharmacies, which are easy to find with their green or red neon signs. Emergency phone numbers vary – the most important ones are on the opposite page. If you lose your documents, contact your consulate or the local police.

The beautiful interior of a traditional pharmacy in A Coruña

In an Emergency

In an emergency call **112** for the police, an ambulance or the fire brigade. You can also call the national police on **091**; the fire brigade on **080** (in main cities); and the ambulance service on **061**.

In a medical emergency for which an ambulance is not required you can go to the hospital casualty department (Urgencias).

Medical Treatment

All EU nationals are entitled to Spanish social security cover. To claim, you must obtain the European Health Insurance Card from the UK Department of Health or from a post office before you travel. It comes with a booklet, Health Advice for Travellers, which explains exactly what health care you are entitled to and where and how to claim.

Not all treatments are covered by the card and some are costly, so it is worth arranging separate medical insurance to cover the cost of, for instance, medication, home visits by a doctor, repatriation or an extended hospital stay. Note that in private hospitals you have to pay unless you have private insurance. Visitors coming to Spain from non-EU countries should arrange cover through a private insurance company.

A Spanish pharmacy sign

Pharmacies

Spanish pharmacists (farmacéuticos) are well trained and have wide responsibilities. They can advise and, in some cases, prescribe medication without consulting a doctor. In a non-emergency a pharmacist is a good person to see first. It is easy to find one who speaks English.

The farmacía sign is a green or red illuminated cross.

The addresses and telephone numbers of pharmacies open at night are listed in the windows of all the local pharmacies. If you need a pharmacy on a Sunday, look for farmacías de guardia. Do not confuse pharmacies with perfumerías, which sell toiletries only.

Personal Security

Violent crime is rare in Spain but visitors should avoid walking alone in poorly lit areas. Men occasionally make complimentary remarks (piropos) to women in public, particularly in the street. This is an old custom and not intended to be intimidating.

To protect yourself against theft, be sure to keep your credit cards, money and documents well hidden and close to your body. Wear a bag or camera strap across your body, not on your shoulder. When visiting a café, restaurant or bar, keep your handbag on your knees – never leave it on the tabletop or the chair opposite.

Police

There are three types of police in Spain. The Guardia Civil (national guard) are in charge of policing rural areas, and their responsibilities include enforcing traffic restrictions on main highways.

Guardia Civil   Policía Nacional   Policía Local

A patrol car of the Policía Nacional, Spain's main urban police force

A patrol car of the Policía Local, mainly seen in small towns

A Cruz Roja (Red Cross) ambulance

A fire engine with the emergency number painted on its side

It's better and safer to pay by card, where possible, than to carry large amounts of cash.

Public Conveniences

Public pay-toilets are rare in Spain. Department stores are often good places to find a toilet, as are petrol stations, cafés, bars, restaurants and museums. Most cafés and restaurants will allow you to use their toilet (ask for *los aseos* or *los servicios*). Sometimes toilets are kept locked, in which case you should ask for the key (*la llave*).

DIRECTORY

Emergency Numbers

Emergency: all services
Tel 112 (toll-free).

Policía Nacional
Tel 091 (nationwide).

Fire Brigade (Bomberos)
Tel 080 (in all large cities).

Ambulance
Tel 061.

Hospitals

Hospital Quirón (private)
Calle Londres 2, A Coruña
(Galicia). Tel 981 21 98 00,
902 32 22 33.

Hospital Xeral (public)
Calle Pizarro 22, Vigo (Galicia).
Tel 986 81 11 11.

Hospital Central de Asturias (public)
Carretera de Rubin, "La Cadellada",
Oviedo (Asturias).
Tel 985 10 80 00.

Clínica Quirón (private)
La Esperanza 3 01002 Vitoria
(Basque Country).
Tel 945 25 25 00.

Policlínica Guipúzcoa (private)
Paseo Miramón 174 San
Sebastián (Basque Country).
Tel 943 00 28 00.

Clínica Universitaria de Navarra (private)
Avenida Pío XII 36 Pamplona
(Navarra). Tel 948 25 54 00.

Hospital San Pedro (public)
Calle Piqueras 98 Logroño
(La Rioja). Tel 941 29 80 00.

The Policía Nacional (national police) are the main force charged with dealing with crime in towns of over 30,000 people. In addition, in two of Northern Spain's autonomous regions, many of the duties of the Policía Nacional and the Guardia Civil have now been taken over by regional forces, the red-uniformed Ertzainta in the Basque Country and the blue-uniformed Mossos d'Esquadra in Catalonia.

Local police forces (Policía Local, Policía Municipal or Guardia Urbana or Guardia Local), operate in each town, with their own structure and uniforms. They are responsible for dealing with parking and associated town by-laws.

In the event of an incident, any of the three police services will either help or direct you to the relevant authority that can deal with your problem.

Personal Property

Before travelling to Spain it is worth arranging holiday insurance to protect you from the loss or theft of property. The moment you discover a loss or theft, report it to the local police station and obtain a report. To claim on insurance, you must act within 24 hours.

Banking and Local Currency

The official currency of Spain is the euro. You may enter Spain with any amount of money, but if you intend to export more than €10,000, you should declare it. Travellers' cheques may be exchanged at banks and *cajas de cambio* (foreign currency exchanges), but it is difficult to find hotels and shops that accept them. Banks generally offer the most favourable exchange rates. The cheapest rates may be offered on your credit and debit card, which you can use in cash dispensers (ATMs), which are open 24 hours, but check before you travel on the charges made by your card provider for cash withdrawals.

A 24-hour cash dispenser

Banking Hours

Hours vary between Spanish banks, but most are open Monday to Friday from 8:30am to 2pm. In cities and larger towns, they may stay open longer in the afternoon. Very few banks open on Saturday mornings, and never on Saturdays in the summer.

Changing Money

Money can be exchanged in a bank *(banco)* or savings bank *(caja de ahorro)*. Most banks have a foreign exchange desk with the sign *Cambio* or *Extranjero*. Always take your passport as ID to effect any transaction.

In the tourist areas of Spanish towns and cities you'll find bureaux de change *(casas de cambio)*, which stay open later than banks. The exchange rates they offer can vary considerably, so it's best to shop around.

Some department stores, such as El Corte Inglés, have their own bureaux de change

TELEBANCO

An ATM logo

that have the same opening hours as the store.

Avoid changing money in hotels, as they almost always levy heavier fees or have poorer rates than banks.

Cheques and Cards

Travellers' cheques in euros can be purchased at **American Express**, Thomas Cook or your own bank before starting your trip. When cashing a cheque at a bank, you will need to show your passport or another form of photographic ID.

The most widely accepted credit cards in Spain are **VISA**, **MasterCard** and (less so) **Diners Club** and American Express. You must show photo ID, such as your passport, when paying by credit or debit card.

Cash Dispensers

If your card is linked to your home bank account, you can use it with your PIN to withdraw money from cash dispensers.

All take VISA or MasterCard; cards with Cirrus and Maestro logos are also widely accepted in Spain.

When you enter your PIN, instructions are displayed in English, French, German and Spanish. Many ATMs are located inside buildings, and to gain access you will have to run your card through a door-entry system. This type of cash dispenser is the safest to use, especially at night or in crowded places.

DIRECTORY

Banks

Banco Popular
 bancopopular.es
Tel 902 30 10 00.

Banco Santander
Tel 902 24 24 24.
bancosantander.es

BBVA
Tel 902 22 44 66.
bbva.es

Kutxa
Tel 900 44 55 66.
kutxa.net

Lost Cards and Travellers' Cheques

American Express
Pl de Las Cortes 2, 28014 Madrid.
Tel 900 81 45 00.

Diners Club
Tel 902 40 11 12.

MasterCard
Tel 900 97 12 31 (toll-free).

VISA
Tel 900 99 11 24 (toll-free).

The entrance to a branch of the Banco Pastor

The Euro

The euro (€) is the common currency of the European Union. It went into general circulation on 1 January 2002, initially for 12 participating countries. Spain was one of those countries. EU members using the euro as sole official currency are known as the Eurozone. Several EU members have opted out of joining this common currency.

Euro notes are identical throughout the Eurozone countries, each one including designs of fictional architectural structures and monuments. The coins, however, have one side identical (the value side), and one side with an image unique to each country. Both notes and coins are exchangeable in each of the participating countries.

Bank Notes

Euro bank notes have seven denominations. The 5-euro note (grey) is the smallest, followed by the 10-euro note (pink), 20-euro note (blue), 50-euro note (orange), 100-euro note (green), 200-euro note (yellow) and 500-euro note (purple). All notes show the 12 stars of the European Union.

5 euros

10 euros

20 euros

50 euros

100 euros

200 euros

500 euros

2 euros

1 euro

50 cents

20 cents

10 cents

5 cents

2 cents

1 cent

Coins

The euro has eight coin denominations: 2 euros and 1 euro (silver and gold); 50 cents, 20 cents and 10 cents (gold); and 5 cents, 2 cents and 1 cent (bronze). The reverse side of euro coins is the same in all euro-zone countries, but the front varies by country.

Communications and Media

With the proliferation of smartphones, the number of public telephones and cybercafés is gradually diminishing. Several service providers in Spain offer both mobile and Internet services, and there are plenty of places to find free or inexpensive Wi-Fi for those travelling with their own devices.

The Spanish post office provides an efficient service, and there are also courier firms for urgent communications.

There are numerous TV and radio stations in Spain, some state-run and others private.

Public payphone booths, with their characteristic blue tops

Logo of Movistar, the main telephone company in Spain

Public Telephones

Public telephones, operated by the main telephone company **Movistar**, are easy to find. Most accept credit cards, or pre-paid telephone cards (*tarjetas telefónicas*) instead of coins. You can purchase phonecards from tobacconists, supermarkets and newsstands.

When calling from a fixed line, there are four charge bands for international calls. The cheapest calls are to numbers within the European Union; slightly more expensive are calls to non-EU countries and northwest Africa, followed by calls to North and South America; the most expensive calls are to the rest of the world.

Reverse-charge calls from Movistar phone boxes (*cábinas*) can be made through the operator or by prefixing the number with 1409 (if calling a fixed line number) or with 210 (when calling a mobile number).

When calling Spain from abroad, dial the international code for Spain (+34), followed by the nine-digit number.

Mobile Phones

A 3G broadband mobile (or a mobile operable in frequencies GSM 900/1800) will work in Spain, but check costs with your service provider first. If you plan to make frequent calls, it will probably work out cheaper to get a Spanish number. You can have your phone unlocked and get a pre-paid SIM card, or buy a pre-paid phone with a number of minutes included. The Bic Phone, an inexpensive disposable phone that comes fully charged and with a small amount of phone credit, is available at petrol stations, supermarkets and tobacconists in larger towns and cities.

The most popular mobile phone providers in Spain are Movistar, **Vodafone**, **Orange** and **Yoigo**. Their products can be found at their own shops, online, at El Corte Inglés stores and at **Phone House**. For a simple handset plus SIM card (allowing free incoming calls to Spain), expect to pay about €50. Rates for national calls are around 5 cents per minute; most providers also offer pre-paid Internet data cards that start at around €5 for 300MB.

To add more credit to your phone, purchase a scratch card from supermarkets and shops, online at your provider's website, or by phone using your credit card. Mobile phone top-ups are also available from most ATMs.

If you have a Wi-Fi connection, you can also use popular videochat and call programs or apps, such as Skype, Google Hangout or Viber.

Internet

Wi-Fi is available in all airports, most hotels and an increasing number of cafés and restaurants, as well as in many of the well-known international fast-food and coffee chains. Increasingly, Wi-Fi is offered for free. Some larger cities, such as Bilbao, also provide a free Wi-Fi service, as

Useful Spanish Dialling Codes

- Within Spain, you must always dial the nine-digit number in full.
- Numbers beginning with 900 are toll-free, with 902 are inexpensive information lines, and with 80 are the most expensive lines. Those beginning with 6 are mobiles (cell phones).
- To make a call to Andorra, dial 00 376 followed by the full number (omitting the initial 0).
- To make an international call from Spain, dial 00, then the country code, the area code (omitting the initial 0) and the phone number.
- Country codes: Spain 34, UK 44, Eire 353;

France 33; US/Canada 1; Australia 61; New Zealand 64; South Africa 27.
- Information services of mobile operators: Movistar 1004; Orange 1414 (470 from an Orange line); Vodafone 607 123 000 (123 from a Vodafone line); Yoigo 1707 (622 from a Yoigo line).
- International directory enquiries (Movistar) – 11825.
- Speaking clock/wake-up calls/weather (Movistar) – 1212.
- To report a technical fault on Movistar lines, dial 1002 (Movistar).

do many public libraries. There is a smattering of Internet cafés (cibercafés) in the main resorts and towns across the region, and you can usually find computers with Internet access (for a charge) in privately owned call centres (locutorios).

Postal Services

Correos, the Spanish postal service, is identified by a crown insignia in blue on a yellow background. Correos has a network of around 2,500 post offices, including some outposts at major railway stations and airports. Main post offices open 8:30am–8:30pm Monday to Friday and 9:30am–2pm on Saturday. Branches in the suburbs and small towns and villages open 8:30am–2:30pm Monday to Friday and 9:30am–1pm on Saturday.

Although you can buy stamps in Correos offices, it is quicker and easier to buy them at a tobacconist's (estanco). Postal rates fall into three price bands: Spain; Europe and North Africa; and the rest of the world. Parcels must be weighed and stamped at Correos offices.

Registered post can be sent from all post offices. If you want to receive post while you are in Spain, poste restante letters should be addressed care of the Lista de Correos in the relevant town. You can collect them from main post offices.

In cities, Spanish postboxes (buzón) are yellow pillar boxes, often with separate slots for local (ciudad) and other destinations (otros destinos). Elsewhere, postboxes are small and wall-mounted.

A number of courier firms operate in Spain, including **FedEx**, **DHL** and **Seur**.

Newspapers and Magazines

Spanish national dailies (periódicos), such as El País, ABC or El Mundo, are of a high standard.

The various regions also have their own

A postbox (buzón)

local newspapers. Some of these are written in regional languages (for instance, Gara, a Basque newspaper), while other local papers have non-Spanish sections (such as La Voz de Galicia, which provides readers with a digital version in Gallego). There are both Catalan and Spanish editions of Catalunya's La Vanguardia and El Periódico newspapers.

Most newspapers cost around €1 to €1.50. Weekend papers with colour supplements are more expensive (€2 to €2.50).

Newsagents and kiosks in town centres often stock periodicals in English. Many foreign newspapers, such as The International Herald Tribune, The Financial Times and The Guardian, as well as German, French and Italian newspapers, are widely available in Spain.

Television and Radio

Televisión Española, Spain's state television company, broadcasts on two main channels, La Una and La Dos, and also provides a children's channel, Clan.

Most comunidades (regions) have their own television channels, which broadcast in the language of the region – for instance, TVG (Televisión de Galicia) in Galicia, ETB (Euskal Telebista) in the Basque Country and TV3 in Catalunya. There are also many national private TV stations, including Antena 3, Cuatro, Tele-5 and La Sexta. Most foreign films shown on Spanish television and in cinemas are dubbed, but films are sometimes shown in their original language with Spanish subtitles, indicated by the letters "VO" (versión original) in newspaper listings.

The state radio company, Radio Nacional de España, has six stations. The various regions also have their own radio stations, which broadcast in the language of the region (Radio Galega, for instance, broadcasts in Galician). There are hundreds of private radio stations, too.

A kiosk selling newspapers and magazines in Vitoria-Gasteiz, Basque Country

Addresses

In Spanish addresses, the house number follows the name of the street. The house number is followed by the flat number. Therefore, Calle Luna 6, 4–2° means: No. 6, Luna Street, Fourth floor, Flat 2. The letters "s/n" mean sin número (no number).

TRAVEL INFORMATION

Spain has an increasingly efficient transport system. All the major cities have airports, and many international flights arrive at Madrid and Barcelona. One third of visitors to Spain arrive by air. Aside from scheduled flights, and charter flights in summer, budget airlines fly to many Spanish cities throughout the year. Within Spain, too, especially when travelling long distances, flights are the best option – comfortable, fast, and increasingly cheap. Both the road and rail networks were greatly improved during the 1980s and 90s. Intercity rail services are efficient, but coaches are a faster and more frequent option between smaller towns. In much of rural Spain, however, public transport is limited and a car is the most practical solution for getting about. Ferries connect mainland Spain with the UK.

Arriving by Air

Spain is served by most international airlines. Iberia, the national airline, has scheduled flights daily into Madrid from all western European capitals, and once or twice weekly from most east European capitals.

All the major European airlines (Alitalia, Air Europa, Air France, British Airways, CSA, Iberia, KLM, LOT, Lufthansa, Malev and Swiss) fly direct to Madrid and Barcelona, Spain's two main international airports. British Airways offers scheduled flights to Madrid and Barcelona daily from London Heathrow. **Vueling** (a low-cost Spanish airline) flies from London Heathrow to A Coruña and Bilbao.

Low-cost airlines run many additional services. EasyJet has direct flights from London Stansted to Bilbao and Oviedo (Asturias); Ryanair flies from London Stansted, Frankfurt and Rome to Santander, Santiago de Compostela and Zaragoza; and Air Berlin has connections from Germany's major cities to Santiago de Compostela, Oviedo (Asturias), Logroño and Bilbao. Increased competition among the budget airlines has forced all of the carriers to lower their prices.

Of the US airlines serving Spain, Delta Air Lines and American Airlines fly to both Madrid and Barcelona. Iberia has a comprehensive service from the USA, as well as an indirect service from Canada.

International Airports

Most international services operate from Madrid and Barcelona. Barajas airport in Madrid, serving 49 million passengers each year, is 12 km (8 miles) from the city centre, which can be reached by metro or shuttle bus. A taxi from the airport to the city costs around €25–30.

Terminal 1 operates some international flights (**Ryanair**, **Delta** and **easyJet**, among many others); Terminals 2 and 3 operate domestic flights; and Terminal 4, designed by British architect Richard Rogers, operates most international and some domestic flights (including Iberia, American Airlines, British Airways and Vueling). Terminal 4 is a long way from the others, but a free shuttle train runs between it and the Metro station next to Terminals 1 and 2. Allow an extra 30 minutes if you are travelling by public transport to Terminal 4.

Barcelona's El Prat international airport is located 12 km (7.5 miles) from the city centre, to which train services run every 30 minutes and buses every 15 minutes. Terminal 1 deals with Star Alliance, Sky Team and One World flights and most intercontinental flights, while terminal 2 operates departures on low-cost and other international airlines, such as **Jet2**, **Ryanair** and **Wizzair**. There are two bus services from the city centre to Terminal 1 and Terminal 2 and between terminals, too. A train also runs between the city centre and Terminal 2.

Altogether, Spain has 48 airports. Of those located in the north, the following have the status of international airports: Oviedo (Asturias), Bilbao, A Coruña, Pamplona, San Sebastián, Santander, Vigo and Vitoria. However, most

Bilbao's modern international airport

A Brittany Ferries service from Plymouth to Santander

international flights go through Madrid or Barcelona. The biggest international airport in Northern Spain is Bilbao, which has direct flights to several major European cities.

There are also domestic airports in León and Logroño. Iberia flies from Madrid and Barcelona to Gijón (Asturias), Bilbao, A Coruña, Logroño, León, Pamplona, San Sebastián, Santander, Santiago de Compostela and Vigo. **Iberia Express** (a low-cost airline) flies from Madrid to Santiago de Compostela and Vigo (as well as to Dublin and Edinburgh), and there are plans to add additional routes over the next few years. Vueling flies daily between Madrid, Barcelona, Málaga and Santiago de Compostela.

IBERIA
Iberia logo

Air Europa has regular flights from Oviedo (Asturias), Bilbao, Santiago de Compostela, Vigo, Valladolid and Zaragoza to the islands. Domestic flight times vary from 50 minutes (Madrid–Bilbao) to 90 minutes (Barcelona–A Coruña).

Air Fares

The price of air tickets to Spain depends on the time of year, whether the trip includes a weekend, and how far in advance the booking is made. The prices fluctuate according to demand. Air fares are typically highest during the summer months. Special deals, particularly for weekend city breaks, are frequently offered in the winter and may include a number of nights in a hotel.

Generally, the earlier you book, the cheaper your fare. The lowest fares are available only when you book direct with the airline via its website. Look out for **Iberia's** reduced air fares, and check easyJet and Ryanair for competitive deals. Christmas and Easter flights are often booked up well in advance.

Charter flights from the UK are sometimes available. These can be very cheap, but less flexible, and often fly at inconvenient times. Make sure your agent is ABTA bonded before booking. Local car hire companies may offer good deals at resort airports, but read rental terms carefully.

Ferries

Brittany Ferries has regular connections between Plymouth and Portsmouth and Santander in Cantabria and Bilbao. The *Pont-Aven* and *Cap Finistère* ferries leave two to three times weekly, the crossing lasting 20 or 24 hours. Tickets are best purchased in advance, on the Internet if possible. It is wise to book early if you plan to travel in summer or around big public holidays.

Ferries are equipped with cabins, restaurants, cafés, casinos, cinemas, disco and gym, beauty parlours and other facilities for passengers.

DIRECTORY

Info on Spanish Airports

Aena
Tel 902 404 704.
W aena.es

Spanish Airlines

Air Europa
Tel 902 40 15 01.
W aireuropa.com

Iberia
Tel 901 11 15 00.
Tel 020 3648 3774 (UK).
W iberia.com

Iberia Express
Tel 901 10 04 24.
W iberiaexpress.com

Vueling
Tel 807 20 01 00.
W vueling.com

International Airlines

Delta
Tel 902 810 872.
W delta.com

easyJet
Tel 902 599 900.
W easyjet.com

Jet2
Tel 902 881 269.
W jet2.com

Ryanair
Tel 0871 246 0000 (UK).
W ryanair.com

Wizzair
Tel 807 44 40 41.
W wizzair.com

Ferries

Brittany Ferries
Estación Marítima,
39002 Santander.
Tel 902 10 81 47,
0871 244 0744 (UK).
W brittany-ferries.co.uk

Ferry Reservations

W brittanyferries.com
W aferry.co.uk
W directferries.co.uk

Travelling by Train

The Spanish state railway, RENFE *(Red Nacional de Ferrocarriles Españoles)*, operates a service that is continually improving, particularly between cities. The fastest intercity service is operated by AVE and TALGO – with high-speed, luxury trains. *Intercity* trains, between major destinations, are quick and comfortable. *Largo recorrido* (long-distance) and *regionales y cercanías* (regional and local) trains operate slower services, many stopping at every station, but they are much cheaper than the high-speed trains.

Arriving by Train

There are several direct train services from France to Northern Spain. The main western route runs from Paris through Hendaye in the Pyrenees to San Sebastián. The eastern route now has a high-speed direct connection from Paris to Barcelona twice daily (6.25 hrs) and also daily from Toulouse and Lyon into Barcelona, with stops in Figueres and Perpignan. For journeys from Switzerland, Germany, the Netherlands, Belgium and the North of Italy to Barcelona, you need to change trains in France. The best websites to find connections and buy tickets are www.logitravel.com or renfe.com. There is also a direct rail connection between Lisbon and Madrid that stops in Ávila and Salamanca, and a direct overnight rail connection between San Sebastián and Lisbon, with stops in Vitoria, Burgos and Valladolid among others. Both overnight lines are run by Renfe Trenhotel,

and offer three categories of bed compartments, in addition to regular seats.

Exploring by Train

Spain offers many options for train travellers, and the TALGO and AVE services make it easy to travel long distances between cities quickly. These luxury trains run at speeds of up to 200 km/h (124 mph). Journeys are comfortable, and the standard of service is high. Ticket prices compare favourably to high-speed train fares in other European countries.

Long-distance trains *(largo recorrido)* are significantly cheaper. Those that run at night offer a *cochecama* (a compartment with two *camas* or beds) or a *litera*, a compartment with four seats that convert into bunk beds. Both types cost extra and should be reserved when booking your ticket. Tickets for overnight trains should be booked well in advance.

Regional trains *(regionales)* and local trains *(cercanías)* are

frequent and cheap, however, numerous stops can lengthen journey times considerably.

Train tickets can be bought on the **RENFE** website and from station ticket offices and ticket machines.

Most RENFE lines converge on Madrid.

Train Stations

Most large cities in Northern Spain have train stations served by all categories of train. Some cities have two stations.

DIRECTORY

Regional Railways

ET
Tel 902 54 32 10.
 euskotren.es

FGC
Tel 900 90 15 15.
 fgc.es

Ticket Reservations

RENFE
Tel 902 32 03 20; for disabled passengers, 902 24 05 05.
 renfe.com

Main Train Stations

A Coruña
Calle Joaquín Planelles Riera.

Bilbao
Estación de Abando, Plaza Circular 2.

Burgos
Avda. Príncipe de Asturias.

León
Calle Astorga.

Logroño
Calle Marqués de Larios 1.

Oviedo
Calle Uría s/n.

Pamplona
Avda. San Jorge.

San Sebastián
Estación del Norte, Paseo de Francia 22.

Santander
Plaza de las Estaciones.

Santiago de Compostela
Rúa de Hórreo 75.

The Estación Santander de Bilbao

The railway station in Padrón

The main RENFE routes from Madrid to Northern Spain are: Madrid to A Coruña route via Ávila, Medina del Campo, Zamora, Ourense and Santiago de Compostela; Madrid to Santander via Ávila, Medina, Valladolid and Palencia; Madrid to Bilbao via Burgos and Miranda; and finally Madrid to San Sebastián via Guadalajara and Pamplona.

Regional Railways

As well as the RENFE services there are also two separate local rail companies in Northern Spain. They are run by different regional governments, the **FGC** (Ferrocarrils de la Generalitat) in Catalonia and the Basque **ET** (Eusko Tren).

Eusko Tren includes not only trains but also trams, buses, cable cars and even a steam train (tren de vapor) which departs from the Basque Railway Museum (Museo Vasco del Ferrocarril) in Azpeitia.

Fares

Web fares are the same as the fares on offer in the RENFE ticket offices. The lowest fares available are Promo or Tarifa 4, when four passengers travel together, but it is advisable to book in advance. Fares for rail travel in Spain are structured according to the speed and quality of the service. Tickets for the TALGO and AVE are most expensive.

A range of rail passes, among them Interrail (www.interrail.eu), is available from major travel agencies in Europe and from RENFE ticket offices in Spain. For further information see www.raileurope.com. Take proof of your identity and age when booking.

Booking Tickets

TALGO, AVE and any other tickets for long-distance trains (largo recorrido) may be booked and bought on the RENFE website or at any of the major railway stations from the ticket office (taquilla). Reservations can be made up to 59 days prior to the date of

travel. Tickets for regional services (regionales) and local services (cercanías) cannot be reserved. You can buy them on the RENFE website or from the station taquilla. In large stations there are ticket machines (cajeros automáticos).

For a one-way ticket ask for a billete de ida; for a return ask for a billete de ida y vuelta (sold at 20 per cent discount).

Timetables

RENFE timetables, available from RENFE offices, change in May and October each year. Most timetables are broken down into the various types of journey: intercity, largo recorrido and regionales. Cercanías timetable are posted on boards at local train stations. Timetables can be accessed in English via the RENFE website.

A regional RENFE train

Tourist Train Routes

In addition to daily service, RENFE also offers tourist routes. The luxurious Transcantábrico takes passengers on a splendid eight-day journey along Spain's north coast between Santiago de Compostela and León or San Sebastián, passing important sights along the way. Passengers travel in style in 14 period carriages built between 1900 and 1930, and restored to their former glory. Visit www.renfe.com/trenesturisticos for more

Cremallera mountain train in the Pyrenees

information.

For a much shorter, but still stunning journey, the Catalan FGC runs the Cremallera mountain train up to Nuria and Queralbs, with beautiful views. Other tourist trains are La Robla (Bilbao–León) and a few routes in Galicia (www.renfe.com/trenes turisticos/otros-trenes-galicia.html).

Travelling by Road

Spain's fastest roads are its *autopistas*. They are normally dual carriageways and are subsidized by *peajes* (tolls). *Autovías* are similar but have no tolls. The *carretera nacional* is the countrywide network of main roads or highways with the prefix N. Smaller minor roads are generally less well kept but provide a more leisurely and enjoyable way to see rural areas of Spain. These pages tell you how to use the roads, tolls and parking meters, and explain important driving regulations.

A national highway sign

Arriving By Car

Many people drive to Spain via the French motorways. The most direct routes across the Pyrenees pass through Hendaye on the western flank (Basque Country) and Port Bou in the east (Catalonia). Other, rather more tortuous routes may be used, from Toulouse through the Vall d'Aran, for instance. The mid-Pyrenees route through Puerto de Somport to Jaca is beautiful, for those with time to spare. From the UK there are car ferries from Plymouth and Portsmouth to Santander, and from Portsmouth to Bilbao in the Basque Country (see p245).

What to Take

Spanish law requires you to carry with you at all times your vehicle's registration document, a valid insurance certificate and your driving licence. You must always be able to show a passport or a national identity card as ID. You must also display a sticker with the car's country of registration on the rear of the vehicle.

The headlights of right-hand-drive vehicles will have to be adjusted or deflected. This is done with stickers that can be bought at ferry ports and on ferries. You risk on-the-spot fines if you fail to carry two red warning triangles, spare light bulbs, a first-aid kit and a reflective vest. In winter you should carry chains if you intend to drive in mountain areas. In summer, it is a good idea to take drinking water with you if you are travelling in a remote area.

Buying Petrol

In Spain petrol stations (*gasolineras*) sell both unleaded petrol (*gasolina sin plomo*) and diesel (*gasóleo*). Petrol stations are usually self-service. Automatic card-operated pumps often reject foreign credit cards. It's better to fill up at a staffed station. You will need to show ID if you pay by credit card.

A petrol station belonging to the Repsol chain

Rules of the Road

Spain has a few road rules and signs that may be unfamiliar to some drivers from other countries. To turn left at a busy junction or across oncoming traffic you may have to turn right first and cross a main road, often across traffic lights, over a bridge or through an underpass. If you are going the wrong way on a motorway or a main road with a solid white line, you are allowed to do a u-turn where you see a sign for a *cambio de sentido*.

At any crossing you must give way to traffic on the right unless a sign indicates otherwise. It is compulsory always to wear seat belts in front and rear seats. Oncoming drivers may flash their headlights at you, which means they are claiming the right of way and you should let them go first.

Sign for an *autovía*, a fast toll-free road

Speed Limits and Fines

The speed limits on Spanish roads for cars without trailers are as follows: 120 km/h (75 mph) on motorways, 100 km/h (62 mph) on dual carriageways, 90 km/h (56 mph) on main or secondary roads, and 40 km/h (25 mph) in built-up areas.

Speed traps and tests for drink-driving are increasingly common. The latter are especially frequent at weekends by motorway exit roads.

The legal limit for blood alcohol is 30 mg per millilitre (0.05 per cent).

Motorways

Spanish motorways come in two varieties: *autopistas* (designated "AP", followed by the route number) and *autovías* ("A"). *Autovías* are toll-free. Most *autopistas* are toll roads; they are expensive, with tolls calculated per kilometre. They have service stations every 40–50 km (25–30 miles), mostly

The toll-booth barrier at the entrance to an *autopista*

with fuel, shops and toilets, and emergency telephones every 2 km (1.2 miles).

Car Hire

International car hire companies operate all over Spain. **Hertz**, **Avis** and **Europcar** are the most popular, and they have branches at airports and in most large towns. The best-known Spanish car hire company is **National-Atesa**. When signing a car-hire agreement, you will be required to show your driving licence, credit card, and passport or other ID.

The logos of the larger car hire companies

Paying Tolls

When you join a motorway you pick up a ticket from a toll booth (*peaje*, also called *peaxe* in Galicia or *peatge* in Catalan); when you leave the motorway, you surrender the ticket along with the appropriate fee. Over some short stretches of motorway, a fixed price is charged but in most cases you pay according to the distance you have travelled.
There are three types of motorway toll booths: *telepago* (tourists should avoid this l ane as it is only for motorists

who subscribe to a special prepaid credit system), *automático* (for motorists who can pay by credit card) and *manual* (for motorists who require change from an attendant).

Other Roads

Spain's main roads *(carreteras nacionales)* have black and white signs and are designated N plus a number. Those with Roman numerals (N-III) start at the Puerta del Sol in Madrid. The distance from the Kilómetro Zero mark at the Puerta del Sol appears on kilometre markers. Those with ordinary numbers (N-3, N-12 etc.) have kilometre markers giving the distance from the provincial capital. Some *carreteras nacionales* are dual carriageways, but most are single-lane roads. Secondary roads *(carreteras comarcales)* have a number preceded by the letter C. Other minor roads have numbers preceded by the letters representing the name of the province, such as the L-200

A long-distance coach, part of the fleet run by Alsa

in Lleida. In winter, especially in the Pyrenees and around Burgos, minor roads may be closed.

Travel by Coach

The cheapest way to travel to Spain is by coach. **Eurolines** operates routes throughout Europe and runs services to Madrid and Barcelona.
   Alsa is part of the British group National Express and operates most intercity routes in Spain and Europe.
   Coach services within Spain are comfortable and efficient. Coach companies operate many long-distance routes, as well as short routes and special sightseeing trips for tourists. Spanish coaches are clean and usually air-conditioned.

Hitchhiking

Hitchhiking in Spain is not recommended as a safe method of transport, though young people, mainly tourists, are often seen hitchhiking around, especially during the summer.

DIRECTORY

Alsa
Tel 902 42 22 42.
W alsa.es

Avis
Tel 902 18 08 54.
W avis.com; avis.es

Eurolines
Tel 902 40 50 40.
Tel 0871 781 8178 (UK).
W eurolines.co.uk

Europcar
Tel 902 50 30 10.
W europcar.com; europcar.es

Hertz
Tel 902 40 24 05.
W hertz.com; hertz.es

National-Atesa
Tel 902 10 01 01.
W atesa.es

Traffic Information
Tel 011. W dgt.es

Getting Around Cities

As ever more people in Spain move from the countryside to the towns and cities, they are becoming increasingly crowded. Getting around the cities by car can be challenging, with many one-way streets, pedestrianized streets, and heavy traffic during rush hour. It's generally far better to use the very efficient local transport systems, which comprise buses, trams, the metro and taxis. The historic centres of towns and cities in Northern Spain are best explored on foot, as they are compact enough to see easily.

On Foot

Most of the sights are clustered together within walking distance of each other, so exploring on foot is the best option. Many of the streets are closed to traffic (calles peatonales), and even if they are not, finding a parking space can be difficult.

Taxis

There is no central system for taxis in Spain. Every city and/or region has its own operation and tariffs for its taxis. All display a green light if they are available.

Taxis are a comfortable means of transport. Most taxis are metered, and at the start of the journey a minimum fare will be shown on the meter. Ask at the hotel reception or in a nearby shop for the name and number of a local taxi company. Only in the smallest villages is it possible that you'll encounter unmetered

Signs to a city's historic sights and accommodation

taxis, in which case you should negotiate the fare before setting off.

In cities there are taxi ranks at the airports, the railway and bus stations and usually the main shopping areas.

Visitors with luggage may have to pay an additional charge of approximately €1–2 per item. You should remember this, especially when travelling to or from an airport. An average fare from an airport to a city centre is around €20–30. To travel an average distance by taxi within a city you should expect to pay around €7–12. Tips of approximately €1 will be acceptable.

Bicycles, Mopeds and Motorbikes

Bicycles are becoming more common on Spanish streets, but be very careful if you cycle in traffic, as many drivers do not make allowances for cyclists. An increasing number of Spanish cities have excellent cycle lanes.

Motorbikes and scooters – much loved by the Spanish – continue to be a fashionable way to avoid traffic jams and also reach one's destination quickly.

Cycling trips through the Spanish countryside are also popular. Visitors can easily hire a bike from an alquiler de bicicletas.

Bicycles may be carried on local trains (cercanías, after 2pm only), on all regional trains (regionales) with goods compartments, and on all overnight long-distance trains (largo recorrido). Sometimes you may have to send your bicycle as luggage and pay a baggage charge.

Buses

Local bus routes and timetables are posted at bus stops. Single tickets can be bought from the driver when you board the bus (always through the front doors), but in most cities multi-journey tickets (bonobus or tarjeta) valid for 10 journeys on local buses and – where there is one – the Metro system are preferable. You buy these in advance from bus offices, automatic machines or estancos (tobacconists). They work out a lot cheaper, and save a lot of time whenever you board a bus.

Trams

Tram systems are a rarity in Spanish cities (Valencia has one), but one of the most modern tram services in Northern Spain is the Basque **EuskoTran**, part of the EuskoTren company, which operates trains and trams in and around Bilbao and Vitoria. There is a fast and elegant service within and beyond the borders of the city, for instance, to the town of Hendaia (Hendaye) on the French-Spanish border,

The modern green EuskoTran in Bilbao

The futuristic entrance to a metro station in Bilbao

to the spa of San Sebastián, as well as to several beach resorts, including Zarautz and Bermeo.

Metro

Bilbao's excellent metro system is a pleasure to use. It enables you to reach your destination quickly, providing a good alternative to overground transport. The station entrances, especially in the city centre, are very impressive. Viewed from afar, both during daytime and at night, they resemble giant shrimps and are among the boldest examples of modern design to be seen in Bilbao. The stations, which perfectly complement the city's showpiece Museo Guggenheim (see pp128–9), were designed by Norman Foster.

Driving

Driving in Spanish cities is not a pleasant experience, especially for visitors unfamiliar with the surroundings. In the more crowded cities motorists tend to drive aggressively. Signs are often misleading or missing, service stations are few and parking is usually difficult. Read the map before setting off, but watch out for one-way systems, tunnels and overpasses. In rush hour, traffic often comes to a standstill. If you get lost while driving, hail a taxi, shout the address and follow the driver.

Parking

Parking spaces are especially scarce in the summer season. Free parking is almost impossible to find, while metered parking is expensive. To park on the street, you normally need to find a blue pay-and-display parking space. Be sure to remember when your time-limit expires. In most cities in Northern Spain, parking is free between 8pm on Friday evening and 8am on Monday morning. Underground car parks provide an alternative to metered on-street parking. You collect a ticket when you enter, retain it, and then pay the attendant, or at the machine, as you drive out. Underground parking is convenient, but tends to be expensive. Parking your car for just a few hours may cost more than €10.

50

Speed limit sign in a small village

ESTACIONAMIENTO
LIMITADO Y CONTROLADO
TICKET DE CONTROL OBLIGATORIO
DE 9 A 14 Y DE 16,30 A 20 H.
EXCEPTO SABADOS TARDE Y FESTIVOS

A sign with information on parking regulations

Parking Penalties

Be sure to park in designated spaces only. Exceeding your pay-and-display time limit may incur a penalty of up to €40. When a vehicle receives a penalty ticket it is automatically registered on the computer system. Any further infringements or traffic violations may result in the car being clamped or towed.

Parking is controlled by the local police in each town, and it is to them you have to go to pay a fine or retrieve your car if it's been towed away.

DIRECTORY

Taxi Companies

Oviedo
Radio Taxi Ciudad de Oviedo
Tel 985 25 00 00.

A Coruña
Tele Taxi Tel 981 28 77 77.

Santander
Tele Taxi Tel 942 36 91 91.
Radio Taxi Tel 942 33 33 33.

Bilbao
Radio Taxi Nervión
Tel 944 26 90 26.
Radio Taxi Bilbao
Tel 944 44 88 88.
Radio Taxi Getxo
Tel 944 91 53 53.

San Sebastián
Radio Taxi Donostia
Tel 943 46 46 46.

Logroño
Radio Taxi
Tel 941 22 21 22.
Tele Taxi
Tel 941 50 50 50.

Trams

Bilbao
EuskoTran
Tel 902 54 32 10.
Ⓦ euskotren.es

Metro

Bilbao
Plaza Miguel de Unamuno.
Tel 944 25 40 25.
Ⓦ metrobilbao.net

General Index

Page numbers in **bold** type refer to main entries

Acknowledgments

Dorling Kindersley and Hachette Livre Polska would like to thank the following people and institutions, whose contributions and assistance have made the preparation of this guide possible:

Publishing Manager Vivien Antwi, Kathryn Lane
Managing Art Editor Kate Poole, Jane Ewart
Publisher Douglas Amrine
Senior Cartographic Editor Casper Morris
Senior DTP Designer Jason Little
DTP Designer Jenn Hadley, Natasha Lu
Editorial Assistance Alexandra Farrell
Production Coordinator Louise Minihane
Jacket Design Tessa Bindloss
Senior Picture Researcher Ellen Root
Assistant Picture Researcher Rachel Barber
Consultant Nick Ryder
Factchecker Lola Carbonell
Proofreader Stewart J Wild
Indexer Hilary Bird

Additional Photography

Max Alexander, Frank Greenaway, Zuzanna Jakubowska, Krzysztof Kur, Ian O'Leary, Grzegorz Micuła, Małgorzata Omilanowska, Ewa Szwagrzyk.

Revisions Team

Umesh Aggarwal, Emma Anacootee, Chris Barstow, Kate Berens, Tessa Bindloss, Paula Canal, Emer FitzGerald, Anna Freiberger, Mary-Ann Gallagher, Camilla Gersh, Lydia Halliday, Mohammad Hassan, Christine Heilman, Claire Jones, Bharti Karakoti, Juliet Kenny, Sumita Khatwani, Alison McGill, George Nimmo, Scarlett O'Hara, Jane Oliver-Jedrzejak, Susie Peachey, Rada Radojicic, Azeem Siddiqui, Conrad Van Dyk.

Special Assistance

The publisher would like to thank the following for their kind assistance and permission to photograph at their establishments, and to reproduce photographs from their collections and archives:

Ayuntamiento de Oviedo and Carmen López; Aranecie Sacristan and Miren Begoñe; Centro de Atracción y Turismo de San Sebastián; Centro Información Turística del Principado de Asturias El Camino Real; Federación Internacional de Pelota Vasca and Fundación de los Ferrocarriles Españoles union; Amaya Asiain and Vías Verdes programme - www.viasverdes.com; La Rioja Alta S.A. and Gabriela Rezoli; Museo de Altamira and Eusebio Dohijo; Museo de Bellas Artes de Álava and Itziar Ruia de Erentxun; Museo Provincial de Lugo; Josi Martinez; the staff of www.ordesa.com; Sahatsa Basque Dance Group and Juan Luis Izabe; Santuario de Loyola and Txakel Urarte; Teatro Arriaga; Turgalicia; Turismo Rural de Cantabria and Francisco Javier San Jóse from www.cantabriarural.com.

Picture Credits

a = above; b = below; c = centre; f = far; l = left; r = right; t = top.

Works of art have been reproduced with the permission of the following copyright holders: Eduardo Chilida © DACS, London 2012 127cl, 130-1; Salvador Dali © Kingdom of Spain, Gaia – Salvador Dali Foundation and DACS, London 2012 193tc; Benjamin Palencia © DACS, London 2012 8-9; © Succession Picasso/DACS, London 2012 22bl; Richard Serra © ARS, NY and DACS, London 2012 124br; Zubiaurre © DACS, London 2012 143cla.

The publisher would like to thank the following individuals, companies and picture libraries for permission to reproduce their photographs:

4Corners: Olimpio Fantuz / SIME 174; Günter Gräfenhain 134–135.

Agence Vu: Christina Garcia Rodero 21bc; AISA - Archivo Iconografico S.A., **Barcelona:** 40br, 42tc, 69br, 121cb; Catedral de Sevilla *Ignacio de Loyola* Alonso Vazquez 142br; **Ajuntamiento de Oviedo:** 92clb; **Alamy Images:** Adams Picture Library/Eric Farrelly 227tc; age fotostock 52, 98br; Alan Copson City Pictures/Alan Copson 158cla, 159bl; Arcaid/Inigo Bujedo Aguirre 248bl; Sébastien Baussais 32tr; Mark Baynes 147bl; Bildarchiv Monheim GmbH/Markus Bassler 43crb; Chris Cameron 159cr; Cephas Picture Library/Mick Rock 169br; Cephas Picture Library/Neil Phillips 36bl; Ashley Cooper 107crb; Jean Dominique Dallet 40tl; Andrew Darrington 188bc; Roger Day 32bl, 224cl; Danita Delimont 121bl; Elizabeth Whiting & Associates 107bl; Paul Hobson 188cb; Peter Horree 238cl; imageBROKER 12tc, 239tl; John Warburton-Lee Photography/Ian Aitken 226cra; John Warburton-Lee Photography/John Warburton-Lee 227crb; Christian Kober 232tl; Mike Lane 188bl; M. J. Mayo 227cr, 229tl; Melba Photo Agency 158t, 159tl; Philip Mugridge 188clb; Alice Mutasa 229cr; Joris Van Ostaeyen 100–101, 218bl; Point-of-view 133ca; Radharc Images 239clb; Robert Harding World Imagery 32cr; Alex Segre 26cl, 211tc, 213tr; Stephen Saks Photography 124cl; © TNT Magazine 158bl, 158clb; Dave and Sigrun Tollerton 188tc; Colin Underhill 239cl; vario images GmbH & Co.KG/Rainer Unkel 242tr; VIEW Pictures Ltd 2-3 ; Andrew Watson 159tr; Kevin Wheal 239cla; WildPictures 189br; **Arcaid:** Paul Rafferty 128bl; **Amaya Asiain:** 232b; ALSA Group S.L.L.C: 249bc. **Hotel Andria:** 222tr. **AWL Images:** Danita Delimont Stock 122; Shaun Egan 62–63, Hemis 18, Carlos Sanchez Pereyra 84.

Baqueira-Beret: 193t; Helene Binet: 168tr. **Martin Berasategui:** 220bc.

Hotel Bosque Mar: 203tl, 204bc. **Hotel Calle Mayor:** 207bl, Montse Jalon and Jose Salguiero 202tl.

Carlos Viana: 215ftr. Casa de Juntas de Gernic: 26–27c. A Casa Dos Martinez: 216bc. Centro de Arte Reina Sofia: *Bertsolaris* Zubiaurre 147cla. Centro Información Turística del Principado de Asturia: 92b. Cephas Picture Library: Mick Rock 28tr. Corbis: Oriol Alamany 30tr, 30bl, 31c, 188cl; © Archivo Iconografico S.A. 43tr, 45t; Philip de Bay 45crb; © Bettmann 44t, 46crb, 159br; Michael Busselle 23tr, 57b, 61bl; © Christie's Images 42bl; Demotix /Hugo Ortuño Suárez 47cb; Dusko Despotovic 47tr; Owen Franken 211c; Darrel Gulin 33bl, 33br; © Hulton-Deutsch Collection 46t; Maurizio Lanini 30cr, 107cl; George D. Lepp 189tl; Lothar Lenz 33crb; George McCarthy 189bl; Tania Midgley 30clb; © Francesca Muntada188–9c; Gianni Dagli Orti 38; Jacques Pavlovsky 27cr; Reuters /Joseba Etxaburu 175b, Ruggero Vanni 44bl; Nick Wheeler 58b; Martin B. Withers 33clb; Adam Woolfitt 23t. Joe Cornish: 172tr. Cuadrilla De Anana: Antonio Garcia Ruíz 146cl.

Dreamstime.com: Steve Allen 148; Eugenesergeev 247cr; Roberto Atencia Gutierrez 198-199; Hanmon 144cl, 243tr; Karol Kozlowski 127br; Lunamarina 15br; Juan Moyano 12br; Natursports 48–49; Agustin Paz 14br, 184-185; Photoshot44 19b; Vítor Ribeiro 234–235; Pere Sanz 11bl; Alena Stalmashonak 13tr; Typhoonski 10br; Maria Vazquez 14tl, 201br.

ECB: 241cra. Edilesa: 117br. Meson Egues: 221tr. El Camino Real: 97tl. Estrella Galicia: 215bc.

Federación Internacional de Pelota Vasc: Josean Iraundegui 27br; Francisco Javier San Jóse: 202b. © FMGB Guggenheim Bilbao Museoa, 2012: 128br, 219tl, Erica Barahona Ede 128tr, 129bl, 129tc.

Darrio Garrido: 37bl, 137tc, 147cr. Getty Images: AFP/ Pedro Armestre 144bl; Bloomberg 242cla. Gran Hotel Sardinero: 200bc, 205tr.

Humberto Bilbao: 79b, 147cl.

Iberia: 245c. Imagestate: AGE Fotostock 176br, 187cra, 187crb, 231cra; Incafo: J A Fernandez 51clb; JA Fernandez & Cde Noriega 147br; Index Fototeca: 46bc, 46br; X. Correa 39crb;

La Rioja Alta S.A.: 168b.

Pasqualino Marchese: 215cr, 215br. Marques de Riscal: 169cr. Hotel Miró: TBE Agency 206tr. Museo de

Altamira: 112–13; Victor Gascón 113clb. Museo de Bellas Artes de Alva, Vitoria: 145cra. Museo Provincial de Lugo: 80cla.

Naturpress: Jose Martinez 31cla.

Omega Foto: 34br; Oronoz: 41tr, 121br, 170bc; Biblioteca National. Madrid *Isabel la Catolica* Luiz Madrazo 44bc; Museo Prado 45bl; *Alrededores de Bilbao* Benjamin Palencia 8–9; *Interior de la Catedral de Santiago* Villaamil Perez 24–25tc; *Guernica* Pablo Picasso 26bl.

Parque Nacional Ordesa: 189tr, 189cr; Paweł Pasternak: 215tr, 226bl, 227tcl. Photoshot/NHPA: Manfred Daneggar 31tc; Pictures Colour Library: 30br; Prisma, Museo de Bellas Artes, Zaragoza *Principe de Viana* Jose Moreno Carbonero 156bc.

Reuters: Jim Hollander 35c; Pablo Sanchez 139br; Javier Anton Riestra: 209b.

Robert Harding Picture Library: Christophe Boisvieux 15tl, Tim Graham 167br, Javier Larrea 11tr, 140t, Juergen Richter 10crb.

Sahatsa Basque Dance Group: 27tl. Maria Angeles Sanchez: 29t, 37cr. San Telmo Museoa: Eliza Morella Munoz 13bl. Santuario de Loiola: 142clb. Anna Skrzyńska: 31cra. Stockphotos: Heinz Hebestein 35bc; Mikael Helsing 238br; Pixtal 210cl.

Las Termas: 208cla, 217tr. Teatro Arriaga: 230cla. Torre del Remei: 223br

Alan Williams: 28br.

Front End Paper
4Corners: SIME / Olimpio Fantuz br. Alamy Images: Danita Delimont ftl. AWL Images: Danita Delimont Stock tr; Carlos Sanchez Pereyra tl. Dreamstime.com: Steve Allen ftr.

Jacket:
Front: DK Images: Peter Wilson bl; Getty Images: Walter Bibikow main; Spine: Getty Images: Walter Bibikow

All other images © Dorling Kindersley. For further information see: **www.dkimages.com**

Phrase Book – Spanish

In an Emergency

Help!	¡Socorro!	soh-koh-roh
Stop!	¡Pare!	pah-reh
Call a doctor!	¡Llame a un médico!	yah-meh ah oon meh-dee-koh
Call an ambulance!	¡Llame a una ambulancia!	yah-meh ah oonah ahm-boo-lahn-thee-ah
Call the police!	¡Llame a la policía!	yah-meh ah lah poh-lee-thee-ah
Call the fire brigade!	¡Llame a los bomberos!	yah-meh ah lohs bohm-beh-rohs
Where is the nearest telephone?	¿Dónde está el teléfono más próximo?	dohn-deh ehs-tah ehl teh-leh-foh-noh mahs prohx-ee-moh
Where is the nearest hospital?	¿Dónde está el hospital más próximo?	dohn-deh ehs-tah ehl ohs-pee-tahl mahs prohx-ee-moh

Communication Essentials

Yes	Sí	see
No	No	noh
Please	Por favor	pohr fah-vohr
Thank you	Gracias	grah-thee-ahs
Excuse me	Perdone	pehr-doh-neh
Hello	Hola	oh-lah
Goodbye	Adiós	ah-dee-ohs
Goodnight	Buenas noches	bweh-nahs noh-chehs
Morning	La mañana	lah mah-nyah-nah
Afternoon	La tarde	lah tahr-deh
Evening	La tarde	lah tahr-deh
Yesterday	Ayer	ah-yehr
Today	Hoy	oy
Tomorrow	Mañana	mah-nya-nah
Here	Aquí	ah-kee
There	Allí	ah-yee
What?	¿Qué?	keh
When?	¿Cuándo?	kwahn-doh
Why?	¿Por qué?	pohr-keh
Where?	¿Dónde?	dohn-deh

Useful Phrases

How are you?	¿Cómo está usted?	koh-moh ehs-tah oos-tehd
Very well, thank you	Muy bien, gracias.	mwee bee-ehn grah-thee-ahs
Pleased to meet you	Encantado de conocerle.	ehn-kahn-tah-doh deh koh-noh-thehr-leh
See you soon	Hasta pronto.	ahs-tah prohn-toh
That's fine	Está bien.	ehs-tah bee-ehn
Where is/are ...?	¿Dónde está/están ...?	dohn-deh ehs-tah/ehs-tahn
How far is it to ...?	Cuántos metros/ kilómetros hay de aquí a ...?	kwahn-tohs meh-trohs/ kee-loh-meh-trohs eye deh ah-kee ah
Which way to ...?	¿Por dónde se va a ...?	pohr dohn-deh seh bah ah
Do you speak English?	¿Habla inglés?	ah-blah een-glehs
I don't understand	No comprendo	noh kohm-prehn-doh
Could you speak more slowly please?	¿Puede hablar más despacio por favor?	pweh-deh ah-blahr mahs dehs-pah-thee-oh pohr fah-vohr
I'm sorry	Lo siento.	loh see-ehn-toh

Useful Words

big	grande	grahn-deh
small	pequeño	peh-keh-nyoh
hot	caliente	kah-lee-ehn-the
cold	frío	free-oh
good	bueno	bweh-noh
bad	malo	mah-loh
enough	bastante	bahs-tahn-the
well	bien	bee-ehn
open	abierto	ah-bee-ehr-toh
closed	cerrado	thehr-rah-doh
left	izquierda	eeth-key-ehr-dah
right	derecha	deh-reh-chah
straight on	todo recto	toh-doh rehk-toh
near	cerca	thehr-kah
far	lejos	leh-hohs
up	arriba	ah-ree-bah
down	abajo	ah-bah-hoh
early	temprano	tehm-prah-noh

late	tarde	tahr-deh
entrance	entrada	ehn-trah-dah
exit	salida	sah-lee-dah
toilet	lavabos, servicios	lah-vah-bohs, sehr-bee-thee-ohs
more	más	mahs
less	menos	meh-nohs

Shopping

How much does this cost	¿Cuánto cuesta esto?	kwahn-toh kwehs-tah ehs-toh
I would like ...	Me gustaría ...	meh goos-ta-ree-ah
Do you have?	¿Tienen?	tee-yeh-nehn
I'm just looking, thank you	Sólo estoy mirando, gracias.	soh-loh ehs-toy mee-rahn-doh grah-thee-ahs
Do you take credit cards?	¿Aceptan tarjetas de crédito?	ah-thehp-tahn tahr-heh-tahs deh kreh-dee-toh
What time do you open?	¿A qué hora abren?	ah keh oh-rah ah-brehn
What time do you close?	¿A qué hora cierran?	ah keh oh-rah thee-ehr-rahn
This one	Éste	ehs-the
That one	Ése	eh-seh
expensive	caro	kahr-oh
cheap	barato	bah-rah-toh
size, clothes	talla	tah-yah
size, shoes	número	noo-mehr-oh
white	blanco	blahn-koh
black	negro	neh-groh
red	rojo	roh-hoh
yellow	amarillo	ah-mah-ree-yoh
green	verde	behr-deh
blue	azul	ah-thool
antiques shop	la tienda de antigüedades	lah tee-ehn-dah deh ahn-tee-gweh-dah-dehs
bakery	la panadería	lah pah-nah-deh-ree-ah
bank	el banco	ehl bahn-koh
book shop	la librería	lah lee-breh-ree-ah
butcher's	la carnicería	lah kahr-nee-theh-ree-ah
cake shop	la pastelería	lah pahs-teh-leh-ree-ah
chemist's	la farmacia	lah fahr-mah-thee-ah
fishmonger's	la pescadería	lah pehs-kah-deh-ree-ah
greengrocer's	la frutería	lah froo-teh-ree-ah
grocer's	la tienda de comestibles	lah tee-yehn-dah deh koh-mehs-tee-lehs
hairdresser's	la peluquería	lah peh-loo-keh-ree-ah
market	el mercado	ehl mehr-kah-doh
newsagent's	el kiosko de prensa	ehl kee-ohs-koh deh prehn-sah
post office	la oficina de correos	lah oh-fee-thee-nah deh kohr-reh-ohs
shoe shop	la zapatería	lah thah-pah-teh-ree-ah
supermarket	el supermercado	ehl soo-pehr-mehr-ah-doh
tobacconist	el estanco	ehl ehs-tahn-koh
travel agency	la agencia de viajes	lah ah-hehn-thee-ah deh bee-ah-hehs

Sightseeing

art gallery	el museo de arte	ehl moo-seh-oh deh ahr-the
cathedral	la catedral	lah kah-teh-drahl
church	la iglesia	lah ee-gleh-see-ah
	la basílica	lah bah-see-lee-kah
garden	el jardín	ehl hahr-deen
library	la biblioteca	lah bee-bloh-teh-kah
museum	el museo	ehl moo-seh-oh
tourist information office	la oficina de turismo	lah oh-fee-thee-nah deh too-rees-moh
town hall	el ayuntamiento	ehl ah-yoon-tah-mee-ehn-toh
closed for holiday	cerrado por vacaciones	thehr-rah-doh pohr bah-kah-cee-oh-nehs
bus station	la estación de autobuses	lah ehs-tah-thee-on deh owtoh-boo-sehs
railway station	la estación de trenes	lah ehs-tah-thee-ohn deh treh-nehs

Staying in a Hotel

Do you have	¿Tienen una	tee-eh-nehn oo-nah
a vacant room?	habitación libre?	ah-bee-tah-thee-ohn lee-breh
double room	habitación doble	ah-bee-tah-thee-ohn doh-bleh
with double bed	con cama de matrimonio	kohn kah-mah deh mah-tree-moh-nee-oh
twin room	habitación con dos camas	ah-bee-tah-thee-ohn kohn dohs kah-mahs
single room	habitación individual	ah-bee-tah-thee-ohn een-dee-vee-doo-ahl
room with a bath	habitación con baño	ah-bee-tah-thee-ohn kohn bah-nyoh
shower	ducha	doo-chah
porter	el botones	ehl boh-toh-nehs
key	la llave	lah yah-veh
I have a reservation	Tengo una habitación reservada.	tehn-goh oo-na ah-bee-tah-thee-ohn reh-sehr-bah-dah

Eating Out

Have you got a table for …?	¿Tienen mesa para …?	tee-eh-nehn meh-sah pah-rah
I want to reserve a table	Quiero reservar una mesa.	kee-eh-roh reh-sehr-bahr oo-nah meh-sah
The bill please	La cuenta por favor.	lah kwehn-tah pohr fah-vohr
I am a vegetarian	Soy vegetariano/a	soy beh-heh-tah-ree-ah-no/na
waitress/ waiter	camarera/ camarero	kah-mah-reh-rah/ kah-mah-reh-roh
menu	la carta	lah kahr-tah
fixed-price menu	menú del día	meh-noo dehl dee-ah
wine list	la carta de vinos	lah kahr-tah deh bee-nohs
glass	un vaso	oon bah-soh
bottle	una botella	oo-nah boh-teh-yah
knife	un cuchillo	oon koo-chee-yoh
fork	un tenedor	oon teh-neh-dohr
spoon	una cuchara	oo-nah koo-chah-rah
breakfast	el desayuno	ehl deh-sah-yoo-noh
lunch	la comida/ el almuerzo	lah koh-mee-dah/ ehl ahl-mwehr- thoh
dinner	la cena	lah theh-nah
main course	el primer plato	ehl pree-mehr plah-toh
starters	los entremeses	lohs ehn-treh-meh-sehs
dish of the day	el plato del día	ehl plah-toh dehl dee-ah
coffee	el café	ehl kah-feh
rare	poco hecho	poh-koh eh-choh
medium	medio hecho	meh-dee-oh eh-choh
well done	muy hecho	mwee eh-choh

Menu Decoder

baked	al horno	ahl ohr-noh
roast	asado	ah-sah-doh
oil	el aceite	ah-thee-eh-teh
olives	las aceitunas	ah-theh-toon-ahs
mineral water	el agua mineral	ah-gwa mee-neh-rahl
still/sparkling	sin gas/con gas	seen gas/kohn gas
garlic	el ajo	ah-hoh
rice	el arroz	ahr-rohth
sugar	el azúcar	ah-thoo-kahr
meat	la carne	kahr-neh
onion	la cebolla	theh-boh-yah
beer	la cerveza	thehr-beh-thah
pork	el cerdo	therh-doh
chocolate	el chocolate	choh-koh-lah-the
red sausage	el chorizo	choh-ree-thoh
lamb	el cordero	kohr-deh-roh
cold meat	el fiambre	fee-ahm-breh
fried	frito	free-toh
fruit	la fruta	froo-tah
nuts	los frutos secos	froo-tohs seh-kohs
prawns	las gambas	gahm-bahs
ice cream	el helado	eh-lah-doh
egg	el huevo	oo-eh-voh
cured ham	el jamón serrano	hah-mohn sehr-rah-noh
sherry	el jerez	heh-rehz
lobster	la langosta	lahn-gohs-tah
milk	la leche	leh-cheh
lemon	el limón	lee-mohn
lemonade	la limonada	lee-moh-nah-dah

butter	la mantequilla	mahn-teh-kee-yah
apple	la manzana	mahn-thah-nah
seafood	los mariscos	mah-rees-kohs
vegetable stew	la menestra	meh-nehs-trah
orange	la naranja	nah-rahn-hah
bread	el pan	pahn
cake	el pastel	pahs-tehl
potatoes	las patatas	pah-tah-tahs
fish	el pescado	pehs-kah-doh
pepper	la pimienta	pee-mee-yehn-tah
banana	el plátano	plah-tah-noh
chicken	el pollo	poh-yoh
dessert	el postre	pohs-treh
cheese	el queso	keh-soh
salt	la sal	sahl
sausages	las salchichas	sahl-chee-chahs
sauce	la salsa	sahl-sah
dry	seco	seh-koh
sirloin	el solomillo	soh-loh-mee-yoh
soup	la sopa	soh-pah
pie/cake	la tarta	tahr-tah
tea	el té	teh
beef	la ternera	tehr-neh-rah
toast	las tostadas	tohs-tah-dahs
vinegar	el vinagre	bee-nah-greh
white wine	el vino blanco	bee-noh blahn-koh
rosé wine	el vino rosado	bee-noh roh-sah-doh
red wine	el vino tinto	bee-noh teen-toh

Numbers

0	cero	theh-roh
1	uno	oo-noh
2	dos	dohs
3	tres	trehs
4	cuatro	kwa-troh
5	cinco	theen-koh
6	seis	says
7	siete	see-eh-the
8	ocho	oh-choh
9	nueve	nweh-veh
10	diez	dee-ehth
11	once	ohn-theh
12	doce	doh-theh
13	trece	treh-theh
14	catorce	kah-tohr-theh
15	quince	keen-theh
16	dieciséis	dee-eh-thee-seh-ees
17	diecisiete	dee-eh-thee-see-eh-teh
18	dieciocho	dee-eh-thee-oh-choh
19	diecinueve	dee-eh-thee-nweh-veh
20	veinte	beh-een-the
21	veintiuno	beh-een-tee-oo-noh
22	veintidós	beh-een-tee-dohs
30	treinta	treh-een-tah
31	treinta y uno	treh-een-tah ee oo-noh
40	cuarenta	kwah-rehn-tah
50	cincuenta	theen-kwehn-tah
60	sesenta	seh-sehn-tah
70	setenta	seh-tehn-tah
80	ochenta	oh-chehn-tah
90	noventa	noh-vehn-tah
100	cien	thee-ehn
101	ciento uno	thee-ehn-toh oo-noh
102	ciento dos	thee-ehn-toh dohs
200	doscientos	dohs-thee-ehn-tohs
500	quinientos	khee-nee-ehn-tohs
700	setecientos	seh-teh-thee-ehn-tohs
900	novecientos	noh-veh-thee-ehn- tohs
1,000	mil	meel
1,001	mil uno	meel oo-noh

Time

one minute	un minuto	oon mee-noo-toh
one hour	una hora	oo-na oh-rah
half an hour	media hora	meh-dee-a oh-rah
Monday	lunes	loo-nehs
Tuesday	martes	mahr-tehs
Wednesday	miércoles	mee-ehr-koh-lehs
Thursday	jueves	hoo-weh-vehs
Friday	viernes	bee-ehr-nehs
Saturday	sábado	sah-bah-doh
Sunday	domingo	doh-meen-goh

Phrase Book – Basque

In an Emergency

Help!	**Lagundu!**	*lah-goon-doo!*
Stop!	**Gelditu!**	*gehl-dee-too!*
Call a doctor!	**Sendagile bati deitu!**	*sehn-dah-gee-leh bah-tee deh-ee-too!*
Call an ambulance!	**Anbulantzia bati deitu!**	*ahn-boo-lahn-tzee-ah bah-tee deh-ee-too!*
Call the police!	**Poliziari deitu!**	*poh-lee-zee-ah-ree deh-ee-too!*
Call the fire brigade!	**Suhiltzaileei deitu!**	*suh-eel-tzah-ee-leh-ee deh-ee-too!*
Where is the nearest telephone?	**Non dago telefonorik gertuena?**	*nohn dah-goh teh-leh-phoh-noh-reek gehr-too-eh-nah?*
Where is the nearest hospital?	**Non dago ospitalerik gertuena?**	*nohn dah-goh ohs-pee-tah-leh-reek gehr-too-eh-nah?*

Communication Essentials

Yes	**Bai**	*bah-ee*
No	**Ez**	*ehs*
Please	**Mesedez**	*meh-seh-dehs*
Thank you	**Eskerrik asko**	*ehs-keh-rreek ahs-koh*
Excuse me	**Barkatu**	*bahr-kah-too*
Hello	**Kaixo**	*kah-ee-sho*
Goodbye	**Agur**	*ah-goor*
Good night	**Gabon**	*gah-bohn*
Morning	**Goiza**	*goh-ee-sah*
Afternoon	**Arratsaldea**	*ah-rah-tsahl-deh-ah*
Evening	**Arratsaldea**	*ah-rah-tsahl-deh-ah*
Yesterday	**Atzo**	*ah-tzoh*
Today	**Gaur**	*gah-oor*
Tomorrow	**Bihar**	*bee-ahr*
Here	**Hemen**	*eh-mehn*
There	**Hor**	*ohr*
What?	**Zer?**	*zehr?*
When?	**Noiz?**	*noh-ees?*
Why?	**Zergatik?**	*zehr-gah-teek?*
Where?	**Non?**	*nohn?*

Useful Phrases

How are you?	**Zer moduz?**	*zehr moh-dooz?*
Very well, thank you.	**Ondo, eskerrik asko**	*ohn-doh, ehs-keh reek ahs-koh*
Pleased to meet you.	**Pozten nau zu ezagutzeak**	*pohz-tehn nah-oo zoo eh-zah-goo-tzeh-ahk*
See you soon.	**Gero arte**	*geh-roh ahr-teh*
That's fine.	**Ados**	*ah-dohs*
Where is/are…?	**Non dago/daude …?**	*nohn dah-goh/dah-oo-deh …?*
How far is it to…?	**Ze tarte dago hemendik …-ra?**	*seh tahr-teh dah-goh eh-mehn-deek …-rah?*
Which way to…?	**Nondik joaten da …-ra?**	*nohn-deek joh-ah-tehn dah … -rah?*
Do you speak English?	**Ingelesez badakizu?**	*een-geh-leh-sehs bah-dah-kee-zoo?*
I don't understand	**Ez dut ulertzen**	*ehs doot oo-lehr-tzehn*
Could you speak more slowly please?	**Mantsoago hitz egin dezakezu, mesedez?**	*mahn-tsoh-ah-goh ee-tz eh-geen deh-sah-keh-zoo, meh-seh-dehs?*
I'm sorry.	**Barkatu**	*bahr-kah-too*

Useful Words

big	**Handia**	*ahn-dee-ah*
small	**Txikia**	*txee-kee-ah*
hot	**Beroa**	*beh-roh-ah*
cold	**Hotza**	*oh-tzah*
good	**Ona**	*oh-nah*
bad	**Txarra**	*txah-rah*
enough	**Nahiko**	*nah-ee-koh*
well	**Ondo**	*ohn-doh*
open	**Zabalik**	*sah-bah-leek*
closed	**Itxita**	*ee-txee-tah*
left	**Ezkerra**	*ehs-keh-rah*
right	**Eskuina**	*ehs-koo-ee-nah*
straight on	**Zuzen**	*zoo-zehn*
near	**Gertu**	*gehr-too*
far	**Urrun**	*oo-roon*
up	**Goian**	*goh-ee-ahn*
down	**Behean**	*beh-eh-ahn*
early	**Goiz**	*goh-eez*
late	**Berandu**	*beh-rahn-doo*
entrance	**Sarrera**	*sah-reh-rah*
exit	**Irteera**	*eer-teh-eh-rah*

toilet	**Komunak**	*koh-moo-nahk*
more	**Gehiago**	*geh-ee-ah-goh*
less	**Gutxiago**	*guh-txee-ah-goh*

Shopping

How much does this cost?	**Zenbat balio du honek?**	*zehn-baht bah-lee-oh. duh oh-nehk?*
I would like…	**… gustatuko litzaidake**	*… guhs-tah-too-koh lee-tzah-ee-dah-keh*
Do you have?	**Ba al daukazue …-rik?**	*bah ahl dah-oo-kah-zoo-eh … -reek?*
I'm just looking.	**Begiratzen nago, besterik ez.**	*beh-gee-rah-tzehn nah-goh, behs-teb-reek ebs*
Do you take credit cards?	**Txartelik onartzen al duzue?**	*txahr-teh-leek ohn-nahr-tzehn ahl doo-zoo-eh?*
This one.	**Hau**	*ah-oo*
That one.	**Hori**	*oh-ree*
expensive	**Garestia**	*gah-rehs-tee-ah*
cheap	**Merkea**	*mehr-keh-ah*
size, clothes	**Neurria, arropa**	*neh-oo-ree-ah, ah-roh-pah*
size, shoes	**Neurria, oinetazkoak**	*neh-oo-ree-ah, oh-ee-neh-tahz-koh-ahk*
white	**Zuria**	*zoo-ree-ah*
black	**Beltza**	*behl-tzah*
red	**Gorria**	*goh-ree-ah*
yellow	**Horia**	*oh-ree-ah*
green	**Berdea**	*behr-deh-ah*
blue	**Urdina**	*oor-dee-nah*
antiques shop	**Antigoaleko gauzen denda**	*ahn-tee-goh-ah-leh-koh gah-oo-zehn dehn-dah*
bakery	**Okindegia**	*oh-keen-deh-gee-ah*
bank	**Bankua**	*bahn-koo-ah*
book shop	**Liburu-denda**	*lee-boo-roo dehn-dah*
butcher's	**Harategia**	*ah-rah-teh-gee-ah*
cake shop	**Gozotegia**	*goh-zoh-teh-gee-ah*
chemist's	**Farmazia**	*far-mah-zee-ah*
fishmonger's	**Arrandegia**	*ah-rahn-deh-gee-ah*
greengrocer's	**Frutategia**	*froo-tah-teh-gee-ah*
grocer's	**Janari-denda**	*jah-nah-ree dehn-dah*
hairdresser's	**Ile-apaindegia**	*ee-leh ah-pah-een-deh-gee-ah*
market	**Azoka**	*ah-zoh-kah*
newsagent's	**Kioskoa**	*kee-ohs-koh-ah*
post office	**Postetxea**	*pohst-eh-txeh-ah*
shoe shop	**Zapata-denda**	*zah-pah-tah dehn-dah*
supermarket	**Supermerkatua**	*soo-pehr-mehr-kah-too-ah*
tobacconist	**Tabako-denda**	*tah-bak-koh dehn-dah*
travel agency	**Bidaia-agentzia**	*bee-dah-ee ah-ghehn-tzee-ah*

Sightseeing

art gallery	**Arte-galeria**	*ahr-teh gah-leh-ree-ah*
cathedral	**Katedrala**	*kah-teh-drah-lah*
church	**Eliza**	*eh-lee-zah*
garden	**Loretegia**	*loh-rah-teh-gee-ah*
library	**Liburutegia**	*lee-boo-roo-teh-gee-ah*
museum	**Museoa**	*moo-seh-oh-ah*
tourist information office	**Turismo bulegoa**	*too-rees-moh boo-leh-goh-ah*
town hall	**Udaletxea**	*oo-dhal-eh-txeh-ah*
closed for holiday	**Oporretan gaude**	*oh-poh-reh-tahn gah-oo-deh*
bus station	**Autobus-geltokia**	*ah-oo-toh-boos gehl-toh-kee-ah*
railway station	**Tren-geltokia**	*trehn gehl-too-kee-ah*

Numbers

0	**Zero**	*zeh-roh*
1	**Bat**	*baht*
2	**Bi**	*bee*
3	**Hiru**	*ee-roo*
4	**Lau**	*lah-oo*
5	**Bost**	*bohst*
6	**Sei**	*seh-ee*
7	**Zazpi**	*zahz-pee*
8	**Zortzi**	*zohr-tzee*
9	**Bederatzi**	*beh-deh-rah-tzee*
10	**Hamar**	*ah-mahr*

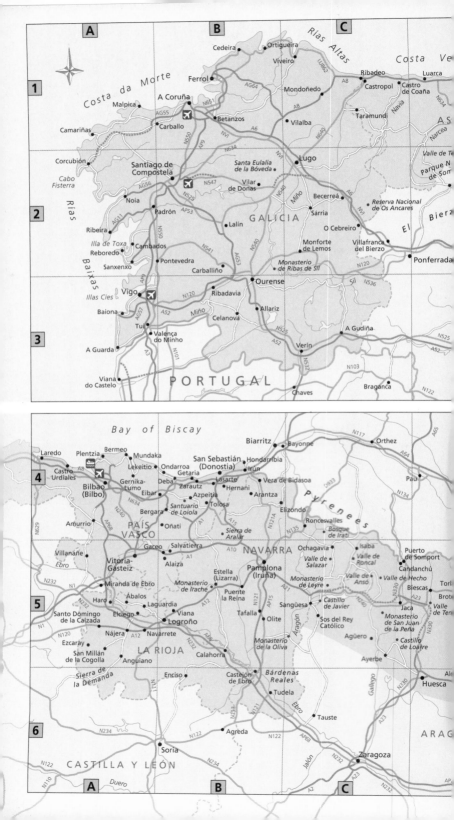